THE LORE
OF THE
UNICORN

THE UNICORN IN CAPTIVITY   (*Metropolitan Museum of Art, New York*)

THE LORE
OF THE
UNICORN

ODELL SHEPARD

DOVER PUBLICATIONS, INC.

NEW YORK

Published in Canada by General Publishing Company, Ltd., 30 Lesmill Road, Don Mills, Toronto, Ontario.

Published in the United Kingdom by Constable and Company, Ltd., 3 The Lanchesters, 162–164 Fulham Palace Road, London W6 9ER.

Bibliographical Note

This Dover edition, first published in 1993, is an unabridged republication of the work originally published by George Allen & Unwin, Ltd., London, in 1930. The frontispiece was originally in color.

Library of Congress Cataloging-in-Publication Data

Shepard, Odell, 1884–1967
      The lore of the unicorn / Odell Shepard.
            p.   cm.
      Originally published : London : Allen & Unwin, 1930.
      Includes bibliographical references (p.   ) and index.
      ISBN 0-486-27803-4 (pbk.)
      1. Unicorns.   I. Title.
      GR830.U6S5   1993
      382'.469—dc20   93-27712
                                                                      CIP

Manufactured in the United States of America
Dover Publications, Inc., 31 East 2nd Street, Mineola, N.Y. 11501

TO THE MEMORY OF

MY FRIEND

FREDERIC WALTON CARPENTER

WHO LOVED ALL ANIMALS

REAL AND IMAGINARY

NOTE

In my study of the unicorn legend I have been helped in various ways by the following persons: Mr. Edward Thompson of Oxford University, Mr. Robin Flower of the British Museum, Professor Gilbert Murray, Sir Flinders Petrie, Miss Rachel Elfreda Fowler of Oxford, Dr. Edward Hungerford of Northwestern University, Miss Lucy Perkins of Hartford (Connecticut), Mr. Paul Parsons of the Loomis Institute, Professor Paul Spencer Wood of Grinnell College, Mr. Carl Beecher of the Northwestern School of Music, Professor C. H. Grandgent, Mr. Walter de la Mare, my son, and my wife. To each of these, and also to the librarians and custodians of the British Museum, I take pleasure in expressing thanks.

O. S.

"Now I will believe that there are unicorns."
                                        —*The Tempest.*

TABLE OF CONTENTS

TABLE OF PLATES AND FIGURES

THE LORE
OF THE
UNICORN

THE LORE OF THE UNICORN

INTRODUCTION

ON the table before me there lies a long straight wand of ivory.
Cut to the length of a walking-stick, it is somewhat more than two
inches in diameter at the top and it tapers evenly to a blunt point.
Smooth-backed ridges, not more than a quarter of an inch in height,
spiral round it counter-clockwise, making about two turns and a
half between one end and the other. As a whole, it is a twisted spear.
One can fancy that it has been taken in powerful hands and wrung,
as one wrings a wet cloth. Thomas Fuller, having seen another
such ivory wand as this, said excellently that to his dim eyes and at
some distance it seemed "like a taper of wreathed waxe".

This walking-stick has been fitted at the upper end with a gilded
silver cap which bears the arms of a certain noble house and a motto
in Welsh. Four inches below the cap a hole has been bored through
the stick—one would say, at first, to receive the cord to which some
gentleman of the grand old days attached the silken tassel that
adorned his cane. I scarcely think, however, that this particular stick
ever tapped its way along Birdcage Walk or through the gardens
of Versailles, partly because there are no signs of wear on its point
and partly because it weighs something like three pounds. More
probably, the cord that went through this hole was used not to
carry a tassel but to hang the stick against the wall in some great
house of three or four centuries ago.

And yet I do not doubt that some of the former owners of this wand carried it about with them, but when they did so they carried it neither for comfort nor display; rather, it was their companion on dark nights and in perilous places, and they held it near their hearts, handling it tenderly, as they would a treasure. For indeed it was exactly that. It preserved a man from the arrow that flieth by day and the pestilence that walketh in darkness, from the craft of the poisoner, from epilepsy, and from several less dignified ills of the flesh not to be named in so distinguished a connection. In short, it was an amulet, a talisman, a weapon, and a medicine-chest all in one. Small wonder that such a wand as this, in the days when such things were appreciated, sold for twenty times its weight in gold, and that one alone, as Thomas Dekker said, was "worth a city". Small wonder that perfect sticks like this were to be seen only in the treasure-chambers of popes and emperors and kings, or, when some opulent church like St. Mark's of Venice did manage to acquire one, that it should be shown to the public only on gala days and beneath a pall of purple velvet. The stick before me, although of ivory, was not cut from an elephant's tusk or even from the tusk of a mammoth or mastodon. It grew as it is, and according to the most learned opinion of many generations it grew single on the brow of a beast so glorious, so virtuous, so beautiful, that heaven vouchsafed the earth, as in the case of the phoenix, only one specimen at a time. For this is the horn of the unicorn.

To retrace the devious ways by which this piece of ivory, so reverently handled, has come to lie here on my writing-desk, I shall have to tell a story that ranges back through more "wild centuries" than we can count—a story that begins with a time before cities or agriculture, when barbarous tribes wandered with their herds from summer to winter pasturage and back again, a tale that includes at one end the most primitive myths and the first stirrings of the moral sense and at the other the trickery of the charlatan and the mountebank. Into the web of this tale I shall have to catch up many strands of the history of exploration, of medicine, of art, of commerce, and of scientific thought. The fact is that I cannot explain how this ivory wand came to lie before me—I purchased it not long ago from a London dealer in antiques for about three guineas—without indicating, in one vivid example, the ways by which magic rose into religious dogma and this gradually succumbed, or is succumbing, under the attrition of modern science. But even then, of course, I shall fall short of a full explanation, and any reader of these words who cherishes the few relics of superstition that we have left to us may be assured that this book will not "murder to dissect", will not substitute a dull explanation for one of the most beautiful legends in the world. The remote and solitary strangeness of the unicorn is perfectly safe from me, and I think from any one; for even if I did not prefer to do so I should have to let him stalk away, at the end, into the mystery out of which he comes.

The lore of the unicorn is enormous in range and variety, not only because of the great expanse of time it covers but because it involves so many different departments of knowledge, and the literature dealing specifically with the topic is surprisingly extensive. Like most of my predecessors, I have hunted the unicorn chiefly in libraries, realizing the delightful absurdity of the task quite as fully as any one could point it out to me. A zoologist would have written on my topic a different and probably a shorter book, but for me the unicorn is interesting almost entirely as a denizen of "the Monarch Thought's dominions". Whether there is or is not an actual unicorn—and this is one of the questions upon which I shall merely quote the opinions of others—he cannot possibly be so fascinating or so important as the things men have dreamed and thought and written about him. A dream, if it is no more than that, of such great age and beauty as this of the unicorn, is far more worthy of consideration than the question whether we shall have one species more or less in the earth's fauna. And the dream, at any rate, is an unquestionable fact, a phenomenon of the mind; it has grown like a tree, striking deep roots in thought and spreading huge boughs against our mental sky. This book about the unicorn is a minute contribution to the study of the only subject that deeply and permanently concerns us—human nature and the ways of human thought.

In view of the fact that I am tracing what has been thought and said about the unicorn and that most of the literature concerned is found in rare and forgotten books, it has seemed necessary to quote more freely than would otherwise have been desirable. After reading hundreds of pages of unfounded and ignorant recent writing on my topic I have no apology to make for the care I have taken to prove my points by exact citation of authority. The lore of the unicorn owes much to the work of accurate scholars, and I have tried to present their opinions with an accuracy they would have approved; but the mere apparatus of scholarship is a scaffolding that should always be kept as much as possible out of sight, and my notes will be found at the back of the book, where they will trouble no one for whom they are not intended.

Perhaps it would not be inappropriate to explain how I first struck into a footpath so far, at least in appearance, from any of the highways of contemporary research. Some time ago, while reading Petrarch's treatise *De Vita Solitaria*, I came upon a vivid description of the noon-day meal in the house of an Italian tyrant in the fourteenth century. Like most things in Petrarch's Latin prose, this description is derivative, its main source being St. Ambrose's *De Abstinentia*, but a sentence or two in the middle of it stood out as a rather startling bit of personal observation. "Among all these yellow and black and livid lumps of flesh", says Petrarch, who was himself a vegetarian, "the diligent taster goes exploring for the suspected and not undeserved bit of poison. But another kind of precaution has been taken against secret plots: between the wines and the viands project the livid horns of serpents skilfully fastened to little gilded trees, so that it is a wonder to see how Death himself stands guard, as it were in the very stronghold of pleasure, against the death of this miserable man."

What the horns of serpents might be doing on a rich man's dinner table I had no idea, and I determined to find out. A few hours of excavation in the pages of Pietro de Abano, Ardoynus, and Cardinal Ponzetto taught me all that I cared to know about the devices once used in Italy for detecting poison at the table—devices such as that of the cerastes's horn which Petrarch mentions, the vulture's claw, the "sealed earth", the crystal goblet, the eagle-stone, the snake's tongue, and others of the same sort. But while I read, the terror of those evil times when death might lie at the bottom of any cup took hold of me, and, still more powerfully, a sense of pity for the wild and ignorant ways in which the danger was encountered. Gradually, however, I found myself moving out into a purer air along a path not entirely strange even then, for the unicorn's horn was long the chief defence against poison of those who could pay the huge prices at which it was held. And then several other questions arose: How did this horn acquire its great reputation? How was it supposed to act in detecting poison? How could it maintain its prestige while the princes and dukes of Italy who owned it were dying on every hand suddenly and from no apparent cause? Where did these horns come from, and what was the nature of the traffic that purveyed them? Was the belief in their powers a vulgar super-stition only or was it held by learned men and perhaps even by physicians? How old was this belief, and what was its origin? These are some of the questions I asked myself and shall try in this book to answer.

CHAPTER I

THE GORGEOUS EAST

WE may never know precisely when or where or how the legend of
the unicorn began. It pervades recorded time and may be dimly
visible even in the clouds that hover just above history's sunrise.
The mystery of its origin, leaving a wide field for speculation and
surrounding even the facts of which we are certain with bands of
twilight, is one of the legend's most evident charms, but it precludes
the possibility of tracing that legend from its beginnings. We can
best take up the tale of the unicorn at the point where it first emerges
into the literature of the western world, early in the fourth century
before Christ.

Few need to be reminded that at just this time Mediterranean
civilization was sweeping rapidly up to one of the summits, perhaps
the highest, of human achievement. In structures of stone and of
words and of pure thought the Greek world was then creating
marvels which compel us to accept the assurance with which the men
of that world ruled out all who did not belong to it as "barbarians".
There are two aspects of that Greek civilization, however, from
which we barbarians of the modern world are accustomed to draw
a little comfort: in the first place, it was an affair of a few small
cities and, even in these, of few individuals; in the second place, it
was achieved in spite of what we must regard as an abysmal ignorance.
Greece in the Age of Pericles was like the hand's-breadth of lighted

country, surrounded by shadow, that may be seen from a hill-top
on a lowering day. The best minds in the Hellenic world knew
little—and, with a few exceptions, they cared less—about what lay
beyond the circle of their light, and even of what lay within it
their ignorance is likely to seem to us pathetic. This may well
remind us to what a slight extent deep wisdom and high intellectual
attainment depend upon mere information, but the interesting fact
remains. Greek notions of geography, with regard to every part
of the earth's surface remote from the Mediterranean, were grotesquely few and wrong; in the field of zoology there were no clear
ideas about species, and, before Aristotle, no ideas whatever about
orders and genera; with regard to the animals of distant lands where
no Greek had ever been men were completely at the mercy of
travellers' tales.

It was from this civilization and this intermingling of intellectual
brilliancy and ignorance that the physician Ctesias went out in the
year 416 B.C., going eastward from his native town of Cnidus to
accept an appointment at the court of Darius II, King of Persia.
This appointment he owed partly to the already great prestige of
Greek medicine and partly, perhaps, to the fact that he was a member
of the priestly caste of the Asclepiadai in which medicine was a
hereditary profession. He remained in Persia for some seventeen
years, serving both Darius and Artaxerxes. For a single instant he
appears in familiar history, for Xenophon tells us that when Cyrus
broke through the bodyguard of the Great King at Cunaxa and
struck him through his breastplate, it was Ctesias, one of those
fighting near at hand, who healed the wound.[1] * About the year
398 he returned to Cnidus and there wrote his two works, a History
of Persia in twenty-three books, now largely lost, and his *Indica*,
preserved in a fragmentary abstract made in the ninth century by
one Photius, Patriarch of Constantinople.[2]

There is reason to suspect that Photios subordinated the more
commonplace passages of his original and stressed the marvels,
yet that original work was the Mandeville's Travels of its time and

---

* Superior figures refer to the notes which will be found at the back of the book.

even the Greeks who knew the text of Ctesias regarded him as a romancer.[3] It is fair to remember, however, that he wrote, confessedly, about a district which he had never seen, so that he had to depend upon the tales of travellers and the reports of Persian officials, and that his most remarkable stories have usually some discernible foundation in fact. In justice to him we may ask ourselves what would be the present reputation of Herodotus, his great contemporary, if the History had been preserved only in a few selections chosen by a credulous cleric of the Dark Ages. In the thirty-third and final fragment of the *Indica* Ctesias asserts roundly— or perhaps it is Photius who does it for him—that his book is all perfectly true, that he has set down nothing which he has not either seen himself or else heard from the mouths of credible witnesses. Indeed, says he, many more wonderful things than he has put into his book have been left out simply because he does not wish to be thought a liar. We do well to keep this assurance in mind when we come to consider his twenty-fifth fragment, the earliest and one of the most important of European documents relating to the unicorn:—

"There are in India certain wild asses which are as large as horses, and larger. Their bodies are white, their heads dark red, and their eyes dark blue. They have a horn on the forehead which is about a foot and a half in length. The dust filed from this horn is administered in a potion as a protection against deadly drugs. The base of this horn, for some two hands'-breadth above the brow, is pure white; the upper part is sharp and of a vivid crimson ($\phi o \iota \nu \iota \kappa o \hat{\upsilon} \nu$ $\dot{\epsilon} \sigma \tau \iota \nu$, $\dot{\epsilon} \rho \upsilon \theta \rho \grave{o} \nu$ $\pi \acute{a} \nu \upsilon$); and the remainder, or middle portion, is black. Those who drink out of these horns, made into drinking vessels, are not subject, they say, to convulsions or to the holy disease [epilepsy]. Indeed, they are immune even to poisons if, either before or after swallowing such, they drink wine, water, or anything else from these beakers. Other asses, both the tame and the wild, and in fact all animals with solid hoofs, are without the ankle-bone and have no gall in the liver, but these have both the ankle-bone and the gall. This ankle-bone, the most beautiful I have ever seen, is like that of an ox in general appearance and in size, but it is as heavy as lead and its colour is that of cinnabar through and through. The animal is exceedingly swift and powerful, so that no creature, neither the horse nor any other, can overtake it."

Whatever else we may think of this passage, we cannot call it a baseless fabrication. We can believe that Ctesias added to it nothing whatever out of his own fancy, but recorded what he had heard from men who, in their turn, spoke quite honestly and even accurately of what they had seen and heard. Considered from the zoologist's point of view, the fault of the passage is that the facts it contains are strangely combined, but for our present purposes this is just its charm and value. Evidently, Ctesias is describing at least two different animals at once, and it is as though a child, having read descriptions of the lion and the camel, should combine them into a *tertium quid* vaguely like both but exactly similar to neither.

A main ingredient of this compound beast is almost certainly the Indian rhinoceros. The evidence for this lies in what is said of the horn's alexipharmic virtue, that those who drink from beakers made of it are free from certain diseases and from poisons. This belief about rhinoceros horn, still widely current in the Orient, was already old, apparently, in the time of Ctesias, and underneath it there lies a welter of symbolism and superstition exceedingly difficult to comprehend. (See Plate I.) Without attempting to explain it at present, we may accept it as an important datum of our study.

Thinking, then, of the rhinoceros horn, what explanation can be made of the remark about its colours, white and black and red? The actual horns of the rhinoceros vary somewhat widely in hue, and the colour of a carved specimen is really a strange dull red in the thinner parts, deepening toward reddish black where it is thick. At first thought, therefore, it seems possible that Ctesias described the natural colours of the horn by his words μέλαν and ἐρυθρὸν πάνυ, although both epithets are much too strong. This interpretation makes no account, however, of the pure white that is said to extend upward from the brow for two hand's-breadths, for there is no hint of white in the natural horn. The words suggest, by their precision, that Ctesias imagined the horn as having three broad bands of sharply distinct and vivid hues, and this is an effect not of nature but of art. It seems possible that he got his idea of the horn's colouration, not necessarily at first hand, either from some representation of it or else from a horn artificially decorated.

Support for one of these suggestions is given by Manuel Philes, a Greek poet who, although he lived in the thirteenth century, is a mere echo of the ancients. Seeing in the hands of an Indian king a drinking vessel *adorned* with three bands of colour, white and black and red, Philes asks what this cup is made of, and is told that it is the horn of the ὀνάγρος or wild ass.[4] The ultimate source of this passage is Ctesias himself, so that the story in Philes amounts not to a discovery but to an interpretation; yet, considered as such it is both shrewd and plausible. The rhinoceros cups of India may well have been painted with these three colours for symbolic or magical reasons now lost,[5] and the mistaking of such an artificial for a natural colouring would have been only one of several such confusions that we shall meet in unicorn lore.[6]

Yet even this interpretation is not wholly satisfying, for it leaves out of account the remarkable colours of the animal's body. No matter how feeble the colour-sense of the ancients may be thought, no matter how different it may have been from our own or how widely the meanings of colour words may have changed, it seems incredible that any man who had ever seen a rhinoceros could call its body white, its head dark red or purple, and its eyes blue. Taking these hues together with those of the horn, we have a beast coloured like the peacock—and one so gaudy, indeed, that here again we suspect the intervention of art. The splash of vivid dye at the end of the horn, ἐρυθρὸν πάνυ, holds special attention. It recalls a passage in the twenty-first fragment of Ctesias in which we are told that near the sources of the Hyparkhos "there is found a certain flower used for dyeing purposes and not inferior to the Greek purple, giving in fact a far more vivid hue even than that. In the same district there is an animal about as large as a beetle, with very long legs and as red as cinnabar, which the Indians grind into a powder and so use for dyeing the robes and tunics to which they wish to give a purple colour. Their dye-stuffs are better than those of the Persians."

This means, almost certainly, that the Persians of the time of Ctesias imported dyed fabrics from the regions of northern India over which they ruled—fabrics in which a vivid purple was a prominent hue. May it not be that they sometimes found the rhinoceros, a beast unknown to them but familiar to the manufacturers, represented upon these fabrics, and in the strong hues made possible by the native dyes? We know that the animal was so represented, in colours that made no attempt at verisimilitude, by Scythian and Chinese embroiderers of later centuries. The colours of Ctesias's unicorn may, just possibly, have had some such origin.

Undoubtedly there is an appearance of the fantastic in this theory, but we are moving here in a world of fantasy. Ctesias never saw any part of the vast romantic region comprising the Himalaya mountains and Tibet which is what he means by "India", but he heard it talked about for seventeen years, for the most part in languages that he understood imperfectly, by men to whom it was a Land of Cockayne lying many caravan-journeys deep in the gorgeous East. Their gold and ivory and spices and woven fabrics came from there, and concerning the beasts said to inhabit its forests they believed what they were told. Ctesias must have been told something, for his idea about the properties of the onager's horn were not derived from plastic or tectile representation; the suggestion is only that he may have filled in his description with details of an artistic origin. He was not well equipped for criticism of his sources of information, and if it had occurred to him that his unicorned wild ass had an odd look, in particular that it was remarkably polychromatic, he would have quieted his doubts by recalling that it was a native of India.

It may be objected that even in the fourth century before Christ no intelligent man could have assumed the actual existence of a beast such as this on no better evidence than that of a rude representation. Against this objection one may bring forward the exactly similar assumption made by a scientifically trained traveller of the nineteenth century who was converted to belief in the existence of unicorns by the discovery of a primitive picture of what he took for one in a South African cave.[7]

But thus far we have ignored the fact that Ctesias calls his unicorns wild asses (ὄνοι ἄγριοι), and even with such an absurd name as that of the hippopotamus—"river horse"—before us it seems unlikely that either he or his informants could ever have seen anything asinine in the rhinoceros. The wild ass, a native of Persia, as well as of India, should have been familiar to Ctesias by personal observation. It was vividly described by Xenophon[8] and was a favourite quarry of Mesopotamian kings, its great speed and ferocity making the chase of it indeed a royal sport.[9] Ctesias could scarcely have spent seventeen years in Persia without knowing rather definitely what he meant when he referred to the wild ass, and it seems probable that this animal contributed something to his description of the unicorn. In a part of that description which I have not translated above he says that the unicorn fights "with horn, teeth, and heels". This, and what is said of the beast's great speed, suggests the wild ass; but in saying that the unicorn increases its speed as it runs he gives us a closely observed trait of the rhinoceros. Xenophon tells us that the flesh of the wild asses killed by the soldiers of Cyrus in the Arabian Desert was "like the flesh of deer, although more tender", but Ctesias, with obvious reference to the rhinoceros, says that the flesh of his unicorn is too bitter to be eaten.[10] There is even a possibility that the colouration of the real wild ass, which is described as "reddish above" and "silvery grey" on the belly and hinder parts, may have suggested the white body and red head of the one-horned onager.

For a moment, all difficulties seem to be solved, and one is ready to believe that Ctesias or his informants confused and combined the rhinoceros with the wild ass, clapping the artificially decorated horn of the one upon the brow of the other.[11] When this solution is closely examined, however, its plausibility vanishes, for common sense demands a reason why a known animal should have been thus violently transmogrified. Gross inaccuracy with regard to the rhinoceros is what we should expect, but the addition of a horn to a beast that Ctesias must have seen many times, and always horn-less, calls for explanation. Common sense asks how it happened that the horn of the rhinoceros, so obviously on the nose that its position there gave the beast its very name, was transferred to a totally different position, so as to stand ἐν τῷ μετώπῳ. What is needed, apparently, is some intermediary between the rhinoceros and the wild ass, to ease the transference of shape and characteristics from the one to the other.

A vigorous and widespread belief in a unicorn inhabiting the table-lands of Tibet—a region included within the "India" of Ctesias—can be traced in existing documents as far back as the time of Genghis Khan, and there is good reason for supposing that it is much older still. This Tibetan "unicorn", undoubtedly, is the *Antholops Hodgsoni*,[12] a large and fleet antelope the nearly straight horns of which, seen from one side, give the effect of a single horn.[13] It is certain that the natives, who see these animals frequently, have long believed that some individuals in almost every herd—those individuals, naturally, which they have seen in profile and at a distance—are unicorns. May it be that some vague report of these antelopes helped to set the single horn of the Indian rhinoceros upon the brow of the Mesopotamian wild ass? The conjecture looks hazardous at first, and too complex, but it gathers credibility as we consider the evidence bit by bit and as we find much the same sort of thing happening elsewhere. Such a confusion, instead of being unique, might rather be called typical, and typical not of the ancient world alone but of far more recent times. Compared with the juggling of species and the transferences of animal attributes to be found in the mediaeval bestiaries, it approaches scientific exactness.

This confusion, rolling three different beasts into one, need not be attributed to Ctesias. The rumour of the unicorn came up to him over the long trails running westward from a land as strange, as replete with incredible possibilities, as America was to the Spanish conquistadors. His unicorn, like the far less probable beasts of the Arabian Nights, was pieced together by travel-weary men sitting about many a camp-fire, drowsy, uncritical, pooling all that they had seen and heard. We may believe that every contributor meant and tried to tell the exact truth—just as each of the blind men in the proverb intended to give an honest report about the elephant, the discrepancies in their results being due to the fact that one of them had hold of the animal's trunk, another grasped a tusk, and a third was pulling at the tail. Some of these scientists of the camp-fire had seen the rhinoceros, perhaps, or had talked with men who had seen

I. RHINOCEROS HORN BEAKER

II. THE UNICORN OF MEDIAEVAL MANUSCRIPTS

him; others had handled the painted horn and had heard report of its occult virtues; still others, hearing talk about a beast with a single horn, and that a horn of magic properties, would recall the apparently unicorned animals they had seen feeding at a distance with a herd of antelopes, and they might even know that the apparently single horns of these animals were objects of veneration in Tibet and were sold to pilgrims at high prices; finally, the merchants and tax-gatherers of Persia, returning from the lands where such tales were told and trying to make clear what they had heard, might say that the beast with the precious vari-coloured horn standing in the middle of its forehead was a good deal like a wild-ass—a statement practically equivalent to the declaration that it *was* a wild-ass. For all these earnest, far-travelled, and well-intentioned men Ctesias, the court physician, acted merely as amanuensis, freshening and defining his impressions somewhat, perhaps, by means of any figures and images of the unicorn there may have been available.

Or so, at any rate, I make it out. Besides these three actual animals, towering above them all, there may have been a guiding and shaping conception of a celestial and purely symbolical unicorn of which the beast thus compounded was only a feeble earthly representative. Of that I shall have something to say in the proper place. For the present it is enough to have shown how the unicorn of Ctesias may have been constructed out of mundane materials.

The close attention we have paid to one brief passage in an unimportant book is justified by the fact that this passage is one of the two main sources from which the Western legend of the unicorn comes down to us. It was written far back in the Ages of Authority, during which men seldom thought of acquiring opinions of their own by independent investigation and when scholarship consisted largely in the discovery, balancing, and recording of what others had said. This habit of mind made it possible for the passage just considered to reverberate through twenty centuries.

Shortly after the time of Ctesias there arose one supreme authority, "*il maestro di color che sanno*", who might have given the legend of the unicorn its quietus by a single blow. The animal had a narrow escape when Aristotle passed it by with a few scant references merely sufficient to show that he believed in its existence.[14] Why he should have believed in it at all, considering that he thought Ctesias untrustworthy, and what other evidence he may have had, we shall probably never know. He even makes a slight addition to the unicorn lore handed on by Ctesias, for he says: "We have never seen an animal with a solid hoof and with two horns, and there are only a few that have a solid hoof and one horn, as the Indian ass and the oryx. Of all animals with a solid hoof, the Indian ass alone has a talus."[15] Aristotle, then, not only believed in the existence of a one-horned Indian ass but he thought also that the oryx has only one horn and a solid hoof. He was a man whose very errors were to be far more fruitful than most men's correct opinions.—Already there are two different species of unicorns for the echoers of authority to describe.

The unicorn has no place in the classic literature of Greece and Rome, yet during the five hundred years between Aristotle and Aelian its legend somehow made progress. Aristotle knew of only two unicorns, but Aelian and Pliny between them muster seven: the rhinoceros, the Indian ass, the oryx, the Indian ox, the Indian horse, the bison, and the unicorn proper and *par excellence*. Aelian's acquaintance with two or three of these, moreover, is far more extended than that shown by Aristotle or even by Ctesias, but there is no way of discovering how his increments of knowledge came to him. His book about animals, composed in a florid Greek, although he was a Roman and spent his life in Italy, exerted an influence upon later writers on zoology inferior only to that of Aristotle and of Pliny. Every phrase of his three considerable passages about the unicorn was conned and reiterated many times during the following fifteen hundred years and for this reason they deserve careful attention.

In the first of these passages[16] Aelian adds nothing to the statement of Ctesias. In the second he says: "I have found that wild asses as large as horses are to be seen in India. The body of this animal is white, except on the head, which is red, while the eyes are azure. It has a horn on the brow, about one cubit and a half in length, which is white at the base, crimson at the top, and black between.

These variegated horns, I learn, are used as drinking-cups by the Indians—although not, to be sure, by all of the people. Only the great men use them, after having them ringed about with hoops of gold exactly as they would put bracelets on some beautiful statue. And it is said that whosoever drinks from this kind of horn is safe from all incurable diseases such as convulsions and the so-called holy disease, and that he cannot be killed by poison."[17] In the rest of the chapter Aelian speaks of the *black* ankle-bone, of the onager's way of fighting with horn and teeth and heels, and of its bitter flesh.

The foundation of this passage, obviously, is that of Ctesias, but there are significant additions and variations. Aelian adds that the beakers are used only by the great men of India and that they are adorned with gold rings. He diverges from Ctesias in saying that the horn is about a cubit and a half in length instead of only one cubit, and also in asserting that the astragalus or ankle-bone is black. Ctesias, who affirms that he has seen this ankle-bone, declares that it is red like cinnabar. Shall we infer that Aelian had some source of information about unicorns other than the book of the court physician? He might well have increased the length of the horn without authority, as several others were to do after him, but his remark about the gold rings and about the use of the cups by great men alone is hardly of the sort that even a naturally inaccurate man like Aelian evolves from his own mind. His disagreement with Ctesias about the colour of the ankle-bone raises a curious problem. Ctesias gives us the impression that this bone was important by saying in the first place, quite wrongly, that among solid-hoofed animals only the wild ass has it, and secondly that the unicorned onager is hunted in India for the horn and the ankle-bone only. What could have given it this importance? Possibly the use of it as a charm or talisman, for we know that every part of the body of the rhinoceros was thought to have magical virtues; and it may be that the specimen seen by Ctesias had been painted or dyed so as to make it both an ornament and an amulet. The common use of these ankle-bones in the ancient world, however, was for the making of dice, as one is reminded by the Latin word *talus*, which means both "an astragalus" and "a die". There is a bare possibility that Aelian was thinking of the black dice of Italy.

The third passage in Aelian about the unicorn is the most important. "They say", he writes, "that there are mountains in the interior regions of India which are inaccessible to men and therefore full of wild beasts. Among these is the unicorn, which they call the 'cartazon' (καρτάζωνος). This animal is as large as a full-grown horse, and it has a mane, tawny hair, feet like those of the elephant, and the tail of a goat. It is exceedingly swift of foot. Between its brows there stands a single black horn, not smooth but with certain natural rings (οὐ λεῖον, ἀλλὰ ἑλιγμοὺς ἔχον τινὰς καὶ μάλα αὐτοφυεῖς), and tapering to a very sharp point. Of all animals, this one has the most dissonant voice. With beasts of other species that approach it the 'cartazon' is gentle, but it fights with those of its own kind, and not only do the males fight naturally among themselves but they contend even against the females and push the contest to the death. The animal has great strength of body, and it is armed besides with an unconquerable horn. It seeks out the most deserted places and wanders there alone. In the season of rut it grows gentle towards the chosen female and they pasture side by side, but when this time is over he becomes wild again and wanders alone. They say that the young ones are sometimes taken to the king to be exhibited in contests on days of festival, because of their strength, but no one remembers the capture of a single specimen of mature age."[18]

In this passage we part company with Ctesias. Aelian is here describing the rhinoceros and getting much closer to the real animal than Ctesias did, even giving it a name, "cartazon," which is apparently connected with the Sanscrit *kartājan*, lord of the desert. His account is correct with regard to the beast's habitat, size, feet, tail, voice, strength, and solitary habits, although he is wrong in what he says of its mane, its tawny hair, its pugnacity, and its great swiftness. These errors are of little importance, however, in comparison with his assertion that the horn stands between the brows. This horn is black, and it is not smooth but has certain natural rings.[19] It is about a cubit and a half, that is to say about twenty-seven inches, in length. Almost certainly, this is the horn of an antelope. The suggestion made above that the Ctesian unicorn owes something to the antelope is corroborated by Aelian's independent and unconscious recourse to the same animal.

The most influential of Aelian's remarks about the unicorn were those concerning its indomitability, its solitude, its habit of fighting with others of its own species except with females during the season of rut,[20] and the custom of taking such specimens as were captured when young to the king, who exhibited them on public holidays.

By this last touch one is inevitably reminded again of the rhinoceros, which Aelian, as a Roman of the third century A.D., must have seen frequently at the Circus.[21] He had not the slightest suspicion, however, that his "cartazon" of India and the well-known rhinoceros were identical. The one, as he tells us here, has a horn between the eyebrows; in XVII, 40, he discusses the other briefly, saying that it would be ridiculous for him to describe its appearance, because it is familiar to all Greeks and Romans; but he does say that it has a horn on its nose. Thus we see that he describes the rhinoceros, rather accurately in most respects, without knowing that he is doing so, and that in another place he refuses to describe the rhinoceros because it is too familiar. The strange confusion had strange results, lasting on into the nineteenth century. One of the more amusing phases of it is the fact that when Aelian is speaking of the wild ass he makes much of the magical properties of its horn, but when he comes to speak of the "cartazon," or rhinoceros, to which alone those properties were originally attributed, he has not a word to say of them.

Among the several passages in which the elder Pliny mentions unicorned animals, the only one of present importance is that in which he says: "The Orsæan Indians hunt an exceedingly wild beast called the monoceros, which has a stag's head, elephant's feet, and a boar's tail, the rest of its body being like that of a horse. It makes a deep lowing noise, and one black horn two cubits long projects from the middle of its forehead. This animal, they say, cannot be taken alive."[22]

Here, one observes, is a sober account written by a serious-minded man. We may be sure that Pliny had read stories of the horn's prophylactic powers because Pliny read everything, but he does not speak of them, contenting himself with adding another half-cubit to the horn's length and then passing on to other matters. His brief reference to the unicorn is important chiefly because for more than a thousand years his beliefs about animals were the beliefs of almost every reader of Latin in Europe. If he had enlarged, like his Greek authorities, upon the horn's medical values, the western legend of the unicorn, with a full millennium added for the development of its more interesting elements, would have attained an even richer and stranger complexity than it did. Pliny might have transplanted the fascinating Oriental idea of the horn's prophylactic virtues into the hotbeds of western folklore and magic, where it would have flourished mightily, but, having to do without his assistance, that idea came into the popular legend of the West only a few centuries before the awakening science of Europe was ready to cope with it.

The docility with which later writers accepted the opinions of Pliny was shown almost at once by Julius Solinus, whose description of the unicorn has a sonority that makes it worthy of direct quotation: "*Atrocissimum est Monoceros, monstrum mugitu horrendo, equino corpore, elephanti pedibus, cauda suilla, capite cervino, cornu è media fronte protenditur splendore mirifico ad longitudinem pedum quatuor, ita tamen, ut quidquid impetat, facile ictu ejus perforetur. Vivus non venit in hominum potestatem, et interimi quidem potest, capi non potest.*" [23] Whatever rhetoric can do to make the unicorn impressive Solinus has done. In this passage not even Arthur Golding can improve upon his original, for he translates: "But the cruellest is the Unicorne, a Monster that belloweth horriblie, bodyed like a horse, footed like an Eliphant, tayled like a Swyne, and headed like a Stagge. His horne sticketh out of the midds of hys forehead, of a wonderful brightness about foure foote long, so sharp, that whatsoever he pusheth at, he striketh it through easily. He is never caught alive; kylled he may be, but taken he cannot bee." [24]

We observe, to be sure, that Solinus has added another foot to the length of the horn and that he calls the monoceros a "monster"—

an epithet vehemently exclaimed against by the pious of later ages, who considered it both sacrilegious and bad zoology to call any beast monstrous that was mentioned in the Bible. Otherwise, there is nothing new in Solinus, and nothing not to be found in Pliny except the vivid touch of colour on the horn which, as we have seen, may come from the indelible dyes of Upper India.

One really learned and thoughtful man of the ancient world seems to have been confronted with the rhinoceros and with the Indian superstition concerning it at the same time. This was the enigmatic seer, traveller, and rhetorician Apollonius of Tyana, whose life and sayings, as they have come down to us, form the strangest tissue of idle nonsense and lofty wisdom. During his travels in India, says his biographer, Apollonius saw the wild asses that were captured near the Hyphasis and was told that cups made from their horns—single horns, which grew from the brow—were used by the kings of India in the belief that those who drank from them were free for that day from sickness and poison. When Damis, one of the philosopher's companions, asked what he thought of this story, he said : "I should have believed it if I had found that the kings of this country were immortal." [25] By these words the man who has usually been regarded as a mystagogue and a liar, partly because of the attacks of his Christian enemies, takes high rank among the commentators upon the unicorn. He is the first man of whom it is asserted— he does not make the assertion himself—that he actually saw the unicorn, but even this was not sufficient to induce a perfect faith.

Only two further references to the unicorn in ancient literature are worthy of attention. In his long poem on the art of hunting Oppian speaks of certain Aonian (Bœotian) oxen as having solid hoofs and one heavy horn protruding from the middle of the brow.[26] Of these we can only say that if they really did inhabit Bœotia in his time it is strange that we hear nothing of them from Aristotle or Pausanias or even Plutarch, who would scarcely have left such remarkable denizens of his district unheralded. We suspect that Oppian erred about the habitat and even the species of these bulls when we read that their horns are coloured white and black and red, for we seem to remember having heard of this colouration elsewhere.

The other reference occurs in the writings of a man often regarded as the greatest figure of the ancient world. Julius Caesar tells us that in his time there was to be found in the Hercynian Forest—where wonders have always abounded—a huge beast with the form of a stag, from the middle of whose brow and between the ears there stood forth one horn, longer and straighter than the horns known to the Romans.[27] The words are impressive by their precision and directness, and they convince us at least of this, that one of the keenest minds recorded in history believed in the unicorn.

And yet it is clear that the unicorn legend did not really flourish in the ancient Western world. It lived merely from book to book, a literary life, taking no hold and showing no vitality in the popular imagination. It found no place in creative literature or in plastic art; religious symbolism and mythology knew nothing of it; if it ever appeared in the ancient folklore of the Mediterranean it seems to have left no trace; Galen, Hippocrates, Dioscorides even, never mention the prophylactic and therapeutic values of the horn. A thousand such merely literary references as those we have considered, most of them borrowed and reflecting a belief which had vitality only in a distant land, would never, unless by lucky chance, have given the unicorn an important position in true legend. To gain such standing, together with the complexity and strangeness and human significance that would accrue, it had to be brought closer home to the erring, dreamful, devoted hearts of men than the books of the most learned zoologists and the most honey-tongued rhetoricians could ever bring it. The legend had to be helped out of the library into the world.

Such assistance was close at hand.

CHAPTER II

THE HOLY HUNT

In the King James Version of the Bible there are seven clear references to the unicorn, all of which occur in the Old Testament. The animal is mentioned twice in the Pentateuch, once in Job, once in Isaiah, and three times in the Psalms. These passages read as follows :—

"God brought them out of Egypt; he hath as it were the strength of the unicorn."—Numbers xxiii. 22.[1]

"His glory is like the firstling of his bullock, and his horns are like the horns of unicorns : with them he shall push the people together to the ends of the earth."—Deuteronomy xxxiii. 17.

"Save me from the lion's mouth; for thou hast heard me from the horns of unicorns."—Psalm xxii. 21.

"He maketh them [the cedars of Lebanon] also to skip like a calf; Lebanon and Sirion like a young unicorn."—Psalm xxix. 6.

"But my horn shalt thou exalt like the horn of the unicorn: I shall be anointed with fresh oil."—Psalm xcii. 10.

"And the unicorns shall come down with them, and the bullocks with their bulls ; and their land shall be soaked with blood, and their dust made fat with fatness."—Isaiah xxxiv. 7.

"Will the unicorn be willing to serve thee, or abide in thy crib?

"Canst thou bind the unicorn with his band in the furrow? or will he harrow the valleys after thee?

"Wilt thou trust him because his strength is great? or wilt thou leave thy labour to him?

"Wilt thou believe him, that he will bring home thy seed, and gather it into thy barn?"—Job xxxix. 9–12.

One thing is evident in these passages: they refer to some actual animal of which the several writers had vivid if not clear impressions. Although the allusions were made at widely different times, the characterization is consistent, bringing before us a beast remarkable for strength, ferocity, wildness, and unconquerable spirit. Nothing suggests that it was supernatural, a creature of fancy, for it is linked with the lion, the bullock and the calf; yet it was mysterious enough to inspire a sense of awe, and powerful enough to provide a vigorous metaphor.

Much patient toil has been expended in the effort to identify the Biblical unicorn. At the outset of such an inquiry one finds that we owe the word "unicorn" in the King James Version [2] to the μονόκερως everywhere used by the Septuagint to translate the Hebrew *Re'em*, a bit of translation, interesting in itself, which had enduring results. So far as the western development of the unicorn legend is concerned, this translation is like the main jewel of a watch, holding the intricate structure together. One does not like to see it set down, therefore, as a mere blunder, and when we think of the problem with only such light as the Seventy had we are inclined to call it a minor stroke of genius. They did not know what animal the Hebrew seers and poets had in mind when speaking of the *Re'em*, but they found that it was characterized as fleet, fierce, indomitable, and especially distinguished by the armour of its brow. Dim recollections were awakened by these traits, and so the Seventy called the one unknown animal by the name of another. Even from our point of vantage it seems doubtful whether they could have found a closer equivalent for a beast which had been mysterious and awful to the Hebrews than this monoceros or unicorn which was to themselves still strange, remote, and conjectural.

Apart from such appropriateness, we discover another value of a different kind in this translation. For the greater part of their course, and until the scholarship of the late Renaissance brought them together, what may be called the Hellenic and the Hebraic branches of the unicorn legend ran separately, with a cleanness of division that would have satisfied Matthew Arnold himself. This one word μονόκερως, however, with its already accumulated overtones, was a connecting channel between the two, more important in fact than in appearance. For a long time it maintained belief in the Greek tradition by seeming to imply that whatever Ctesias and his successors had said about the unicorn had the sanction of divine authority. The Septuagint translation of *Re'em* by μονόκερως, a translation which meant hardly more than that X = X, was accepted, as the inspired word of God. Ctesias, Aelian, Pliny, and Solinus seemed to be corroborated by Jehovah.[3]

In several passages of the Vulgate the *Re'em* becomes a rhinoceros, losing as much in imaginative value as it gains in clarity of outline. We are hardly to suppose, however, that Jerome derived this translation directly from the Hebrew text in complete independence of the Septuagint version; it is more likely that he, like St. Ambrose, held the μονόκερως of the Greeks to be identical with the rhinoceros —a view in which he was to have many followers and as many ardent antagonists. His word amounts, therefore, to an interpretation of the Septuagint's word, and one feels that it is less good largely because it is more precise. How often Jerome may have attended the Circus during those unregenerate days in Rome which he so bitterly repented we cannot be sure, but if he went at all he probably saw there the animal that he later identified with the Biblical *Re'em*. In superficial appearance it would seem to correspond closely enough.

An attempt to trace the devious and learned arguments by which Biblical scholars have tried to establish the identity of the *Re'em* would lead us too far afield, considering that there is no reason to believe that the Hebrews themselves thought of this animal as one-horned. None of the passages cited above forces such an interpretation, and only one of them, that from the ninety-second Psalm, even suggests it. Elsewhere, as in Deuteronomy xxxiii. 17 and Psalms xxii. 21, the word for "horns" is used in the plural while

"*Re'em*" is singular.[4] Clearly, therefore, this deep and dark little pocket of erudition need not be explored at present, and we may be content with seeing what has been brought out of it.

After the general abandonment of belief in the unicorn during the eighteenth century there was a return to Jerome's view that the *Re'em* was the rhinoceros; but as this animal became better known it was felt that he was not fierce and swift enough, and there was doubt whether the Hebrews were likely to have known him. Another view attributed the whole belief in the *Re'em* to the bas-reliefs of huge mythological beasts seen by the Jews in Egypt and Mesopotamia. Under the leadership of Samuel Bochart, the profoundest scholar who has ever waded these deep waters, a considerable company once contended for the oryx, pointing out that the Arabic name of this animal is still *rîm*; but the value of this discovery was soon destroyed by the announcement of another school that *rimu* was the Assyrian name of the gigantic aurochs or *Bos Primigenius*, a species of wild buffalo which became extinct in the sixteenth century. Cuvier, basing his measurement upon remains of the aurochs much smaller than others since discovered, estimated that this animal was twelve feet long and almost seven feet high; its teeth have been found in a cave on Mount Lebanon; Julius Caesar describes it as indigenous to his prolific Hercynian Forest, and in terms fitting all that is said in the Bible about the *Re'em*;[5] Layard identified the animal with the majestic sculptured bulls of Nineveh.[6] The *Bos Primigenius* now holds the field. Its bulk, speed, and savage ferocity are described by Caesar in words that make it clear why the Hebrews always spoke of the *Re'em* with bated breath. So much, then, for the source of the Septuagint μονόκερως—a word inspired by Apollo if not by Jehovah—and therefore of the Biblical unicorn. One is glad to have found the *Re'em* worthy of his descendant.

Although it seems clear that the writers of the Old Testament did not think of the *Re'em* as one-horned, there is a possibility that the Talmudic writers did come to consider it so. Any horned animal remembered chiefly by its representations in the sculptures of Egypt, Babylon, Nineveh, and Persepolis, was likely, as we shall see, to be regarded sooner or later as a unicorn, and there came a time when Hebrew writers, with no native sculpture to guide them, were dependent upon just such representations. The Talmudic interpreters, it is certain, had never seen the *Re'em*, for they exaggerate its size "out of all reasonable compass", asserting in one passage that it is so tall as to touch the clouds [7] and in another that it was too large to be got into the ark and so had to be towed along behind by a cord tied to its horn. [8] Obviously, the *Re'em* is here seen fading into myth, and so it may have been the original of the wonderful ox three times mentioned in the Talmud as the victim of Adam's first sacrifice—an ox with the interesting peculiarity that it had only one horn on its brow. [9]

The unicorn legend gained valuable and lasting corroboration from the brilliant error of the Septuagint, but this alone would not have won for it anything like its later prestige; another influence was required to carry the unicorn into the centre of Christian myth and symbolism. Fully to understand the second influence that was brought into play we should need to know more than we do about that agglomeration of vice and virtue, wealth and poverty, ignorance and erudition, wisdom and folly, which we call Alexandria. In that city, during the third century after Christ and under Christian influence, there were brought together a number of animal stories, some of them drawn from the wide-spread "Beast Epic" of the world and others apparently concocted to serve the immediate need, each of them fitted with a "moral" somewhat after the fashion of Aesop's Fables. It seems unnecessary to assume that any single individual was responsible for the collection as a whole or that a single original text ever existed. [10]

Readers of Tertullian, Cassiodorus, and even Origen, will not need to be told that the habit of allegorizing not merely everything in the Scriptures but everything outside of them was at this time fastening upon the Christian mind. The world of nature, seldom valued for its own sake by the typical Christian, was more and more regarded as a mere storehouse of edifying metaphors. What we should call facts were felt to be of little worth in comparison with the moral truths that alleged facts could be supposed to signify and

it was considered that God had created the lower animals, particularly those that seemed to have no other use, solely for the moral
and spiritual instruction of mankind. Very little of Aristotle's objec-
tive spirit and method was carried over into the Christian thought
centring at Alexandria, disabled as that was from the start by a
puerile moral-hunting and phrase-making, by the determination to
make facts bend to the uses of edification and to see, almost literally,
books in the running brooks, sermons in stones, and good—or, what
was considered the same thing, moral significance—in everything.

These were some of the conditions surrounding the haphazard
selection, fabrication, and welding together of the stories composing
the Christian Beast Epic. In the primitive forms of that body of
fable, apparently, each article began with a quotation from Scripture
followed by the formula: "But the physiologus [i.e. the naturalist]
says . . . " and then came a description of the major traits, real or
fancied, of some animal, capped by the moral deduction, the lesson
to be learned therefrom. Later copyists seem to have separated the
animal descriptions and the morals from the texts they were intended
to illustrate, so that each article began with the words: "The
Physiologus says." Thus the whole collection, naturally regarded as
the work of one author called Physiologus, came to be called by that
supposed author's name. In later centuries it was called, in Europe,
the "Bestiary".

What sort of thing we may expect from this treasury of animal
lore is indicated by its account of the ant-lion: "Physiologus says
that the ant-lion's father has the shape of a lion and his mother that
of an ant. His father feeds on flesh and his mother on herbs. These
two bring forth the ant-lion, which is a mixture of both, for his
fore part is that of a lion and his hind part that of an ant. Being thus
composed, he can eat neither flesh like his father nor herbs like his
mother, and so he starves to death."

Official Christianity did what it could to repudiate this collection,
for a synod of Pope Gelasius in 496 condemned it as the work of
"heretics", although it had been falsely ascribed to Saint Ambrose.
In spite of this and other attacks it remained familiar and influential
throughout Christendom for over a thousand years, and there are

extant texts in Greek, Arabic, Syriac, Latin, Armenian, Old High German, Icelandic, Old French, Provençal, Ethiopic, Italian, and Anglo-Saxon. It was chiefly by means of these Bestiaries that the popular as distinguished from the learned tradition of the unicorn was disseminated. Not Ctesias and not Aelian but this grist of old wives' tales fathered upon an imaginary "Physiologus" was responsible for scattering the image of the unicorn throughout Europe, making him familiar where books were never read, contorting his shapely limbs on corbels and cornices and miserere seats, depicting him in stained glass and on tapestry, lifting him finally to the British Royal Coat of Arms.

Existing texts of the *Physiologus* vary considerably in minor details, but this is the substance of what they have to relate about the unicorn: He is a small animal, like a kid, but surprisingly fierce for his size, with one very sharp horn on his head, and no hunter is able to catch him by force. Yet there is a trick by which he is taken. Men lead a virgin to the place where he most resorts and leave her there alone. As soon as he sees this virgin he runs and lays his head in her lap. She fondles him and he falls asleep. The hunters then approach and capture him and lead him to the palace of the king.

One may have known this story for years and may have seen it represented a hundred times in Christian art, yet if he has any gift for stubborn wonder he will be surprised at each return by its strangeness, and curious to know by what queer twist of thought or accident of transmission it has taken on its present form. For this tale, absurd though it may be, is not childishly and feebly absurd like that of the ant-lion; there is a suggestion of age about it and a hint of symbolism not wholly due to the fact that it has served for centuries as a Christian symbol. What affinity did the makers of the tale imagine between the unicorn and the virgin? Why should this animal be thought worth so elaborate a ruse? Why is he led "to the palace of the king"? These questions have puzzled a good many acute and learned minds, and they have never been answered.

But these questions arise out of the *Physiologus* story by itself, without reference to the fact that another unicorn legend was already current in the Mediterranean world. The moment we recall that fact, another set of questions comes into view. What strands of connection can be discerned between the two legends? Instead of the proud beast of Ctesias and Aelian—fierce, shaped like an ass or horse, solid-hoofed, dangerous, indomitable—we have here an animal so small that it is likened to a kid, with a divided hoof and a beard as seen in later Christian art, and chiefly characterized by a propensity to fall asleep in virgins' laps. The only discernible likenesses are that in both legends the animal is said to be fierce and not to be taken by the ordinary arts of the hunter, and that the quarry in both belongs to the king; but these similarities are so slight as to seem hardly worth mentioning. Apparently we must conclude that the unicorn legend has had two independent origins, or, in stronger terms, that there are two legends of the unicorn, one of which we may call the Ctesian and the other that of *Physiologus*.

With this not very satisfactory conclusion in mind we may leave, for the present, the larger question of inter-relationship, turning back to the *Physiologus* account for a closer examination. Some light may be thrown upon that account by the allegorical interpretation that usually follows, though in varying forms, the story itself. In its simpler versions this interpretation likens the unicorn directly to Christ: its one horn is said to signify the unity of Christ and the Father; its fierceness and defiance of the hunter are to remind us that neither Principalities nor Powers nor Thrones were able to control the Messiah against His will; its small stature is a symbol of Christ's humility and its likeness to a kid of His association with sinful men. The virgin is held to represent the Virgin Mary and the huntsman is the Holy Spirit acting through the Angel Gabriel. Taken as a whole, then, the story of the unicorn's capture typifies the Incarnation of Christ.[11]

Thus we see the unicorn caught up into the fervours and ecstasies of Christian symbolism and into the very worship of the Virgin. There could be no limit, once this had happened, to the glory of his career. For this reason one is all the more eager to discover, if possible, the origin of the remarkable story upon which the symbolism is based.

The widest variations from the typical unicorn story to be found in what may be called, with caution, the primitive texts of *Physiologus*, are those to be seen in the Syriac and Provençal versions.[12] In the Provençal Bestiary, composed under Waldensian influences, the "properties" of many of the beasts are changed, and the unicorn is made to represent the Devil, the signification of the virgin-capture being that evil can be overcome only by virtue. The Syriac version is so interesting as to deserve quotation:—

"There is an animal called *dajja*, extremely gentle, which the hunters are unable to capture because of its great strength. It has in the middle of its brow a single horn. But observe the ruse by which the huntsmen take it. They lead forth a young virgin, pure and chaste, to whom, when the animal sees her, he approaches, throwing himself upon her. Then the girl offers him her breasts, and the animal begins to suck the breasts of the maiden and to conduct himself familiarly with her. Then the girl, while sitting quietly, reaches forth her hand and grasps the horn on the animal's brow, and at this point the huntsmen come up and take the beast and go away with him to the king.—Likewise the Lord Christ has raised up for us a horn of salvation in the midst of Jerusalem, in the house of God, by the intercession of the Mother of God, a virgin pure, chaste, full of mercy, immaculate, inviolate."[13]

Little assistance in one's search for the origin of the virgin-capture story would seem to be obtainable from this wild tale, which looks like confusion worse confounded, but at least it precludes all possibility that that story was invented *ad hoc* by Christian allegorizers.[14] One is convinced of this partly by the fact that the *significatio* does not here fit the story as told but is forced upon it in accordance with a custom known to be followed elsewhere. More conclusive is the emphasis upon sexual attraction as the source of the power exercised by the "virgin" over the unicorn. If the virgin-capture story had been deliberately composed as a symbol of Christ's incarnation—such a supposition implying, of course, that the virgin was always and from the start understood to represent the Virgin Mary—it would scarcely have been corrupted by Christians in just this way. In this version the Christian interpretation is forced upon

a tale not fully prepared to receive it; old and incongruous elements
—or so one might say if disposed to beg the question—have not
been deleted here as they have in the other versions. The Syriac
version seems to represent an idea about the right method of
capturing unicorns which is older than *Physiologus*; it suggests a
possibility that the origin of the virgin-capture story, if it can be
found, will turn out to be non-Christian and will rest more heavily,
or at least more obviously, upon sexual attraction than the
Christianized form of the story usually does.

This element was not entirely ignored in later Christian writing
about the unicorn. Hildegarde of Bingen and Thomas of Cantipré,
among others, enlarge upon the animal's skill in detecting a virgin
at sight, and in some stories we are told that when the huntress
is not really a virgin she is killed by the beast—a fairly obvious
intrusion of the virginity-test theme. Furthermore, it was held by
some that the hunt was more likely to succeed if the virgin was
naked,[15] and several insist that she must be beautiful. (See Plate II).
Alanus de Insulis, who flourished at the end of the twelfth century,
gives a curious explanation of the story [16] in which the sexual interpretation is made in terms of mediaeval science. He concludes that the
virgin's power is due to a radical difference in "humours", the *cali-
dissima natura* of the unicorn being drawn irresistibly to its opposite,
the *femina frigida et humida*. The unicorn, he says, has an excess of fer-
vent spirits or humours which dilate his heart, and when he comes into
the pure moist air surrounding the virgin he feels such relief and
is so delighted by that feminine atmosphere that he lies down in her
lap. In several early versions, moreover, and notably in the Ethiopic
Bestiary, the virgin is not wholly passive but adds certain calculated
blandishments to the natural attraction of her charms.

The connotations of the virgin-capture story are in fact definitely
erotic, and the Christian interpretation put upon it does not harmonize with the tale exactly but seems to wrench it out of its natural
course of development. In saying that the interpretation does not
harmonize I refer to the difficulty of imagining the Virgin Mary
as lending herself to a deliberate deception of her Son, the omniscient
God. In saying that the story seems to have been wrenched out of

its natural course I am thinking of what would probably have been done with it elsewhere. The Greeks, if they had been at all interested in animal allegories, might have made it a symbol of the over-mastering power of erotic emotion, leading to the ruin of a strong, proud nature; the Hebrew poets might have used it somewhat as they did the great legend of Samson which it so curiously and perhaps significantly resembles—although Delilah is not a good surrogate for the virgin; but in Christian legend the story's original intention has been thwarted, I believe, to serve the purposes of edification. The attempt to point out what that original intention was, and so to solve, in some sense, the long-standing mystery of the virgin-capture story, may be postponed until we have followed the development of the story during the Christian ages.

Probably the earliest narration of the tale in literature outside of the *Physiologus* itself is that in the Commentary on Saint Basil's *Hexaemeron*, long attributed to Saint Eustathius of Antioch, who died about A.D. 330.[17] This curious work weaves about Basil's poetic account of creation a tissue of popular legend which makes it good hunting-ground for the student of folklore. In most of its discussions of animals it drags a wide net through the sea of Levantine super-stition, but the unicorn passage follows *Physiologus* in every detail, its only importance for our purpose consisting in the fact that here we see the virgin-capture story moving out into literature under its own sail, without assistance from allegory.

The next mention of the tale was far more influential, for it occurred in a work that was read, copied, imitated, and learned almost by heart for centuries, a work used as quarry and foundation by most of the "encyclopaedists" of the Middle Ages—writers who tried, not so unsuccessfully as might be supposed, to compress all human knowledge within a single book. Isidore of Seville, who died in 636, was one of the men who have exerted an influence upon human thought out of all proportion to their powers chiefly because of their strategic positions in time or place. Played upon by many forces, which he is incapable of criticizing or relating, his tendency is to shovel together rather helplessly all that he has read and heard.

This tendency is evident in his important account of the unicorn, which I give myself the pleasure of quoting in John of Trevisa's English:—

"Rynoceron in grewe [i.e. in Greek] is to meanynge an Horne in the nose. & Monoceros is an Unycorne: and is a ryght cruell beast. And hath that name for he hath in the mydull of the forehed an horne of foure fote long. And that horne is so sharpe & so stronge that he throwyth downe al or thyrleth al that he resyth on. . . . And this beest fyghtyth ofte wyth the Elyphaunt and woundyth & stycketh hym in the wombe, and throwyth hym downe to the grounde: And the Unycorn is so stronge that he is not take with myghte of hunters. But men that wryte of kynde of thinges meane that a mayde is sette there he shall come: And she openyth her lappe and the Unycorne layeth theron his heed, and levyth all his fyerinesse & slepyth in that wyse: And is taken as a beest wythout wepen & slayne wyth dartys of hunters." [18]

It is sometimes said that Isidore took the unicorn to be the rhinoceros, but this statement is due to a careless reading of his two first sentences;[19] the fact is that he *confused* the two animals, which is a quite different thing, as we have seen in considering the third passage from Aelian. In what is said of the unicorn's fight with the elephant and of the great strength of its horn he is dependent upon one or more of the several accounts of the rhinoceros to be found in late classical writers, and especially in Pliny. Unlike Aelian, he had probably never seen a rhinoceros; he had no means of knowing that this animal supplied most of the details of his description of the unicorn, and so he is not entirely responsible for the ridiculous picture he gives us of a rhinoceros slumbering in the lap of a virgin. That picture, in all its gay absurdity, we owe to his mingling of two diverse traditions.

Isidore's account of the unicorn is important, as I have said, because of its influence on later writers, and it was copied, usually with slavish exactness, by most of his successors in the long line of mediaeval encyclopaedists.[20] His passage, indeed, may almost be said to have established a third tradition in which what I have called the Hellenic and Hebraic branches come together; one not confined to the learned like that emanating from Ctesias, nor yet to the ignorant like that of *Physiologus*, but familiar to the many persons, mostly monks, who could read Latin but had little power of discrimination in what they read. A few of the encyclopaedists, such as Vincent of Beauvais,[21] showed greater independence, but in general it may be said that Isidore determined middle-class opinion about the unicorn, giving the animal an authenticity it could not have won from *Physiologus* and a vogue it would not have gained from Ctesias, Aelian, or even Pliny.

Intimately associated by the Bestiaries with the central mystery of the Christian faith, and corroborated by a document which even the semi-learned regarded as authoritative, the unicorn was at length firmly fixed in the popular imagination of Europe. The fact that no one ever saw a unicorn did not disturb belief in the slightest degree. No one in mediaeval Europe ever saw a lion or an elephant or a panther, yet these beasts were accepted without question upon evidence in no way better or worse than that which vouched for the unicorn. The stories everywhere told and believed about these three actual animals were not at all less marvellous than those that recommended the unicorn to popular attention; all were upon exactly the same footing so far as credibility was concerned, and side by side with them stood the griffin, the dragon, the amphisboena—a snake with a head at either end—the basilisk, the salamander that lives in fire, and a score of other beasts similarly spawned in the fertile fancy of man and swept together out of all past time. By virtue of his beauty and beneficence, but chiefly because he had the holiest associations, the unicorn was probably the most important of these, yet he was only *primus inter pares*. He was not regarded as in any sense or degree a mythical, legendary, or supernatural animal—any more than the horse or cat or cow, the hydra or kraken or were-wolf was so regarded; neither was he thought of as a symbol in any degree in which any other animal might not be symbolic. The peculiarity or weakness, call it which one will, which made him so susceptible to the wiles of virgins was merely his "property" or "*natura*", his idiosyncrasy, exactly analagous to the "property" attributed by mediaeval science to every other creature.

And yet it is probably true that the unicorn attracted more attention during the Middle Ages than any other single beast except the ass. He is the only imaginary animal of *Physiologus* that passed over into the Renaissance and the most important figure in those menageries of the fancy, gathered for the most part out of *Physiologus*, that began to swarm in the Cathedrals of Europe during the thirteenth century. From the time of Isidore to the present day he has been more significant to the imagination, and more prominent therefore in literature and art, than any other beast that man has made more or less "in his own image".

Anything like a full presentation of the literature devoted to the virgin-capture story would involve an intolerable amount of repetition, for all this writing was done when it was still sound doctrine that

> Who-so shal telle a tale after a man,
> He moot reherce, as ny as evere he can,
> Everich a word.

To take a few examples: the versified Bestiary of Philippe de Thaun tells the tale rather feebly in perfect accord with Isidore and develops the allegory at considerable length;[22] that of William, Clerk of Normandy, carries the *significatio* to great length and complexity;[23] and Richard de Fournival in his *Bestiaire d'Amour* manages to inject some novelty into the theme by using it as a symbol of the courtly instead of the celestial love—an audacious thing to have attempted in the middle of the thirteenth century.[24] Richard's poem is a protracted wooing in terms of animal symbolisms, and the lady, quite as learned in the lore of beasts as the lover himself, replies in kind. The lover says in the unicorn passage: "I have been drawn to you by your sweet odour alone, as the unicorn falls asleep under the influence of a maiden's fragrance. For this is the nature of the unicorn, that no other beast is so hard to capture, and he has one horn on his nose which no armour can withstand, so that no one dares to go forth against him except a virgin girl. And as soon as he is made aware of her presence by the scent of her, he kneels humbly before her and humiliates himself as though to signify that he would serve her. Therefore wise huntsmen who know his nature set a virgin in his way; he falls asleep in her lap; and while he sleeps the hunters, who would not dare to approach him when awake, come up and kill him. Even so has Love dealt cruelly with me; for I have been the proudest man alive with regard to love, and I have thought never to see the woman whom I should care to possess. . . . But Love, the skilful huntsman, has set in my path a maiden in the odour of whose sweetness I have fallen asleep, and I die the death to which I was doomed." [25]

In this charming passage one sees that Isidore's confusion of the rhinoceros and the unicorn has done its work: the horn of Richard de Fournival's unicorn is *en la narine*. Rudolf von Ems places the horn on the brow—

> Emmiten an der stirnin sin
> hat er ein horn reht als ein glas,
> vier füze lanc, als ich ez las—

but in other details he depicts the rhinoceros. Thus it happens again and again, as though by a fatality, that the unicorn slips back, as it were, into the rhinoceros; and even the virgin-capture story, violently incongruous as it is with that huge and ugly beast, is often involved in the confusion. It was not that these writers thought the two animals identical, for most of them were almost passionately convinced that the two were different; but no sooner have they finished insisting upon the differences than they describe the one in terms that apply only to the other.[26] Thus the nose-horned beast of India, lumpish and gross and mud-wallowing, looms always just behind the delicate unicorn, related to it as fact to dream, as actuality to the ideal, as Sancho Panza to Don Quixote.

Rudolf von Ems makes as clear a statement as any one of the belief that the ruse of the hunters can succeed only when the girl chosen for the decoy is really a virgin. If she is not, the unicorn shows great anger and runs her through with his horn to punish her deceit.[27] A similar power of distinguishing at sight between the true and the pretended virgin is attributed in folklore to several other

animals such as the stag and elephant and lion, and among the many
"virginity-tests", all supposed to be unerring, one of the simplest
was that of setting the woman in the way of one of these beasts:
if she was killed, then she deserved her death; if she lived, over-
coming the animal's natural ferocity, it could be only through
chastity's magic power. Such ideas, so pervasive and enduring as
to have had echoes even in Milton's *Comus*, were widely current
during the centuries when the virgin-capture story was growing,
and it would have been strange if they had not found expression
there; but one cannot believe that they had a shaping, not to say an
originating, influence upon that story. Suggestions of the virginity
test are rare in unicorn literature, and they are late; any argument
based upon them would be strongly countered by the frequently
seductive conduct of the woman herself. In the Syriac Bestiary, as
we have seen, the decoy is so obviously not a virgin that no
unicorn with the slightest discernment in such matters should
have been deceived by her, and we learn, also, from a Greek
grammarian of the twelfth century, that the animal can be taken
as well by a young man dressed in a maiden's garments as by the
maiden herself.[28]

The feminine garments of this youth, we are told, must be heavily
perfumed, and this reminds one that in fully half of the virgin-
capture narratives in which any explanation is vouchsafed of the
virgin's powers of fascination she is said to attract her victim by
what may be called the odour of chastity—a scent which could be
purchased, apparently, like feminine beauty in our own time, of any
good chemist. This idea appears subordinately in the elaborate
explanation already cited from Alanus de Insulis. John of San
Geminiano says that the unicorn, while stepping along through the
forest, "smells the odour of a virgin".[29] Philippe de Thaun remarks
that the animal is attracted by the odour of the maiden's breast.[30]
Richard de Fournival makes his unicorn aware of the maiden "*au
flair*". The list is a long one, extending from Albertus Magnus, who
ascribes the whole phenomenon to the unicorn's keen sense of
smell—and here again one is reminded of the rhinoceros—to a
learned pharmacist of the seventeenth century, Laurens Catelan

who decides, after deep thought and expenditure of much erudition, that the maiden can attract her prey only by the odour which is peculiar to virgins.

Laurens Catelan, however, had not the strange mediaeval belief—a belief which endures to-day in some districts—in the attractive and holding power of the eye. The Abbess Hildegarde of Bingen felt quite at home in mysteries such as this, and her explanation is therefore more confident than most. She believes that several virgins wandering together in a wood are much more attractive to unicorns than a single virgin can be. (Considering that almost all other authorities say that the virgin must be left *alone*, some even asserting that she must be naked and bound to a tree, is it permissible to suggest that the Abbess may have been led to take this view by her responsibilities as head of a houseful of nuns?) Hildegarde makes it clear that these virgins should be no mere rustics but well born, and neither too old nor too young. When the unicorn sees a bevy of such damsels wandering about, gathering flowers or engaged in some other such maidenly pursuit, he stops at once in his tracks and eyes them; they eye him; then he advances very slowly, crouches on his hind legs and looks at them for a long time from a distance. He is surprised at the fact that although they have in general the appearance of human beings yet they have no beards; he loves them because he sees, forsooth, that they are gentle and kind; and while he is gazing at them, all his wild and innocent heart drawn forth in adoration, the hunters steal up behind and slay him and cut off his horn.[31]

Hildegarde's naïve remark that the unicorn loves the maidens because they are gentle and kind, so charmingly oblivious of the purpose of those maidens, recalls the fact that not once in all the hundreds of references to the virgin-capture story is there dropped the slightest hint that this device of venery is somewhat lacking in "sportsmanship". The girl always plays her detestable rôle, drawing the unicorn to his death by acting upon his highest nature, without the slightest compunction,[32] and in the faces of the virgins that were painted in this tableau during the Middle Ages there is always an expression of profound serentiy.[33] One feels that some of the supernal charm of chastity might be dispensed with if we could have a little more of the sense of fair play in its place.

The force of this feeling is increased when we turn to consider the use to which the virgin-capture story was put in Christian symbolism. To secure clarity of presentation, I have thus far ignored as much as possible the allegorical meanings put upon the story even in *Physiologus* and this separation is justified by the fact that the story is sometimes told without any reference to those meanings; yet the vogue of the unicorn legend was largely due to its symbolism, and the efflorescence of the story in the thirteenth and fourteenth centuries synchronized significantly with the increase of devotion to the Virgin Mary. During those centuries the story that I have called the Virgin-Capture was elaborated swiftly, in the fervid devotional spirit of the time, into a form which, though the same in origin, seems to deserve another name, and which I shall call the Holy Hunt. Beginning in *Physiologus* as an allegory of the Annunciation alone, the story came to comprehend in one rich and compact symbol the total life and death of Christ and to shadow forth the whole divine plan of redemption. In its final form it is one of the strangest and one of the most compressed symbols or allegories ever devised—and it sprang, as we shall see, from a strange seed.

The scope of the Holy Hunt allegory may be shown most readily by a paraphrase of an extended passage in an old German book written in honour of the Virgin.[34] A very great king, it is said, had two noble sons. One of them wilfully stabbed himself to death, and the other brought himself so near to death by his misconduct that his life was despaired of. The father, though angry with this second son, was determined to do all that was possible for him, and so sent abroad for the advice of physicians. The wisest of these counselled that no medicine would avail except the blood of a unicorn poured upon the wound. The King therefore inquired how a unicorn might be captured, and he was advised to seek out the most beautiful maiden in his dominions and to seat her in a garden with six other maidens about her; then he should find four swift dogs, set a huntsman over them, bind them two and two together, and cause them to drive the unicorn toward the maiden. This device was successful. In the *geistliche auszlegong* or spiritual interpretation of this story we are told that the King is God the Father, the first son Lucifer, the second son Adam and his seed; the chief maiden is Mary and those about her are the personifications of her virtues; the huntsman is the Holy Ghost, represented by the Angel Gabriel; the four dogs are strangely identified with the four winds of heaven. In other narrations and frequently in the numerous Holy Hunt tapestries and stained glass windows these dogs are called *Veritas*, *Justitia*, *Pax*, and *Misericordia*—strange names indeed, considering the purpose the animals serve. The coupling of the dogs, which usually takes place after the unicorn's death, signifies that whereas Mercy and Truth, Justice and Peace, were formerly foes they are now united. (See Plate III.)

When once the story of the Holy Hunt had attained such complexity as this it was likely to occur anywhere in the vast literature written in praise of the Virgin and of chastity in general. We find it, for example, in a thoroughly detestable book celebrating virginity written by one Heinrich Kornemann early in the seventeenth century.[35] Here the huntsmen who slay the unicorn are called Jews and the "palace of the king" to which the animal is taken after its death is identified with heaven where, *"ante conspectum paterni vultus et civium supernorum"*, it is greeted with appropriate ceremonies like a returning Roman general. The story was never questioned or criticized in any way, for it had been sanctified, and any suggestion that the Virgin acted deceitfully in ensnaring her own Son would perhaps have been regarded as impious. How engaging is the picture of the Angel Gabriel driving the beast into her embraces, with God looking on benignly over the garden wall! And then how ingenious, when the creature has been soothed to rest and slaughtered, to blame its death, which all three of the holy Persons concerned had foreseen and planned and brought about, upon the Jews! The idea suggested by Kornemann that the Son of God, transformed into a unicorn, is harried and hunted through the forests of this world in order to be brought back as a "spectacle" for the citizens of heaven—a faint memory of the Roman Circus—is not so much

"quaint" as it is degraded and brutal. Furthermore, the story as told
by Kornemann and many others is soaked in a peculiarly foul
praise of sexual asceticism which is more base, to all clear and clean
thinking, than honest pornography.

The virgin-capture story is not, for all its interest, a pleasing one,
and in its later ramifications it becomes positively painful. When he
strayed into *Physiologus* the unicorn entered a region not worthy of
him. A creature imagined nobly as terrible, solitary, with the beauty
of power, was transformed under Christian influence into a little
goat-like animal eating out of the hand, going to sleep in maidens'
laps, and serving as a symbol of virginity. Nietzsche could not
have asked for a more brilliant illustration of " slave morality."

The Greek version of *Physiologus* brings before us a trait of the
unicorn which is quite as strange as its weakness for virgins and
which had a development in Europe quite as extensive and bewildering. The statement of this trait is brief and simple, but we shall find
that the explanation of it, in so far as it can be explained, is neither
simple nor brief but will lead us up and down over great stretches
of time and into some of the darkest places of the mind. The Greek
Bestiary says that when the animals assemble at evening beside the
great water to drink they find that a serpent has left its venom
floating upon the surface—a characteristic trick of serpents which is
elsewhere vouched for. They see or smell this venom and dare not
drink,but wait for the unicorn. At last he comes, steps into the water,
makes the sign of the cross over it with his horn and thereby renders
the poison harmless. (καὶ σταυρὸν ἐκτυπώσας τῷ κέρατι αὐτοῦ,
ἀφανίζει τοῦ φαρμάκου τὴν δύναμιν.) The significance of this trait
is elsewhere explained by saying that the animal's single horn
represents the Holy Cross,[36] that the serpent stands for the Devil,
and that the poisoned waters are the sins of the world.

It is remarkable that this trait—which I shall call, somewhat
arbitrarily, the water-conning—exactly suited as it was to the uses
of Christian allegory, was not reported in the Bestiaries of western
Europe. To be sure it was known in the West, but not until late,
and then chiefly in learned circles.[37] Isidore of Seville and his

followers seem never to have heard of it, and it was almost certainly unknown to Hildegarde of Bingen, who would have delighted in its magical connotations. We may be fairly certain, therefore, that the trait was not mentioned in the primitive versions of *Physiologus* and that it entered the Greek version from a source to which the other Bestiaries had not access.

The two themes of the water-conning and the virgin-capture were seldom brought together in a single account except in contexts professedly erudite, but a remarkable exception to this rule is found in a rather famous poem on hunting written by Natalis Comes in Latin hexameter about the middle of the sixteenth century. Here a large amount of unicorn lore is packed into little space :—

Far on the edge of the world and beyond the banks of the Ganges,
Savage and lone, is a place in the realm of the King of the Hindus. . . .
Where there is born a beast as large as a stag in stature,
Dark on the back, solid-hoofed, very fierce, and shaped like a bullock.
Mighty and black is the horn that springs from the animal's forehead,
Terrible unto his foe, a defence and a weapon of onslaught.
Often the poisoners steal to the banks of that swift-flowing river,
Fouling the waves with disease by their secret insidious poisons;
After them comes this beast and dips his horn in the water,
Cleansing the venom away and leaving the stream to flow purely
So that the forest-dwellers may drink once more by the margin.
Also men say that the beast delights in the embrace of a virgin,
Falling asleep in her arms and taking sweet rest on her bosom.
Ah! but, awaking, he finds he is bound by ropes and by shackles.
Strange is the tale, indeed, yet so, they say, he is taken,
Whether it be that the seeds of love have been sown by great Nature
Deep in his blood or for some more hidden mysterious reason.[38]

Having seen in some detail the development of the unicorn legend during the Middle Ages, we may now turn to the difficult question regarding the origin of that part of the legend, the Virgin-Capture and the Holy Hunt, which is the special topic of the present chapter. Speculation about that origin has engaged a good many pens since the time when men began once more to ask questions about things instead of taking them on trust, for every thoughtful writer about the unicorn has been perplexed by the story and has wanted to know whence it came. The result of all this speculation may be summed up in the words of one of the most learned men who have ever touched the problem: *"unde nostra fabella orta sit, ignoro"* [39]—whence our fable comes I know not. There are two attempts at a solution, however, to be recorded—one of them puerile, but the other, to say the least, highly ingenious.

The statement of Aelian will be recalled that the unicorn lives at strife with animals of its own species except during the season of rut, when the males make a temporary truce with the females. This is not a surprising or even a peculiar trait, but it has caught the attention of a number of scholars as a possible explanation, in default of a better, of the virgin-capture story. Such explanation may have been vaguely suggested by Manuel Philes in the thirteenth century;[40] it was accepted by Andrea Bacci and by Conrad Gesner the zoologist; Samuel Bochart, the greatest scholar who has ever discussed the unicorn legend, added the weight of his name;[41] even Dr. Friedrich Lauchert, a trained literary student of our own time, adopts it without hesitation.[42] In spite of this impressive array of names, however, the theory is too absurd to be seriously entertained, and even if it were credible in other respects, we should reject it on the ground that Aelian came too late into the world to affect the fundamental stories of the *Physiologus*,[43] and also on the ground that his influence was primarily rhetorical. There is hardly any likeness between the kid-like unicorn of *Physiologus* and the "cartazon" of Aelian, and it is to the last degree improbable that a single minor trait was adopted from Aelian's unicorn and given such extensive and surprising development while major differences were neglected. Finally, the distinction between the taming of an animal during the season of rut by the females of his own species and the taming of him by a human virgin is a difference "of all the sky".

The second attempt to account for the virgin-capture story requires more respectful attention. Professor Leo Wiener of Harvard University points out the striking similarity between the *Physiologus* account of the *antholops* or antelope and that of the unicorn.[44] The former, as told in a Latin manuscript of the eleventh century, runs thus: There is an animal called *antholops* which is so exceedingly fierce that none of the hunters is able to approach him. He has long horns in the shape of a saw with which he can cut down the largest oaks. . . . When he is thirsty he goes to the great river Euphrates and drinks. Now there grow in that place certain soft and pliable branches of the vine [*sunt autem ibi virgae viticeae subtiles et molles*], and while he is playing about he entangles himself in them by the horn. When he is firmly caught by both horns he cries out with a great voice, because he is unable to escape from the slender branches [*virgulis*]; and then the hunter, hearing his voice, runs up, finds him bound, and kills him.

The analogies between this story and that of the unicorn are obvious. The *antholops* is very fierce and defies the hunters; he is remarkable for the armour of his brow, and this brings about his death; the hunters wait until he is *hors de combat* before advancing to dispatch him; furthermore, he is caught and held, according to this Latin text of *Physiologus*, by *virgae*—in the spelling common in old manuscripts, *virge*. Professor Wiener believes, if I understand him correctly, that the story of the virgin-capture arose from a misreading, or perhaps a scribe's error, which substituted for *virge*, "twigs" or "slender branches", the word *virgo*, "a virgin".[45] He also thinks that the *antholops* story itself is a retelling of Aesop's story of the Stag Caught by its Horns in the Forest, and that certain minor details of the unicorn story as told in *Physiologus*, are of Arabic origin. He sums up thus: "The *autolops*, after drinking from the Euphrates, goes into the woods and there plays with the branches, *virgae*. . . . The *Physiologus* or its source read *virgo* instead of *virgae*, and thus produced the story of the unicorn which plays with its horn in the bosom of the *virgo*, maiden, and thus is caught. This, then, shows beyond a chance of doubt that the unicorn story arose only after the Arabs came in contact with Latin, which was after 711, and thus the earliest date of the *Physiologus* is established."

I have spared the reader as much as possible of the amazing involution in Professor Wiener's argument, but I cannot mitigate the surprise he will feel at seeing the virgin disappear, like Daphne, into a tree; I can only ask him to share my own disappointment that after such gigantic labours the mountain of scholarship should bring forth only this ridiculous mouse of an alleged mistranslation. Convinced that the *Physiologus* as we know it cannot be of earlier date than A.D. 711, Professor Wiener is constrained to argue that the narrations of the virgin-capture story in Gregory's *Moralia* and in Isidore's *Etymologiae* are interpolations made after that date. He does not mention the fact that the story was told by Saint Eustathius of Antioch almost four hundred years before, nor does he explain how Pope Gelasius could have condemned in the fifth century a work that was not produced until the eighth. The words upon which his argument chiefly rests—"*sunt autem ibi virgae viticeae*"—are found only in a manuscript of the eleventh century, and this seems to me much too late for our present purposes. I do not believe, therefore, that the Latin phrasing of the *antholops* story gave the original suggestion for the story of the virgin-capture.[46] There is a considerable difference between a unicorned animal and one with two horns fitted with saw-tooth edges,[47] and Professor Wiener's explanation that the *antholops* may break off one of his horns in his struggle with the *virgae*, thereby making himself an artificial unicorn, does not seem to meet the needs of the case. We shall do well to look farther.

In considering the Syriac version of *Physiologus* we have found reason to suspect that the emphasis there laid upon sexual attraction indicates some non-Christian influence. A story similar to that in Syriac is found in Arabic literature of the fourteenth century. Al Damîrî says that "a virgin or a beautiful girl" is put in the way of the unicorn, and that as soon as he sees her he leaps into her lap making signs for milk, of which he is naturally very fond. After he has been suckled he lies down drunk, as though with wine, and at this moment the hunters rush in and bind him without resistance.[48] This Arabian unicorn has fallen even below the poor creature of *Physiologus*, for he is captured because he is drunk, and on milk! Equally interesting is the implication that if no virgin is available any beautiful girl will do as well. Now it seems remotely possible that this Arabian version is a degraded form of the Christian story, and that virginity has been subordinated because the Mohammedans are

der hystori von dem einhorn.

III. THE HOLY HUNT

IV. ADAM NAMING THE ANIMALS

V. THE WATER-CONNING

VI. DEATH OF THE UNICORN

not Mariolaters and have never laid quite the Christian emphasis upon chastity; but it is certainly far more probable that we have here and in the Syriac version the relics of an older story which the Christians of Alexandria shaped to their purpose. The mention of the virgin in the Arabic tale is due, no doubt, to Christian influence, but her presence is so incongruous with the tale itself as to suggest that she has been imported from another form of the story.

In that case, we must abandon all effort to explain the virgin-capture story in terms of itself and its variants, and we are driven back into the sea of the world's folklore without compass or chart, there to make what accidental landfalls we may. We are seeking an explanation of the elective affinity between virgins and beasts with single horns, or, if virginity is not a primary notion, of the attraction, whether sexual or of some other sort, between women and horned beasts. Virgins undergoing sundry tests, beautiful girls seated lonely and receptive under trees, unicorns, rhinoceroses, faithful lions, elephants, appear and disappear in the mists. Bartholomew Anglicus says that "Elephants be hunted in this wise: there go in the desert two maidens all naked and bare, and these maidens begin to sing alone; and the beast hath liking when he heareth their song, and cometh to them and licketh their teats and falleth asleep anon for liking of the song; and then one maiden sticketh him in the throat and the other taketh his blood in a vessel, and with that blood the people dye cloth. This is useful information, but it is not directly to the purpose and the fog closes in again. We learn that the horn of the young female rhinoceros, taken before she has mated, sells both in Siam and in South Africa at a price at least ten times as great as that given for the horns of mated animals of either sex, on the ground that they are much more powerfully prophylactic. We delve into the myth of Diana the virgin huntress and ponder her connection with the horned moon which has had control over poisons since the beginnings of superstition. In all this rather aimless beating up and down one may learn much about the mental habits out of which the virgin-capture story arose, but the actual source of it eludes one. The suspicion grows upon the seeker that he is looking for the origin of a belief which has never had any single beginning and that all the success he can hope for will be like that of one who looks for the source of a great river—and finds it in half a dozen different springs separated, it may be, by hundreds of miles, or in the rain-wind, or in the wandering cloud. And just as it is a hazardous thing to say that the Nile or the Mississippi or the Amazon springs out of precisely this or that hillside, so it would be rash to assert that the virgin-capture story must have had just this or that origin and no other. Such confident assertions are seldom made by those who have looked long into the mists of the primitive imagination where vague shapes are constantly forming and dissolving again.

And yet, though the ultimate origin of the story remains hidden, we have already traced that story somewhat behind the form it took on in *Physiologus*. It is possible to take one long step farther still, and then we shall have done what we can.

The sudden expansion of the known world during the sixteenth century and the consequent opening of new lands to exploration and conquest, gave to the imagination of Europe an impetus which had among its many results a sort of modern mythology. We are accustomed to think of this expansion in connection with the western hemisphere alone, but the sea route to India and the Far East contributed quite as much as America to European fancy. India, which had been a land of chimera to Ctesias and had remained such during all the intervening centuries, was no less marvellous now that the Portuguese were bringing back a cargo of wonders in every ship that rounded the Cape. By one of the stranger accidents in the history of legend, some of the tales that had once been told of India were transferred to a nearer land, Ethiopia, which had been confused with the great peninsula even in Virgil's time. Most of these tales moved westward with the fabulous Court of Prester John, which had originally been located somewhat vaguely in "India". Ever since the forged letter describing this Christian court had been received, and answered, by Pope Alexander III, Christian missionaries had been much interested in it, and they were none the less so in the early seventeenth century when there seemed to be grave danger that Prester John—at that time approximately five hundred years of age—would fall into heresy. These are the circumstances surrounding the several accounts of Ethiopia that we owe to Jesuits of the period, the best known of which is that of Jeronimo Lobo. Most of the Jesuit travellers to the Court of Prester John have something to say about the Abyssinian unicorn, and Father Lobo has a great deal. From one of them, Fray Luis de Urreta, we get an unmistakable clue to the original nature of the virgin-capture story.

This clue is found in a book packed with unheard-of matters and quite worthy of its noble title: *Historia de los Grandes y Remotos Reynos de la Etiopia, Monarchia del Emperador llamado Preste Iuan.*[49] Well beyond the middle of it there is a clear description of the rhinoceros, which Fray Luis says has been made familiar to Europe by many pictures.[50] He describes it as an extremely wild animal, very fierce and brave and proud, and so powerful that it can be killed only by one ruse or trick. The way of killing it is this: The hunters go into the province of Goyame, which is at the base of the Mountains of the Moon whence the Nile springs, for there alone, in all Africa, are these beasts to be found. When they learn that one is near at hand they load their muskets and they take a female monkey which they have trained for this kind of hunting, and they bring her to the place. She begins at once to run about looking for the rhinoceros, and when she sees him she leaps here and there and dances as she goes toward him, playing a thousand monkey-tricks. He is much delighted in watching this entertainment, so that she is able to approach until she can throw one leg over his back. Then she begins scratching and rubbing his hide, and this gives him keen pleasure. At last, jumping to the ground again, she starts to rub his belly, and then the rhinoceros is so overcome with ecstasy that he stretches himself out at length upon the ground. At this point the hunters, who have been hidden all the while in some safe place, come up with their cross-bows or muskets and shoot him.

Here is such a tale as hunters may have told round the camp-fire, time out of mind, as a matter-of-fact statement of the method by which a valuable animal, too tough for darts and arrows, might be killed. One who lays the two side by side will have little doubt, I think, that the tale reported by Fray Luis springs from the same root as the virgin-capture story, for they correspond not merely here and there but at every point. With regard to the question as to which of the two is probably the older, one sees that Fray Luis's relation, as compared with the other, verges everywhere toward the probable, even the realistic. Instead of the unicorn we have here the rhinoceros, his grossly actual *doppelgänger*. In place of the virgin we are given a monkey—a female monkey, be it observed, and one specially trained in the appropriate feminine blandishments. Instead of depending upon such vague lures as the odour of chastity or the power of the eye, this decoy sets to work with seduction of the most physical kind. Instead of the sleep of the unicorn, which is usually left unexplained by the narrators of the other tale, we have here the natural stretching-out of the beast to enjoy itself to the fullest extent.

Now it seems unlikely that this account is a degraded or broken-down version of the virgin-capture story. Usually, when a myth or legend has reached such an elevation of the supernatural as that attained by the virgin-capture tale, it maintains itself at that level, if only because simple minds find it easier to remember and perhaps easier to believe. This rule—which has, of course, many exceptions—holds particularly for myths and legends that have become entangled with religious beliefs. Numerous written texts of the virgin-capture story, and very numerous representations of it, have existed for a long time to preserve it from corrupting influences. The variations from that story in the account of the rhinoceros hunt, moreover, are not of a sort to be accounted for by assuming a gradual decomposition of the Christian tale as it was tossed from tongue to tongue during the centuries. The two stories answer to each other point for point, so that one who tried to prove that the monkey-capture is a debased version of the virgin-capture story would be obliged to assume a conscious act of euhemerization for which he could scarcely assign a sufficient motive. But the most cogent argument against such a theory is the vaguest and the hardest to state: such a patient unravelling of a developed legend and the substitution, strand by strand, of baser materials, is simply foreign to the thought-habits of the times and the minds concerned. Such cynical performances are amusing to a Lucian or an Anatole France, but we cannot atttribute them to African hunters of the seventeenth or of any earlier century. And this tale of the rhinoceros hunt is a hunter's tale. As such, it is probably ancient, for during historic times the rhinoceros of India—where the story first was told—was captured chiefly by great drives, such as that organized by Tamerlane in the fourteenth century, in which hundreds of men took part on foot and horseback.

We must conclude, then, that the tale told by Fray Luis is not derived from the account of the unicorn in *Physiologus*. But the two stories are related to each other, and closely related. Either they spring separately from a single root or else the Christian legend is the product of a more or less deliberate allegorizing of the heathen belief. The second of these possibilities seems to me to harmonize with the little we can safely surmise about the methods and purposes of the shapers of *Physiologus*. There may have been some intermediary forms of the story that are now lost, and there were probably some forms of the monkey-capture story more primitive and even less pleasing than that related by Fray Luis, for early Arabian tales about the monkey were often obscene. To pursue the story into the jungles of Siam would be an absorbing adventure, no doubt, but it would not advance our knowledge of unicorn lore. We have traced the Christian legend of the unicorn back, if not to its source, at any rate to a form as primitive, in all likelihood, as that in which the early Christians found it, and this should be sufficient.

The conclusion at which we arrive is a surprising one. On the one hand we have the rich and mystical beauty of the Holy Hunt comprising in one packed symbol the conception, life, and death of Christ—a symbol branching out into literature, flowering profusely in the arts, entangled with the central religious passion of the Middle Ages. On the other hand we have a ludicrous tale about the antics of a she-monkey trained to decoy the rhinoceros by scratching his belly and back. Our inference that the religious symbol is derived from the gross hunter's tale may be repugnant to some sensibilities, but the apparent contrast is exactly of the kind that confronts us everywhere in our probing toward the bases of life, of beauty, even of love. Ultimately we have to decide whether we shall think less highly of the flower or contrive to think somewhat better of the earth from which it grows.

CHAPTER III

SHAPING FANTASIES

THE unicorn is one of the most beautiful of the "shapes that haunt
thought's wildernesses", but he did not attain his beauty all at once.
As soon as we begin to inquire how he looked to the imagination
of the Ages of Faith we are reminded that his ancestry is mixed,
that he descends from the horse and the ass on the side of the Greeks
and from the goat on that of *Physiologus*. The results of this misce-
genation were a series of hybrid variations as perplexing as those
governed by the Mendelian law. Aristotle had said that the unicorn's
hoof is solid, on the excellent ground that animals with divided
hoofs have two horns when they have any horns at all; but on the
other hand, *Physiologus* declared that the unicorn resembles a little
goat, and the goat has a divided hoof. The faithful did not know
what to think, and in default of a Thomas Aquinas to resolve the
apparent discrepancies between Aristotle and *Physiologus* they tried
to believe in a unicorn somewhat like a goat and somewhat like a
horse at the same time. Early representations of the animal show
cloven hoofs on the fore feet and solid hoofs behind, or *vice versa*;
they show a goat's beard on a horse's head or even the body of a
goat with the head of a horse. A more perfect example of the divided
allegiance of the Renaissance could hardly be imagined;[1] yet, in
spite of these difficulties, the artists of the time made the unicorn
at least as credible as the animals they had before their eyes, and
usually far more graceful.

From the thirteenth century to the sixteenth, representation of the unicorn in ecclesiastic decoration was continuous and widespread. Formerly he had been depicted chiefly in manuscripts,[2] and it is clear that his increased popularity was due in some degree to the rapid intensification of Mariolatry.[3] Although the animal's figure was not so much used in England as in Europe, I have seen him represented on misericords in Lincoln Cathedral, in St. George's of Windsor, in the chapel of Durham Castle, in St. Botolph's of Boston, and in at least half a dozen parish churches. Mrs. Jameson describes an elaborate representation of the Holy Hunt which stands over the altar in Breslau Cathedral,[4] and the same subject is treated in stained glass at Bourges,[5] Erfurt, Caen, Lyons, and many other places. Representations of the unicorn on old altarcloths, corbels, and capitals are almost numberless.[6]

A subject so popular as this was certain to be adopted by secular art, as the *Physiologus* story was used by Richard de Fournival and others in erotic poetry, for it was only necessary to lay a slightly additional emphasis upon the theme of the hunt and to subordinate the holy symbolism in order to make the transition from sacred to profane.[7] Perhaps the most sumptuous representations of the unicorn ever made are those in the "Millefleur tapestries" produced about the year 1480 for François de la Rochefoucauld. (Plates IV, V, VI.) Here we are shown a pure white animal, vaguely equine but smaller than a horse, with goat's beard and cloven hoofs and the spiralled horn. Although the monogram "A.M."—Ave Maria—appears in each scene, the atmosphere of the whole series is not devotional but that of an elaborate hunt in the French manner. The death of the unicorn is shown, but we do not find the Virgin in her conventional position, and there are other indications that the theme is tending toward a purely secular treatment. The same tendency is observable in the superb Flemish tapestry, based probably upon an Italian cartoon and now in the Academy of Fine Arts at Florence, which shows the naming of the animals by Adam—most of the beasts trooping by in pairs, but the unicorn, significantly leading the procession, without a mate. (Frontispiece.) The unicorn is singled out for such special honour in many another representation, as, for example, in the large picture by Tintoretto in the Church of San Rocco at Venice, which shows the Saint healing animals in the desert. Here the unicorn stands at the forefront of the group, very shaggy about the head but horse-like and with a striated horn. A purely secular treatment is seen in the familiar and beautiful d'Aubusson tapestries known as *La Dame à la Licorne*, probably intended to illustrate the metrical romance of that title, which is now in the Musée de Cluny, for in these the animal is scarcely more than ornamental.

Most influential in this secularizing of the unicorn were the numerous illustrations made, from the second quarter of the fifteenth century onward, for Petrarch's *Trionfi* (Plate VII). In only one of the divisions of his poem does Petrarch mention a triumphal car, but his illustrators—probably because a "triumph" necessarily meant for them a chariot with allegorical figures—provided such cars for each of the divisions. The chariots depicted by them to illustrate the "Triumph of Chastity" are always drawn by unicorns—two, four, or six in number—and these unicorns, if I may judge from the scores of examples that I have seen in woodcuts and on canvas, are always equine, cloven-footed, bearded, and with striated horns. Copies and editions of Petrarch's *Trionfi* were to be found in every European language during the Renaissance, and wherever they went some engraving on wood or metal of the Chariot of Chastity drawn by unicorns went with them. Many of the foremost painters of the age tried their hands at a subject which for several decades was second in popularity only to the well-worn Biblical themes. These allegorical Triumphs are to be found not in painting and engraving only but on tapestry, pottery, bas-reliefs in bronze and wood and ivory, marriage chests and birth-trays. Splendid and familiar examples of them are to be seen at the Victoria and Albert Museum in the two great tapestries—Flemish, of the sixteenth century—from a set illustrating Petrarch's poem.   Other tapestries from the same design, once the property of Cardinal Wolsey, are at Hampton Court. Eugéne Müntz, the historian of art, has collected over a thousand examples of them in the volume he has devoted to the subject, and in each of these examples the figure of the unicorn is necessarily prominent. Obviously, the influence of all this work would be to withdraw the unicorn from his exclusive association with sacred themes and history. The illustrators of the *Trionfi*, furthermore, developed and fixed the equine shape of the unicorn as we see it to-day in heraldic insignia.

For beauty of the higher sort I know of nothing in the artistic representation of the unicorn superior to the famous Santa Justina of Moretto, painted about 1530 and now in the Belvidere Gallery at Vienna. (Plate VIII.) In this serene and noble picture the animal is again depicted as white, equine, and with cloven hoofs, but the horn is for once the black horn described by Pliny.

The unicorn of heraldry was devised by men who had rather more confidence in the classic writers of antiquity than they had in the Bestiaries, and therefore their animal has more of the horse than of the goat in his composition; yet the prominent position of the unicorn in heraldry is primarily due, of course, to the moral attributes that he acquired from the *Physiologus* tradition. Primarily, but not entirely. Several streams of influence converged to make him the chief emblem of purity: the identification with Christ and association with the Virgin first of all, but, in addition, the water-conning trait and the world-wide reputation of the horn as a drug and a magical prophylactic. Considering that chastity was one of the foremost chivalric virtues, we are not surprised to find the unicorn figured on many knightly seals and coats of arms. There was something essentially aristocratic about him. His kinship to the horse, always associated with knighthood, was suggestive, but more important was the headlong enthusiasm of his devotion to beautiful women. He was fierce and proud and dangerous to his foes, as a knight should be, and he was also gentle; he had the dignity of solitude; he was beautiful and strong; most significant of all, he was a protector and champion of other beasts against the wiles of their enemies. In all the range of animal lore there is no other story conceived so completely in the aristocratic spirit as that of the unicorn stepping down to the poisoned water while the other beasts wait patiently for his coming, and making it safe for them by dipping his magic horn. Here was a perfect emblem of the ideal that

European chivalry held before itself in its great periods—the ideal according to which exceptional power and privilege were balanced and justified by exceptional responsibility. The lion, for all the heroic courage falsely attributed to him, the panther with his sweet breath, the bear with his mighty strength, had no such chivalric significance as the unicorn, which might almost seem to have been imagined precisely to serve as an emblem of the "verray parfit gentil knight".

John Guillim, who wrote his famous book on heraldry at a time when his subject had chiefly antiquarian interest, makes clear his own feeling that the unicorn is aristocratic and a fit subject, therefore, for a gentleman's crest. "Some," he admits, "have made doubt whether there be any such beast as this or no, but the great esteem of his horn (in many places to be seen) may take away that needless scruple." The animal's invincibility and virtue are praised, and then Guillim writes: "The greatness of his mind is such that he rather chooseth to die than to be taken alive: wherein the unicorn and the valiant-minded soldier are alike, which both contemn death, and rather than they will be compelled to undergo any base servitude or bondage they will lose their lives."[8]

Later heraldic writers rival even the historians of art in the extent and variety of their misinformation about unicorns, perhaps because they are so accustomed to discussing creatures of which almost anything may be asserted that they do not know how to respect a beast with a definite legend. We are gravely told, for example, by a writer of the nineteenth century, that the whole notion of the unicorn was derived from the spike in the middle of the "tester" or head-armour of the horse,[9] although this spike was not regularly used in Europe until late in the fifteenth century. It is true that the "panache" has been used since ancient times as a decoration of the war-horse's head, but one would prefer to believe that if there is any connection this was suggested by the unicorn.[10] For dense and audacious error, however, the palm should be awarded to John Brand, who says of the unicorn: "This fabulous animal of heraldry . . . is nothing more than a horse with the horn of the pristis, or sword-fish, stuck in his forehead."[11]

Before the accession of James I to the throne of England a great variety of "supporters" had been used for the Royal Arms, but a lion had for several generations been one of the two. Henry VI used the lion and the antelope; Edward IV the lion and bull; Richard III the lion and boar; Henry VII and Henry VIII the lion and dragon; Mary and Elizabeth the lion and greyhound. On the Royal Arms of Scotland the unicorn had been employed as consistently as the lion in England. It is often said that the lion and unicorn were chosen as supporters of the British Arms because of the belief in the natural animosity of these two beasts and as a symbol of the reconciliation between England and Scotland. James I was a learned man to whom such a symbol might well have been interesting, but the presence of these two historic foes in the British Royal Arms is really no more than a fortunate accident. James kept his Scottish unicorn and he chose the English lion merely because it had been the most persistent supporter of the English Arms before his time. He kept the lion dexter as it had been on Elizabeth's Arms, and he retained all its heraldic insignia. His unicorn remained, as it had been in Scotland, argent, armed, crined, unguled, gorged with a coronet of *crosses patées* and *fleur-de-lis*, with a chain extending from the crown between the forelegs and reflexed over the back, all or. Since their adoption by James the British supporters have been used continuously, except that the seal of the Exchequer in the time of Charles I shows as supporters a stag and an antelope, chained and ducally collared.[12]

No small amount of lore is implicit, to the pausing eye, in this heraldic unicorn as one may see him to-day on the first page of an English newspaper or rampant over the Old State House in Boston, Massachusetts. He owes his horse's head and neck and mane to Pliny and to certain artists of the Italian Renaissance, his graceful legs to a series of mediaeval writers who will be named in due course, his beard and divided hoofs in part to *Physiologus*, his tail either to the oryx or else to the aesthetic taste of the College of Heralds, and the spiral twistings of his horn to a marine mammal of the northern seas. Here is a creature fearfully and wonderfully made, and yet, in spite of his compound ancestry, one more than a match in beauty for the megalocephalic lion, and one so credible, or rather so probable, in appearance as to make the hardiest doubter feel that if there is no such animal then an excellent opportunity was overlooked in the process of creation. He seems to fill a gap in nature.

One can readily understand that during the Middle Ages, when coats of arms were not confined to stationery and table-silver but were pictures in vivid hues that went everywhere in the world—flaunting in state processions, resplendent at Court, rallying soldiers about their lords in battle—the frequent use of the unicorn upon heraldic crests would do much to increase the animal's vogue and to make it seem certain, if there had ever been any doubt, that he was as real as any beast of field or forest. It is certain that the presence of the unicorn on the British Royal Arms, reproduced as they are millions of times in every year and scattered throughout the world, has tended to maintain interest in the animal and to develop a curiosity about its tradition even in our time.

One of the fundamental facts concerning lions and unicorns is that they hate each other by instinct, as Englishman and Scot once did, and that they never meet without fatal consequences. This is matter for later discussion, but in the meantime we may pause to wonder at the chance that brought such deadly opposites into accord, uniting majesty with gentleness and beauty with strength. To the adult observer they seem to be now at peace, but the familiar nursery rhyme will not have it so, for there, until recently,

> The lion and the unicorn
> Were fighting for the crown;
> The lion chased the unicorn
> All round the town.

I should never have doubted for a moment that this bit of doggerel was suggested by the British Royal Arms if I had not come upon the following remarkable passage: "In one of the rooms of the Borromeo Palace on the Isola Bella in Lago Maggiore are two large tapestries—say fifteen feet by twelve feet—apparently of the sixteenth century or earlier. The first represents a lion and a unicorn engaged in combat for a crown lying between them. The second shows the lion chasing the unicorn round a mediaeval walled town drawn quite small in the centre of the tapestry, the lion and the unicorn being on a much larger scale."[13] These assertions are so surprising and indeed inexplicable that I have gone many miles out of my way on a journey through northern Italy in order to verify them—only to find them false. The Borromean Palace does contain two excellent Flemish tapestries in which the lion and the unicorn are prominently figured, but in neither of them can I find either a crown or a pursuit round a walled town. Both tapestries show the two animals fighting: in one the unicorn has gored the lion and is lifting him off his feet, and in the second the unicorn is attacked from behind by two lions while goring a third. The tapestries may have been intended to bear some symbolic significance, for the unicorn is prominent in the Borromean arms—a huge unicorn of stone stands on the summit of the palace gardens—but there can be no connection between them and the English nursery rhyme.

There is much to be surmised, but little that a cautious investigator would care to affirm positively, about the symbolic meanings ascribed to the unicorn in pre-Christian times.[14] Several bits of evidence concur, however, in the suggestion that for a very long time one-horned animals have been regarded as emblematic of unlimited or undivided sovereign power. We have made nothing as yet of the curious statement which occurs in nearly all the older texts of *Physiologus* that when the unicorn is captured he is "taken to the palace of the king"[15]—a remark which, as I have said, is one of the few traces of a connection between the *Physiologus* unicorn and that of the Greeks. Philostratus makes it clear in the passage cited above from the life of Apollonius that only the kings of India hunt the unicorn and only they possess the beakers made from its horn. Aelian also tells us that only the potentates own these beakers, and he says in another place that the young of the "cartazon" are taken to the king. Of course there is abundant evidence that the larger animals of the chase are regarded in many parts of the world as belonging to the king,[16] but the rule seems to apply with special force to unicorns as it does also to the rhinoceros. On his voyage to the East Indies in 1592 James Lancaster sent commodities to the King of Junsaloam, off the Straits of Malacca, "to barter for Ambergriese and for the hornes of Abath [rhinoceros] whereof the king only hath the traffique in his hands." In South Africa the so-called "kerry", a sort of wand or sceptre made from the horn of the white rhinoceros—which, however, has two horns—is so well recognized a symbol of sovereignty that quarrels arising from disputes over the ownership of it have led to more than one Kaffir war in recent times. In China, again, the unicorn, or Ki-lin, has been associated for ages with emperors, the appearance of one of these animals being accepted as a certain prophecy of a beneficent reign. Plutarch tells us of a ram's head with only one horn that was brought to Pericles from his farm as a sign that he would become the single ruler of the Athenian state.[17]

But the most remarkable and conclusive evidence for this ancient symbolism is to be found in the Bible. In the Book of Daniel (chapter viii) there is recorded this strange vision: "And behold, an he goat came from the West on the face of the whole earth, and touched not the ground; and the goat had a notable horn between his eyes. And he came to the ram that had two horns . . . and ran unto him in the fury of his power. And I saw him come close unto the ram, and he was moved with choler against him, and smote the ram, and brake his two horns: and there was no power in the ram to stand before him, but he cast him down to the ground and stamped upon him." Later in the same chapter we are given an interpretation of this vision: "And the rough goat is the king of Grecia, and the great horn that is between his eyes is the first king."

The one-horned goat of Daniel's vision, in other words, stands for Alexander the Great, and the whole allegory depicts his triumph over the hosts of the Persians, represented by the two-horned ram. The interesting thing is that the one horn should be chosen as a symbol of superior power. One can readily understand it as a symbol of single and supreme sovereignty, and it is permissible to paraphrase the sentence quoted above so as to make it read:

"The great horn that is between his eyes signifies that he is the supreme king."[18] Exactly the same symbolism is found in the pseudepigraphic first book of Enoch, in the ninetieth chapter: "And I saw till horns grew upon these lambs, and the rams cast down their horns; and I saw till there sprouted a great horn of one of these sheep, and their eyes were opened. And it looked at them and it cried to the sheep, and the rams saw it and all ran to it." The one-horned sheep of this passage, according to the notes of R. H. Charles, must be Judas Maccabaeus.

One recalls in this connection several Biblical references to horns, apparently single, which make it clear that they were symbols of power. In 1 Samuel ii. 1 are the words "By Jehovah my horn is exalted," and in Psalms lxxxix. 17 "By thy favour our horn is exalted." "Lift not up your horn," says David again as a caution of humility, and in Jeremiah we read: "The horn of Moab is cut off." In these passages the horns concerned, whether actual or metaphorical, were those not of animals but of men. Frequently, no doubt, they were actual; that is to say, they were high head-dresses of some sort related to the tall peaked caps worn by Persian and Assyrian kings and by the members of their households. Such symbolic adornments for the head were used by the *flamines martiales* of Rome, and they seem to have consisted of single horns. Bishop Taylor, writing at the end of the eighteenth century, says that he saw Sepoys in India who wore single spikes or horns on their foreheads attached to flat leather helmets. Perhaps the most familiar example of this symbolic head-dress is the peaked cap of the Doges of Venice, which seems to have been derived from the Orient.

"No one", says Coleridge, "has yet discovered even a plausible origin for this symbolism as to horns",[19] but the problem is not quite so difficult as he suggests, now that we know a little more about the habits of primitive minds. Very simple men think of the power of a horned beast as residing in the horns with which it defends itself and attacks its enemies; to such men, therefore, horns are a natural symbol of vigour, power, strength of any kind, and they have been used as such a symbol for ages. Homer makes Achilles push the Trojans with his horns.[20] Horace says that wine adds horns to a man of lowly condition;[21] the Lamb of the Apocalypse is equipped with seven horns, the perfect number, to signify omnipotence;[22] the famous horns of Moses, whatever they were originally intended to signify, have usually been interpreted as symbols of power.[23] All these horns are double, but it will be readily understood that when the strength of two horns is concentrated in one that one is very strong indeed and a perfect emblem of strength.[24]

We may take it as highly probable, then, that one-horned animals were regarded in the pre-Christian world, in many widely distant places, as symbols of sovereignty. Turning to the symbolism of the unicorn in Christendom we are on firmer ground. Partly because of its association with the Virgin, partly because of its service as a purifier of poisoned waters, and to some extent on account of the reputation of its horn, it came to be regarded as an emblem of purity. An instance of this is seen in its association with Saint Justina,[25] and even clearer examples are found in the numerous illustrations of Petrarch's *Triumph of Chastity* and in the remarkable engraving made by an unknown artist for the *Hypnerotomachia* of Poliphilo in which the triumphal chariot of Diana is drawn by eight unicorns. (Plate VII.) So widely variable is symbolism of this kind, however, that Leonardo da Vinci makes the animal a type of incontinence, or what he calls *Intemperanza*.[26] Still another symbolic significance of the Christian unicorn is that of solitude—a significance derived not from *Physiologus* [27] but from Pliny and Aelian, and one, therefore, which is found only in the more learned tradition. Several of the early Fathers and of their followers drew the unicorn into their praise of solitude,[28] and in later centuries the animal was generally understood to be an emblem of the monastic life. There is still preserved at St. Fulda a pastoral staff supposed to have belonged to Saint Boniface, and, if genuine, dating therefore from the seventh century, on which the unicorn is shown kneeling at the foot of the Cross. Many monastic seals are still to be seen on which the animal is the central figure. I have already referred to the strange metaphor connecting the unicorn's horn with the central beam of the Holy Cross—a metaphor struck out, probably, in the disordered African fancy of Tertullian but used also by Irenaeus and by Justinus,[29] to mention only two of many.

By far the most important emblematic significance of the unicorn, however, was that in which he stood for Christ. This signification is stated in *Physiologus* and in most of the passages derived therefrom, it is implicit in the pictorial allegory of the Holy Hunt, and the Church Fathers, with their enormous influence upon a millennium of thought and life, spread it broadcast. "Who is this Unicorn," says Saint Ambrose, "but the only-begotten Son of God."[30] "The unconquerable nature of God is likened to that of a unicorn," writes Saint Basil.[31] More extended interpretations were not uncommon, such as that in which we are told that the unicorn represents the Hebrew people as a whole, its one horn standing for their single law wherewith they are to toss aside all other nations.[32] Speaking in general, however, one may say that from the third century of our era to the period of the Reformation the unicorn represented the person of Christ.[33] Whether the pre-Christian symbol had any direct influence upon the Christian allegory one hesitates to say.

Only in recent years has the legend of the unicorn been turned over to avowed and professional dreamers; throughout the greater part of its history it has been shaped chiefly by practical men—hunters, physicians, explorers, and merchant-adventurers—who regarded mere poetry with the healthy contempt shown by Shakespeare's Theseus. Yet the literary allusions to the animal are of course very numerous. I can choose only such examples as seem typical or otherwise important, and these may be arranged in an approximately chronological order.

Several of the earlier references to the unicorn occurring in what we may call imaginative literature—although it seemed no such thing to its authors—appear in the numerous mediaeval stories of Alexander. In one of these [34] we hear that among the gifts sent by Queen Candace to the Conqueror there was a unicorn, valued not so much for itself as for the precious stone growing at the base of its horn. No translation can rival the rudeness of the original, but this is the sense of the lines :—

> I had from this rich queen
> A beast of proud and noble mien
> That bears in his brow the ruby-stone
> And yields himself to maids alone.
> But few such unicorns are found
> On this or any other ground,
> And only such are ever captured
> As stainless virgins have enraptured.
> No man of woman born
> Endures the terror of his horn.

The ruby or "carbuncle" in the brow of Queen Candace's unicorn is an adornment which seems to have been of Levantine origin, and it reminds us that Pfaffen Lamprecht, the author of the poem, was a contemporary of the Crusaders, who brought back many such exotic marvels. For the rest, the meagre lines follow *Physiologus* except for the naïve admission that the unicorn is scarce in this land (*der ist luzzil in diz lant*), which may possibly be a reminiscence of Aelian.

In Wolfram von Eschenbach's *Parzifal* there is another reference to the unicorn's ruby (*karfunkelstein*), here used as one of the several medicines, including also the animal's heart, employed to cure the wound of Anfortas, King of the Grail:—

> We caught the beast called Unicorn
> That knows and loves a maiden best
> And falls asleep upon her breast;
> We took from underneath his horn
> The splendid male carbuncle-stone
> Sparkling against the white skull-bone.[35]

The unicorn story found expression even in a poem called, by one who should have known the word's precise meaning, a *Volkslied*.[36] Although this poem does not seem to me to bear the marks of the popular ballad, it has beauty and a definite value for the present purpose, so that it seems worth while to attempt a translation:—

> I stood in the Maytime meadows
>   By roses circled round,
> Where many a fragile blossom
>   Was bright upon the ground;

And as though the roses called them
    And their wild hearts understood,
The little birds were singing
    In the shadows of the wood.

The nightingale among them
    Sang sweet and loud and long,
Until a greater voice than hers
    Rang out above her song;
For suddenly, between the crags,
    Along the narrow vale,
The echoes of a hunting horn
    Came clear upon the gale.

The hunter stood beside me
    Who blew that mighty horn;
I saw that he was hunting
    The gentle unicorn—
But the unicorn is noble,
    He knows his gentle birth,
He knows that God has chosen him
    Above all beasts of earth.

The unicorn is noble;
    He keeps him safe and high
Upon a narrow path and steep
    Climbing to the sky;
And there no man can take him,
    He scorns the hunter's dart,
And only a virgin's magic power
    Shall tame his haughty heart.

What would be now the state of us
    But for this Unicorn,
And what would be the fate of us,
    Poor sinners, lost, forlorn?
Oh, may He lead us on and up,
    Unworthy though we be,
Into His Father's kingdom,
    To dwell eternally!

The most interesting feature of this poem is the drawing of the
unicorn into a local *mise-en-scène*. The landscape is that of Switzer-

land or Upper Germany, the opening stanzas are those of a secular poem dealing with a hunt, and the unicorn is visualized by the writer as a chamois. In spite of its conventional prettiness, the poem gains from these peculiarities a certain freshness and charm.

As I have already pointed out, the unicorn provided a useful metaphor to the erotic verse of the later Middle Ages and the early Renaissance. Burkhardt von Hohenfels calls himself a unicorn because a woman has lured him to his doom, Guido Cavalcanti says the same thing in a sonnet addressed to Guido Orlandi, and Thibaut, Count of Champagne, writes :—

> The unicorn and I are one:
> He also pauses in amaze
> Before some maiden's magic gaze,
> And, while he wonders, is undone.
> On some dear breast he slumbers deep,
> And Treason slays him in that sleep.
> Just so have ended my life's days;
> So Love and my Lady lay me low.
> My heart will not survive this blow.[37]

One of the most familiar literary allusions to the unicorn is that in Rabelais. Pantagruel says, in narrating his adventures in the Land of Satin: "I saw there two-and-thirty unicorns. They are a cursed sort of creature, much resembling a fine horse, unless it be that their heads are like a stag's, their feet like an elephant's, their tails like a wild boar's, and out of each of their foreheads sprouts a sharp black horn, some six or seven feet long. [Pliny, whom Rabelais follows in most other particulars, had made the horn only three feet in length.] Commonly it dangles down like a turkey-cock's comb, but when a unicorn has a mind to fight or put it to any other use, what does he do but make it stand, and then it is as straight as an arrow."[38]

The unicorn has a less prominent rôle in the romances of the Middle Ages than one might expect, considering his potentialities, but this fact merely reminds one again that he was not regarded as exceptionally romantic or wonderful. The title of *Le Romans de la Dame à la Lycorne et du Biau Chevalier au Lyon* [39] arouses expectations which are not fulfilled, for here the animal's function is largely symbolic. He is given to the heroine by *Li Diex d'Amours* in recognition of her *tres grant purté*, and all that he has to do in the course of eighty-five hundred lines is to swim the moat surrounding the Castle of Chief d'Or with his mistress on his back—the lion belonging to the hero, similarly mounted, paddling proudly beside him.

Far more interesting than this merely ornamental beast is the unicorn we meet towards the end of the charming Old French prose romance called *Le Chevalier du Papegau*.[40] King Arthur, wandering on his maiden adventure, has been stranded on a strange coast, and there he finds a square red tower, without door or window, in which a dwarf is living. The dwarf tells Arthur that he and his wife had been set on shore there many years before by the Lord of Northumbria, and that his wife had died shortly after giving birth to a son. "When my wife was dead and I had buried her," says he, "I put my food into my overcoat, wrapped up my child as best I could, and then went through the forest looking for a hollow tree where I might rest and find shelter from the rain and the night and the wild beasts. At last I found one with a hollow large enough for six knights to lie in, and within the hollow there were new-born fawns, each one with a little horn in the middle of its brow. And when I saw these fawns I went inside and looked at them for a long time with wonder, and I sat down among them. While I was sitting there the mother came—a huge beast, as large as a large horse, with a horn in her brow as sharp as any razor in the world and with fourteen great udders of which the smallest was as large as the bag of a cow, and when this beast saw me she looked at me so terribly that I leaped up and dropped my child and fled. The child began to cry bitterly—and you are to know that it was the finest and fairest infant that ever was seen—so that the beast was touched with pity and she came into the hollow, while I lay hidden behind a root looking to see what she would do to the child. She lay down before him and put the nipple of her udder in his mouth and nursed him until he fell asleep. All that night I lay there without sleep and without daring to move for fear that the beast might kill me, and the child lay sleeping among the fawns. In the morning the unicorn went out to feed and I arose and took up the child, but while I was swaddling him she returned again. This time, however, she showed me such affection that I stayed with her; and when my son and the fawns had been suckled, the beast, who saw that I was little—for I am a dwarf—seemed to think that I must be young, and she made a motion with her head toward one of her udders that was still quite full. Being very thirsty, I did as she wished, and I found she had the best milk and the sweetest that ever I had drunk. Sire, I lived thus while my food lasted, and my son was so well fed that he shows it still, I thank God. But when my food was gone I grew weak, and one day as I was looking out of the hole in our tree I saw a great stag going by, and I was so hungry, after living a long while on milk, that I cried out: 'O Lord God, how I wish that I had a steak from that stag, well cooked!' The unicorn overheard me; she dashed out of the hollow tree, made after the stag, and cut him in two with a single blow of her horn."

To make this delightful but rambling story as short as possible, the unicorn helped the dwarf gather firewood for cooking the stag, she helped him build a hut of boughs, she slew for him many other beasts as the needs of his larder required them. The child throve mightily on unicorn milk, and when he was weaned the dwarf fed him on the flesh of bears. Before long he had grown into a giant, able to uproot huge trees at a single jerk, and finally he built the square red tower, making it very tall and without doors or windows so that wild beasts would not eat the father while the giant boy was off at play. And everywhere he went the mother unicorn went with him.

While Arthur stands at the foot of the tower talking up to the dwarf, this son arrives, carrying a freshly killed bear in one hand and his club in the other. Introductions are made, the giant lifts Arthur to the top of the tower, and the three dine off the bear, the giant standing on the ground alongside. Next morning the giant and the unicorn drag Arthur's ship off the sands and the whole company sets sail for Windsor Castle.—*Cy finit le conte du papegaulx*.

The unicorn is mentioned several times by Luigi Pulci in *Il Morgante Maggiore*, but no accurate treatment of the legend is to be expected from this burlesque upon romance. In one passage [41] a strange combination is made of the water-conning trait with the ideas underlying the use of the horn at table, for we are told that the animal watches its own horn after dipping it to see whether it perspires :—

> Ma non si fidi all' acqua, e non gli creda
> Se non vi mette il corno prima drento,
> E se quel suda sta a vedere attento.

Elsewhere [42] we see Morgante and Margutte shoot and cook and eat a unicorn, taking advantage of the poor beast just as he is dipping his horn, in defiance of all the best authorities. The remarks of Luca Pulci, Luigi's brother, concerning unicorns are equally inaccurate, for he tells us [43] that one of his characters by the name of Severe was turned into a unicorn by Diana to punish him for falling in love with a nymph; he ran straightway to a river's brink to look at his own reflection and while standing there was pierced by an arrow from the nymph's own bow which transformed him into the River Sieve.

Turning now to English literature, we come to the characteristically elaborate simile of Spenser :—

> Like as a Lyon whose imperial powre
> A proud rebellious Unicorn defyes,
> T'avoid the rash assault and wrathful stowre
> Of his fiers foe, him to a tree applyes,
> And when him ronning in full course he spyes
> He slips aside: the whiles that furious beast
> His precious horne, sought of his enemyes,
> Strikes in the stocke, ne thence can be releast,
> But to the mighty victor yields a bounteous feast.[44]

George Chapman provides an interesting variant of this lion-capture story by substituting a man for the lion :—

> I once did see
> In my young travels through Armenia,
> An angrie Unicorne in his full carier
> Charge with too swift a foot a Jeweller,
> That watcht him for the Treasure of his browe;
> And ere he could get shelter of a tree,
> Naile him with his rich Antler to the Earth.[45]

Shakespeare is obviously referring to this same story in the words: "Wert thou the unicorn, pride and wrath would confound thee, and make thine own self the conquest of thy fury." [46] In the two other references to the animal to be found in Shakespeare's plays the speakers express disbelief. We may safely infer that Shakespeare himself did not believe in the existence of unicorns, and this is an interesting fact when one considers that thousands of his contemporaries, as well educated and as well read as he, accepted the animal apparently without a doubt. [47] The shallower critics of Shakespeare have entertained us for many decades with speculations as to whether he did or did not believe in witches, fairies, ghosts, and other "night fears", some of them contending that so wise a man could not have entertained such childish superstitions, and others, more plausibly, that he was a man of his times with all that fact implies. Sound criticism will of course point out that he believed in these things at least imaginatively with an intensity adequate to his artistic needs. If an imaginative faith in the unicorn had been required of him by the day's work, such a faith would have been forthcoming, much as Milton's belief in the Ptolemaic system stood forth bold and clear when he saw that it would serve his purpose. As matters turned out, however, Shakespeare never had to write a play involving a "temporary suspension of disbelief" in the unicorn, and so he lets us see that belief in the animal is to his thinking a minor mark of easy credulity. Thus Decius Brutus, showing how easily Caesar may be swayed by old wives' tales, says:—

> He loves to hear
> That unicorns may be betrayed with trees. [48]

A more revealing passage is that in which Alonso and his followers are entertained by Prospero with strange music and a phantom banquet, after which the irreverent Sebastian remarks, in the tone of a worldling whose scepticism is shaken:—

> Now I will believe
> That there are unicorns. [49]

Little would be gained by an attempt to trace the later history of the legend in literature. It is true that a group of poets has recently pushed the hunt of the unicorn so actively that one critic has felt obliged to advocate a closed season, but most of this writing has been done in ignorance or neglect of the earlier legend. One reference to recent writing must suffice, and I make this chiefly because it suggests an aspect of the subject, never clearly expressed but often implied, which I do not care to consider extensively. Readers of Aubrey Beardsley's prose will recall that the Abbe Fanfreluche found in Queen Helen's library a pamphlet entitled "A Plea for the Domestication of the Unicorn," and that at the end of the story Helen goes out to feed her pet unicorn Adolphe—"milk-white all over except his nose, mouth, and nostrils".[50] This is about all, but, as in nearly every other detail of the morbidly lascivious story, more is meant than meets the eye.

CHAPTER IV

EAST AND WEST

In the scientific discussion of any animal one of the prime essentials is the determination of its habitat, and we must not proceed farther with the study of the unicorn without naming the places where he has been supposed to be found.

Ctesias placed the unicorn, as we have seen, in "India", then as for long after a very inclusive term, and this location sufficed for his Greek and Roman followers. The *Physiologus* does not commit itself on this question, but when we consider that all the other animals it mentions—or all, at any rate, not concocted in libraries, like the ant-lion—were thought to belong to Egypt, we may infer that the unicorn also was regarded as a local species. Few of the Christian echoers of *Physiologus* have any notion of animal habitat, so that they give us little help.

Ethiopia had been confused with India even by Virgil, and therefore, if for no other reason, it was so confused during the Middle Ages. The bewildering transfer of "Prester John's Court" from India to Ethiopia, already referred to, helped on this confusion, and the transfer had a definite influence, as it happened, upon the legend of the unicorn. In the first letter supposed to have been addressed by him to one or other of the potentates of Europe, Prester John is made to describe himself as an Indian monarch, and in this letter, furthermore, he mentions the unicorns to be found in his realm. Fifty years later, that is to say about A.D. 1200, we find him established as a king and priest in Ethiopia,[1] and it was naturally assumed that he had taken his unicorns with him—all the more because later versions of his letter, dated from Ethiopia, continued to mention these animals as prominent in the local fauna. But there were other influences at work to draw the unicorn into North Africa. For one thing, the people of Abyssinia had their own version of *Physiologus*; for another, the Arabs among them had a well-developed unicorn legend; finally, the Portuguese missionaries and merchants of a later time went into Ethiopia with unicorn lore gathered from India itself, and when they found in this new land much the same legends and beliefs as those with which they had become familiar at Goa it is not strange that they were convinced.

Fray Luis de Urreta, whose account of rhinoceros hunting in Abyssinia we have already considered, places the unicorn—which he insists is an entirely different animal—in the Mountains of the Moon.[2] He was by no means the first to hold this view. Cosmas Indicopleustes saw four brazen figures of the unicorn at the court of the King of Ethiopia in the sixth century of our era. A Mappa Mundi, made in the fifteenth century and now hanging on the wall of Hereford Cathedral, shows the unicorn, with a horn almost as long as its body, standing in the region of the Upper Nile. The Arabian zoologist Al Damîrî testified to the same effect.[3] John Bermudez reported unicorns in Abyssinia.[4] Marmol Caravaial found them *"en las sierras de Beht, o de la Lune"*.[5] An English traveller of the sixteenth century asserts: "I have seen in a place like a Park adjoyning unto prester Iohns Court, three score and seven-teene Vnicornes and eliphants all alive at one time, and they were so tame that I have played with them as one would play with young Lambes."[6] Father Lobo handed on an extended account of the Abyssinian unicorn.[7] Job Ludolphus accepts these earlier declarations.[8] We shall see also that a French consular officer of the nineteenth century corroborates them by a long and judicious letter about the unicorn of Central Africa addressed to a learned society.

Quite apart from this abundance of testimony, there is a fitness in the association of the unicorn with the enormous mountain ranges of Abyssinia. The Queen of Sheba is supposed to have hidden her treasure somewhere in those terrifying gorges, and they are a good place in which to hide any precious thing. The very name "Mountains of the Moon", which they owe to Ptolemy, makes them seem a proper home for wonderful beasts. If the unicorn does live among the snows held up for ever on the line of the Equator then it is clear why the world should know so little about him. An Arabian writer says that a great king once sent out a host of men to discover the sources of the Nile, but that they brought back no report because when they reached these mountains the heat reflected from their snows was so great that every man was reduced to ashes.

No sooner has one accustomed himself to think of the Mountains of the Moon as the unicorn's native place, however, than he finds that a case at least equally good may be made out for Tibet. An unknown Chinese traveller of the eleventh or twelfth century informs us that about eighty *li* from H'lari there is a lake in the vicinity of which unicorns are found in great abundance.[9] Again, we are told by several Eastern historians that when the conqueror Genghis Khan set forth in 1224 to invade Hindustan he was met at the top of Mount Djadanaring by a beast with but one horn which knelt thrice at his feet as though in token of respect. The conqueror fell to brooding over this strange event, and he concluded that the beast was an incarnation of his father's spirit come to warn him against the expedition; therefore he turned his army about and marched down the mountain, leaving Hindustan unharmed.[10] Centuries after this, Captain Samuel Turner, one of the most dependable of the earlier authorities upon Tibet, was solemnly told by the Rajah of Bootan that he had once owned a horse-like creature with a single horn in the middle of its forehead.[11] The most famous of all travellers in Tibet, a learned man of the nineteenth century, was entirely convinced that the unicorn is to be found there.[12] A certain Major Latter of the British Army wrote home in 1820 that he had found the unicorn beyond a doubt in Tibet.[13]

Next one comes to the numerous reports of the unicorn in South Africa, where Garcias ab Horto heard it described—equipped with a single horn which it could raise and lower at will—on his voyage round the Cape in the middle of the sixteenth century.[14] Somewhat over a century later Father Jerom Merolla da Sorrento, a Capuchin missionary, saw it in the region mentioned by Garcias.[15] Baron von Wurmb writes from the Cape of Good Hope toward the end of the eighteenth century that he expects to see a unicorn any day, as the reports of it are all about him.[16] Sir John Barrow, a well-trained observer, found so universal a belief in the animal among the natives of South Africa that he himself was inclined to believe, and his faith was rewarded by the discovery of a cave-painting, which he reproduced, of a beast with a single horn.[17] Sir Francis Galton is half-convinced by the persistent reports he hears in Africa,[18] and Dr. William Balfour Baikie finds his former scepticism "partly shaken".[19]

Returning to the Near East, one finds a similar abundance of unicorns, either seen or surmised. One John of Hesse, a priest who visited the Holy Land in 1389, had the good fortune not only to see one but to witness the water-conning performance in actual operation.[20] Felix Fabri, who made pilgrimage to the Holy Land a century later saw, on September 20, 1483, with his own eyes—as did all the members of his company—a unicorn standing on a hill near Mount Sinai, and he observed it carefully for a long time.[21] Lewis Vartoman, regarded for centuries as an exceptionally veracious traveller, gives a careful description of two unicorns that he says he saw at Mecca about the middle of the sixteenth century [22]—but it is to be observed that these two had been sent to the Sultan as a present by the King of Abyssinia. Vincent Le Blanc, who set out on his travels in 1567—at the age of fourteen—saw only one unicorn at Mecca, the other one mentioned by Vartoman having died, but by way of atonement he saw two at the Court of Pegu.[23]

Not to make too intolerably long a list, there is the unicorn of Tartary reported by a British traveller of the eighteenth century[24] and explained one hundred and fifty years later by Lieutenant-Colonel Prejevalsky.[25] There is the unicorn of Persia, said to have been kept as a pet by the Sophy in his private gardens at Samarkand.[26] There is the unicorn of the Carpathians made known by Antony Scheneberger in a letter quoted by Conrad Gesner. There is the unicorn of India, distinct from the rhinoceros, clearly depicted on a map of the Orient published with the English translation of Linschoeten's *Voyages*.²⁷ There is the unicorn of Poland reported by Aldrovandus, the unicorn of Scandinavia of which we learn in the *Historia Naturalis* of Johnston, the unicorn of Florida made known to Europe by the Spanish conquistadors, the unicorn of the Canadian border described by Olfert Dapper, and finally there is the unicorn of China. (Plate IX.)

Chinese writers do not assert that the unicorn or ki-lin ²⁸ is a native of their land; on the contrary, they say that it comes from afar, presumably from heaven, and only at long intervals of time. They regard it, so to speak, as an intermittent animal, and its appearance on earth is considered a certain omen of a beneficent reign or of the birth of some great man comparable with a good emperor in importance. According to the testimony of Tse-Tche-t'ong-kien-kang-mou, the ki-lin was first seen in the year 2697 B.C., in the palace of the Emperor Hoang-ti, on which occasion it was a truthful prophet of national felicity. Another appeared to the mother of Confucius just before the sage's birth, holding in its mouth a great tablet of jade on which there was engraven a dithyramb in praise of the man her son was to become.²⁹ Events of this sort have occurred so many times and the prophecy has always been so unerring that pictures of the unicorn are now pinned or pasted in the women's quarters of millions of Chinese houses in the hope that they may exert pre-natal influence and induce the birth of great men, or at least of boys rather than of girls. They are also affixed to the red chair in which the bride is borne to her husband's house, and the gods that oversee the distribution of desirable babies are often depicted riding upon the ki-lin. To say of any man that a ki-lin appeared at the time of his birth is the highest form of flattery.

The question is asked in the Lî-Kî: "What were the four intelligent creatures?" and the answer is given: "They were the Phoenix, the Tortoise, the Dragon, and the Ki-lin."³⁰ The last, though not so popular as the dragon, is commonly regarded as the king of beasts.³¹ No hunter has ever killed one; and it is seldom captured or even wounded, although we are told that one was injured by a hunter just before the death of Confucius. Like an exceptionally good Buddhist, the ki-lin eats no living thing, either animal or vegetable, so that its diet is severely restricted. It will not even tread upon an insect or a living blade of grass. It has the body of a stag, the hoof of a horse—conforming in these respects to the European tradition —the tail of an ox, and a single horn twelve feet long springing from the middle of its brow, which has at the end a fleshy growth.[32] The most significant thing about the ki-lin's physical appearance, however, is the fact that he is resplendent in the five sacred colours, which are the symbols of his perfection.[33]

The ki-lin is supposed to spring from the centre of the earth, and perhaps he was originally a representative of the earthy element as the phoenix represents fire, the dragon air, and the tortoise water. All commentators enlarge upon the excellence of his character. He knows good from evil, is reverential towards his parents and piously attached to the memory of all his ancestors; he is harmless, beneficent, and gentle, the fleshy tip of his horn indicating clearly that that otherwise formidable member has only symbolic and aesthetic uses. Like the Western unicorn, he keeps the dignity and the mystery of solitude, never mingling promiscuously even with those of his own kind and never treading upon soil tainted by the human foot unless he comes on a mission. He is not violently haled by hunters into the court of the sovereign, but arrives as one king visiting another. Unlike the Western unicorn, the ki-lin has never had commercial value; no drug is made of any part of his body; he exists for his own sake and not for the medication, enrichment, entertainment, or even edification of mankind.

We must infer that this Oriental unicorn was conceived on a higher plane of civilization than that which produced the European legend. Our Western unicorn does us credit in many ways, but when we compare him with the ki-lin we see that there is after all a good deal of violence and deceit and calculation implicit in the stories we have told of him. The ki-lin legend was developed by men who had got beyond fear and calculation in their attitude toward wild nature—by men not unlike those who painted the pictures and wrote the poetry of the Sung period in which Nature is loved for her own sufficient self almost a thousand years before the West learned to look at her without terror.

While speaking of the ki-lin's beneficence I may mention a detail of his legend which, although less firmly authenticated than one could wish, presents a surprising parallel with the legend of the West. The Chinese, we are told, preserve a tradition to the effect that the ki-lin "is to come in the shape of an incomparable man, a revealer of mysteries, supernatural and divine, and a great lover of all mankind. He is expected to come at about the time of a particular constellation in the heavens, on a special mission for their benefit."[34] If this belief really exists—and it corresponds exactly with what we learn from better sources of the ki-lin's nature—then two apparently quite separate unicorn legends have worked out, in regions far apart, the same ultimate symbolism. Both in the East and in the West the unicorn comes to typify a Messiah. Shall we call this an accident, or shall we attribute it to the infiltration of Christian influence? A third possibility, one to which some slight support will be given in later pages, is that the two legends came to similar fruition because they sprang from a single root. It may appear that from the very beginning the unicorn has been conceived as beneficent, holy, in some sense divine, always striving for the healing of the nations.

Distinct as the ki-lin seems at first to be from the Western unicorn, and especially from the unicorn of *Physiologus*, it is hardly possible to think of him at last as an entirely independent creation. His different colouring, his more actively humane disposition, even the subtle but significant change in his horn—difficult to reconcile with our notions of physiology, but clear enough in allegorical intent—all these are due to his Chinese environment. On the other hand, he has the body of a stag and the solid hoof of a horse, like the unicorn of Aelian and Pliny and Solinus. Like all Western unicorns, he is solitary, and he cannot be captured. The Chinese are so certain of this last characteristic, indeed, that they never go forth against him even with virgins for bait. It seems likely, therefore, that the ki-lin and the unicorn of the West have a common ancestor.

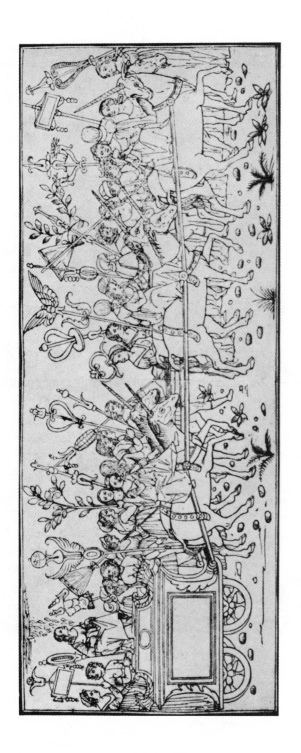

VII. THE CHARIOT OF CHASTITY

VIII. MORETTO'S SAINT JUSTINA

IX. THE ORIENTAL UNICORN

X. THE UNICORN OF AMERICA

Chinese writers enumerate six different sorts of unicorns: the King, the Kioh Twan, the Poh, the Hiai Chai, the Too Jon Sheu, and the Ki-lin; but it seems probable that all six are derived from a single original.[35] The great age of some of the classics in which these animals are described proves that the unicorn legend is old in China, and this fact alone accounts for the existing discrepancies. In spite of these, the ki-lin is more consistent than the Western unicorn; it varies little in appearance and not at all in habits or temperament, being always gentle, beneficent, delicate in diet, regular and stately in pace, and with a call "which in the middle part thereof is like a monastery bell".

The ki-lin, moreover, does not show the tendency to sink down and fade away into the rhinoceros which is so deplorable in the Western unicorn, for the Chinese know the rhinoceros perfectly well and describe it accurately as a totally different species.[36] From the time of the Han dynasty to our own day they have been the carvers of the rhinoceros horn, and old Chinese writers have much to say of the prophylactic value of this horn. During the T'ang dynasty (A.D. 618–905) the official girdles of mandarins were studded with pieces of it, used as charms somewhat in the way of the Japanese *natsuke*. Through all the many centuries that the commerce in rhinoceros horns has been going on, however, those who have had to do with it have known that the horns came from the rhinoceros, and the ki-lin has been kept apart from such associations. Uncontaminated by trade, never regarded as a drug or as an emblem of moral virtue, he has moved serenely all this while in the central recesses of the Oriental imagination.[37]

One of the rarer titles in the "Americana" that have so strongly attracted the cupidity of book-collectors in recent decades is a well-printed and brilliantly illustrated volume called *Die Unbekante Neue Welt*, by Dr. Olfert Dapper.[38] The most accurate pages in this entertaining book are those that deal with New Amsterdam and the present site of New York City, so that a casual reader is the more surprised when he finds, immediately after those pages, a lively representation of the American unicorn in its native haunts—the suggestion is that they must have been in the general region of the Bronx—with an unmistakable American eagle upon its back. (Plate X.) In the accompanying letterpress, however, and under the appropriate rubric *Seltsame Tiere*, the Doctor places this unicorn somewhat farther afield. "On the Canadian border", he says, "there are sometimes seen animals resembling horses, but with cloven roofs, rough manes, a long straight horn upon the forehead, a curled tail like that of the wild boar, black eyes, and a neck like that of the stag. They live in the loneliest wildernesses and are so shy that the males do not even pasture with the females except in the season of rut, when they are not so wild. As soon as this season is past, however, they fight not only with other beasts but even with those of their own kind."

While one reads this fairly accurate paraphrase of Aelian one's thoughts slip back more than two thousand years behind Dr. Dapper to another physician sitting in his library at the court of Darius and describing as accurately as he could the animals of another distant and wonderful land. (Without the medical profession the lore of the unicorn would have been far less rich than it is.) Here we see the animal's range enormously extended at a single leap, so that we may think of the unicorn as roaming, if not Manhattan Island, at any rate the woods of Maine and the Canadian border—that is to say, the region of the moose.

But it had not been reserved for Dr. Dapper to discover the American unicorn. His account is more than a hundred years too late for that, in addition to the fact that it has a strong smell of the lamp. We are told in the legends of the conquistadors that Friar Marcus of Nizza set out from Mexico in 1539 with Stephen the Negro to find the "Seven Cities of Cibola", and that when he got there the inhabitants showed him, among other wonders, "an hide halfe as big againe as the hide of an Oxe, and said it was the skinne of a beast which had but one horne upon his forehead, bending toward his breast, and that out of the same goeth a point forward with which he breakes any thing that he runneth against."[39] Furthermore, Sir John Hawkins writes in his account of his voyage of 1564: "The Floridians have pieces of unicornes hornes which they wear about their necks, whereof the Frenchmen obtained many pieces. Of those unicornes they have many; for that they doe affirme it to be a beast with one horne, which comming to the river to drinke, putteth the same into the water before he drinketh. Of this unicornes horne there are of our company, that having gotten the same of the Frenchmen, brought home thereof to shew. . . . It is thought that there are lions and tygres as well as unicornes; lions especially; if it be true that is sayd, of the enmity betweene them and the unicornes: for there is no beast but hath his enemy . . . insomuch that whereas the one is the other cannot be missing."[40]

This passage helps one to see how notions of a new country's fauna developed even in the minds of intelligent men less than four centuries ago. Objects of horn or bone worn on necklaces by the natives of "Florida" proved that there were unicorns in that region, and in that case there must be lions too, for a beast cannot be left without its natural enemy. No man endowed with the divine faculty of reason required, or even wished, to see an actual American lion in order to be convinced; the bits of bone strung round the necks of the Floridians were a sufficient proof of lions to satisfy him. And if any one should be inclined to doubt the veracity of Captain Hawkins, now that his sword is rust, he has left a remarkable bit of "convincing detail" in a marginal rubric accompanying the text just quoted: "Unicornes hornes, which ye inhabitants call Souanamma." He brought home, then, one hard bit of fact—a name. We see how he read what he thought he knew into the unknown, but that unknown belief of the Floridians may after all have been something worth finding out.

Twenty-three years after the voyage of Sir John Hawkins, John Davis, seeking a north-west passage to India, found a "unicorn's horn" in the hands of a savage on the coast of North America, in latitude 67 degrees. "Of them," he says, "I had a darte with a bone in it, or a piece of Unicornes horne, as I did judge. This dart he [the savage owner] made store of, but when he saw a knife, he let it go, being more desirous of the knife than of his dart."[41]

So much, then, for written records, by means of which we have traced the unicorn legend through the greater part of the world. And now, if one might shake off for a moment the necessity of finding definite authority for every opinion, if one might indulge his own fancy on this topic as thousands of others have done, and if it were not for the fear of being taken quite seriously, one would like to toy with the notion that the original home of the unicorn was the Lost Atlantis. Let us consider what may be said for this. Here we have a very ancient and persistent legend concerning a beast that seems to have vanished from the earth. The belief is of long standing that this beast, although as actual as the mammoth or the sabre-tooth tiger, was destroyed by the flood. Now it is generally agreed among Atlanteans that the world-wide tradition of the Flood—which Hebraizers will persist in calling "Noah's Flood"—is a racial memory of the submergence of the Atlantic Continent. Most significant are the few but startling evidences that the aborigines of the Western Hemisphere had their own legend of the unicorn, and that they actually used its supposed horn for magical ends. Legends so similar and so peculiar, found in both hemispheres, must have spread East and West from a common distributing centre, and that centre may well have been the vast region that has been covered for at least ten thousand years by the Atlantic waves. The Sargasso Sea has been for time out of mind the port of missing ships. Why may it not cover the primeval habitat of missing animals?

Here is an argument in support of Plato's theory about the Lost Atlantis that would have commended itself to the enthusiastic genius of Ignatius Donnelly; but one of the several objections to it is that we cannot really prove the existence of a unicorn legend among the American aborigines. One is sorry for this, feeling that Atlantis would have been as appropriate a habitat for the unicorn as even the Mountains of the Moon. We should solve several difficult problems if we could place him there with assurance.

CHAPTER V

THE TREASURE OF HIS BROW

ALTHOUGH men have often been uncertain where unicorns were to be found, there has never been the same difficulty with regard to unicorns' horns.* These have never been plentiful and they have usually been very dear, but they have been known. Almost any well-read or widely travelled European of the sixteenth century would have been able to name eight or ten whole horns kept in cathedrals, monastic houses, or kings' treasuries, not to mention the innumerable smaller pieces to be found in the hands of the wealthy. The study of these horns, of their distribution, origin, and use, leads into the centre of unicorn lore.

"Come we now", in the words of Thomas Fuller, "to the fashion and colour of the Horn, conceiving it no considerable controversy concerning the length and bignesse thereof, quantity not varying the kind in such cases." It is hard to know just what Thomas Fuller, who lived victoriously and contentiously through the English Civil Wars, may have understood by a "considerable controversy", but this one has been long and earnestly waged. Ctesias gives the length of the horn as one cubit or eighteen inches, Aelian as a cubit and a half, Pliny as two cubits, Solinus and Isidore as four feet, Cardan as three cubits, Rabelais as six or seven feet, and Albertus

---

* In order to avoid repeated cacophony I shall use the word "alicorn" to mean "unicorn's horn" wherever it seems convenient to do so in the following chapters. This is not quite a neologism; it is an adoption of the Italian word *alicorno*.

Magnus as ten feet. At this point the growth of the horn was checked, for the animal that bore it was obviously becoming top-heavy and needed, as several sceptics pointed out, to be "as big as a ship" merely to carry such a formidable bow-sprit. Arabian writers showed less retraint, for Al Damîrî, among others, asserts that the unicorn, for all its great strength, is unable to lift its head because of the great weight of its horn. Other Arabian authorities inform us that he often carries about on this horn the bodies of several elephants which he has "perforated". Although the spoils went to the victor in these contests, they were frequently—as in human affairs—quite as lethal as defeat, for Alkazuwin says that when once the unicorn has gored the elephant he is unable to remove the corpse from his horn, so that he either starves to death or else dies of the putre-faction. (Here was material for a powerful pacifistic allegory, if the Arabs had been given to such things.) The end comes when the roc, seeing the unicorn with one or more elephants impaled upon his horn, swoops down and bears the whole mass of flesh away as a titbit for its young.

Concerning the length of the alicorn, then, one could think almost whatever one liked. The time was to come when specimens almost if not quite as long as that described by Albertus Magnus were to be seen in Europe, and undoubtedly the respect in which the unicorn was everywhere held was maintained by the effort to imagine a beast to which a horn ten feet in length would be proportionate.

Before the sixteenth century there was general agreement among the learned that the true horn was black, as Aelian had said, but after a long period of vacillation the opinion that it was white or of the colour of old ivory definitely triumphed.[1] Less bookish persons had thought of it as white for a long time, if we may judge from the numerous pictures of the unicorn to be seen in mediaeval manuscripts. Andrea Bacci recalled the assertion of Aelian and Pliny, but had to admit that all the specimens he had seen were not black but more nearly white. His dilemma was really distressing, for he had, on the one hand, the Renaissance scholar's profound respect for ancient authority and, on the other, he felt obliged to avoid saying anything that would cast a doubt upon the genuineness of the horn, a white one, belonging to his patron, Don Francesco di Medici. He does the best he can in saying that *"niger"* does not necessarily mean pure black,[2] but with all his learning he cannot make the word mean anything like white. Thomas Fuller suggests that the differences in colour may be due to age—"white when newly taken from his head; yellow like that lately in the Tower, of some hundred years seniority; but whether or no it will ever turn black, as that of Aelian's and Pliny's description, let others decide."[3] But the most ingenious solution of these discrepancies was the view that the true horn is white within and black outside, on account of the "bark" that covers it, so that the same horn may be described as either black or white according as the bark has been left on or stripped off.[4]

By far the strangest thing in the history of opinion about the alicorn's appearance is the age and persistence of the belief in the natural spiral twistings or striae. These are clearly delineated in every picture of the unicorn that I have seen in mediaeval manuscripts, some of which were drawn in the twelfth century. It is possible that Aelian meant to describe them in his phrase ἐλιγμοὺς ἔχον τινὰς καὶ μάλα αὐτοφυεῖς for the word ἐλιγμούς may mean either "rings" or "spirals".[5] Even the horns of the unicorned animals shown in bas-relief on the walls of Persepolis seem to show these twistings. There is nothing said about them, however, in Ctesias, Pliny, Solinus, Isidore, or *Physiologus*; aside from the mysterious passage in Aelian, there seems to be no ancient authority for them whatever, and learned writers do not mention them until after the close of the Middle Ages. Erudite Europeans were converted to the "anfractuous spires and cochleary turnings"—to adopt Fuller's charmingly pedantic phrase—at about the time when they admitted a possibility that the horn might sometimes be white, but Arabian writers had accepted them somewhat earlier. Alkazuwin says, for example, that the unicorn has one horn on its head, sharp at the top and thick below, with raised or convex striae outside and hollow or concave striae within.

Arabian notions of the inside of the alicorn are highly interesting. Ibn Khordâdhbeh asserts that when the horn is split longitudinally one finds inside of it, on a black background, the white figures of a man, a fish, and a peacock or some other bird.[6] Algiahid, in his *Book of Holy Things*, makes much the same remark, and Al Damîrî affirms in more detail that when one cuts the alicorn lengthwise there are found in it various figures in white on black, as of peacocks, goats, birds, certain kinds of trees, men, and other things wonderfully depicted.[7] Horns with such remarkable interior decorations were more prized, of course, than those without them, and the Arabs tell us that a good one was worth over four thousand shekels of gold and that they were used by the Chinese mandarins on their girdles.

This whole belief is certainly one of the most curious confusions of art with nature. Michelangelo seems to have found it helpful to imagine that his statue already existed in the stone block before him, so that his task was merely to strip away the superfluous material. Arabian travellers in the Orient could understand the work of the Chinese ivory carvers in no other way.

While considering the physical characteristics of alicorns we should not neglect the abundant testimony that they are not always fixed solidly in the skull, but that some unicorns have them "plyable", as Arthur Golding says in speaking of the one-horned bulls of Inde, "to what purpose they liste". There was the best authority for movable horns in general, Aristotle having ascribed them to the Indian bull[8] and Solinus asserting that the Erythian ox could raise and lower its horns at will. The same advantage was enjoyed by the Yale, whose horns normally projected one forward and one backward, but who could switch them about to suit the exigencies of the moment in fighting.[9] Cosmas Indicopleustes informs us that the rhinoceros's horn is normally so loose that it shakes and rattles when he walks, but that when he is in a rage it is suddenly tightened to such a degree that he can tear up rocks and trees.

The unicorn does not suffer in this comparison. Garcias ab Horto, rounding the Cape of Good Hope about the year 1550, heard of an amphibian on the eastern coast of Africa that could raise and lower its single horn and swing it to right or left as caprice or necessity dictated,[10] and some years later André Thevet reported another amphibian unicorn—it had webbed feet behind and cloven hoofs before and lived on fish—from the Island of Molucca, with a three-foot horn that waved about like the crest of a cock.[11] In this connection we must not forget the mobile horns observed by Pantagruel upon the unicorns of the Land of Satin. Finally, a consular agent of France writes a long letter in the middle of the nineteenth century to prove that the unicorn of the ancients has been discovered in Central Africa, and that it has a movable horn—*"une corne unique, mobile, susceptible d'érection en ce sens qu'elle peut recevoir de la volonté de l'animal une position variable relativement à la surface du front".*[12]

There is one more thing, perhaps the most instructive of all, to be said about the physical characteristics of the alicorn. For two or three centuries many learned men, quite as intelligent as those of their kind to-day, measured and weighed and tasted these objects, speculated about them, subjected them to various tests, bought and sold them for great sums, wrote astonishingly erudite books about them—all the while calling them "horns". Not one of these men guessed, until the seventeenth century brought in new habits of thought, that the objects they had before them, ninety-nine times in the hundred, were not composed of horn at all but of ivory.

By the year 1600 Europe and England contained at least a dozen famous alicorns that were known to all travellers, were frequently exhibited on state occasions to the people, and were carefully described again and again. Most of these were kept in great churches or monasteries. They were regarded as sacred objects, and were sometimes used as pontifical staffs.

Best known of all was the horn of St. Denis, near Paris, seven feet long and weighing over thirteen pounds.[13] This was included in the monastery's inventory of its treasures, together with other sacred relics, and was one of the "worthies" of Europe. Even John Evelyn speaks of seeing it—"a faire unicorne's horn, sent by a K. of Persia, about 7 foote long".[14] The popular belief was that it had been presented to the monastery by André Thevet, the famous traveller, who was thought to have had it from the King of Monomotapa with whom he was said to have gone unicorn hunting; but this opinion was groundless, for Thevet speaks of having seen the horn of St. Denis *"en ma grand' jeunesse"*, he never went unicorn hunting with the King of Monomotapa, and in fact he did not much believe in unicorns.[15] How this alicorn was acquired we do not know, but it was lost during the general looting of old treasures, particularly those of the Church, during the Revolution of 1793.[16] It was kept in a dark vault of the sanctuary, one end of it resting in water. We hear that "this water is given to drink to those that go under the hollow arch; and so soon as they have drunk they suddenly fall into a great sweat".[17]

Cardan has left a careful description of the St. Denis alicorn which he saw during a visit paid to the monastery in company with the monks' physician. "After we had seen the sepulchres of the kings", he writes, "and the statues and other marble ornaments, I studied very closely the unicorn's horn hanging in the sanctuary. It was so long that I could not touch the top of it with my hand, but its thickness was slight in proportion to its length, for it was easily possible to surround it with the thumb and first finger. . . . It was smooth all over, but was marked by bands running from end to end as on a snail-shell. . . . Nature makes nothing else that I know of like this." [18]

Almost equally celebrated were the two horns of St. Mark's in Venice, said to have been taken at the fall of Constantinople in 1204 as part of the Venetian share in the spoil.[19] It is true that many of the treasures of St. Mark's were thus acquired, and the two horns have long been associated by tradition with the blind Doge Enrico Dandolo who, although ninety-seven years of age when Constantinople was taken, is said to have been the first man over the wall; but against this romantic and persistent tradition stand certain awkward facts. On the silver-gilt handle of one of these alicorns is the inscription: Ἰωάννης . Παλαιολόγος . βασιλὲ + Ἐλιουμκόρνι . ἀντι . φάρμακον. (John Palaeologus, Emperor. Alicorn good against poison.) Now the first Emperor of the East named John in the Palaeologus dynasty was John V, who ruled 1341–1391; the only other, ignoring the non-dynastic John Cantacuzenus, was John VI, 1425–1448, and there are several reasons for believing that the alicorn in question belonged to him. For one thing, the Greek inscription upon it, although crude in several ways, is comparatively modern in lettering. It bears on the handle the familiar design of the double-headed eagle —probably Hittite in origin and perhaps brought into Europe by the Crusaders—which was adopted in the arms of the Emperor of the Romans not earlier than 1414. Finally, this John VI made a famous visit to the West, and especially to Venice, to seek aid for his crumbling empire, and we are told by the chronicler Phrantzes that when he appeared in St. Mark's Basin the Venetian galleys went out to meet him adorned with the design of the double-headed eagle—a gracious courtesy on the part of the city that had caused most of his distress. It seems to me more than possible that the alicorn bearing his name was brought to Venice by him on this occasion, although it is hard to see how it could have fallen, as it must have done, into the hands of the wealthy jewel merchant Giorgio Belbava. At any rate, St. Mark's Library contains a record that in 1488 this alicorn was given by the son of Belbava to Doge Barbarigo, and that the Doge at once handed it over to the Procurators of the Cathedral, "*ut illud in Thesauris Sanctuarii in Celebritatibus portandum curarent*".

The second alicorn of St. Mark's, like the first about one metre in length, is made of three pieces joined together. This also has a Greek inscription, but one that gives no hint of the horn's origin, so that one can believe, if one likes, that it was brought back by Doge Dandolo in 1204. Both of these alicorns have been coloured with vermilion for several inches from the points, and on this colour have been written various devotional ejaculations in Arabic, of no present interest except as they serve to indicate once more that the objects were regarded as sacred. Clearly, however, the Greek and Arabic inscriptions alike would be felt to increase the alicorn's magic power, and the phrases $"A\gamma\iota\sigma s$. $\Theta\epsilon\grave{o}s$. $"A\gamma\iota\sigma s$. $\grave{\iota}\sigma\chi\upsilon\rho\grave{o}s$. $"A\gamma\iota\sigma s$. $\grave{a}\delta\acute{a}\nu\alpha\tau\sigma s$ on one of them were probably intended as a charm.

These two alicorns are still shown to visitors as they were when the hero of *The Cloister and the Hearth* saw them centuries ago, and when properly understood they are among the most interesting relics of the past to be seen in Europe. One's guide asserts that they were formerly used by admirals of the Venetian fleet as batons of office, and this, whether true or not, shows that they have long been popularly regarded as symbols of supreme power and leadership. The spiral ridges of both have been smoothed away to such an extent that Andrea Marini thought them not genuine, but the grain of the ivory may still be seen to run in counter-clockwise spirals, leaving one in no doubt as to their nature. This smoothing was not done, as some have surmised, to improve their appearance, but to get medicinal powder, and there exists a highly interesting, not to say amusing, decree of the august Council of Ten: "That the Procurators are to have the Alicorns decorated with silver from the points to the silver-gilt handles so that the marks of former scrapings may be concealed, and they are to prohibit any further scrapings except in cases allowed by unanimous vote of the Council of Ten." [20]

There is in the St. Mark's Treasury still another alicorn, more than twice as long as the other two, unscraped, and without inscriptions. The history of this one can be traced accurately for a long period, although it is probably not so old as the others. In the year 1597 Francesco Contarini, ambassador from Venice to the Court of France, wrote to the Council of Ten advising the purchase from the Maréchal de Brissac of his alicorn, held at thirty thousand ducats. Francesco argued, like a Venetian, that in this way the Republic could get back some part of the debt owed to it by France. Venice seems to have offered the sum demanded, but for some reason did not get the alicorn until 1668, when it was sold to a descendant of Francesco Contarini by the Brissac family. In his will, dated 1684, Alessandro Contarini left it to the Treasury of St. Mark's, adding the information that it had been taken by the French in the sack of Turin. When given to the Treasury this alicorn stood on a pedestal of wrought silver, which gave it the appearance of a gigantic candle, but about the middle of the nineteenth century the pedestal was put to other uses. [21]

Milan Cathedral also had its famous alicorn; the church at Raskeld somehow acquired several; St. Paul's in London and West-

minster Abbey each had one or more before the Dissolution, when
they were probably either taken into the royal treasury or else sold
to the highest bidders.[22] The inventory taken by order of Cromwell
in 1536 of the property owned by the tiny Church of St. Swithun
at Winchester shows: "One Rectors staf of Unicorns horn"—a
proud possession indeed for one of the smallest churches in England
at a time when the alicorn was still "worth a city". Chester
Cathedral still keeps its alicorn, but I am told by the Dean that
it has been in the Chapter's possession only since the eighteenth
century.

The long association of the unicorn with Christianity and the
Church is amusingly illustrated by an attempted act of vandalism
in which the beast fully justified the ancient belief that he could not
be captured. In a forgotten book of travels I find this passage:
"Our leader having taken a great fancy to the unicorn which stands
on one side of the great entrance to the Church of Saint John in
Malta, wishing to place it as a figure-head to his brother's yacht, he
resolved to have the animal, and his refractory crew were desired
to be in attendance the next night. . . . The rope was placed round
the unicorn's neck, and all of us began, with a true sailor-like
'one, two, three, haul!' to dislodge our victim. It was, however, so
well fastened on its pedestal that we did not succeed." [23]

A feeling that the horn had some vague sanctity, due perhaps to
the symbolism of the unicorn, must certainly be assumed to explain
the possession of these objects by so many churches and monasteries and the veneration in which they were held; but a quite
different feeling lay behind the eager quest of them by popes and
kings and emperors during the Renaissance. Andrea Bacci says that
in his time—the second half of the sixteenth century—there was not
a prince in Italy, to say nothing of those outside of it, who had not
at least a piece of the horn in his possession.[24] He describes in
detail the alicorn belonging to the Grand Duke Francesco Medici,
which he seems to have had before him while writing his book, and
others belonging to the Pope, to the Duke of Mantua, to Ruberto
Ricci of Florence, and to the King of Poland—this last a very famous

specimen. Echoing Bacci, J. F. Hubrigk asks rhetorically: "Is there any Prince, Duke, or King in the world who has not either seen or possessed, and regarded as among the most precious of his possessions, a unicorn's horn?" [25] Such men there may have been, but if so it was not for lack of desire but of funds.

Among the earliest references to the alicorns of kings' treasuries are those in the royal accounts of France. There we find recorded, for the year 1388, the sum paid to a goldsmith *"pour avoir atachié une espreuve de lincorne et mise sur une chayenne d'argent doré et enchaçonée."* [26] This was early indeed, for the alicorn was not to reach the height of its reputation for more than a century to come. Just eighty years after the King of France paid for the decoration of his horn, Edward IV of England gave a sumptuous dinner to his sister, the Princess Margaret, on the occasion of her wedding to the Duke of Burgundy, and in the contemporary description of the furniture prepared for the dinner we read: "In the myddis a copeborde, in triangle of IX stagis hight. On every corner unnycorns horns, the poyntes garnysshid, and othe thre in other places, accomplissinge the coopborde." [27] One of the most amusing glimpses into remote history afforded us by unicorn lore is the possibility that at least one of the numerous alicorns at this wedding dinner was brought over from France by the bridegroom himself. This we may perhaps infer from the inventory of the Dukes of Burgundy made in 1467, the year before the wedding, for there we find described: *"Une licorne garnye autour du bout, par dessoubz, d'or, à la devise de MS., et à la pointe garnie d'argent doré et depuis l'un des boutz jusques à l'autre garnye de plusieurs filetz d'or."* [28] Perhaps the Duke felt even on his wedding journey and while sitting beside his bride that he preferred to trust his own horn, for the times were troubled and one did not know how English alicorns might act. However this may have been, these people were certainly much interested in the alicorn. In September of 1472 Louis de la Grantehuse came to England as ambassador to Edward IV from the Duke of Burgundy. The highly interesting account of this visit records that "When the masse was doon, the Kinge gave the sayde Lorde Granthuse a Cuppe of Golde, garnished w^t Perle. In the myddes of the Cuppe ys a greate Pece

of Vnicornes horne, to my estimacyon, VII ynches compas." [29]
Somewhat after this, Commines relates that de Ballassat, plundering
the palace of Pietro de' Medici in 1495, "took, among other things,
a whole unicorn's horn worth six or seven thousand ducats, and
two large pieces of another".[30] D'Aubigné, also, narrating the
exploits of one of his noble ruffians, says that he found in a villa
he was plundering *"pour butin principal une licorne estimée à quatre-
vingt mille escus"*.[31]

These, however, were the alicorns of subjects, and comparatively
humble things. The gorgeous popes of the Renaissance acquired
a number of horns by one means and another, descending when
necessary even to outright purchase, and they were accustomed to
have them set with appropriate splendour in silver and gold. In his
account of how he worsted his rival Tobbia, Benvenuto Cellini
enables us to see how carefully this work of the goldsmith was
done. He says that Pope Clement VII commanded him and Tobbia
"to draw a design for setting an unicorn's horn, the most beautiful
that ever was seen, and which had cost him seventeen thousand
ducats: and as the Pope proposed making a present of it to King
Francis, he chose to have it first richly adorned with gold: so he
employed us both to draw the designs. When we had finished them
we carried them to the Pope. Tobbia's design was in the form of
a candlestick: the horn was to enter it like a candle, and at the
bottom of the candlestick he represented four little unicorn's heads
—a most simple invention. As soon as I saw it I could not contain
myself so as to avoid smiling at the oddity of the conceit. The
Pope perceiving this, said, 'Let me see that design of yours.' It was
a single head of an unicorn fitted to receive the horn. I had made
the most beautiful sort of head conceivable, for I in part drew it in
the form of a horse's head and partly in that of a hart's, adorned
with the finest sort of wreaths and other devices; insomuch that no
sooner was my design seen but the whole court gave it the preference.
However, as some Milanese gentlemen of great authority were
witnesses of this contest, they said: 'Most Holy Father, if you propose
sending this noble present to France, you should take it into consideration that the French are an undiscriminating tasteless people

and will not be sensible of the excellence of this masterly piece of Benvenuto's. But they will be pleased with these grotesque figures of Tobbia's, which will be sooner executed; and Benvenuto will in the meantime finish your chalice.' " [32] Whether for the reasons given or not, this advice was accepted: in 1553 Pope Clement met François I at Marseilles and there gave him the horn which had been decorated by Tobbia, the occasion being the wedding of the Pope's niece, Catharine de' Medici, to the son of François, the later Henry II of France.

Temporal princes were not less eager purchasers than Pope Julius III, who bought a horn for ninety thousand *écus* for the Vatican museum. At the coronation of the Emperor Theodore Ivanovitch in Moscow, 1584, he wore "a bejewelled robe—worth two hundred pounds, his staff imperial in his right hand of an unicorn's horn of three and one half feet in length beset with rich stones bought of merchants of Augsburg by the old Emperor in 1581, and cost him seven thousand marks sterling." [33] We hear also that the Sultan of Turkey sent twelve alicorns as a gift to Philip II of Spain,[34] feeling, no doubt, that Philip needed them as much as any man in Europe. (This story was doubted by Caspar Bartholinus, who could not believe that even the Sultan was rich enough to own twelve horns at a time.)

One might write an entire book, and not a dull one, about the alicorns of kings' treasuries; but the present book has a longer road to travel, and I can only mention a few of the horns that have been owned by British sovereigns.

In 1303, while King Edward I of England was fighting far in the North, he learned that a large part of the immense treasure which he had hidden, before setting out, under the Chapter House at Westminster, had been stolen. As soon as he could return to London he set on foot a strict investigation, and the trial that followed proved the guilt of some of the Westminster monks. Under the bed of one of the chief culprits, the keeper of the palace gate, there was discovered a unicorn's horn which had been stolen from the treasury,[35] and for centuries thereafter the skin of a fair-haired and light-complexioned man was to be seen nailed to the place in the wall where the entrance had been made—intended, no doubt, "to encourage the others".

An inventory taken in 1497 of the possessions of James III of Scotland shows: "In unicornis [i.e. in the coins of that name] nyne hundreth and four score. Item a serpent toung and ane unicorne horne, set in gold. Item a covering of variand purpir taster, browdin with thressilis and a ùnicorne."

But by far the most famous of all British alicorns was the great "Horn of Windsor" which the German traveller Hentzner saw in 1598 and valued, if his Latin text is to be trusted, at one hundred thousand pounds.[36] We know exactly when and where this horn was discovered; it was picked up on the twenty-second of July, 1577, on an island in Frobisher's Strait, and we are told that when it reached England it was "reserved as a jewell by the Queen's Majesty's commandment, in her wardrobe of robes." [37] We have also a dark hint as to what became of it, for Thomas Fuller, speaking of it and of the Tower Horn, both of which he had seen in his youth, remarks: "It belongs not to me to inquire what became of them", and then somewhat later he says that a unicorn's horn has been presented to his Majesty "to supply the place of that in the Tower which our Civil wars have embeseled".[38] We may infer that the Horn of Windsor was "embeseled" at the same time.

Fuller's words imply that the Tower Horn also belonged among the Crown jewels, and it deserved a place there if contemporary estimates of its value were not exaggerated. "In 1641 the Marquis de la Ferte Imbaut, Marshal of France, saw in the Tower of London a unicorn's horn covered with plates of silver and estimated at the enormous sum of forty thousand pounds." [39] Such an estimate as this, at so late a date, must have been due largely to the goldsmith's work, for the value of alicorns fell away rapidly after 1625. The one belonging to Charles I and kept by him at Somerset House was valued at only five hundred pounds,[40] although it was an exceptionally fine specimen. Pierre Pomet tells us that it was seven feet long and weighed thirteen pounds, so that it equalled the famous horn of St. Denis.[41]

The cost of "true unicorn's horn" (*verum cornu monocerotis*) in its best period was a little over ten times its weight in gold when sold in small pieces or in powder, but whole alicorns sometimes brought twice as much as this.[42] The inventory of Lorenzo the Magnificent, recently opened to the public in the new Medici Museum at Florence, shows that the most precious of his possessions after the famous Tazza Farnese was his alicorn, three and one-half braccia in length and valued by him—probably on the basis of what it cost him—at six thousand gold florins. About the year 1560 a group of German merchants offered an alicorn for sale in Rome and other Italian cities for ninety thousand scudi—the scudo being then worth about four shillings—and finally sold it to the Pope. We are told that the King of France refused one hundred thousand écus for the horn of St. Denis, although we are not told how it came to be in his control.[43] A horn picked up on the coast of Wales in 1588 by a poor woman was sold for a great but unspecified sum.[44] Edward Topsell could say in 1607 that "the price of that which is true is reported at this day to be of no less value than gold".[45] The famous alicorn belonging to the city of Dresden was valued at seventy-five thousand thalers. Ordinarily it was kept on display, strongly protected, in the museum which was known to the more leisured classes as the *exotikothaumatourgematatameion*, and there was a strict municipal regulation that whenever raspings were taken from it for medicinal uses two persons of princely rank should be present in the room. Pierre Pomet tells us that a horn given to the King of France in 1553 was said to be worth twenty thousand pounds sterling.[46] The Republic of Venice in 1597 offered for a whole horn the sum of thirty thousand ducats—ten times the price of Shylock's pound of flesh—and did not get it.[47]

Many things in the history of commerce are less interesting than the curve of market quotations on unicorns' horns. The means that were taken to increase and then to maintain the price of them we can only infer from a number of minute details, but the reasons why that price rather swiftly declined are more open to examination. By 1734 a well-informed writer could say that horns which formerly brought many thousands of dollars could then be had for twenty five;[48] yet this same writer makes it clear that even in his time there was still an active sale, and it is certain that long after the wealthy had lost all interest in alicorns the poor continued to buy them. Something of this commercial history is indicated by the fact that the Book of Rates for the first year of Queen Mary, 1531, gives the import duty as *"cornu unicorni* ye ounce 20 shillings"*, and that in 1664 the French duty on unicorn's horn was fifty sous per pound.

There is something delightfully humorous, to the modern view, in the idea of adulterating and "faking" the unicorn's horn. The rewards of success were enormous, and human nature was almost as prevalent in the sixteenth century as it is to-day, so that one finds in all the more responsible and socially minded writers upon our topic bitter complaints about the frequency of counterfeiting, warnings that purchasers must be constantly suspicious, and tests by which the true horn may be known from the false. Andrea Bacci makes it clear that fraud was very common in his time, though he thinks it can only be practised in the sale of powdered horn and of fragments, for which, he says, various kinds of horn and pounded stone were sold; but even this would be impossible, he reminds his readers, if only the public would realize that the true horn is rarer than precious stones, so that none but great princes can hope to possess even a large piece. Bacci does not show his usual knowledge and acumen, however, in saying that the horn cannot be imitated in the whole piece, for there is evidence that the wicked knowledge of how this could be done was possessed and used in his time all over Europe. Amatus Lusitanus, following Dioscorides, says that if ivory is boiled for six hours in a decoction of mandragora it becomes soft so that one can bend and work it as he likes,[49] and Cardan tells us that elephants' tusks were often so treated. One source of the supply of alicorns is revealed by Hector Boëthius in his *History of Scotland,* where he asserts, after a grotesque account of walrus hunting, that the tusks of the beasts are straightened artificially and sold in Europe as unicorns' horns.[50] André Thevet affirms that he has actually seen this artificial straightening performed by clever Levantine artisans on an island in the Red Sea, a distributing station for both East and West.[51] Antony Deussing admits that such fraud is possible, and he suspects that it is a good deal practised.[52] Andrea Marini, always a sceptic, goes so far as to imply that even the sacred horns of St. Mark's, in his own city, are not above suspicion.[53] For powdered alicorn the common substitutes seem to have been burnt horn, whalebone, various kinds of clay, the bones of dogs and of pigs, lime-stone, and, most important of all during the later history, stalactites and the bones of fossil animals.[54] Edward Topsell, with all these facts in mind, advises that alicorn be bought "out of the whole horn if it may be done, or of greater crums, and which may describe the figure of the horne".

Under these deplorable circumstances there was an obvious need of tests by which the true horn might be known and counterfeits detected. The scientist set himself once more to his ancient and endless task of outwitting and exposing the charlatan, with the result that we may study the nascent "experimental method", as applied to the alicorn, in examples much earlier than Francis Bacon. In these tests we see the fumblings of infant science: it does not ask what seem to us the fundamental questions; for a long time the effort was not to find out whether unicorns existed, nor yet, supposing that they did, whether the magical properties attributed to their horns really belonged to them. Unicorns and magical properties were assumed, so that the only question for scientific investigation was the practical one: is this particular horn genuine *cornu monocerotis*? Nevertheless, groping and childish as these experiments seem to us, it is with them that the unicorn legend enters its final phase. It had come through the "theological" period, to adopt Comte's famous generalization, and through another which we may perhaps call, by a somewhat violent wrenching of the term, the "metaphysical"; now it slowly emerges into the "positivistic" period, into the modern scientific world in which, after a long time and many hesitations, it was to be forgotten. Thus the history of human thought, so far as we have yet gone, is implicit and epitomized in the lore of the unicorn.

A full account of the alicorn tests would fill many pages, and I must choose a few examples that seem typical of their respective periods. One of the most curious passages concerning them is that given by one David de Pomis, who describes himself with no false modesty as "a Hebrew physician and philosopher of the Tribe of Juda, and a member of the noble family of Pomaria which the Emperor Titus led captive from Jerusalem to Rome." His book[55] is at first sight somewhat bewildering. The fact that it is written in three languages—Hebrew, Latin, and Italian—contributes something to this effect; it is paged backward, the indexes run backward, and the title-page stands at the end; David uses the full-stop only when he is quite through with a topic, to mark a period in the exact sense, and he employs the comma for all other punctuation. All this is darkened rather than illumined for me, in the only copy I have seen, by the numberless marginalia in the hand of Isaac Casaubon, who improves upon his polyglot author by adding a vocabulary in Arabic. But it is precisely in such "quaint and curious volumes of forgotten lore" as this—how Edgar Allan Poe would have loved it!—that we have to delve for unicorn lore, and David of the Tribe of Juda does not disappoint one.

"The unicorn", says he,[56] "is a beast that has one horn in its brow, and this horn is good against poison and pestilential fevers. But one is to observe that there is very little of the true horn to be found, most of that which is sold as such being either stag's horn or elephant's tusk. The common test which consists in placing the object in water to see whether bubbles will rise is not at all to be trusted, and therefore, wishing to benefit the world and to expose the wicked persons who sell worthless things at great prices, I take this occasion to describe a true test by which one may know the genuine horn from the false. The test is this: place the horn in a vessel of any sort of material you like, and with it three or four live and large scorpions, keeping the vessel covered. If you find four hours later that the scorpions are dead, or almost lifeless, the alicorn is a good one, and there is not money enough in the world to pay for it. Otherwise, it is false."

A series of alicorn tests is given by Laurens Catelan:[57] the true horn, when thrown into water, sends up little bubbles, "like a pearl"; the water seems to boil, though cold, and one can hear the boiling; the horn gives out a sweet odour when burned; poisonous plants and animals, when brought near it, burst and die; it sweats in the presence of poison. This Catelan, we are to remember, was an eminent pharmacist of the seventeenth century, and he had a whole "true horn" of his own, yet he names these five tests in apparent good faith. The physician Jordanus in his book *De Peste* speaks of seeing a Jew enclose a spider in a circle drawn on the floor with an alicorn, and he says that the spider could not cross the line, and starved to death inside it. Basil Valentine, in his *Triumphal Chariot of Alchemy*,[58] specifies that the circle should be drawn, not with the horn, but with the flesh of the animal; and Ambroise Paré relates that the test was sometimes made by soaking the horn in water, dipping a finger in this water, and then drawing a circle with it on a table.[59] This was something like the test that John Webster had in mind in the lines :—

> As men, to try the precious unicorn's horn,
> Make of the powder a preservative circle,
> And in it put a spider.[60]

These tests were not always accepted, however, by more thoughtful writers. Ambroise Paré, like Andrea Marini, says that he has tried all of them and that those that cannot be explained on natural grounds do not work.[61] Cardan gives his own set of tests, according to which the true horn is always striated, is extremely hard, very heavy, of the colour of boxwood, and able to save the life of a pigeon poisoned with arsenic.[62] In the last of these tests we approach modern methods. It was used more and more frequently as time went by and gradually supplanted all rivals. Thus Andrea Bacci tells us that the Cardinal of Trent had an alicorn richly adorned with gold and gems which he used very generously —"and I am able to affirm that on one occasion, several signors being present, he put it to this test: he gave arsenic to two pigeons, and then to one of them he fed as much as it would take of powder scraped from the horn. This one, after a few symptoms of sickness, revived and lived; the other died in two hours." [63] And again we read that on the 3rd of October, 1636, the Professors and College of Physicians of Copenhagen were present at an experiment made by a pharmacist of that city named John Woldenberg. He gave arsenic to two doves and two kittens, and then administered scrapings of alicorn to one of the doves and one of the kittens. According to Ole Wurm, who was present, the test was "not entirely unsuccessful", for the dove to which the alicorn was given survived, but both kittens died.

This brings us to the most interesting, the strangest, and the central belief about the unicorn—that its horn has a mysterious alexipharmical or prophylactic "virtue". It was supposed to be a detector of the presence of poison. Opinions varied concerning the mode of its operation and the causes of its power, but that power itself was seldom questioned or subjected to intelligent investigation. The faith in it rested upon authority, tradition, and common consent, which have always been and are still the strongest influences governing belief; destruction of this faith took a century and a half of time and the gradual substitution of new habits of thought for old.

For a clear English statement of this faith we may go to John Swan, an unquestioning though late believer. "Monoceros", he writes, "is a beast with one horne, called therefore by the name of an unicorne . . . which hath naturally but one horne, and that a very rich one, which groweth out of the middle of his forehead, being a horne of such virtue as is in no beast's horne besides; which, while some have gone about to deny, they have secretly blinded the eyes of the world from their full view of the greatness of God's works. . . . This horne hath many sovereign virtues, insomuch that being put upon a table furnished with many junkets and banqueting dishes, it will quickly descrie whether there be any poyson or venime among them, for if there be the horne is presently covered with a kind of sweat or dew." [64]

For two full centuries at least, roughly speaking from the final decades of the fourteenth century to those of the sixteenth, this belief was almost universal and unchallenged throughout Europe;

but even in the fourteenth century it was already ages old, for one sees at a glance that it must be closely related to the belief reported by Aelian about the beakers used by Indian potentates. After the sixteenth century it lingered on, in spite of repeated attacks, almost into our own time. At present we may focus attention upon the period of its undisputed sway.

As one would expect, considering the constant search of mediaeval medicine for a panacea, so remarkable an object as the alicorn was not allowed to remain a mere detector of poisons. To the basic faith in its supernatural properties there was added the belief that it had a more general prophylactic power, and at length, invading the other great department of medicine, it was widely accepted as a powerful therapeutic agent. Before the sixteenth century closed the alicorn had an important place in *materia medica*, for we learn from an accurate and scholarly physician of the time that it was then prescribed as a cure for all poisons, for fevers, for bites of mad dogs and scorpions, for falling sickness, worms, fluxes, loss of memory, the plague, and prolongation of youth. Charlatans were even known to assert that it could raise the dead.[65]

One of the earliest indications that this superstition was beginning to form in Europe is to be found in the writings of Hildegarde of Bingen (1098–1179). A most remarkable woman—by no means a saint, though often called so, and scarcely a "mystic", proper regard being had to her pathological condition—Hildegarde lays strong claim to the respect of those who can be just to brilliant reasoning based upon false premises. The centre of her encyclopaedic interests was medicine, so that she could scarcely have ignored the alleged virtues of the alicorn if she had ever heard of them. I find no mention of them in her works,[66] but I do find discussion of other matters closely allied. Hildegarde believed that not the horn alone of the unicorn, but the whole animal was medicinal: under its horn, she says, it has a piece of metal[67] as transparent as glass in which a man may see his face; she tells us how to make an unguent of the yolks of eggs and powdered unicorn's liver, which unguent is a sovereign cure for leprosy—"unless the leper in question happens to be one whom Death is determined to have or else one whom God will not allow to be cured". (As Hildegarde is the only woman who has ever written anything important about the unicorn, the suggestion of the cook-book in her "yolks of eggs and powdered unicorn's liver" is the more welcome.) A belt made of unicorn's skin, she says, will preserve one from fevers, and boots of the same material assure one of sound legs and immunity from plague.[68] All this is good to know, and it comes with the authority of one who, as head of a large religious house, had the health of a whole community in her keeping.

Albertus Magnus (1193–1280), as mighty in his influence as in learning, a cautious and even thoughtful writer considering his times, makes little of the horn's magical virtues and thinks they should be investigated further.[69] Peter of Abano (*c.* 1250–1318), who carried on the work of Albertus in "conciliating" the remains of Aristotelianism with Aristotle's Arabic commentators, was a man of different stamp. Generally regarded as a magician, he seems to have saved himself from the stake only by an opportune death. During his exploration of Arabic lore he acquired a firm faith in the alicorn which he transmitted to many others,[70] and indeed if one were asked to name a single writer to whom the European belief might be attributed with least exaggeration, one could not do better than to choose this Peter. The fact is, of course, that no single writer was even largely responsible, for the belief grew up at a time when no scholar ever expressed an original idea if he knew what he was doing. It may well be that the Crusaders returning from the East did more to spread the faith in the alicorn through Europe than all the books put together, but at any rate that faith was well established among the learned before 1350, and by the end of the same century it was accepted by the wealthier classes of Europe and Great Britain. The poor and ignorant were to have no practical interest in it for at least two centuries to come.

Detached expressions and indications of the belief are almost innumerable. The writer known as "Dame Juliana Berners" says

that "venym is defended by the horne of the Unycorne",[71] and
James I of Scotland speaks of

> the lufare unicorne
> That voidis venym with his evoure horne.[72]

We hear that the inquisitor Torquemada always kept a piece of
alicorn on his table as a precaution against the wiles of his numerous
enemies; [73] it was carried by Spanish and English explorers of
America as conscientiously as quinine is carried to-day by travellers
in tropical countries; Cabeza de Vaca writes that during his journey
down the Paraguay River in 1543 there were three attempts made
to poison him with arsenic, but that he foiled them all with a bottle
of oil and a piece of alicorn.[74] When the Elizabethan adventurer,
Edward Webbe, was at the point of death from poison administered
to him by "some lewd gunners"—one sympathizes with those
gunners, for they were probably worn out by the man's outrageous
lies—"his phisitian gave him speedily Unicorne's horne to drinke",
with the deplorable result that he lived on.[75] A whole ship's company
of Englishmen was poisoned in Elizabethan days "by the roots
of Mandioca, but by a piece of Unicornes horne they were
preserved".[76] It seems probable that even Francis Bacon, reputed
"father of the experimental method", shared the belief of his time
in the alicorn, although he admits that the general confidence in
it was in his day declining.[77] When the Apothecaries' Society of
London was founded in 1617 two unicorns were chosen as the
supporters of its arms, and the common sign of the apothecary's
shop, both in England and in Europe, during the seventeenth
century was the figure of a unicorn or that of its head and horn.[78]
Laurens Catelan lists the names of a dozen foremost medical authorities who had not only used the alicorn in their practice but had
praised it in their writings.[79] Conrad Gesner, a zoologist of great
influence, says that the horn, especially that "*ex novis insulis allatum*",
works miracles against poison.[80] Even at Venice and in the middle
of the seventeenth century there was a general belief that the remarkable sweetness of the water in a certain well was due to bits of
alicorn that had been thrown into it years before.[81] In 1639 James

Primerose of Hull said that the horn was still more trusted than the bezoar-stone, although less common.[82] But there is no need to extend this catalogue farther in order to show that the belief in the alicorn's magical properties was at least as general as the contemporary belief in witchcraft. I may end it by quoting the words of one of the most learned and witty of Englishmen. Thomas Fuller, having at one time doubted the stories of the horn's virtue, reconsiders his doubts, and concludes delightfully: "It is improbable that the vigour of Nature should extrude that so specious to sight which is not also sovereign to service." [83]

Long before Fuller's time there were of course disbelievers abroad, as the Reverend Edward Topsell makes clear—"A vulgar sort of Infidels who scarcely believe any herb but such as they see in their own gardens, or any beast but such as is in their own flocks, or any knowledge but such as is bred in their own brains . . . so that of the true Unicorn, because of the nobleness of his horn, they have ever been in doubt: by which distraction it appeareth unto me that there is some secret enemy in the inward degenerate nature of man which continually blindeth the eyes of God his people from beholding the greatness of God his works." [84] We shall have to hear from several base heretics of this kidney in their turn, but in the meantime there is no doubt what was the orthodox belief.

The rapid development and spread of this belief and the correspondingly rapid increase in the prices paid for alicorns synchronize curiously—one cannot help thinking, significantly—with another equally swift development, that in the art or profession of poisoning. Working upon the few poor hints left them by ancient writers,[85] and urged on by the peculiar needs created by their political institutions, the Italians of the Renaissance carried this art and profession to wonderful heights. When every possible allowance has been made for the exaggeration caused by contemporary fear and by the romantic fancies of a later age, it remains clear that, during just those two centuries in which the interest in alicorns culminated, poison was a tool of social and political ambition very commonly used in Italy, always to be considered and provided against, never to be ignored.

We need not believe in all the alleged crimes of the Borgias in order to recognize in the very nature of the Italian tyrannies a direct incitement to this basest and most cowardly form of murder, for the violence and crime and subterfuge by which the tyrant frequently gained his power often gave the suggestion, sometimes almost the excuse, for the insidious violence of his taking off, and there can be no doubt whatever that many of the noblemen of Italy lived in constant fear. The "poison-rings", the amulets and charms against poison, the crystal cups and the goblets of Venetian glass that have come down to us would alone show that. Between the early years of the fourteenth century, when Peter of Abano wrote his treatise *De Venenis*, and the appearance in 1586 of Andrea Bacci's book of similar title, scores of Italian scholars and physicians, most of them in the pay of great lords, pitted their learning and wits against the secret skill of the poisoner. The pharmacopœia was ransacked, ancient texts were searched, superstitions older than civilization were revived—but nothing would serve; the dukes and counts and captains and cardinals of Italy continued to die suddenly, mysteriously, and, at least in one sense, prematurely. Medical science could not then detect the nature of the poison by which a man had died, and could not even make certain that he had been poisoned at all; but this uncertainty did not mitigate the fear. If suspicion outran the facts, this did not slow down the search for antidotes and precautions.

Francis Petrarch, who lived for many years in the palaces of cardinals and dukes and who knew their hunted lives at first hand, left a vivid picture of one of them at his noon-day meal to which I have already referred. There is exaggeration in that picture, but the facts were terrible enough. Those who think that our northern ideas of Italian poisoning are chiefly due to misinterpretation of Machiavelli and to diseased fancies, such as those of Webster, Tourneur, and Beddoes, may be recommended to study the career of the Milanese poisoner Aqua Toffana, who although she lived long after what may be called the best period of her art, is said to have disposed of more than six hundred persons during her halt-century of practice, before she was publicly strangled at the age of seventy. When cases of poisoning were traced to her, she took refuge in a convent—as her only dangerous rival, the Marquise de Brinvilliers, also did in like straits—and from that point of vantage, the convent authorities refusing to give her up, she went on selling her Acquetta di Napoli for twenty years more. And on every bottle of this deadly poison—tasteless, odourless, without colour—there was painted the image of a saint.

French poisoning on a grand scale is usually supposed to have come, like most of the other arts, from Italy—or such, at any rate, is the opinion of French scholars,[86] who trace it confidently to the advent of Catharine de' Medici and her crowd of Italian retainers. Her family had been remarkable even in Italy for its frequent resort to poison and for equally frequent deaths from poisoning—one reason for the equality being, perhaps, the fact that the family had a way of practising upon its own members. The famous "laboratory" in the palace of Cosmo I, which none but he ever entered, has often been supposed to have been devoted to the manufacture of poisons. Cosmo's son, for whom Andrea Bacci wrote his book on the unicorn, died in agony of unascertained cause, followed in fifteen hours by his wife, and it was observed at the time that his brother, Cardinal Ferdinand de' Medici, made what seemed undignified haste to divest himself of his robes so as to succeed him. The handsome alicorn mounted in gold which, as we have seen, was given by Pope Clement VII to the bridegroom's family when Catharine de' Medici married the Dauphin, was therefore a most appropriate wedding gift, all these things considered, for it might certainly have been taken as a graceful intimation that Catharine was not expected to practice her family's talents upon her husband's kin— or that, in case she did so, they might be prepared. However this may have been, rumour was still kept busy with her name; she was often charged with the poisoning of the Queen of Navarre in 1572 and even with the death of her own son, the Duke of Anjou, who died very suddenly in 1585, just after his valet had "forgotten" to test his wine with an alicorn.

All the arts blossomed somewhat later in France than in Italy, and it was not until after the middle of the seventeenth century

that the Marquise de Brinvilliers, by slaying with poison, and chiefly
for money, her father, her husband, her sister, and her two brothers,
threatened Italy's "bad eminence". With better luck, or if she had not
stolen out of her convent to meet the "lover" who was really an
officer of the law, she might have gone as far as Aqua Toffana. The
steady increase of criminal poisoning led Louis XIV to establish
a committee, the so-called *Chambre Ardente*, which sat for three
years investigating what had become almost a major social problem.
But France has never rivalled the secret society of women, mostly
young, discovered at Rome in 1659, the sole purpose of which was
to kill by poison the husbands of all the members. These women are
said to have met regularly at the house of one Hieronyma Spara,
who found the drugs and gave directions for the dosing. An archaic
touch in the story of this quaint sisterhood, which takes it quite out
of the atmosphere of our more chivalrous modern times, is that
twelve of the lot were hanged and most of the others were publicly
whipped through the streets of Rome.[87]

England was still more backward than France at the time of the
Renaissance. The art of poisoning was not one of those brought
back by the "Italianate Englishman", although it was among those
that Roger Ascham feared, and if it had been it would have found
scant encouragement at home. An Act of Parliament passed in
1531 made poisoning treason, and provided that those proved guilty
of it should be boiled to death. The first person to suffer this penalty
was a certain cook named Richard Roose, convicted of trying—
unsuccessfully—to poison the Bishop of Rochester, and two other
persons at least were executed in this way at Smithfield before
the Act was repealed in 1547. Even in England, however, rumours
of poisoning in high places were always flying about. There were
several such tales of attempts upon the life of Elizabeth; James I
was suspected of having poisoned Prince Henry, and Charles I of
having poisoned his father; it was thought by many that Cromwell
had done away with the Princess Elizabeth, and Cromwell himself
was supposed to have died of poison. Several of the fourteen physicians who waited upon Charles II gave the opinion that he had
been poisoned, and many tales were current as to the culprit.[88]

One has no difficulty in understanding, therefore, how the demand for the alicorn, as for several other articles used to detect the presence of poison, was built up and maintained, and the prices paid for alicorns no longer seem incredible when we think of them with the history of poisoning in mind. All a man hath will he give for his life, and it is a safe inference from what we know that more than one Italian city already groaning under taxation had to melt its silver spoons in order that its lord might pay some northern merchant the sum he asked for an alicorn. The naïve device of employing pregustators or "tasters" which had been sufficient for the ancient Romans had to be abandoned in a time when, according to general belief, a clever poisoner could compound a drug that would kill in an hour, a week, or a month, as pleasure and convenience might dictate. Belief in the poisoner's powers reached fantastic heights. So sensible and well-trained a man as Ambroise Paré, trusted physician to the Court of France—and, it must be said, to Catharine de' Medici herself—thought that it was possible to kill a man by placing poison under the saddle on which he habitually rode.[89] Pope Clement VII, who owned several alicorns and gave away as many more, was thought to have been killed by the odours of a poisoned torch. Poison might be hidden in flowers, in gloves, in rings and bracelets, in cosmetics. How could it be escaped? Almost all the old writers on poisons and their antidotes—an important department of the "Advice to Princes" type of literature—begin by saying that the best security a prince can have is found in living a righteous life and in making no enemies; but this counsel was felt to be unworldly and the practice of it too onerous. There was no real security unless one could find a means of detecting poison the instant it was brought near one, and upon this task, therefore, huge erudition and great sums of money were for a long time expended.

Besides the alicorn, about a dozen different substances and objects were used during the Renaissance in the halls of Italian princes and elsewhere for the detection of poison. These were, in something like the order of importance: the bezoar-stone, the cerastes's horn, snake's-tongue, griffin's claw, *terra sigillata*, vessels of crystal and of Venetian glass, aëtites or eagle-stone, snake-stone or ophite, the stone called "stellio", the toad-stone, the vulture's or raven's claw hung over a burning candle, rhinoceros horns, walrus tusks, parrots, and various limestone formations having the appearance of horns. Although a consideration of these may seem a digression, it will help to clarify the central problem of the alicorn.

The bezoar-stone was a calculus, composed of calcium phosphate and hair, found in the intestines of certain Oriental sheep, goats, monkeys, and hedgehogs. Similar concretions might have been found, of course, in European animals, but either this fact was not known or else objects found near at hand were not valued. Hunters and plainsmen of the western United States still believe in the magical properties of the "mad-stone", an object of the same kind found in deer and put to similar uses, and there seems to have been an active belief in such objects in Peru before the Spanish conquest. Long known in the Orient and still used there, these stones were brought to Europe in large quantities by Portuguese traders from India and were often sold for ten times their weight in gold.[90] They were usually enclosed in delicately wrought baskets of gold filigree hung on chains so that they might be dipped into wine. There are frequent references to the bezoar owned by Queen Elizabeth and to many others belonging to European monarchs. During the great plagues in Lisbon bezoar-stones were hired out to sufferers for ten shillings per day.

The cerastes is a small poisonous serpent of the Sahara and Mesopotamia which has two very short protuberances, vaguely like horns, above its eyes. The belief of the ancients was that it buried itself in the sand, leaving only these "horns" above it, and that with them it killed instantly any creature that stepped upon it. The passage quoted above from Petrarch illustrates the use of these horns in the late Middle Ages and the Renaissance, when they were set in elaborate goldsmith's work and placed on the dining-table where all might see them, in the belief that when poison was brought near them they would break into perspiration. The similarity between this belief and that regarding the alicorn is obvious, and a contemporary writer has even ventured to assert that the cerastes gave the

UNICORNS HORN

Now brought in Ufe for the Cure of Difeafes by an Experienced DOCTOR, the AUTHOR of this Antidote.

A Moft Excellent Drink made with a true *Unicorns Horn*, which doth Effectually Cure thefe Difeafes :

Further, If any pleafe to be fatisfied, they may come to the Doctor and view the *Horn*.

Viz.
> *Scurvy, Old Ulcers,*
> *Dropfie,*
> *Running Gout,*
> *Confumptions, Diftillations, Coughs*
> *Palpitation of the Heart,*
> *Fainting Fits, Convulfions,*
> *Kings Evil, Rickets in Children,*
> *Melancholly or Sadnefs,*
> *The Green Sicknefs, Obftructions,*

And all Diftempers proceeding from a Cold Caufe.

The Ufe of it is fo profitable, that it prevents Difeafes and Infection by fortifying the Noble Parts, and powerfully expels what is an Enemy to Nature, preferving the Vigour, Youth, and a good Complexion to Old Age : The Virtue is of fuch force, as to refift an Injury from an unfound Bedfellow ; None can excel this, for it is joyned with the Virtue of a true *Unicorns Horn*, through which the Drink paffeth, and being impregnated therewith, it doth wonderfully Corroborate and Cure, drinking it warm at any time of the Day, about a quarter of a Pint at a time, the oftner the better, the Price is 2 s. the Quart.

2. Alfo as a preparative for this excellent Drink, and good againft the Difeafes above mentioned, and all Crudities in the Body, is ready prepared twelve Pils in a Box to be taken at three Dofes, according to Directions therewith given, the Price is 2 s. the Box.

3. Likewife he hath Admirable Medicines for the Cure of the P O X, or Running of the Reins, with all Simptoms and Accidents thereto belonging, whether Newly taken or of long Continuance, and (by God's Bleffing) fecures the Patient from the danger of the Difeafe prefently, and perfects the Cure with the greateft Speed and Secrefie imaginable, not hindering Occafions, or going abroad : Whofoever makes Ufe of thefe Admirable Medicines, may have further Advice from the Doctor without Charge.

The Doctor Liveth in Hounfditch, *next Door to* Gun-Yard, *having a Back Door into the Yard, where any Patient may come*

TH. BARTHOLINI
DE
UNICORNU
OBSERVATIONES

XII. THE BARTHOLINUS FRONTISPIECE

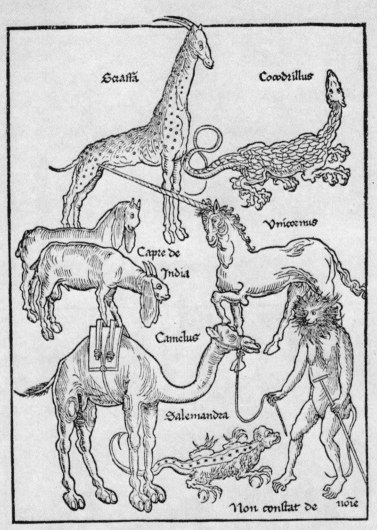

Seraffa

Cocodrillus

Vnicornus

Capre de India

Camelus

Salemandra

Non constat de nõie

Hec animalia sunt veraciter depicta sicut vidimus in terra sancta.

XIII. BEASTS OF THE HOLY LAND

Tab. X

Monoceros Unicornu
Einhorn.

Capricornu Marinq
Meer Steinbock.

Monoceros Unicornu
Einhorn.

XIV. THREE SPECIES OF UNICORN

original suggestion for the whole unicorn legend [91]—thus solving at a stroke to his own satisfaction a problem which, as he accurately says, "has long perplexed humanity".

Albertus Magnus himself had spoken without complete incredulity of the "virtue" of the cerastes, Peter of Abano gave it his full support, and all later writers on poisons and antidotes echo in chorus, the belief spreading from book to book without the slightest reference to actual experience. The prevalence of the superstition is illustrated by the belief that the gates of Prester John's palace were composed of sardonyx mixed with cerastes' horns, so that no poison could be brought through them undetected.

Even more commonly used than the horns of the cerastes, probably because they were more easily obtained, were snaketongues. These tongues were suspended, to the number of thirty or more, on elaborate and often costly dining-table ornaments, usually in the form of golden trees, and such *languiers* or "tongue-stands" are sometimes seen to-day in museums.[92] It was thought that these also perspired in the presence of poison, and because of the belief that they should be kept as dry as possible they were usually placed near the salt—and therefore near the master of the house. In many instances, indeed, the salt-cellar itself was covered with snake-tongues.[93] Powdered snake-tongue was sold in all the apothecaries' shops of Europe during the sixteenth century as an antidote and a protection against poison.

One of the axioms of magical belief everywhere in the world is that an object bearing a close resemblance to another object has the "virtue" or "property" of that other. A curious illustration of this is seen in the use of the stone called "Glossopetra" or "tongue-stone", really the petrified tooth of a shark. "This stone", writes Boëthius de Boodt, "is so like a tongue in shape that the vulgar not only call it snake's tongue but actually think it is that. . . . Many people make much of it for its supposed power against poisons and for keeping off the evil eye. They say that when poison is brought near to it a sweat or dew breaks out upon it, thus revealing the intended crime." [94]

This recalls the very ancient and still existing belief of the East

Indians in a stone with similar properties, sometimes vaguely called in Europe the "Smaragdus", to be found in a serpent's head. Philostratus relates in his life of Apollonius that the snake-charmer lures the snake out of its hole by incantations, lulls it to sleep, cuts off its head with a hatchet, and then extracts the jewel.[95] This stone or jewel is said to contain "a thin crescent-like fibre which oscillates unceasingly in the centre." [96] In other words, the fibre resembles a snake's tongue, and the resemblance has suggested, in the first place, that it is powerful against poison, and, in the second place, that it is to be found in the head of a snake.[97]

From these stones of the Indian snake the transition is easy to the toad-stones of Europe, commonly worn in finger-rings as amulets and prophylactics. No doubt because of the representations made by those who had them for sale, most of the poison-detecting agents were thought to be very difficult to obtain unless one knew the magic formula, and just as there was only one way of capturing unicorns so there was only one quite correct way of securing toad-stones. There were a number of books produced in the late Middle Ages, many of them attributed to Aristotle, which divulged these magic formulae, and in one of these books those who wish to secure a toad-stone are instructed to "put a great or overgrown toad (first bruised in divers places) into an earthen pot, and put this same in an ant's hillock, and cover the same with earth, which toad at length the ants will eat. So that the bones of the toad and stone will be left in the pot." [98] And the test of the toad-stone, to determine whether it was genuine, was equally simple. "You shall know whether the toad-stone called Crapaudine be the right and perfect stone or not. Hold the stone before a toad so that he may see it, and if it be a right and true stone the toad will leap toward it and make as though he would snatch it from you, he envieth so much that a man should have the stone." [99] Most of the toad-stones in actual use seem to have been greenish-brown objects about the size of a large pea, and some were certainly the fossilized teeth of the sting-ray. Finger-rings containing them are still not uncommon.

Similarly used but more difficult to obtain was the "griffin's claw"—in reality the horn of an ibex or a buffalo. There seem to be few exceptions to the rule that when we can trace back the history of a griffin's claw to the time when it came into human possession we come to a saint or some dignitary of the Church, and it is safe to assume a belief that these claws could be secured only by some holy man who cured a griffin of a grievous disease and claimed a claw as his fee. Such a story, which has more than one parallel in folklore, is told of Pope Cornelius in relation to the claw now kept at Cornelimünster on the Inde.[100] In the old Cottonian Library there was a claw inscribed *"Griphi unguis divo Cuthberto Dunelmensi sacer"*, and the supposition is that Saint Cuthbert acquired it in the regular way. Until the French Revolution the monastery of St. Denis had a claw which seems to have had a similar history. All three of those mentioned, and most of those to be seen in various parts of Germany, have been made into drinking-horns. They were thought to act like the beakers mentioned by Ctesias and Aelian when poisoned liquor was drunk from them.[101]

The old belief concerning cups of crystal and of Venetian glass, that they would crack when poison was poured into them, is too familiar to require more than mention. It is a well-known fact, also, that the carbuncle or ruby—the names were commonly interchangeable in the Middle Ages—was thought to have an unerring faculty of detecting poison.[102] More interesting than these was the aëtites or eagle-stone—so-called because, according to Pliny, it was to be found only in the eagle's nest, and was therefore exceedingly rare. The eagle placed it there, as she also sometimes did the amethyst, to watch over her young while she was absent, and it was able to do this because of the great antipathy felt toward it by all serpents. We are told that if a plate containing poison was placed over this stone no man would be able to eat the food upon the plate.[103]

Another belief which carries us far back into primitive magic is that concerning the vulture's foot, an object that seems to have been in common use on the dining-tables of the Middle Ages, perhaps because of its comparative cheapness. The foot was hung in such a way that the claws surrounded the flame of a candle, and it was supposed that whenever poison was brought upon the table it would clutch and extinguish the flame.[104]

Perhaps the most important of all these amulets and prophylactics, considering its great age and universal dispersion, is the
terra sigillata, "stamped earth", or earth of Lemnos. This was originally a red clay dug from a certain hill in the isle of Lemnos on the
6th of August in every year, with appropriate ceremonies performed
by priests in honour of Diana. Dioscorides informs us that after
the clay was dug it was mixed with goat's blood and stamped with
a seal bearing the image of the goddess. When properly prepared
and sent forth with this hall-mark, the little cakes of clay, a quarter
of an inch in thickness and ranging from the diameter of a sixpence
to that of a half-crown, were regarded by the ancients, and by the
people of the Middle Ages and of the Renaissance as well, as perfect
antidotes for all kinds of poison. The clay was also made into cups,
which were thought to render harmless the most deadly drugs.
This earth was one of the seventy-three ingredients of the *theriaca*,
altogether the most famous and the most astonishing concoction
of ancient and mediaeval pharmacy. As the Christian centuries wore
on the image of the heathen goddess was displaced by other emblems
—among them I have seen the figure of the unicorn—and other
clays, even some from England, were found to be quite as effective
as those of Lemnos; the pagan ritual and the goat's blood were felt
by all good Christians, one need hardly say, to have less than no
value; yet, with all these changes, the general faith in the substance
held on with surprising tenacity. Writers of the sixteenth century
who have only contempt for toad-stones and vultures' claws retain
a deep respect for *terra sigillata*. They had never known it to do
the slightest good, but it was mentioned by Dioscorides and it came
out of that ancient Greek world which was still regarded, and quite
rightly, as the source of almost all sound medical theory.

The two substances remaining to be mentioned, the walrus tusk
and the horn of the rhinoceros, point back in the direction of the
alicorn. Among the many different objects passed off by charlatans as
verum cornu monocerotis, probably the most common was the tusk
of the walrus, usually called the "morse" or the "rohart" in old
books. I have already mentioned an amusing passage in Hector
Boëthius about the hunting of the walrus among the northern isles.

This great fish, he says, swims about for a long time without taking any sleep, but at last, overcome with drowsiness, he turns to the shore, finds a convenient bush or tree, hooks his down-curving teeth over a bough, and falls into a deep slumber. Then the hunters approach and bind him with ropes, and after cutting off his teeth, set him free to grow another pair.[105] The tusks are then straightened artificially and sold as alicorns. Again, we are told by Dr. Giles Fletcher, writing in 1598, that the fish-tooth which is called in Russia the Riba-Zuba is used there, and among the Persians and Bougharians as well, to make the knife and sword-hafts used by noblemen. "Some use the powder of it against poison, as the Unicornes horn. The fish that weareth it is called a morse, and is caught about Pechora." [106] André Thevet asserts that he has actually seen the conversion of walrus tusks into alicorns performed by charlatans of the Red Sea district,[107] and the shrewdest of sixteenth-century writers on the unicorn suspects that the "horns" bought in his day are really marine in their origin.[108]

The walrus tusk was not regarded as a substitute for the alicorn but as the thing itself, and the rhinoceros horn owed much of the vogue it had in Europe to the same estimation. Andrea Marini asserts, indeed, that the rhinoceros horn had no reputation whatever in his time except that which it owed to the unicorn [109]—a situation not without ironic humour for one who realizes how much the legend of the unicorn, and especially the belief in the magic virtues of the horn, owes to the rhinoceros. It seems certain, however, that Marini exaggerates, and that the rhinoceros cup was rather frequently used in Europe by those who had heard of its Oriental reputation. Portuguese merchants would not neglect so attractive a commodity. There is still preserved in the Copenhagen Museum a rhinoceros beaker which Rudolph II of Germany (1575–1612) had prepared for his own use; another was owned by the Medici family, and another still, I believe, by the Visconti of Milan. Many more there probably were, but one cannot distinguish them in the records because they were one and all described as alicorns.

The description of the furniture used at the wedding dinner

given by Edward IV for his sister and the Duke of Burgundy illustrates one method of using the alicorn. Like the horn of the cerastes, the snake's tongue, the aëtites, and other objects, it was simply set upon the table, or near it, so that any change in its appearance might be instantly seen. We may imagine that the gaiety of mediaeval feasts was somewhat sobered by the necessity of keeping the eyes fixed upon such objects, and that the grisly suggestions of the vulture's claw might somewhat impede the flow of soul, but the Middle Ages seem to have liked strong contrasts. More commonly, and for a much longer time, the alicorn was used to touch the food and drink before the meal began, being carried about the table by an officer of the household detailed for that important trust. When so employed it was called in mediaeval French *"une espreuve de lincorne"*, [110] and was generally attached to a cord or chain by which it might be hung against the wall when not in use. References to these *espreuves* are numerous in old inventories, and the descriptions of them often indicate the use to which they were put. Thus we read in an inventory, taken in 1416, of the Dukes of Burgundy: *"Une tousche, en quoy a esté mis une piece de lichorne, pour touschier la viande de Monseigneur.* Even the inventory of the Emperor Charles V refers to *"une touche de licorne, garnie d'or, pour faire essay"*—certainly an interesting article to find in the possession of a man who seems to have eaten himself to death.

One can readily imagine that there was a stateliness in this old ceremony of testing the great man's food and drink that would cause it to be kept up long after the belief in its magical efficacy had been abandoned by intelligent people, and one is not surprised, therefore, to learn that it was maintained in the Royal household of France until 1789, when the Revolution made a clean sweep of all such antiquated customs. [111] To what extent those who saw this ceremony performed at the end of the eighteenth century believed in its supernatural value, and to what extent it was for them merely a graceful ritual, interesting because it was old, we cannot say. Most of them, probably, could not have said themselves. The question, however, is an attractive one because it reveals a situation common to all periods of dying beliefs—and this is to say all periods whatsoever, "for each age is a dream that is dying". Even here, almost at the end of its history, the unicorn continues to illumine the ways of human thought. The ceremony of touching the king's food and drink, in its various effects upon different minds, was closely analogous, we may be sure, to the celebration of the Mass or of any other Christian sacrament. By some, that is, it would be accepted at "face value" and without question; the more sophisticated would feel that although they themselves could not believe in it, yet it would have a wholesome effect upon the simple-minded and would tend to keep them in order; others would think that it ought to be abolished because it had no foundation in fact; a few, the most sophisticated of all, would wish to see it preserved simply because it was old and dignified and had aesthetic charm. As we look out across the Christian world of to-day, are not these the chief varieties of religious opinion that we discover?

Two hundred years before the ceremony was abandoned—with the heroic assistance of Madame Guillotine—Chapelain, physician to Charles IX of France, had said "that he would willingly take away that custome of dipping a piece of Unicorn's horne in the King's cup, but that he knew that opinion to be so deeply ingrafted in the minds of men that he feared it would scarce be impugned by reason." [112] Many physicians, he continued, who had themselves no belief in the alicorn felt obliged to prescribe it because, if they did not do so and their patients died, they never had any peace from the surviving relatives. And besides, said he, any man who undertakes to discredit opinions that have been long accepted puts himself in the position of an owl that shows itself in daylight in some prominent place and is persecuted by every other kind of bird.[113] Chapelain and his numerous kind therefore held their tongues, and those who think that the beliefs of the people should never be disturbed will no doubt be charmed with the results—two hundred years were added to the alicorn's lease of life.

Unicorn lore provides an exact parallel also for the feeling of a certain group, well represented in every age, that orthodox belief has a salutary and stabilizing effect upon the public at large, tending to make it patient of conditions that agnostics and free-thinkers might not so quietly tolerate. There is reason to suspect that even in the sixteenth century the more enlightened tyrants of Italy maintained the use of the alicorn, not because they themselves had any faith in its direct action, but rather because they wished others to have such faith, thinking that it would tend to discourage poisoners. This assertion is definitely made by Andrea Marini, who wrote freely in Venice, expressing his own mind; it is strongly implied even by Andrea Bacci, who wrote under the patronage of the Medici and therefore without any freedom whatever. Bacci's pen was hired, and his book on the unicorn is a vivid example of what can happen to a man of sense and learning who is pulled one way by his respect for truth and another way by what he takes to be his interests.

According to Aelian, as the erudite were sure to know, the unicorn's horn was properly used only in the form of a drinking-vessel. Here arose a difficulty, for the alicorns of Europe were seldom more than two inches and a half in diameter at the base, so that it was impossible to shape satisfactory beakers from them. The difficulty was evaded by making cups in which a few slices of the horn were inset, or slabs of it were fitted together to form a tankard.[114] Among the objects once belonging to Queen Elizabeth that were given by James I to his queen was "one little cup of unicorn's horn, with a cover of gold, set with two pointed diamonds and three pearls pendent, being in weight 7½ ounces".[115] The King of England gave to the Duke of Brittany in 1414: *"une grande coupe d'or . . . et y a au fons une licorne et autres choses contre venin"*.[116] Such citations might be continued indefinitely, but all that one can find show that these cups, like the *espreuves* and the other objects into which the alicorn was fashioned, belonged solely to the great and wealthy. The unicorn maintained its aristocratic associations almost to the end—and this not merely because of the great price of its horn, but also because only the great fear poison. Seneca had phrased the situation long before in one pregnant line: *Venenum in auro bibitur.*[117]

Slices of the horn were fitted into the handles of table-knives and salt-cellars, they were shaped into "test-spoons" and sunk in the silver of table dishes, but in all these forms the alicorn was known only to the wealthy. Poorer men used it in powdered form and as a therapeutic. Pharmaceutical ideas were so loose and so uncontrolled by scientific tests that there was no difficulty whatever in this transfer from one department of medicine to the other. Such a transfer, indeed, was inevitable, for the set of beliefs underlying the faith in the alicorn's supernatural properties were just such as would lead to the acceptance of it as a valuable antidote and drug. If it was "indicated" as an antidote against poison, then it seemed to follow that it would be equally good against the so-called "poisonous diseases". Of these the most important was the Plague or Pest.

There is no more pitiful record in the world than that in the scores of books composed during the Middle Ages on methods of avoiding and curing the Plague. It is a record both disgusting and ludicrous, but one's prevailing mood in reading it is that of compassion. Unicorn's horn is certainly the most pleasing of the *materia medica* mentioned in it, and it is as effective as most. I take up the *Monumenta Sinoptica de Peste Preservanda et Curanda*, written long after the Middle Ages had closed by John Collis, and published in 1631. This book names thousands of drugs sold over the counters of England and Europe less than three centuries ago as the best means known to science of saving the lives of one's family and friends from the pestilence that never quite died out. Many of these drugs are too foul to name and others too ridiculous to believe in. Hoofs of asses and elks, horns of wild goats and of stags, viper's flesh and Mathiolus's celebrated oil of scorpions, dust of scorpions, powdered swallow's heart—one hardly knows whether to laugh or to weep. For the thought will emerge as one reads that although these people held views about *materia medica* which we have abandoned —quite recently—yet they loved their children somewhat as we do ours. It was by such means as these that they tried to keep them.

"Noble and powerful against all poisonous and pestilential diseases is the unicorn's horn", says a physician of the time when the Plague took its toll of thousands every year. "Kings and princes and men of wealth all own it, and they should preserve it for the use of future generations. Furthermore, as I know from personal experience, it is highly effective against poisons and all malignant evils." [118] Powdered alicorn was recommended as a specific against the Plague by many of the best physicians of Europe during the sixteenth and seventeenth centuries. In the English version of Johann Schröder's important *Pharmacopœia Medico-Chymica* [119] we are told of the "Vertues" of the horn that "it is Sudorifick, Alexi-pharmacal, and Cordial, hence it is commended good against Poysons, infectious diseases, etc. It is also accounted profitable in the Epelepsie of Infants. The Dose from 4 grains to half a scruple, sometimes a whole scruple and more." According to Andrea Bacci the proper dose is ten grains scraped from the inside of the horn— or a piece might equally well be worn as an amulet. [120] Bacci also says that the Cardinal of Trent, a most "public-minded" man, often gave away filings from his alicorn "in cases of suspected poisoning, mushrooms, fever, and pest, for the most part with excellent success". Laurens Catelan warns his readers that the alicorn, whether in the piece or powdered, must never be put into hot water, for this destroys all its virtue, and Conrad Gesner is equally emphatic in saying that only fresh powder can be used successfully. When the daughter of Henry II of France fell ill with smallpox in 1557, Anne de Montmorency sent to her nurse a piece of alicorn with directions that it should be "dissolved" in cold water and drunk. The water commonly called *eau de licorne* and sold under that name throughout Europe was not made in this expensive way, but merely by standing one end of the horn in a vessel of water, as at St. Denis. Sometimes a hole was bored through the length of the horn and water poured through it, but in either case the water was held to be highly bene-ficial and found a ready sale. (Plate XI.) In this way it was made possible to "drink the horn". Intelligent people, however, seem to have preferred to take their alicorn in powdered form. How intelligent these people were may be inferred from a certain illu-minating fact of medical history: the English Royal Society of Physicians was required to issue, at intervals, lists of the drugs to be carried by every registered pharmacist in London, and all of the twelve or fifteen lists issued thus officially between 1651 and 1741 named the unicorn's horn. The general editor of the last issue including this drug was no less a person than Sir Hans Sloane.

In the edition of 1746 it was tacitly dropped.[121] At about the same time that the Royal Society of Physicians decided to abandon the horn, Hogarth expressed his layman's attitude toward it by placing it in a prominent position in the shop of the quack doctor presented in the series *Mariage à la Mode*.

It must be admitted that the English Society was "not the first to lay the old aside", for Italian and French physicians had been protesting against the alicorn for almost two centuries before this. Andrea Marini had ridiculed the whole belief as early as 1566; Christofle Landré had done all that a courageous and clear thinker could do to kill it even eight years before that; [122] Ambroise Paré, one of the most influential physicians of all time, attacked it repeatedly; Laurent Joubert, another physician to the Court of France, had classed it contemptuously with powdered pearls and potable gold; [123] even Pierre Pomet, a foremost authority, had spoken of it in 1694 as entirely out of date.[124] Decidedly, England did not err on the side of precipitation.

How much responsibility for this lingering of the drug should be attributed to the apothecaries we can only guess. One of the more interesting phases of medical history is that of the relationships between apothecaries and physicians. Often the two parties have been at league, "for ech of hem made other for to winne", but quite as often they have been at strife,[125] and both league and strife might be illustrated, probably, if we knew enough, from the history of the alicorn. One cannot help thinking it significant that forty years after Paré's *Discours* and almost sixty years after Marini's *Falsa Opinione dell' Alicorno*, the French apothecary Catelan, who had certainly read both of these opponents of the whole superstition, brought out his *Histoire de la Licorne*, arguing with apparent conviction not only for the real existence of the animal but for the medical value of its horn. Considering that he was an intelligent man and a leader in his profession,[126] it seems fair to recall that he had alicorn powder to sell and also that he owned a whole alicorn of which he was very proud—though not to such a degree that he would have refused to part with it for a suitable sum of money. All the early opponents of the alicorn were physicians, and no apothecary spoke against it until the time of Pierre Pomet, who had something "just as good" to offer in its stead.

Whatever the apothecaries of Europe may have done to foster the belief we have been tracing, they certainly did little or nothing to establish it, for we have seen that the belief goes back at least to the fourth century before Christ, and it is probably much older still. This can be said, however, only of India, and the question arises, therefore, when and by what means the superstition came into the Western world. Ctesias had made no such assertions about the horn of his onager as those quoted above from European physicians concerning the alicorn. Aelian had spoken only of the beakers made from the horn of his "cartazon". The ancient physicians upon whose works, for the most part grossly misunderstood, mediaeval medicine was chiefly based, had said nothing of this marvellous drug. There is no mention of it in *Physiologus*, in the patristic writers, in Isidore, or in the Bestiaries. Hildegarde of Bingen, although she seems not to have heard that the alicorn had any peculiar medical value, was apparently the first European writer who thought of the unicorn as possessing magical properties.[127] To her, as I have pointed out, its entire body was medicinal, as that of the rhinoceros was thought to be in India.

From what source is Hildegarde most likely to have derived an idea of this kind? I should say from the Arabian writers whose influence was beginning to be felt, through the medium of Latin translation, in just her time. The unicorn legend had an early and an elaborate development among the Arabs, who dominated European medicine, both for good and for ill, from the beginning of the thirteenth century to the revival of learning, sending out successive waves of influence from the Court of Frederick II, from Salerno, and from many centres in Spain. Adding little to Western surgery, anatomy, or nosology, their chief contribution lay in the field of *materia medica*, and even this was made possible chiefly by their contacts, direct and indirect, with the Orient. Indian physicians are known to have lived at the Court of Bagdad in the time of Haroun al-Raschid, and there is evidence that they

added Oriental ideas to those that Arabic medicine owed chiefly
to the Greek tradition. Arabic influence is already discernible in
Albertus Magnus and it is controlling in Peter of Abano. Can it be
a mere coincidence that these two are among the earliest European
writers who show full knowledge of the belief in the alicorn? The
probability is that this belief, in its popular form, entered Europe
with the Mohammedan invasion of Spain, spreading from Bagdad
—whither it had been taken by Indian physicians or brought back
by Arabian travellers—to Cordova, Seville, Granada, and finally
to Salerno, from whence medical theory radiated through all of
Europe.[128]

If this seems no more than a conjecture, it is strengthened, at
least, in the definite ascription of the whole belief, by a man who
should have known the facts, to Arabian physicians. Andrea Marini
makes the charge, with anger and contempt, that the use of the
alicorn in medicine was due to the *setta de gli Arabi*.[129] We should,
of course, remember that by 1566 the "arabistes" were in low repute
throughout Europe, so that anyone who wished to condemn a
medical theory would naturally attribute it to them; but Marini's
charge, if that is the right word, is too plausible to be set aside for
such reasons, and it is supported by the not infrequent references
to Arabian authorities made by European writers on the alicorn.[130]

There is evidence of another kind which, although not conclusive by itself, lends further support to the theory of an Arabian
origin for this belief. In the Italian dialects of the fourteenth century and later the unicorn was variously called *licorno, liocorno,
leocorno,* and *leoncorno*. In French the name has always been *licorne*
or *lincorne*. I cannot accept the derivation given by Littré's *Dictionnaire* in which *licorne* is traced to the whole Latin word *unicornu*.[131] A tenable etymology is suggested by Alfred Hoare,
according to which the ordinary Romance article was prefixed to
the Latin *cornu* "and the resulting word was altered, perhaps under
the attraction of *Leone*, lion". Accepting this derivation, we may
draw from it two significant deductions. It seems clear, in the first
place, that when the basic word *licorno*—which could mean nothing
but "the horn"—was made, the animal to which the horn belonged

was unknown. After the development of the unicorn legend the word was applied, not very appropriately, to the animal,[132] and it has done this double service, both in French and Italian, ever since. We shall find it worth remembering that, if the present argument is sound, then "the horn" was known in Italy and was important enough to name in the most vivid and striking way, before any animal was known or imagined to which it could be fitted. The second deduction is that this horn must have seemed in some way impressive to its namers, else they would not have spoken of it with the simple definite article so as to suggest that it was *the* horn *par excellence*.[133]

But these are not the only conjectures that may be based upon etymology. Much more commonly used than any of the Italian names for the unicorn cited above, and outlasting them all, is the word *alicorno*, backed by the Portuguese *alicornio*. Hoare explains this form without hesitation by saying that it is due to a prefixing of the Arabic article. He refers, of course, to the definite article *al*, seen in many English words of Arabic origin such as "algebra" and "alcohol". *Alicorno*, however, is not of pure Arabic origin; it is a hybrid word. The Arabic article has apparently been prefixed to the Romance word *licorno* already formed, thus giving the word two definite articles fused together. From these facts I think we may infer rather plausibly that the Arabs found when they came to Europe some sort of horn sufficiently remarkable to have attracted attention, and, secondly, that they took enough interest in this horn and made it sufficiently their own so that their capping of its name with an additional definite article from their own language was generally accepted.[134] It seems to me that these etymological considerations, taken together with the evidence to the same effect presented above, make a "strong case" for my theory that the European belief in the alicorn's magical properties was of Arabian origin.

That belief was given considerable impetus, centuries later, by the reports made by Portuguese traders returning from India. The Portuguese were the chief carriers of bezoar-stones—according to contemporary belief because the people of their nation were more afraid of poison than others, but really because they found a huge profit in the trade. They also brought back most of the rhinoceros horns to be found in Europe during the sixteenth and seventeenth centuries, so that they would find it to their interest to spread and deepen the superstitions already existing about horns. Furthermore, they had been, without realizing the fact, in the very land where that superstition had its largest early development and where it was still accepted most widely. There is abundance of contemporary testimony regarding the influence of these traders: "The men of our Portuguese nation", writes Amatus Lusitanus, "who have penetrated the interior of India, are unable to tell us anything about the unicorn itself, but they say that its horn is greatly prized by the Indian kings; and also those who have practised medicine for some time in that country and have then returned home say that in India there is no stronger or more dependable antidote against poison than the horn of the unicorn." [135]

Merely to understand how this idea may have come into Europe gives one a little satisfaction, but one would rather know how so strange a notion ever entered the human mind, and why, once it had found entrance, it was not instantly thrust forth again. Questions of this kind, involving the mental habits of men who lived thousands of years ago, one does well to handle with the least possible suggestion of dogmatic finality. One can only gather all the facts that seem pertinent, enter into those facts imaginatively, strive to think as much as possible in the way of primitive peoples, and then make his conjecture—cautiously, tentatively, as who should say "How will this do?" But whatever the difficulty and danger, the question lies too squarely across our way and is too near the centre and source of unicorn lore to be evaded now.

"Beginning doubtfully and far away", I should like to point out that there has existed from early times and in many parts of the world a vague notion that horns in general, almost any kind of horns, are somehow prophylactic. For ages the most highly valued drinking vessels, used by kings as well as cow-herds, were made of horn, [136] and it is possible that the belief in the medicinal value of such vessels arose in part from what was said of the wholesomeness of their contents. I have myself encountered in western America the idea that nothing drunk from a cow's horn can ever harm the drinker. Lying even behind this belief there was, and is, the almost world-wide use of horns as charms and amulets, into which I need not go because the subject has been recently treated with ample though somewhat too audacious scholarship.[137] Throughout Italy at the present time, and especially in the south, the "corno"— an amulet representing a single horn and made of coral, silver, nickel, bone, and other materials—is used in many ways as a charm against the evil eye. One sees it even as a watchguard and at the end of a chain hung round the neck and on the coat-lapel. Roman and Neapolitan cab-drivers place it on the headgear of their horses, so suspended that it is constantly in motion and pointing forwards; carters and carriers hang a large single horn under their wagons; in Italian shop-windows one often sees fifty or more of these amulets, certainly more popular than those of any other form, exhibited for sale. Old women of the peasant class frequently wear many of them at once, concealed beneath their clothing. From this ancient superstition some suggestion and support, one cannot say how much, was derived by the notion before us. For the sake of clarity one may allow himself to say that all horns came to be regarded as medicinal because they were vaguely associated with beneficent supernatural powers, although in reality there was no relationship of cause and effect but merely an overlapping. Such overlapping and confusion is unmistakable when one looks, for example, at the pharmacopœia of a Zulu medicine man, which consists usually of nothing but fifteen or twenty short antelope horns tied together by thongs. With this outfit the savage physician attacks all devils and diseases alike, making no distinction between the one group and the other. These horns are charms and medicines at the same time, and they are medicines because—for one can scarcely avoid the word—they are also charms or devil-fighters.

The belief that all horns have medicinal value and that this value is of a supernatural sort lasted on, demonstrably, into modern times. André Thevet, a man of fine intelligence and wide knowledge, could say at the end of the sixteenth century that "*quand tout est dict, il ne se trouve guere beste . . . dont la corne n'ait quelque merveilleux effect pour la santé des hommes.*" [138] As an example he names the *pyras-souppi* found in the region of the River Plate, large as a mule and with very long horns which the savages use to cure wounds caused by poisonous beasts and fishes. He says also, as do many other early authorities, that if one burns ordinary stag's horn and scatters the ashes on the ground he will rid the place where they are scattered of all snakes.

Thevet's mention of stag's horn brings us nearer to the centre of our problem, for many writers about the alicorn asserted, during the period when faith in it was breaking down, that the horn of the stag was really quite as effective. Powdered stag's horn was commonly prescribed to the poor as a prophylactic during the whole period of the alicorn's popularity among the wealthier classes, and it is still used in China in the same way. [139] Although all horns whatever were regarded as having medicinal properties, those of the stag were the most important substitute for the alicorn. [140] Now there is no great difficulty in tracing the process by which the stag's horn acquired this reputation, and the knowledge gained in tracing it will provide a clue to the solution of our main problem.

In reading the old zoologists one finds a great deal made of "natural enemies", and what is said of them rests upon one of the fundamental conceptions in the mediaeval and ancient theories of nature. Lucretius, to take the most familiar example, tries to explain the material universe as a system of sympathies and antipathies. There was no attempt to get behind the assumed loves and hates of primordial atoms and of all that they composed; no one thought to inquire whether such loves and hates actually existed; they were axiomatic. One assumed that every object in the world had its natural friends and foes, and a main task of science and of magic, during the long period when the two were scarcely distinguishable, was to find out what these were, for one had control over an object and could use it for human ends when its sympathies and antipathies were known. This belief is familiar, yet it is so important for the present discussion that I venture to emphasize it by a quotation.

"By reason of the hidden and secret properties of things", says John Baptista Porta, "there is in all kinds of creatures a certain compassion, as I may call it, which the Greeks call sympathy and antipathy, but we term it, more familiarly, their consent and disagreement. For some things are joyned together as it were in a mutual league, and some other things are at variance and discord among themselves; or they have something in them which is a terror and destruction to each other, whereof there can be rendered no probable reason: neither will any wise man seek after any other cause thereof but only this, that it is the pleasure of Nature to see it should be so, that she would have nothing to be without his like, and that amongst all the secrets of Nature there is nothing but hath some hidden and special property; and moreover, that by this their consent and disagreement, we might gather many helps for the uses and necessities of men, for when once we find one thing at variance with another, presently we may conjecture, and in trial so it will prove, that one of them may be used as a fit remedy against the harms of the other." [141]

This is somewhat to our purpose, but what follows is more so. Porta reminds his readers that the lion is afraid of the cock, that the elephant and the mouse are natural enemies—a belief which is still remembered—and then says: "So likewise those living creatures that are enemies to poisonous things and swallow them up without danger may show us that such poisons [that is the poisonous members of the poison-eating animals] will cure the bitings and blows of those creatures. The Hart and the Serpent are at continual enmity: the Serpent, as soon as he seeth the Hart, gets him into his hole, but the Hart draws him out again with the breath of his nostrils, and devours him.[142] Hence it is that the fat and the blood of Harts, and the stones that grow in their eyes, are ministered as fit remedies against the stinging and biting of Serpents. Likewise the breath of Elephants draws Serpents out of their dens, and they fight with dragons, and therefore the members of Elephants, burned, drive away Serpents. So also the crowing of a Cock affrights the Basilisk, and he fights with Serpents to defend his hens, hence the broth of a Cock is a good remedy for the poison of Serpents. The Stellion, which is a beast like a Lyzard, is an enemy to the Scorpion, and therefore the Oyle of him, being purified, is good to anoint the place which is stricken by the Scorpion. A Swine eats up a Salamander without danger, and is good against the poison thereof."

This idea of "sympathy" and "antipathy" is encountered everywhere in mediaeval medicine, as it is also, of course, in the history of magic. The Consents and Disagreements, as Porta calls them, are often surprising. In addition to those that he mentions, the goat and the partridge were so sympathetic that they could be prescribed as medicine interchangeably; the ram and the elephant were so antipathetic that elephants always ran away from rams, bellowing with terror; the panther and the hyena were so uncongenial that the mere skin of a dead hyena could put the panther to precipitate flight, and if the skins of the panther and the hyena were hung up side by side the former would soon lose all its hair.

But we must not be drawn aside into these arcana. The pertinent fact before us is that "the stag by nature hates all poysonous things, and therefore either the feet or skin or the hornes of a stag, nayled uppon a doore, no Serpent will enter in." [143] Various parts of the stag are accordingly medicinal, [144] and are especially good against the poison of snakes—either for the reason that the stag is a "natural enemy" of snakes or because he eats them and so becomes poisonous himself. To the modern mind these two "reasons" seem quite distinct, as they probably were in origin, but I am not aware that any writer who believed the superstition ever disentangled them; it was not only possible but easy for really acute thinkers to accept both reasons at once, stressing either as occasion served. When the medical action of the stag's horn is explained on the principle of natural antipathy, we have to think of the horn as extremely pure; [145] but when, on the other hand, the principle of sympathy is invoked we are forced to regard it as extremely poisonous in nature. The physicians of four centuries ago could not agree upon the rather fundamental question whether the stag's horn and similar substances were essentially poisonous or essentially pure, but the members of both schools of opinion continued to administer those substances in their medical practice with perfect confidence and probably with good results. When a modern reader first encounters this absurd situation he is moved to what Hobbes calls "a sudden glory" and is tempted to exult a little over the childish fumbling past—but then he recalls the still unresolved conflict between allopathy and homœopathy, which is in essentials the same conflict as that waged in the Middle Ages, and he decides not to laugh.

Medical action by sympathy, as many of the old writers on *materia medica* explain, requires that the alexipharmical or therapeutic agent shall be of a stronger and more concentrated "virtue" than the thing or condition to be affected, so that it will be active and the other passive. This explains the choice of such supposedly powerful and highly concentrated poison-cures as viper's flesh, the ingredient added to the *theriaca* by one of Nero's physicians.[146] It explains, also, most of the prophylactics and poison-detectors of the Middle Ages and Renaissance that I have named above. The cerastes was thought to carry its poison in its horns; these horns were therefore regarded as exceedingly poisonous, and it was believed that they would have power over any poison less potent and concentrated than that which they contained. Snakes were thought to "bite" with their tongues—a belief held by most people to-day—and therefore snake's tongue, whole or powdered, could detect and cure poison. The vulture's entire body was considered poisonous, and its foot particularly so; all toads were thought venomous, and the stones in their heads, like the snake-stones of India, were held to be concentrated venom. The poisonous nature of the eagle-stone was not so easy to detect or explain, but the eagle does not leave this stone in her nest to guard her young against snakes for nothing; her instinct may be trusted.

In all this mountain of error there was, of course, a grain of sound and precious truth, and no one can fail to do honour to the long struggle of thought which finally isolated the principle *similia similibus curantur*. This principle, to be sure, was well understood by the ancients and was taught by Galen, who said explicitly that certain poisons attract poison as the magnet does iron. Aristotle pointed out [147] that poisonous reptiles seem immune to poison and can eat one another without suffering harm. Saint Ambrose says explicitly *"venenum veneno excludatur"*.[148] One of the most satisfactory statements of the principle to be found in early writers is that of Antonio Ludovico, who says that nothing except poison can expel poison and that the antidote is not hostile to the poisonous substance, as some suppose, but is "bound to it by invisible chains of everlasting and indissoluble amity."[149]

The principle, then, was sound, and it had long been familiar, but the applications of it are often highly diverting. Thus there was a general belief, lasting until at least 1700, that the elk is a chronic sufferer with vertigo and that he has been able to discover only one thing that will give him any relief. The inconvenience of this will be imagined when one is told that whenever he is pursued by hunters and dogs he has to sit down and place his left hind foot in his left ear to cure himself of dizziness before he can run away. But this infirmity of elks was simply another proof of Emerson's dictum that "Nature is ancillary to man" and also of the proverb: "God works in a mysterious way his wonders to perform." The left hind hoof of the elk was prescribed for centuries as an unfailing specific for vertigo, epilepsy, falling sickness, *mal de mer*, and dipsomania, with careful directions for distinguishing the left hind hoof from the right.[150] Amulets of this material are still worn in Italy as protection against the falling sickness and the evil eye.

Coming now to our central question, why the alicorn was supposed to sweat in the presence of poison, we may answer, in accordance with what we have learned from the study of stag's horn and other substances, that it does so either because of sympathy or because of antipathy with that poison. Explanation according to the latter principle was of course the more natural one during the centuries when the unicorn was always thought of as a symbol of Christ, as associated with the Virgin, and as a type of purity, but Arabian influence, based upon Galen, seems to have swung opinion over to the other interpretation—that, namely, according to the principle of sympathy, which required that the alicorn be thought of as highly poisonous.

A clear statement of this view is made by Laurens Catelan,[151] although it is not original with him. Those parts of any animal, he begins by saying, are strongest and fullest of the animal's "virtue" upon which its life depends. In horned animals these parts are the horns. Now it is well known—or so Catelan assumes—that horned animals have a keen appetite for poisonous substances both animal and vegetable, and of course the essence of these substances is drawn into their essential members, their horns. All horns, therefore, are necessarily poisonous in a high degree, for all the poisons that their bearers have eaten is concentrated in them. There is no difficulty in seeing, then, why it is that when all the poison that would ordinarily be distributed through two horns is forced into one it is brought to a very strong focus indeed. The alicorn is clearly one of the most poisonous substances in the world, and with all these facts in mind, Catelan submits, no sensible man can fail to believe the marvels related of it. The alicorn sweats when standing near poison, he thinks, because of a desire to mingle with its like, and when taken as a drug it overcomes and carries off such feebler poisons as arsenic and corrosive sublimate by virtue of its own more powerfully poisonous nature. Why it is that so deadly a substance as this does not kill the patient instantly, how it happens that it can be brought into contact with one's food and drink or worn at one's neck as an amulet with impunity, Catelan and his fellows neglect to inform us.

This theory is too ingenious and has too much of the mark of the clever apothecary upon it for one to accept it as a product of primitive minds, and yet it may contain some primitive elements. Catelan's confident assertion that the unicorn eats snakes and drinks poisoned water [152] implies an intimate knowledge of the animal's habits such as few other writers have claimed, but the assertion is helpful in suggesting that the whole mystery may rest upon a matter of diet. Even those who think of the unicorn as essentially pure sometimes attribute his virtues to the food he eats. Thus Hildegarde of Bingen says that once in every year the animal goes to that land in which the juices of Paradise abound and there seeks out the best herbs, digging them up with his hoof; from these he derives his medicinal properties. It will be remembered that Hildegarde thought the whole body of the unicorn medicinal, and also that the same belief is held in India regarding the rhinoceros. Now we learn from Linschoeten's *Voyages*[153] that the horns of the rhinoceros are valued in India according to the *flora* of the district from which thy come. "All Rhinocerotes", says the traveller, "are not alike good, for there are some whose hornes are sold for one, two, or three hundred Pardawes the piece, and there are others of the same colour and greatness that are sold but for three or four Pardawes, which the Indians know and can discerne. The cause is that some Rhinocerotes which are found in certain places in the countrie of Bengala have this virtue by reason of the hearbes which that place only yeeldeth and bringeth foorth, which in other places is not so." A belief so constant as this, common to both schools of interpretation, may well derive from a source far back in time.

The explanation of the alicorn's "virtue" in terms of "sympathy" and "antipathy" was cogent enough for ordinary minds, but it could not stand the scrutiny of a really thoughtful man such as Andrea Marini. He pointed out that poisons are of many kinds, some hot and some cold, some wet and others dry, and that therefore it was absurd to say that one substance could stand in a relation either of sympathy or of antipathy with all of them at the same time. This contention was unanswerable, and it had a deep influence upon later writers. Andrea Bacci, whose book on the unicorn appeared in the same year as Marini's, was forced by it to abandon the sympathy-antipathy explanation altogether and to fall back upon a pseudo-Aristotelean *forma* and *essentia* which really explained nothing. He also accepted a vague Arabian assertion that alicorn somehow "comforts the heart", but the question as to why it sweats in the presence of poison he confuses and avoids as much as possible, finally leaving it unanswered.

Such light as I have thus far been able to throw upon the mystery of the alicorn's magical properties may be helpful in an attempt to solve the further mystery of what I have called the unicorn's water-conning. We are fortunate in having a description of this performance by one who claims to have been an eye-witness. This is John of Hesse, a priest of Utrecht, who visited the Holy Land in 1389 and had the most extraordinary good luck in the things he saw there. "Near the field of Helyon", he says, "there is a river called Marah, the water of which is very bitter, into which Moses struck his staff and made the water sweet so that the Children of Israel might drink. And even in our times, it is said, venomous animals poison that water after the setting of the sun, so that the good animals cannot drink of it; but in the morning, after the sunrise, comes the unicorn and dips his horn into the stream, driving the poison from it so that the good animals can drink there during the day. This I have seen myself." [154]

One may point out in passing the strange coincidence that John of Hesse should have seen this rare spectacle at just the spot made famous by the miracle of Moses [155] to which it provides so striking a parallel. For the bitter waters of Marah in the Bible story we have here the water poisoned at night by unclean animals; Moses and his staff are matched by the unicorn and its horn; the Children of Israel are represented by the clean animals waiting beside the stream. The two stories correspond in every essential detail, so that John's statement amounts almost to a declaration that he saw the ancient miracle re-enacted symbolically upon the spot.—But this is one of those mysteries into which the lay mind may not hope to pierce.

Leaping now almost five hundred years we find a traveller of the nineteenth century giving almost the same account of the water-conning trait as that given by John of Hesse. "One evening," says he, "as I was sitting among the rocks with a party of natives, the conversation turned upon flags. A man sitting there said to a stranger, 'Why do the English put the *wyheed el win*, that is the unicorn, on their flag?' and then related the whole story of it as one well known through the length and breadth of the land. 'The unicorn is found in a vast country south of Abyssinia. There the animals, undisturbed by man, live after their own laws. The water does not flow in rivers, but lives in the bosom of the soil. When the others wish to drink, the unicorn inserts his horn into the earth: with this he scoops a pool, satisfies his own thirst, and leaves what he does not require to the rest. So these English have the privilege of first discovering all things and then the rest of the world may come after.' " [156]

In this late version the trait appears somewhat altered and debased: the unicorn does not purify but merely uncovers the water—one should observe, however, that he does this with his horn rather than with his hoof as another animal would—and his service to other beasts is not so much altruistic as accidental. Yet, for all these changes, the story is recognizably the same as that told by John of Hesse and many others.

Regarding the origin of the water-conning trait I shall make one suggestion here and another, somewhat farther reaching, in a later chapter. Popular beliefs about the stag have already served us well and may do so again. This animal, it will be remembered, is devoted to a diet of snakes, and in general he seems to thrive upon it, but sometimes, as Pliny informs us, a snake gets on the stag's back and bites him cruelly, whereupon he rushes to some river or fountain and plunges into the water to rid himself of his foe.[157] Here we have at least a horned animal, a snake, and water brought together. A few sentences from the subtle and fascinating book by Antonio Ludovico from which I have already quoted, will carry us somewhat farther. Stags are accustomed to increase their strength, says he, upon a diet of serpents, but when they are quite saturated with this food, and before they begin to feel the noxious effects of the poison, they go down to the great rivers and there submerge their bodies, leaving only their mouths above the water. They do not drink a drop, however they may suffer with thirst, but remain standing there until the poison is sweated in the form of tears through their eyes, and then they leave. These tears, hardened into balls, fall by the wayside and are gathered by the people of the country, who value them as antidotes for poison. The barbarians call them bezoars.[158]

It may seem that this story, however interesting in itself, leaves us still a long way from the unicorn dipping its horn into the water, but a little reflection will show, I think, that the analogy is rather close. We have already learned that the poison in the unicorn's body is not dispersed, as it appears to be in the stag mentioned by Ludovico, but is concentrated in the horn—the single horn. It seems natural, then, whenever the unicorn goes to the water to seek relief from an excess of poison, if that is indeed his motive, that he should dip the horn alone. Furthermore, it would follow naturally from the poisonous quality of the horn that whatever venom there might be in the water would be dispersed. This, at any rate, is the explanation of the water-conning trait that Laurens Catelan seems to have had in mind, for he says that the unicorn's well-known fierceness is caused by the great pain he suffers constantly on account of the poison in his horn, and that he knows no other way of obtaining relief except that of returning to the poisoned stream by which his pain is partly caused. (There has never been any lack of allegorical possibilities in the unicorn legend; the difficulty is in avoiding them.)

This is not a completely satisfying explanation of the water-conning trait because it gives no clue to the reason why the water is poisonous and it does not include the other animals which, in nearly all versions of the story, wait beside the water for the unicorn's coming. With these details unaccounted for we cannot feel that we have reached the origin of the story, but the passages quoted do carry us as far back toward that origin as any one in the Middle Ages or the Renaissance ever went, and this must suffice at present. We shall encounter the water-conning trait again, and shall be able, if not to "explain" it, at any rate to set it high among the myths and legends that are so ancient as for ever to defy explanation.

CHAPTER VI

THE BATTLE OF BOOKS

FOR somewhat more than a century unicorn lore was a toy of scholarship with which the "leviathans of learning" loved to play. They played awkwardly, as leviathans are likely to do, the sport consisting in a half-jocose and half-ostentatious lavishing of erudition upon a topic which, with all its charm, had even in their eyes little practical importance. They played according to the rules of the scholarly game as they understood them, rallying "authorities" from all past ages, pitting book against book, regurgitating and chewing over again their own enormous reading, seldom subjecting what they read to the simplest tests of sense experience. It was a good time for the literary scholar, this period between the middle of the sixteenth century and the beginning of the eighteenth—a time when a man of great vitality and determination might still hope to read nearly everything that mattered and to write his foot-note in the world's huge Book of Letters. And the men were worthy of their opportunities, for there were giants in those days. Perhaps it is a little hazardous to assert that they played with the unicorn, for certainly they preserve at all times a profound sobriety of manner and style. The herd of whales lashing the surface of the sea in the distance may be engaged on serious business, however much they may seem to be gambolling, but when such mighty men as Thomas Bartholinus and Samuel Bochart unbend their strength upon our topic one can hardly avoid the suspicion that they are merely amusing themselves by riding a favourite hobby-horse. (And if they were, the author of the present book should be the last person in the world to condemn them.)

They attacked what we should regard as a scientific problem largely by literary methods, yet they had something of the modern scientist's faith that no investigation, however remote from any apparent utility, can be valueless if faithfully performed. To some of these writers, however, the unicorn topic was not interesting primarily as "pure scholarship": one of them, at least, sold his learning and dialectic skill to an Italian tyrant who felt that belief in the alicorn on the part of his subjects would be good for his own health; another had an alicorn of his own, worth a large fortune if properly marketed, for sale; several others set themselves to combat a superstition which they thought too expensive and even dangerous; another group felt that if belief in the unicorn should be abandoned all belief in the Word of God would eventually go with it, and therefore they defended the animal with all that fury of religious conviction which their worthy successors now display in defending the first chapter of Genesis. But when all these controversialists are accounted for there remain a select few who approached the topic disinterestedly, concerned only to know the facts. Even these few, however, do not attempt to go behind the facts; not one of them asks himself how and why the human mind ever came to accept so curious a set of beliefs as those concerning the unicorn; not even in the rich and shadowy mind of Sir Thomas Browne did unicorn lore reveal significance reaching beyond itself. The facts had yet to be determined, and scholarship had not yet consciously turned to the tracing of human thought. For these reasons even the best writers on the unicorn missed entirely that aspect of their topic which is to us of primary concern—the only aspect, indeed, which justifies a survey of that topic in the twentieth century.

Between 1550 and 1700 there were published about twenty-five extended discussions of the unicorn, ranging from long chapters or separate tracts to whole books. Nearly all of this writing is derivative, each successive author feeling it necessary to cite, with or without credit given, every major assertion of his predecessors.

One who is intensely interested in unicorn lore, or even one who is interested in the literary and scholarly ideals of the later Renaissance, may take a definite pleasure in an exhaustive study of this literature—in discovering the relationship between Bacci and Marini for example, the dependence of Ambroise Paré upon both of these, and in running down the many sources of Aldrovandus and of Thomas Bartholinus—but he can scarcely hope to convey this pleasure to a reader, and he has no right to inflict his minute discoveries upon others. My review of the modern classics of unicorn lore must be as brief as possible.

Sebastian Münster, whose *Universal Cosmography* appeared in 1550, knew nothing about the unicorn except what he got from the account by Lewis Vartoman, but his illustrator was able to draw from Vartoman's specifications a sightly and credible picture of the animal.[1] Hieronymus Cardan knew a great deal about the unicorn, as about most other things, and his description of the animal,[2] which appeared in the same year as Münster's, was frequently quoted by later writers and had an authority almost equal to that of the ancients. In other places, as we have seen, Cardan described the alicorn most exactly and speculated with unusual acumen about the sources of its magic powers. The *Zoology* of Conrad Gesner, published in 1551, exerted an influence quite out of proportion to its merits. Gesner's account of the unicorn was a mere compendium of what had been previously written on the subject and gave little evidence of original thinking. He suggested, whether for the first time I do not know, that the unicorn may have been destroyed in Noah's flood, and he quoted a letter from one of his many correspondents and collaborators in which a species of unicorn theretofore unknown to science, a native of the Carpathians, was reported and vaguely described. Gesner's book [3] remained the standard work on its topic for almost ninety years, until it was superseded by Aldrovandus, and during that period few readers, even among the learned, would think of doubting what it said about the unicorn.

Pierre Belon, who discussed the unicorn problem at length in 1553, was a man of different stamp—not a compiler of other men's opinions but an observer, an independent thinker, a daring traveller, a zoologist in advance of his times. He was undaunted by authorities and majorities when convinced that they were wrong, using books intelligently, and seldom allowing them to abuse him. The great alicorns of St. Denis and St. Mark's and of royal treasuries puzzled him and won his admiration, but he would not believe in the powers attributed to them, and he was convinced that most of the smaller horns on the market and in the hands of individuals were of marine origin. For shrewdness, clear thinking, and independence of judgment, Belon's account [4] is the equal of anything in unicorn literature with the exception of the book by Andrea Marini.

Of this admirable writer I know nothing except what may be deduced from his book itself,[5] but this is really a good deal. He had a mind that would find itself at home in a few places in the twentieth century, but he must have been very lonely in the sixteenth, even in Venice. His thought is strong, clear, incisive; there is something thrilling in the manly vigour with which he cuts and crashes his way through thickets of superstition; his prose marches forward, every sentence and word an advance, with something like the irresistible tread of John Dryden. There is not one paragraph break from end to end of his book, and there does not need to be, so perfect is the linking of his thought. One sees that he is angry at heart, although his head is clear. He has the mind of a modern scientist and he loves clarity and precision, but he has no tools to work with, he is more hampered by surrounding bigotry and ignorance and lassitude than the scientist of our time, he has not even the support of his own profession. One may surmise that he chooses the unicorn legend for his attack not because of any special animosity toward it, but merely because it seems to him representative of the innumerable follies about him and of a general human tendency to prefer lies to the truth.

Marini begins by deploring that untrustworthiness of the senses which renders the discovery of natural truth so extremely difficult. The mind is acquainted for the most part, he says, not with the essences of things but only with their external "accidents"; and thence arises the variety of sects in all professions, for ambition or presumption leads men to pronounce as certain the conjectures of a moment or to lead others astray by deliberate deceit. Harmful everywhere, this has worked most harm in medicine, in which that opinion is most popular which most allures and deceives the public. Although the whole profession is guilty here, the Arabian physicians have been boldest in their promises, hoping to prop their failing fortunes by adopting and elaborating popular superstitions. The Arabs have introduced strange drugs, and among them the bezoar-stone and the alicorn, giving it out that these are antidotes for every poison and cures for every incurable disease, notwithstanding that no one knows where these things come from, what they really are, or by whom they were first tried. Things have come to such a pass that no royal treasury is thought complete without its alicorn, and princes are everywhere determined to have one at any price. Clever merchants have not been slow to take the opportunity for deception, seeing that there is no way of making sure what is the true horn. Marini has decided to expose these deceptions partly because he has been asked for his opinion about the unicorn and partly because he dislikes to see men spending great sums for things of no value, and putting trust in drugs that can do them no good.

He proposes, first, to show that we have no certain knowledge of the unicorn, and second, that, even if we had, the animal's horn could not have the powers attributed to it. The first part of his argument is concerned with the wide discrepancies in the unicorn tradition, which convince him that those who have written about the animal have never seen a specimen. The doubt thus cast upon the tradition is increased when one observes the differences in the reputed alicorns of Europe and England. These horns, he believes, have come from different animals, some of them marine, and he suspects that all the alicorns of England have come from the sea, for there is not even a record of a one-horned beast in that country. With a touch of that wonder at the wealth and variety of Nature which was common in his time, he reminds us that the sea is very prolific of animal life and that many of its forms are still unknown. He thinks it likely that the ocean has cast up many objects with the shape and substance of horns.

If the animal is unknown, how can we find and verify the horn?

It will be replied that the learned have found certain infallible tests, but Marini asserts that most of these tests are childish and that all are worthless. He admits that powdered alicorn will delay the death of a poisoned pigeon, but says that any other horn will do the same thing by retarding assimilation.

Even if the animal and the horn were both well known, it would be easy to prove that the assertions made concerning the alicorn's properties are *come una favola di Romanzi*. To say that it is good against all poisons is obviously ridiculous, and an affront to intelligence, for poisons differ so widely in their elements that one substance can be in sympathy or antipathy with only one or two kinds. Poisons operate upon different organs and in various ways, so that no one antidote can counteract them all. The assertion that the alicorn sweats in the presence of poison may be proved a lie by simple experiment, supposing that one can get an alicorn to experiment upon; but we do not need experiment, for reason alone tells us that sweat is an effect of "vegetative vertue", which no horn can have. Marini allows that marble, glass mirrors, and other such objects, collect moisture under certain circumstances, but this is not sweat; it does not come from the intrinsic nature of those objects but from the surrounding humidity.

Coming to the use of powdered alicorn as a medicine prescribed for poisoning, pestilential fever, bites of mad dogs, stings of scorpions, falling sickness, and the like, he admits that it may have some value, though no more than stag's horn. Like all horn, it is "cold and dry" by nature, so that it corrects the putrefactions that are by nature wet and hot. His professional indignation is aroused, however, by the far greater claims of the "Arabistes" that the alicorn can cure all other diseases and even raise the dead to life.

Approaching his close, Marini has of course to face the argument from authority and common consent. It will be objected, he says, that so enduring a fame as that of the alicorn cannot be without foundation, and that it could not last so long unless it contained truth. He points out that the superstitions concerning the Harpies, the Sirens, and the Golden Ass of Apuleius also lasted for a long time. A very slight occasion may give rise, he says, to a lasting belief

XV. BOCHART'S UNICORN

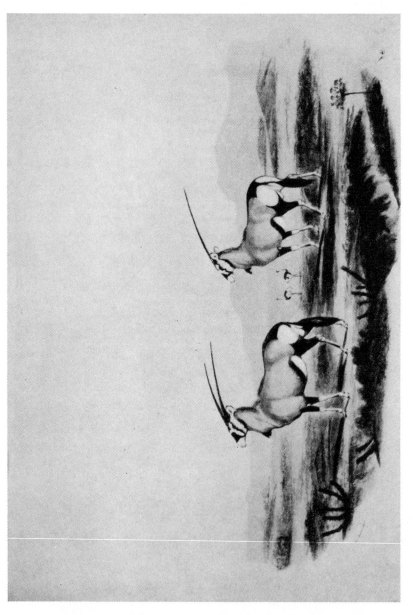

XVI. ORYX CAPENSIS

XVII. THE RAPE OF PROSERPINE

XVIII. THE UNICORN OF PERSEPOLIS

when no person of intelligence and prestige reveals its emptiness. He cannot be sure how the belief in the alicorn arose, but he conjectures most shrewdly that it must be traced back to the custom of the kings in ancient times who drank their wine from vessels of horn. Some person with a speculative turn of mind may have spread abroad the notion that they did this to escape the danger of poisoning; and it may well be, he says, that these kings connived at the spreading of this report, thinking that it would have a discouraging effect upon poisoners. And this is true, he remarks, "even to-day, when those Princes who live in constant fear keep on their table pieces of alicorn or the tongues of serpents or other such things, pretending—or perhaps really believing without any evidence—that they will sweat when poison is brought near". Marini ends his book with the hope that he has crushed this superstition and that men of sense will in future leave the alicorn in the hands of charlatans and make use of some more trustworthy means of protection.

Marini was answered at once by a man of greater reputation; he was called a confirmed sceptic and a sworn foe of all believers in horns;[6] the whole tendency of thought in his time and what may be called the "vested interests" were against him. Nevertheless, his book left an indelible mark upon the literature of the unicorn, he found followers almost immediately, and the ruck of writers whose mental habit was a pious echolalia were put to strange shifts because this one man had broken the rules of the game by doing some independent thinking. The *Discorso* seems to have been translated into Latin by Aldrovandus,[7] who certainly extended its influence by his careful outline of Marini's argument in a book of his own.

Of Marini's chief antagonist, Andrea Bacci, a good deal is known. He was a professional student of botany and a physician to the Pope, very erudite but not successful in medical practice, so that he seems to have lived in poverty until the Cardinal Azzolino Colonna took him into his household. His numerous treatises show a penchant for recondite topics on the border between magic and science.[8] He had far more learning than Marini and a more poetical mind; the total impression that he makes upon one who reads several of his works together is that of an Italian and somewhat less humorous

Sir Thomas Browne; his thought, however, was not active and trenchant, but absorbent, and he loved mystery more than he did the truth.

Bacci's book on the unicorn [9] appeared at Venice in 1566—in the same year and place, that is, as Marini's, and this fact is one of the most curious things about it. Neither of the two writers mentions the other by name or directly alludes to the other's book, yet it is obvious almost at a glance that the two treatises are intimately related. Both begin with an exordium on the inability of reason to discover the essences of natural objects. Bacci presents, and answers, all of the doubts concerning the unicorn named by Marini, and in the same order. Ostensibly, at least, the two writers reach diametrically opposed results: Marini is a sceptic and Bacci would have his readers think that he is a firm believer. I can find no external evidence concerning the relationship between these two books, but internal evidence—most of it too minute to present here—has convinced me that Bacci wrote with the definite purpose of answering and confuting Marini. It seems to me almost certain that he was commissioned to do this by one of his patrons, probably Don Francesco Medici, who feared the weakening of popular belief in the unicorn. For all his grace and skill and learning, Bacci gives everywhere the impression that his pen is hired, his thought dictated, and that he is one of those literary slaves whose miseries were described by Lucian and Aeneas Silvius Piccolomini. He wrote deliberately, I believe, to "keep the Past upon its throne". Did he write dishonestly? Perhaps he could not have answered that question even to his own conscience. He may have felt that a little prevarication, or rather let us say a little stifling of his better thought, would be for the general good. He may have been one of those who honestly believe that multi-millionaires ought not to be poisoned.

If this was indeed his view and if he wrote his book to discourage those who thought otherwise, then it is interesting to observe that he probably failed. The *Discorso* is dedicated *Al Serenissimo Don Francesco Medici, Gran Principe di Toscana*; it may have been written in his house and at his instance; it was certainly written with special reference to an alicorn in his possession. Deeply humiliated Bacci must have been, therefore, when this most serene Don Francesco died according to the belief of the time by poison administered by his brother, the Cardinal Ferdinand, who succeeded him. Fifteen hours later died his wife, the famous Bianca Capello, with whom he had carried on amours for years during the lifetime of his first wife, Jean of Austria. The famous alicorn of the Medici and the brilliant *Discorso* written to corroborate its influence—Bacci says in his Introductory Address that Francesco was almost the author—had failed most dismally.

Bacci's book is clear and orderly in arrangement. "In the first part", says he, "I consider the prime question whether there is such a creature as the unicorn, in regard to which I adduce from one source and another many curious reasonings and finally prove that the animal undoubtedly exists. In the second part we shall decide what sort of animal the unicorn is, and here will be heard the testimony of the ancients and that of all the moderns who have written on the subject so that we may determine what is to be accepted as true. Coming at last, in the third part, to the How and the Why, we shall decide whether the alicorn has any power against poison and how it may be proved that it possesses such power."

Each of the reasons for doubting the existence of the unicorn developed by Marini is considered in a separate chapter with much dialectic skill and adequate learning. Commending those who have expressed doubt not in mere obstinacy but in sincere desire for truth, Bacci points out that the unicorn legend is different from most superstitions in that it has lasted longer and has been shared by the most enlightened minds of all nations. Superstition, he says, lives on the popular tongue alone, but this belief has been maintained by the greatest writers, sacred and profane; furthermore, this belief, instead of growing more monstrous, as superstitions do, has become clearer and simpler and more credible with each succeeding age. The fact that the unicorn is almost unknown does not argue its non-existence but only its rarity. Until recent years the aromatic spices of the East were unknown in Europe; rhubarb and aloes and amber were unfamiliar to the ancients, yet these things existed. We need not wonder that the unicorn is still strange to us when we consider that he cannot be taken alive, that his habit is solitary, that he dwells in remotest mountain fastnesses, and that there are probably very few specimens alive at any one time. The tradition of the unicorn has come down to us precisely as other traditions of actual things have come: first we hear its name from unknown sources and it is confusedly described, but little by little the accounts increase in precision and frequency until we find them everywhere. Notices of the unicorn continue to be confused merely because the beast is very wild and is not found in Europe.

At this point Bacci indulges himself—and at least one of his readers—in an eloquent passage on *due gran segreti della natura*. The first of these is that she contents herself with producing only a few individuals of those species which are especially distinguished by their beauty, and this she does in order that God Almighty may have the greater glory in His works. We acknowledge His glory when we contemplate the frame of this vast machine the earth, when we consider the ranks of the heavens and the concourse of the stars, the composition of the elements, and how He keeps the earth balanced in the air and sets a limit to the sea. In every created thing there is some marvel, more or less. In some things God and Nature have shown their power by the manner of their production—as in gems, which are found in the hidden chambers of the hills and yet are composed of the same substance as the stars. Other things are wonderful for the length of time required to make them, such as gold and precious marbles and many kinds of stones. With respect to animals, those necessary to the maintenance of human life are produced in abundance; others, not necessary or even harmful, are produced sparingly, and to these Nature gives the instinct to flee from the sight of men, as we see in lions, dragons, tigers, and basilisks. And then, too, even the rudest mind must be amazed at the divine beauty of some creations, for not even Solomon in all his glory was arrayed like the lilies of the field and the fowls of the air. The emerald itself is vanquished by the marvellous green of certain beetles; no jewel and no work of man's hands can compare with the natural gems, green and gold and red, to be found in certain humble worms and grubs. Other animals are wonderful for their size, such as the elephant and the whale, huge as the hugest ship; others, again, astonish by their smallness, among which Virgil thought the most wonderful was the zenzala, an animal barely visible but which looks like a hippogriff, at once horse and rider and trumpet, both Perseus and Pegasus. Finally, God and Nature have shown their power by making some things, such as the phoenix and the balsam, exceedingly rare, and thus, apparently, it has pleased the wonder-working Architect and mighty God that the unicorn should be among the rarest works of Nature.

Arguing circularly, Bacci derives from this another "secret". As Nature produces few individuals of the most wonderful kinds and the highest value—witness the phoenix and precious stones—it follows that the unicorn, being so rare, must have great value, and that its horn must have some miraculous virtue (*prerogativa*). As a manifest proof of this, the animal has a strong instinct for solitude, living in deserts so remote that it seems almost a miracle whenever its horn is found. This horn must be washed down from the desert by great rivers in flood, long after the animal's death; naturally, therefore, it is expensive.

The translation of this passage, which has decided beauty in the original, is justified by the brilliant illustration it gives of a habit of thought common in the Renaissance which made belief in the unicorn easy. Men of Bacci's stamp did not draw back from this or that belief about Nature because it was wonderful; they were too well informed, too cultivated and intellectual, one may as well say too scientifically minded, for that. Wonderful things were precisely what they expected of Nature, just as marvels have been expected, and therefore found, by those minds of our own time that have conceived the answering universes of the atom and of outer space. Those who would condemn Bacci and his fellow-believers on the ground that their assertions about the unicorn were too wonderful for belief are less scientific than they suppose.

Like most of his fellows and like the vast majority of educated people of the present day, Bacci is unscientific rather in his method than in his general mental attitude. He lavishes learning and acute thought upon the problem of the alicorn's alleged properties but

says hardly a word about definite experiment, which would have
settled his question in one tenth of the time he gives to it. Here we
have a most vivid example of the tyranny of mental habit. A scholar,
a physician, a trained observer, a man of fine culture and powerful
mind, is sitting in a library with an alicorn before him, and he wants
to find out whether it responds in any way to the presence of poison.
What does he do? He goes to the shelves and pulls down Ctesias,
Aristotle, Aelian, Pliny, Solinus, Dioscorides, Avicenna, Albertus
Magnus, and twenty or thirty other "authorities", and then sets
to work. In the terms of what he finds in these books he thinks with
an acuteness of which only a few of the men we now call scientists
would be capable; but to think in any other terms, to bring a bit
of poison out of Don Francesco's "laboratory" and to set it beside
the alicorn to see what would happen—that is quite beyond him.
Or perhaps we may say, that would not be "pure scholarship".
Perhaps, also, Bacci did not greatly desire to have the truth about the
alicorn demonstrated beyond a doubt. He had seen experiments
performed upon this alicorn by Don Francesco himself, who, as an
amateur chemist, doubtless knew how to get satisfactory results.
Bacci was not being paid to test the alicorn but to write a book
about it.

I shall not summarize Bacci's rather profound but wholly Aristo-
telean chapter on the *Fondamenti di Tutte le virtù delle cose* upon which
he bases his conclusion that the operation of the alicorn is due not
to its "elementary qualities" nor to its "external accidents" but to its
"intrinsic and formal nature or essence" which the mind cannot
grasp or understand. This Aristotelian doctrine of "form" or
"essential nature"—to which we owe, ultimately, the basic and most
obviously false conception of democracy—had lain heavy upon the
world of thought for many centuries, as it does upon society to-day.
As the intrinsic form of a thing is unknowable one may say of it
almost anything that suits his purpose. Bacci derived from the
intrinsic form of the alicorn its alleged powers of detecting poison,
just as the philosophers of eighteenth-century France derived from
the intrinsic form or essential nature of humanity the equally
ludicrous proposition that all men are created free and equal. The

very rarity of the alicorn, says he, is proof presumptive that it has extraordinary intrinsic virtue. This virtue may be judged from its substance: like gems, it has much *forma* in proportion to its *materia*, and its matter, as in the case of gems, is so pure and splendid and starry that none can deny it a heavenly origin. Its virtue may be seen in the excellence of its external accidents, such as its polished density, its odour and taste and colour. The alicorn is the densest of all horns; it is white, pure, uniform, and single for each animal; it works by its own nature and not by assistance of art; it causes heat yet is not hot; it causes cold, yet it is not cold itself. All this means that it must operate by its intrinsic or hidden virtue.

Marini had rendered it impossible for any intelligent man who read his book to explain the operation of the alicorn in terms of "sympathy" and "antipathy", making clear that no single substance could stand in either of these relations to all poisons whatsoever. Bacci therefore abandons the old explanation but not the belief that the alicorn is good against all poisons. He explains its virtue by invoking an assertion which he says he finds in Avicenna's *Treatise on the Heart* that alicorn "comforts the heart" and is a powerful cordial.[10] One sees how this might account for the alleged action of the alicorn as a drug, but it does not seem to explain how it could detect and reveal the presence of poison on a rich man's table.

Bacci ends his book with this strange and significant passage: "Whether the alicorn sweats or does not sweat, whether it makes water boil or does not make it boil, the belief that it does so will do no injury to truth and will be for the good of the state. No man of sound mind should seek to disprove these things by rigour of reasoning, but should allow and discreetly admit them—for the sake, at least, of the Princes whom they will please by such favourable opinion. Thus the common good obliges us to write and to persuade the ignorant that what is said of the Alicorn is true, because such a belief discourages wicked men from evil doing by making them think that the virtue of this horn will easily discover their iniquity and bring about their utter ruin."

Thus Andrea Bacci takes his place among the well-intentioned weaklings who throttle their thought for what they make themselves think the social advantage. Did he, after all, believe in the unicorn and its properties, as he often asserts in the body of his book? After one has read his last paragraph it does not seem to matter what he believed. His patron died, according to contemporary belief, just the death from which Bacci had tried to save him—an apt commentary upon the final value of such endeavours. His book had five editions in twenty-one years,[11] but its influence was far less than that exerted by Marini's *Discorso*, which has never had more than two. It may seem strange that one who is thankful for every legitimate influence that prolonged the life of the unicorn should be sorry for Bacci's advocacy and regard it as a defection from a higher cause, but almost all the writing ever done about the unicorn has been honest, and that of Andrea Bacci apparently was not. One cannot forget that he was a man of first-rate powers, and that, if it had not been "just for a handful of silver", he might have done better work.

He might have done work equal to that of Ambroise Paré who, with less ability but far more courage and character, left a lasting mark upon scientific thought and won for himself the title "Father of French Surgery". Paré knew the temptations to which his Italian contemporary succumbed, for he was first physician to the Court of France during the period of Catharine de' Medici's regime and apparently a friend to Catharine herself. At a dozen different points we find him standing out against hoary abuses, intrenched super-stitions, and ancient ignorances, never failing to act upon and to speak the best he knew through fear that his innovation might be unsafe or untimely. The kings he served used alicorns and bezoar-stones. He did his best to prove to them that such things were useless. In his book on poisons he tells a story which is as well known as anything about him and which illustrates vividly his scientific temper. The king Charles IX, his master, had been given a bezoar in which he had full confidence, but Paré assured him that its reputa-tion was undeserved, suggesting that it be tried on a criminal sentenced to death. The king found that one of his cooks was to be hanged the next day for stealing two silver plates, and this cook gladly agreed to drink poison when he was told by the king that the bezoar would be given him immediately after. The cook died in torment after seven hours, and Paré found by autopsy that the cause of death had been gastroenteritis induced by corrosive sublimate.

The most important of Paré's several passages on the unicorn was written when he was seventy years of age at the request of one of his patients.[12] In 1580 he had successfully treated the Chevalier Christofle des Ursins for an imposthume caused by a fall from a horse, and during his convalescence this patient took great interest in the methods used in his cure, asking particularly why he had not been given mummy to drink. Paré answered this question on both medical and aesthetic grounds, pointing out among other things that it was shameful and *infra dignitatem* for good Christians to eat and drink the dead bodies of pagans. He was then asked why he had made no use of alicorn, and his reply, which brought in by the way certain remarks about poisons and the pest, was so satisfactory that Christofle begged him to write it all out for the good of humanity. The resulting *Discours* rests heavily for both matter and method upon Marini, who is nowhere mentioned.[13] It is moderate, sensible, untechnical in vocabulary, obviously addressed to the general public. Although inferior to the books of Bacci and Marini in almost every important respect, it seems to have had almost as much influence as they.

Paré begins as Marini had done by showing that the existence of the unicorn is doubtful, at least on grounds of ordinary evidence. He admits that an acquaintance of his, a physician of Paris named Louys Paradis, has recently given a minute description of a unicorn which he thought he saw at Alexandria, but even this, and all other human testimony put together, does not shake his scepticism. "If it were not for the witness of Holy Scripture, to which we are obliged to adjust all our beliefs", says he, "I should not think that such a creature as the unicorn had ever existed." He then quotes several of the Biblical references and concludes, almost with a sigh: "*Il faut donc croire qu'il est des Licornes.*"

But the Bible says nothing about the medicinal values of the alicorn, so that Paré is left free to deal with that topic in the way of a scientific man. He sets to work to destroy the superstition by appeal to experience, to authority, and to reason. By "experience" he means experiment. He has drawn circles on a table with water in which the alicorn has been soaked for hours, and he finds that scorpions and toads and spiders have no idea of lying down to die inside of such circles but cross and recross the line of alicorn-water at will. Not content with this, he has put a toad to soak for three days in alicorn-water, and at the end of that time he found the toad—regarded in his day, of course, as a highly venomous creature—*"aussi gaillard que lors que je l'y mis"*. He makes short work of the bubble test for "true horn", asserting that the same bubbles are sent up by the horns of cows, goats, sheep, and other beasts, by the tusks of elephants, by the covers of pots, by tiles, and even by wood. He has tried giving alicorn to pigeons poisoned with arsenic, and the pigeons have always died. The assertion that alicorn sweats in the presence of poison is met, as by Marini, with the observation that glass and marble and other substances with smooth surfaces act in the same way—that is, that they condense the surrounding vapours.

Paré attempts to turn the argument from "authority" against his antagonists by showing that Aristotle, Galen, and Hippocrates never mention the medicinal properties of the alicorn, the strength of this contention being that anything ignored by these three supreme authorities in the field of medicine was not worth mentioning. He cites the testimony of eminent physicians of his own day against the alicorn, and says that physicians of repute continue to use it only because their patients demand it. *"C'est que le monde veult estre trompé."*

Coming to the argument by "reason", Paré accepts Marini's criticism of the alicorn's action by "sympathy" and "antipathy". He goes beyond this and attacks the Arabic theory advanced by Bacci that the alicorn is "cordial" and works by strengthening the heart. Only good blood and good air, says Paré, can do this. Now the alicorn is neither of these, nor is it convertible into either; it is earth, and therefore, according to the old theory of the elements, at the opposite extreme from air; it is dry, while air is moist; it cannot be turned into blood because it contains no flesh or sap. Therefore it cannot affect the heart. Paré believes that the best "alexitery" is to flee from all poisoners as from the plague—*"et les chasser du Royaume de France, et les envoyer avec les Turcs et les autres infideles, ou aux deserts inaccessibles avec les Licornes"*. He did not consider, perhaps, that this drastic policy would have involved the banishment of his royal mistress.

At the end of his *Discours* Paré expresses a hope that those who do not agree with him will bring forward their reasons, for the public good. The wish was gratified. An anonymous champion of the unicorn appeared,[14] reiterated the old superstitions, tried to overwhelm Paré by the weight of authority and tradition and numbers, and—in the way of his kind—treated his antagonist with personal abuse. Paré's reply [15] is a masterpiece of French urbanity. "I say nothing", he writes, "of his apparent animosity, which I suppose must be due rather to his zeal for the truth than to any opinion that he can hold of me"; and at the end of his response he begs his adversary, if he has anything further to advance, *"qu'il quitte les animositez, et qu'il traicte plus doucement le bon vieillard."*

The adversary had taken his stand upon the mediaeval trust in tradition; the fact that unicorns had been believed in for a long time and were still accepted by the vast majority of men was enough for him. All the wise men of the world, he asserted, have believed in the virtues of the alicorn, and, aside from the fact that we are obliged to accept authority, it is better to err with the wise than to think rightly in opposition to them. To the first of these remarks Paré answers that by no means all the wise men of the world have believed in the alleged properties of the alicorn. To the second highly interesting and representative assertion he makes the equally interesting reply: "I say, on the contrary, that I should prefer to be right entirely alone than to be wrong not merely in company with the wise but even with all the rest of the world." (*Quant à la seconde partie, je dy tout au contraire, que j'aimerois mieux faire bien tout seul que de faillir non seulement avec les sages mais mesmes avec tout le reste du monde.*) Clearly, a change is coming over the Western world—a change not yet completed.

The adversary's second point, not easily distinguishable from the first, was that the mere length of time during which the alicorn had been used showed that it must be valuable. Although we do not know this adversary's name, we see and know him quite well enough. His true name is Legion, and he has millions of fellows in every age who think that the antiquity of an error converts it into a truth.

Ambroise Paré did not belong to this school; he was accustomed to
being in a minority of one and to advancing those "minority reports"
which eventually rule the world. "I reply", he says, "that mere
duration of time is not sufficient to prove the value of the alicorn.
Its vogue is founded upon opinion, but the truth depends upon
fact. Therefore it is nothing to the purpose to cite against me the
popes and emperors and kings and other potentates who have kept
the alicorn in their treasuries, for such men are not competent judges
of the properties of natural things."

A pope not a competent judge of everything in the universe?
One is reminded of the contemporary suspicion, certainly well
founded, that Paré was a Protestant, and of the probability that he
escaped the Massacre of Saint Bartholomew because he was too good
a physician for the Court of France to lose. As a Protestant, however,
he does accept the authority of the Bible, and when his adversary
quotes against him the references to the unicorn in the Old Testament
he almost forgets his urbanity. "Any man who tries to bring this
argument against me", he says, "merely shows that he wants to
quarrel, for there is no one who accepts the teachings of the Bible
more faithfully than I do." Thus the champion of personal liberty
was imprisoned by authority after all. He accepted the Septuagint's
word μονόκερως as the "word of God".[16]

Creditable as Paré's discussions of the unicorn were in method
and spirit, they contained little original matter. He depended chiefly
upon Marini, but also upon his contemporary and countryman, the
famous traveller, André Thevet. This writer's *Cosmographie Universelle*, an admirable work, very influential and still highly interesting,
contained a chapter of first-rate importance about the unicorn.[17]
Thevet bases his account upon things he has seen and heard on an
island in the Red Sea which was a port of call for many ships trading
between East and West, and which swarmed with petty traders of
all nations. Here he once met a Turkish ambassador to Abyssinia
who showed him a horn, probably that of an oryx, which was
thought to grow single upon the animal's brow, but which was
decidedly unlike the alicorns of Europe. In the same place and on
the mainland near at hand he has seen the tusks of elephants and of

walruses artificially straightened by charlatans and tricksters and sold
as true alicorns. These and similar observations have made him
doubt almost everything that is asserted about the unicorn. The
story of the virgin-capture reminds him of the chattering of aged
gossips about the winter fire *"avec leurs discours du Melusine"*. He is
not to be intimidated by the authority of Pliny, Münster, Solinus,
Strabo, and all other such men put together, for, wise and learned as
these men were, this tale of the unicorn is not the first nor the
hundredth of their errors and lies. He says with justifiable pride
that if these "authorities" had enjoyed the same knowledge of the
world that he himself possesses and had seen the countries that he has
traversed they would scarcely have forgotten their duty to such an
extent as to hand on to posterity their idle and untested imaginings.
It is unlikely, he thinks, that foreigners can know more about the
fauna of a country than that country's inhabitants know. He has
ranged over the whole territory that the unicorn is said to inhabit
and has heard no rumour of its existence. One-horned animals
may exist, he thinks, like that one described by his Turkish ambassador, but scarcely any such as the unicorn fabled in Europe. The
alicorns of European cathedrals and treasuries are probably, he
thinks, the products of such deceitful arts as he saw practised near
the Red Sea. He does not doubt that they have medicinal value,
but this they share with all other horns whatsoever. The confidence,
not to say the swagger, of Thevet is evident in his concluding words:
*"Voyla donc ce que j'avois de long temps envie d'advertir le Lecteur, pour
oster l'opinion mal fondée de plusieurs hommes doctes, tant Grecs que
Latins, mesmes des Rois, Princes et Monarques, pour le faict de la Licorne."*

From this "vulgar sort of Infidel people", as Edward Topsell
called the writers we have just considered, we may now return to the
faithful, for it is a curious fact that all the chief sixteenth-century
authorities on our topic were sceptical to say the least, and that nearly
all those of the seventeenth century were believers. The Reverend
Edward Topsell is positively devout, and like a few others of his
kind he bolsters his own belief by the conviction that those who do
not agree with him must be bad people. All that he requires to prove
the existence of the unicorn and the truth of everything ever said

of it is the authority of the ninety-second Psalm and of "all the Divines that ever wrote". With these witnesses on his side he feels dispensed from further argument and expatiates in the meadows of unicorn lore at length, thoroughly enjoying himself. There is little in Topsell's account of the unicorn, however, that is not to be found in Conrad Gesner, and he is interesting chiefly for the quaint vigour of his language.[18]

Laurens Catelan's book on the unicorn was of much greater importance.[19] He was an apothecary of note in Montpellier, a city which in his time (1568–1647) was teaching medicine and pharmacy to all of Europe.[20] Besides succeeding as an apothecary, he collected a rather famous small museum of curiosities which contained an alicorn as its greatest treasure, and it is probable, as I have said, that he wrote his *Histoire de la Licorne* not so much as a service to science as with the hope of attracting a purchaser. Catelan is seen at his best in his carefully written *Discours et demonstration des ingrédients de la thériaque*, a valuable book upon a topic of which he was a master. A man of considerable ability and reading, he was both credulous and vain. The chief value of his book on the unicorn is due to the fact that it is the only one of importance written by a practising apothecary.

Catelan divides his book into four parts. In the first he discusses the various names of the unicorn. In the second he treats its appearance, habitat, general characteristics and "virtues" in medicine, giving directions for its chase and capture. The third part is devoted to a fair statement of eighteen objections made by those who think the beast fabulous or the report of its virtues false, and in the fourth division he answers all these objections triumphantly, concluding "*que l'animal Lycorne est, et que grandes et merveilleuses sont les vertus de sa corne, pourveu qu'elle soit de la vraye et legitime.*" It is certain that Catelan had read both Marini and Paré, for he quotes them both as objectors, but they seem to have disturbed his own beliefs not at all.

A year or two after publishing his book on the unicorn Catelan had the pleasure of showing his little museum to a distinguished physician and scholar from Denmark, one Caspar Bartholinus, who was much interested in the apothecary's specimens of one-horned birds and insects. Horns, and particularly single horns, may be said to have "run in the family" of Bartholinus somewhat as music did in the family of Bach and money in that of Rothschild. Nothing one-horned was alien to Caspar or to Thomas his son or to Caspar his grandson. They were fascinated all three by the monocerine idea as it had been exemplified by Nature in various species. If Laurens Catelan gave the elder Caspar the first hint for this strange hobby, then that is the best contribution he made to the lore of the unicorn. It seems probable that he did give that hint and that it was partly due to Caspar's visit to the apothecary's museum in Montpellier that unicorn scholarship passed from the south of Europe to the north.

In 1628 Caspar Bartholinus published his little book about the unicorn and related topics.[21] It is a remarkably clear, sensible, and well-arranged little book, as "scientific" as almost any one living at the time could have made it. In forty-eight compact pages it covers every important aspect of unicorn lore, including several never before discussed. The first chapter is concerned with the question whether unicorns exist, and here Caspar sensibly deplores the tendency of some men to deny the existence of things for no better reason than that they have not seen them; they would do better, he thinks, to trust authority until a thorough ransacking of the planet has shown conclusively what it does and does not contain. For his part, he has no such difficulties, and he recognizes the existence of unicorned insects, birds, snakes, and even men. Among the larger animals he finds eight different unicorns: the oryx, Garcias ab Horto's African amphibian, the sea-unicorn of the north, the Indian bull, the Indian ass, the Indian horse, the rhinoceros, and the monoceros or unicorn proper. The usual argument from the Biblical references is then made and the correctness of the Septuagint translation upheld.

The next four chapters are devoted to discussion of the sea-unicorn, the horn of the rhinoceros, the alicorns of Europe, and the general characteristics of the true unicorn. The sixth chapter denies without qualification all the magical properties attributed to the horn, chiefly because they do not stand the test of experiment. In a covert reference to Bacci, Caspar says that we ought not to allow our opinion in such matters to be swayed by the authority of princes, which is always less important than the truth—"*quae veritati semper est posthabenda*". It is evident that the alicorn has moved into a different political atmosphere. Caspar discusses in his concluding chapters the various substances that were sold as "true horn" in his time and ends with a valuable passage on the nature and use of "fossil alicorn".

But the most interesting of the productions of Caspar Bartholinus was his son Thomas Bartholinus the Elder, Professor of Anatomy at Copenhagen and a man of encyclopaedic learning. The *De Unicornu Observationes Novae*[22] by this son is the most extensive and impressive work ever devoted to the unicorn, and it might have been the best if the author had devoted to it his best powers instead of regarding it as a toy of scholarship. One who knows nothing of Thomas's other books, which are numerous and sound, is likely to think when he glances through the chapter headings of this one that the author was horn-mad. Some of the topics of his thirty-seven chapters are: horned men, the horns of Moses, the causes of horns, horned insects, horned birds and beetles and reptiles and fish, unicorned bulls and asses, the horn of the Holy Cross, the use of horns for beakers, horns as ornaments, horns in medicine, fossil horns. In the second edition of the book this effect of multiplicity is accentuated by a brilliantly executed frontispiece (Plate XII) in which a dozen different sorts of unicorns are pictured or represented. The *Index Auctorum* shows that Bartholinus quotes, in his three hundred and eighty pages from at least six hundred different writers, many of whom are cited many times, and from ten or twelve different languages. This book, the author tells us in his vivacious preface, was written in his youth partly as an act of filial piety—to extend and amplify the work of his father—and partly to while away a tedious interval of time. As I have said, there were giants in those days, and Thomas Bartholinus was one of them. This is the book on the unicorn, more than any other, in which one is convinced that the author is engaged in some sort of erudite play for which we have lost the art and the feeling. The tone of the preface is unmistakably gay and occasionally jocose, and on nearly every later page there is some observation so droll or so almost incredibly erudite as to rouse the suspicion, at least, although we cannot be quite sure, that the unwieldy elephant is wreathing his lithe proboscis to make us sport. The whole work has the look of a giant's jest, and one cannot believe that any sane man could have written it unless he thoroughly enjoyed the task, saw it in relation to serious concerns, and carried it through somewhat in the spirit of play.

I shall not attempt to make even a brief outline of this extraordinary book, which is really a sort of compact encyclopaedia of unicorn lore. It is enough to say that Thomas expanded in all directions the topics discussed by his father, adding illustration and corroboration from his immense hoard of learning, but extending the thought very little if at all. In regard to thought, in fact, the book is disappointing. Thomas presents the opinions of Caspar without change—holding, that is, that the unicorn exists but refusing to believe in the magical horn, trying to mediate between what he considers the credulity of Bacci and the unwarranted scepticism of Marini. His own son, Caspar, in preparing the considerably amplified second edition, left the matter of the first edition almost unaltered but added passages of his own.

The work of the Bartholini was professional scholarship. In France during the seventeenth century scholarship was almost never professional, and no more vivid contrast can be imagined than that between the exhaustive treatment of unicorn lore by Thomas Bartholinus and the contemporary discussion of the same topic recorded in a work, long since forgotten but worthy of remembrance, called the *Recueil Général*.[23] This consists of two hundred and eighty-seven *conférences* or public debates on the widest variety of topics, politics and religion alone excluded. One purpose steadily held is to avoid the acrimony, the pedantry and over-emphasis, the excessive citation of authority and dependence upon it, that still and for long after marked and marred academic discussion. Every speaker strives to show himself at once a scholar and a gentleman—one of the most difficult mediations between extremes—and the result, in its moderation and deference and urbane mingling of scholarship with humour, makes an admirable example of what the learned world owes to the French mind. As compared with the records of the English Royal Society, these papers are literature, and indeed I am not sure that the "Bureau" of debaters was not a fictitious device or "frame" of a single author. The two hundred and fortieth *conférence* is *De la Licorne*.

We have heard the opinions about the unicorn held by the "hirsute scholars in '*us*' "; here we learn what was thought on that subject by the educated public, by men who spent their lives in *salons* rather than in libraries. The two speakers in this debate have read the more important documents of the case. The first, who holds a brief against the unicorn, depends largely upon Paré's *Discours*, though he may have read Marini also, and he concludes: "*ce conte de la Licorne est une fiction*". The second speaker, more representative of the popular views, has certainly read Andrea Bacci. He argues shrewdly that the variety of opinions about the unicorn is no proof that the animal does not exist, for we find the same conflicting views about many indubitable beasts and even about God. He chooses the dog as an example and says tellingly that one who knew only the lap-dog could hardly be persuaded that it belongs to the same species as the mastiff. The argument that the Romans never saw the unicorn at their spectacles does not impress him, partly because it is the "argument from silence", and partly because the animal is, almost "by definition", uncapturable. He believes, with Thevet, that all horns are medicinal, and that the virtue ordinarily distributed through two horns is greatly increased when "united and locked in a single canal, as in the case of the unicorn". In conclusion, he says that occult properties ought not to be denied hastily. We should remember that our knowledge is limited and our reason infirm. Authority, reason, and experiment combine in demonstrating the magical powers of the alicorn.

Ulysses Aldrovandus was the Conrad Gesner of the seventeenth century. His account of the unicorn fills thirty-one folio pages [24] and reviews all the more obvious literature of his time, but he does not commit himself. "Some are doubtful", he says, "whether the unicorn exists; some deny its existence and others affirm it. For my own part,

I shall merely report their opinions faithfully, leaving to each of my readers his own freedom of judgment."

We come next to Sir Thomas Browne—always a delightful thing to do, but in this instance somewhat disappointing. His treatment of the unicorn [25] is badly confused; it is based upon Goropius Becanus, but he reads Goropius carelessly. We feel that the topic was almost made for Browne, and we miss, as frequently in the "Vulgar Errors", the full charm and power of his mystery-loving mind. It is disheartening to see this man who thought, quite rightly, that there are not miracles enough, going about to question and discredit one of the best of the few there were left. He has read his Bartholinus, however, to such purpose that he is by no means to be classed among the "vulgar sort of Infidel people". "Wee are so farre from denying there is any Unicorne at all", says he, "that wee affirme there are many kinds thereof. In the number of Quadrupedes wee will concede no lesse then five." But this hopeful beginning is not maintained, for Browne continues: "Although we concede there be many Unicornes, yet are we still to seeke; for whereunto to affixe this horne in question, or to determine from which thereof we receive this magnified medicine, we have no assurance . . . for although we single but one and Antonomastically thereto assigne the name of the Unicorne, yet can we not be secure what creature is meant thereby, what constant shape it holdeth, or in what number to be received." Further difficulties are that "this animall is not uniformely described", that the "horne we commonly extoll is not the same with that of the Ancients", that "what hornes soever they be which passe amongst us, they are not surely the hornes of one kind of animall", and that "many which beare that name and currantly passe among us are no hornes at all". Even though we were "satisfied we had the Unicornes horne, yet were it no injury unto Reason to question the efficacy thereof. . . . That some Antidotall quality it may have wee have no reason to deny; for since Elkes hoofs and hornes are magnified for Epilepsies, since not onely the bone in the heart but the horne of a Deere is Alexipharmacall . . . we cannot without prejudice except against the efficacy of this. But when we affirme it is not onely Antidotall to proper venomes . . .

but that it resisteth also Sublimate, Arsenick, and poysons which kill by second qualities, that is by corrosion of parts, I doubt we exceed the properties of its Nature, and the promises of experiment will not secure the adventure. . . . With what security, therefore, a man may rely on this remedy, the mistresse of fooles hath already instructed some, and to wisedome (which is never too wise to learne) it is not too late to consider".

One sees, in short, that Sir Thomas Browne the poetic scholar, pondering irresponsibly over the contents of Roman urns which no one had thought of converting into merchandise as "mummy", and Sir Thomas Browne the highly responsible physician of Norwich, estimating the practical worth of a "magnified medicine", were two distinct persons. He had to consider his patients as well as his readers.

In the year after that of the "Vulgar Errors" there appeared a book which one wishes that Browne had written.[26] The *History of Stones. and Gems* by Boëthius de Boodt is one of the more learned productions of a learned age, and all that its author lacked of a complete equipment for his task was imagination. Boëthius adopts the general position of the Bartholini, holding that the unicorn exists— or, at any rate, that its existence should not be denied until the exploration of the planet has been completed—but that the allegations made about its horn are unfounded.

This position, due to the effort of Caspar Bartholinus to mediate between Marini and Bacci, had become orthodox by the time of Boëthius. John Johnston advocated it in his important *Natural History*,[27] and the academic debaters of the second half of the century tended to accept it as axiomatic.

As a usual thing we are safe in assuming, when a given topic is treated in an academic dissertation, that it has lost all the living interest it may once have had, for the learned gentlemen who control the choice of such topics soon develop a sense of smell resembling that of the vulture and the hyena. Intelligent lovers of the unicorn are not delighted, therefore, to find the animal attracting the attention of the universities. In 1660 a Latin dissertation on the unicorn was pronounced at Wittenberg by Johann Frederick

Hubrigk, George Caspar Kirchmayer acting as *Praeses*.[28] Like most successful dissertation writers, Hubrigk avoids, apparently without effort, any suggestion of independent thinking, but his work shows patience, piety, and respect for authorities, so that one feels confident that he secured his degree. His most vigorous utterance refers to a remark of Olaus Magnus in which the unicorn is called a "monster", and to which he responds: "I should have preferred to have Olaus abstain from the use of this word, which seems to cast a slur upon Nature." For the rest, although he does not believe that the horn of the unicorn is a panacea or a universal antidote, he is firmly convinced that the animal exists because the Bible tells him so.

A slightly more important production is the dissertation *De Monocerote* spoken at Leipzig in 1667 by Johann Homilius.[29] This little work strikes a curiously contemporary note, and indeed, except for the tolerable Latin in which it is composed, it might almost have been written by some university student in Tennesse or Oklahoma who had somehow managed to hear of the doubts cast upon the Bible by modern science and had rushed to the defence of Genesis. Homilius has heard of the infidels who doubt the unicorn, and he wishes them to know that "if this animal were really fabulous it would not be mentioned in so many places of the Holy Scripture". In his belief, the translation of the Septuagint is itself inspired, and he asserts, wrongly, that all the Rabbins and Church Fathers accepted it. Like a true Fundamentalist, he will not allow that the unicorn or any other animal or thing mentioned in the Bible was intended as a symbol. He divides the enemies of the unicorn, and therefore of the Bible, into two groups: those who say explicitly that there has never been such an animal and those who deny it implicitly by leaving it out of their descriptions of the earth's *fauna*. In the first group he places Saint Ambrose, Apollonius of Tyana, Andrea Marini, and Ambroise Paré—a strange collocation. Those of the second group he does not name. A third division is composed of the writers who admit that the unicorn existed once, but say that he perished in the flood, and upon these last Homilius is very severe. Like Hubrigk, he objects to having the unicorn called a monster, although it is Solinus rather than Olaus Magnus whom he takes to task for the epithet. He treats the question of the alicorn's properties with great caution, neither denying nor affirming them, but quoting authority on either side.

A third dissertation that may be noticed here is that of Christian Vater, pronounced at Wittenberg in 1679.[30] Vater disarms criticism by saying that he is not old enough to add anything of his own to a subject which has perplexed some of the best minds of the time. Like Homilius and Hubrigk, he considers the Bible a more than sufficient proof of the unicorn's existence, though he deigns to quote some secular authority. The only original part of his remarks is that in which he argues that the alicorn is not dead matter, as most of his predecessors had thought, but a living part of the animal.

As one had feared, the appearance of the unicorn in academic circles was an indication that his best days had gone by. Possibly because the second edition of Thomas Bartholinus's *De Unicornu*, published in 1678, seemed to preclude the possibility of saying anything new on the subject, but more probably because the world had ceased to care about the unicorn, there is no further writing of importance on the topic for a hundred and fifty years. The eighteenth century ignored the unicorn almost entirely feeling, no doubt, that he was a "Gothick" beast, and yet he lingered on at least in the nursery. English children learned their zoology in the eighteenth century from a curious little work by a bookbinder named Thomas Boreman, *A Description of Three Hundred Animals, viz. Beasts, Birds, Fishes, Serpents, and Insects, With a Particular Account of the Whale-Fishery*, a book which appeared in 1730, and had at least seven editions in the next forty years. The author has some difficulty in making up his three hundred, even with the assistance of the Lamia, the Manticora, the Allocamelus, and several varieties of Dragons. In the first edition the unicorn is the eighth beast, and of him we read: "*The Unicorn*, a Beast which though doubted of by many writers yet is by others thus described: He has but one Horn, and that an exceeding rich one, growing out of his Forehead. His Head resembles an Hart's, his Feet an Elephant's, his Tail a Boar's, and the rest of his Body an Horse's. His voice is like the lowing of an Ox. His Horn is as hard as Iron, and as rough as any File, twisted and curled, like a flaming sword; very straight, sharp, and everywhere black, excepting the Point. Great Virtues are attributed to it, in expelling of Poison, and curing of several Diseases. He is not a Beast of prey."

One generalization to be made upon this series of monographs is that the last items in it, the academic dissertations, are greatly inferior in acumen and independence to the first. Even allowing for the fact that the academic dissertation is one of the most degraded and degrading forms of written discourse, they are feebler than one would expect. A main reason for this is that they were not written, like Marini's book, freely and with the whole mind. The Ages of Faith in which one believed what one was told had gone by; the brief period of the Renaissance in which a few minds for a few years followed the light of knowledge and reason was gone too. These young scholars were all Protestants, so that they felt obliged to maintain the authority of the Bible; but they belonged also to the seventeenth century, they lived well on the hither side of the great watershed of time raised by the beginnings of modern science, they were aware of certain recently discovered facts that did not seem to square with God's word concerning unicorns. Facts, moreover, were no longer so malleable as they had seemed to the makers of *Physiologus*; they had taken on a validity of their own quite independent of human desires. The times, in short, were more difficult for a thinking man than those that had gone before. Isidore could accept the unicorn without hesitation because no inconvenient knowledge of facts impeded him; Marini could reject the unicorn almost as freely because he was a physician living in Venice at the end of the Renaissance, and so, for all practical purposes, a pagan; but what could be said on this cardinal topic by young men of the seventeenth century before an audience of Lutherans—by young men seeking academic advancement in a community very literate and very "fundamentalist"? Only such tame and jejune things as Hubrigk and Homilius and Vater did say. The situation was new to them. It is painfully familiar to us.

Nothing if not well read, these young men knew how the unicorn got into their Bibles, and they felt obliged to accept not only the plenary inspiration of the original Biblical text but that of the successive translations as well. If Martin Luther, for example, wrote the word *Einhorn* in translating Deuteronomy xxxiii. 17, that was equivalent to divine assurance that the unicorn exists, and any doubt on that point might open the way to infidelity as the crevice in a Dutch dike may let in all the sea. If the people who believed this had been considerably cruder and more bigoted than they were, and if they had had the power, they might have enacted "unicorn laws" controlling public education like the so-called "monkey laws" of certain American states, for the controversy was in fact a tiny model of the great quarrel over Darwinian theory. However trifling the issue may seem in comparison, a real conflict was involved between Biblical authority and experience or observation, and this is precisely the conflict that has been going on since the appearance of *The Origin of Species* and *The Descent of Man*.

An example of the stress and strain that could be caused by this conflict in earnest minds is found in the writings of Ambroise Paré about the unicorn. When his adversary attempts to overwhelm him with authority and tradition and mere numbers, Paré returns the thrilling reply that he would rather think rightly quite alone than think wrongly with all the rest of the world. One unbroken road runs between that remark and Emerson's *Self-Reliance* two hundred and fifty years in the future, but it was and is a narrow road, full of obstacles, and few there be that find it. Paré's words sound like a final declaration of intellectual independence, but as such they were premature. As a student of nature and as a thinking man Paré had accumulated several reasons for disbelieving in the unicorn. In one place he wrote explicitly: "The so great variety of dissenting opinions easily induceth me to believe that this word Unicorne is not the proper name of any beast in the world, and that it is a thing onely feigned by painters and writers." [31] Somewhat later, however, in the *Discours*, he is obliged to consider the Biblical references to the animal, and these wrench from him the reluctant admission: "*Il faut donc croire qu'il est des Licornes.*" There is a conflict here, and it is being waged inside of one mind. Paré's intellectual condition is that of millions of men who have been drawn one way by know ledge and reason and the whole current of their times and drawn another way by authority, tradition, vested interests, and fear of public opinion. Like them, Paré strove to believe two contradictory things at the same time and not to let the left lobe of his brain know what the right lobe was thinking. We may say that since nothing but unicorns were involved this did not much matter, but Paré and his time were right in feeling that when one begins to doubt the Biblical unicorn there is no convenient place to stop doubting. One might almost say that the cause of Fundamentalism was lost when the unicorn, vouched for by Scripture, was aban doned—for if we cannot trust the translations of the Bible as equally authentic with the original Hebrew, which few Fundamentalists take the trouble to learn, then the door is thrown open to Lower and Higher Criticism, to allegorical interpretations, to scholarship, to facts, to thinking, and, in short, to "infidelity".

The Septuagint's translation of the Hebrew *Re'em* by the word μονόκερως kept the faith in the unicorn alive somewhat longer than it would otherwise have endured, and that bit of translation may have had an effect even upon trade and commerce and medical theory; but the most interesting of its effects is seen in its production of a minor conflict between the old faith in Biblical authority and the new faith in reason and experiment. One cannot say that the problem thus presented was ever definitely solved. Such problems seldom are. They are forgotten.

"To any ordinary reader", says an author of our own time, "the appearance in the sacred writings of creatures which are nowadays known to have had no real existence is bewildering, and probably not a little unsettling. . . . It is much to be regretted that several monstrosities have been permitted to enter the pages of Holy Scripture." [32] This writer gives it as his "earnest advice" that one whose religious faith is endangered by the Biblical unicorn and basilisk and cockatrice should study some good Natural History— "and his difficulties will be swept away". Thus, for example, a close study of whales, with particular attention to the size of the whale's gullet and its powers of digestion, may be recommended for those who are having "difficulties" with the story of Jonah; and others who are shocked by Jacob's trick with the ringstraked cattle—not by the morality of the tale, of course, but by the notions of heredity involved—may be confidently referred to the Mendelian Law. In Paré's time our notions about Nature were tested by the Bible; in our own time it is still asserted that the Bible will stand the test of our notions about Nature. The sooner we admit that it will not stand any such test the sooner we shall be free to put it to higher uses. "When half-gods go, the gods arrive."

Confronted by such a dilemma as that caused by the conflict between authority and experience, the mind seeks avenues of escape, and one such was found for those who wished to believe both the Biblical unicorn and "science": the suggestion was thrown out that although there had once been unicorns they had all been drowned in the Flood. I have been unable to discover who first made this suggestion,[33] but there would be no difficulty in naming many who answered him, for he had the usual fate of the peace-maker and was howled down for his pains. "Is it not wrong", says Hubrigk of Wittenberg, "to think that a single species perished and became extinct when such a great God took in hand the charge of all? Over the whole earth it is a common saying that the unicorn perished and became extinct at the time of the Flood, and that not a single individual of the monocerine species survived. We shall correct this iniquity, and with God's help we shall find a means of putting a stop to this universal blasphemy." [34]

The philosophic answer was made by Julius Caesar Scaliger, a man able to bear down almost any opinion by the sheer weight of his prestige. We have God's word, says he, to prove that the unicorn existed at one time, and God cannot lie. If it existed once, then it exists still, for otherwise a vacuum would have been made in nature, which is absurd, for every one knows that nature abhors a vacuum. Therefore unicorns exist.[35] Later writers extended this argument by quoting the Biblical assertion that Noah took with him into the ark representatives of every existing species, and that God then closed the door so that none could get out.[36] They argued also that God's creation was, to begin with, necessarily perfect—meaning by this, apparently, that it contained every possible species of animal— and that He would not allow it to decline into imperfection.[37] This cheerful faith in the conservation of species was undisturbed by the discovery of the fossil bones of animals such as the mammoth that were being made at the time throughout Europe.

A possible excuse for the original blasphemer was that a beast with a horn ten feet in length, such as that reported by Albertus Magnus, seemed too large to accommodate in the ark. This difficulty did not occur to the makers of the window in the Church of St. Etienne du Mont in Paris, where the animal is shown snugly housed, nor to the monks who painted cross-sections of the ark in miniature, showing unicorns comfortably munching in their stalls. Nevertheless the difficulty was felt, and the question regarding the room available in the ark exercised several acute minds. Sir Walter Raleigh spent some of his leisure in the Tower making a mathematical calculation that set his own doubts at rest; he shows that the ark contained forty-five thousand cubic feet of space, that there were only eighty-nine non-aquatic species to be got into it, that the total number of individual beasts it carried—including many very small ones—was only two hundred and eighty, so that there was room and to spare both for them and for their provender.[38] He would have seen no justification for the statement of the *Talmud* that the *Re'em* had to be towed behind by a rope tied to its horn.

The idea that the unicorn may have perished in the Flood was probably suggested by the discoveries of fossil remains which began to puzzle Europe in the sixteenth century. What the ignorant thought of these we do not hear; some of the learned thought them the bones of Ajax or of Orestes, but the most widely accepted opinion was that they were the skeletons of Hannibal's elephants. The teeth of the mammoth were attributed to Saint Christopher; but Governor Dudley of Massachusetts, when a mastodon's tooth was found near Albany in 1705, could not be so precise as this because the giants of America had no names. He could only assert that this tooth would "agree only to a human body, for whom the

Flood alone could prepare a funeral; and without doubt he would as long as he could keep his head above the clouds, but must at length be confounded with other creatures". The great size and unfamiliar shapes of these remains laid a severe strain upon the faith of some investigators, but the faithful insisted that whatever else they might be they were certainly not the bones of animals that had perished from the earth. "Exactly so many species as were originally created from the protoplasm will endure to the end of the world", says one of these orthodox writers.[39] This was generally considered axiomatic.

In the middle of the sixteenth century Conrad Gesner suggested that the "bones" recently discovered in Germany were the horns of unicorns washed together there during Noah's Flood. This opinion was often ridiculed, but it gained many adherents and had a lasting effect upon *materia medica*. The belief in fossil unicorn's horn, coming at just the time when such corroboration was most needed, helped greatly to sustain the animal's claims to existence, and this belief lasted well into the nineteenth century. In one of the thousands of books written during that century to combat religious doubt I find these words: "At Castle Rising, near to Lynn Regis in Norfolk, where the sea is making rapid encroachments on the land, in sinking for water there were found at a depth of six hundred feet horns perfectly straight, supposed to be those of the unicorn. These were two feet long, an inch in circumference, and hollow." [40]

The modern reader finds it difficult to make out just what the substances studied and sold and prescribed by physicians under the general name of "fossil unicorn" really were. In some instances they were certainly fossil bones, as in the rather famous find at Quedlinberg Cave in 1663, but the "Hercynian fossil unicorn" mentioned by Gesner and scores of others was probably carbonate of lime in stalactite and stalagmite formations. Others were petrified wood. The distinction between animal, vegetable, and mineral subterranean forms was not clearly made by most writers, although a few had known the truth before the sixteenth century.[41] All kinds were called "fossil unicorn", it was assumed that all had the medicinal values ascribed to the alicorn—for no better reason than that they resembled it—and accordingly we find the *lapis ceratites* [42] or horn-stone everywhere advanced to an important place in the pharma-copœia. Boëthius de Boodt, to be sure, ridicules this confusion of substances, saying that he has had more than twenty pieces of the *lapis ceratites* given him as true alicorn and that most of them were merely petrified wood. He knows how such objects are formed as well as we do, and yet at the end of his account of them he says that all kinds of fossil unicorn have medicinal value against poison, fever, and pest.[43] Caspar Bartholinus tells us that he has used the horn-stone successfully in his practice as a sudorific, for bites of snakes and venomous animals, for fevers and plague, and to "comfort the heart" —in short, for all the purposes for which true alicorn was used.[44] Ole Wurm, a scholar of high attainments, could say precisely the same thing thirty years later.[45]

The seventeenth century did not possess three men better fitted to pronounce upon this topic than Boëthius de Boodt, Caspar Bartholinus, and Ole Wurm, and all three asserted that the horn-stone had precisely the same medical properties as alicorn. They asserted this, so far as I can see, for no better reason than that the horn-stone vaguely resembled the alicorn, so that they seem to have thought somewhat in the way of the primitive medicine man collecting his magical simples. But Ole Wurm, at any rate, did not believe in the alleged properties of the alicorn itself, and he had done more than any other man to discredit the whole unicorn legend. In other words, he rejected the substance and accepted the shadow. The deeper one delves into unicorn lore the more clearly one sees that its chief interest lies in the revelations it makes of the human mind.

Citation of the praises of "fossil unicorn" might be extended to great length. Daniel Sennert gave it a qualified commendation.[46] Fallopius and Francis Joëles considered it a sovereign cure for the plague.[47] John Bausch wrote a whole book about its medical properties,[48] and Paul Sachs asserted that "nothing is better than Hercynian unicorn, taken in drink, as a sudorific and for expelling poison, as I know from personal experience".[49] All of these writers, indeed, base their remarks upon actual experience with the drug, and one soon concludes that they cannot all be lying. By a route extending through thousands of years of superstition men had

come upon a substance of real medical value. "Fossil unicorn" is not
by any means the only example of this. The substance sometimes
vaguely called "ossifrage", hollow tubes of carbonate of lime usually
found fractured—it was perhaps identical with *lapis ceratites*—was
considered good for broken bones because it resembled them, and
it really was so because it contained lime.

In adding "fossil unicorn" to her pharmacopœia Europe was
merely trailing once more behind China. For a great length of time
one of the most valued medicines of China has been "dragons'
bones", the fossilized remains of mastodon and elephant, hippo-
therium and rhinoceros.[50] When Dr. Henry Fairfield Osborn was
excavating for fossils in China in 1923 he heard himself and his
company described as "the American men of the dragon bones".[51]
The beliefs underlying this ancient superstition may have been
similar to those we have found supporting the use of the alicorn,
for there seems to have been an opinion that some parts of the
dragon, in spite of its general beneficence, are poisonous.[52]

In the year 1663 there was discovered in a limestone quarry near
Quedlinberg in Germany the "skeleton of a unicorn". We are told
that it was crouched upon its hind-quarters with its head thrown
back, and that it had on its brow a horn as thick as a human shin-
bone and seven feet and a half in length. The workmen broke it up
and extracted it piece-meal, but the head and horn together with
some of the ribs and the spine were handed over to a responsible
person and were later accurately described.[53] Somewhat before the
middle of the eighteenth century a similar skeleton was found in
the so-called Einhornloch at Scharzfeld in the Harz Mountains, and
this one was seen and described by no less a person than the philosopher Leibniz. Admitting that recent treatises and discoveries have
caused him some doubts in the past concerning the real existence
of the unicorn, Leibniz says that the Quedlinberg skeleton and this
of Scharzfeld have converted him entirely. He publishes a drawing,
intended to represent his reconstruction of the animal, which does
not "carry conviction".[54] It is interesting enough, however, to find
one of the most brilliant minds of the eighteenth century convinced
of the unicorn's existence.

CHAPTER VII

RUMOURS

THE first point that research into a doubtful matter should try to determine, as Andrea Bacci wisely observes, is whether the thing in question really exists; and if we were concerned in this book with the unicorn itself rather than with unicorn lore there could be no excuse for having postponed for so long the question concerning the animal's actuality. That question cannot be entirely ignored because the doubts that have been expressed and the affirmations made in reply are themselves an important part of unicorn lore.

To anyone not instructed in comparative anatomy the unicorn is so credible a beast that it is difficult to understand why anyone should ever have doubted him. Compared with him the giraffe is highly improbable, the armadillo and the ant-eater are unbelievable, and the hippopotamus is a nightmare. The shortest excursion into palaeontology brings back a dozen animals that strain our powers of belief far more than he does. What may be called the normality of the unicorn is just as evident when we set him beside the creatures of fancy. Compared with him the griffin is precisely what Sir Thomas Browne calls it, "a mixed and dubious animal".

Yet it is well known that the unicorn has been doubted, and that not by natural infidels like Paré and Marini and Cuvier alone, but by natural believers living far back in the Ages of Faith. Saint Ambrose, for example, disbelieved in the animal for the strange reason that it was not to be found, or so he thought, in nature—"*non inveniatur*".[1]

One might have made sad havoc in the theological creed of Ambrose or any other early Christian by applying that brutal test, and we can imagine the flood of invective he would have poured forth upon the pagan who dared to write *"non inveniatur"* against the Apostolic miracles. However, I wish to devote this chapter to affirmations, recording the testimony of those who have kept the good faith and of the many others who, having fallen away into agnosticism or free-thinking or positive infidelity, have been brought back into the fold. The list of these affirmations will necessarily involve some writers that I have mentioned elsewhere.

One of the earliest of these, aside from the Ctesian and the *Physiologus* traditions, was that of Cosmas Indicopleustes, a Greek of Alexandria who spent his young manhood travelling as a merchant in Ethiopia, the Red Sea, and the Persian Gulf. In his *Christian Topography*, written about A.D. 550, Cosmas writes: "Although I have not seen the unicorn, I have seen four brazen figures of him in the four-towered palace of the King of Ethiopia, and from these figures I have been able to draw a picture of him as you see. People say that he is a terrible beast and quite invincible, and that all his strength lies in his horn. When he finds himself pursued by many hunters and about to be taken he springs to the top of some precipice and throws himself over it, and in the descent he turns a somersault so that the horn sustains all the shock of the fall and he escapes unhurt." [2]

Cosmas's ingenuous admission that he has not seen the living animal inclines one to believe that he did see the brazen images. These must have been figures in the round rather than bas-reliefs, so that their single horns could not well have been due to the well-known convention of ancient art which often led to the representation of one horn where two were to be understood; we may be fairly confident, therefore, that there existed in Ethiopia during the sixth century of our era an active belief in a one-horned animal. The drawing of this animal which accompanies the text in the Vatican manuscript of Cosmas[3] is more interesting than the description. It shows a beast of the antelope kind, apparently not large, very spirited in bearing, with a horn almost as tall as itself jutting per-

XIX. A GAME OF DRAUGHTS

XX. THE LUNAR UNICORN

pendicularly from between its brows. The moment one sees this drawing the unicorn of *Physiologus* comes to mind. One remembers that the feat of absorbing the shock of a fall by an elastic or possibly spring-like horn has been attributed also to the ibex, to the African oryx, and to the Rocky Mountain goat. Finally, it is not to be ignored that Cosmas found these brazen unicorns in the palace of a king.

In the year 1206, we are told, the conqueror Genghis Khan set out with a great host to invade India. His army had marched for many days and had climbed through many mountain passes, but just when he reached the crest of the divide and looked down over the country he intended to subjugate there came running toward him a beast with a single horn which bent the knee three times before him in token of reverence. And then, while all the host stood wondering, the Conqueror paused in his march and pondered. At last he said, as we are told in the vivid narrative of Ssanang Ssetsen: "This middle kingdom of India before us is the place, men say, in which the sublime Buddha and the Bodhisatwas and many powerful princes of old time were born. What may it mean that this speechless wild animal bows before me like a man? Is it that the spirit of my father would send me a warning out of heaven?" With these words he turned his army about and marched back again into his own land. India had been saved by a unicorn.[4]

In several versions of the Alexander Romance we read that Alexander's host, while travelling near the Red Sea, met a number of beasts with single horns, sharp as swords, on their foreheads. They were very strong and fierce and charged the host again and again, but they were killed by arrows. The description is not clear enough to show that they were the unicorns we know.[5]

The Friar Felix Fabri, who went on pilgrimage to the Holy Land in 1483, says that on the twentieth of September in that year he and his company saw standing on a hill near Mount Sinai a large animal gazing toward them. (Plate XIII.) At first they took it for a camel, but their guide told them that it was a unicorn and pointed out the great single horn on its brow, so that they examined it as closely as they could and were sorry that it was too far away to be seen quite clearly. They lingered there a long while watching the beast, which seemed to enjoy the sight of them as much as they did the sight of it, for it did not leave until they did. This beast, the friar adds, is remarkable in many ways: it is exceedingly wild and destroys everything that comes in its way; it sharpens its horn on stones; the horn has a brilliant hue and is set in gold and silver; the animal can be captured only by using a virgin as a decoy.[6]

The most important of all descriptions of the unicorn given by the few who claim to have seen the animal is that of Lewis Vartoman (Ludovico Barthema), of Bologna, who travelled in 1503 through the countries of the Near East. Vartoman's *Itinerario* is a book of sustained interest and some historical value, although the modern reader is unlikely to share Scaliger's opinion that its author was a man worthy of trust.[7] At the city of Zeila in Ethiopia he saw certain cattle with single horns about a palm and a half in length rising from their brows and bending backward,[8] but much more important than these were the unicorns in a park adjoining the temple at Mecca.[9] There were two of these animals, "shewed to the people for a miracle, and not without reason for the seldomenesse and strange nature. The one of them, which is much hygher than the other, yet not much unlyke to a coolte of thyrtye moneths of age, in the forehead groweth only one horne, in maner ryght foorth, of the length of three cubites. The other is much younger, of the age of one yeere, and lyke a young Coolte: the horne of this is of the length of foure handfuls. This beast is of the coloure of a horse of weesel coloure, and hath the head lyke an hart, but no long necke, a thynne mane hangynge only on the one syde. Theyr legges are thyn and slender, lyke a fawne or hynde. The hoofes of the fore feete are divided in two, much lyke the feet of a Goat. The outwarde part of the hynder feete is very full of heare. This beast doubtlesse seemeth wylde and fierce, yet tempereth that fiercenesse with a certain comelinesse. These Unicornes one gave to the Soltan of Mecha as a most precious and rare gyfte. They were sent hym out of Ethiope by a kyng of that Countrey, who desired by that present to gratifie the Soltan of Mecha." [10]

This passage was almost as influential among modern writers as the remarks of Aelian about the unicorn had been during the Middle

Ages. One is to observe that the hoofs of Vartoman's unicorns are divided on the fore feet and, apparently, solid behind—a peculiar characteristic faithfully observed by the artist who drew the unicorn picture for Conrad Gesner's *Historia Animalium* and by all who imitated him. We should observe also that these unicorns came from Ethiopia and that they were sent as a present from one sovereign to another.

I have placed Vartoman, as others do, among those who claim to have seen the unicorn, but although he does say that he saw the one-horned cattle of Zeila, he makes no such assertion about the two animals at Mecca and it has been inferred that he saw these only from the extreme minuteness of his description. Edward Webbe, an Elizabethan traveller whom no one has ever called trustworthy, does not wish to leave his readers in any doubt on this point. "I have seene," says he, "in a place like a Park adjoyning unto prester Iohn's Court, three score and seven-teene unicornes and eliphants all alive at one time, and they were so tame that I have played with them as one would play with young Lambes." [11]

Vincent Le Blanc, who set out on his travels through the Orient in 1567, was still more fortunate, for he declares: "I have seen a unicorn in the seraglio of the Sultan, others in India, and still others at the Escurial. That there are some persons who doubt whether this animal is to be found anywhere in the world I am well aware, but in addition to my own observation there are several serious writers who bear witness to its existence—Vartoman among others, who says that he saw some at the same place in Mecca." [12] In the seraglio of the King of Pegu he saw a unicorn with a tongue "very long and like a file". (This probably means that he had read Marco Polo on the rhinoceros.) He was told that these beasts were tormented cruelly by huge serpents which were very fond of their blood because it had a delicious odour, and that when one of them was wounded in the chase the hunters always sent as much of its blood as they could collect to the king, enclosed in a little box. No one had ever seen the unicorn dip its horn in the water when drinking. A Brahmin told Le Blanc that he had been present at the capture of a very old unicorn which defended itself so fiercely that it broke off

its horn on the branch of a tree and which, when it had been taken
and bound, was led to the palace of the king; but this animal had
been so severely beaten by the hunters for having wounded the
king's nephew that it died in a few days. The queens of India,
Le Blanc reports, wear bracelets of unicorn bone, and the King of
Casubi showed him a horn much lighter in hue than those he had
seen elsewhere in the Orient.[13] His remarks are a strange compound
of things seen and heard and read thrown together without any
attempt at criticism or sorting.

Another Oriental traveller, Dr. Leonard Rauchwolf, who saw
the countries visited by Le Blanc a few years after him was told by
a Persian "that the Sophi King of Persia had several Unicorns at
Samarcand . . . and also in two islands . . . which lay from
Samarcand nine Days Journey, some Griffins which were sent him
out of Africa from Prester John." [14]

In the same year in which Vincent Le Blanc began his travels
there was published a famous book on the drugs and spices of India
by Garcias ab Horto. Here we find a description of an amphibian
unicorn which the author says he has had from men worthy of belief.
They have told him that between the Cape of Good Hope and the
promontory commonly called Currentes (Cape Corrientes, opposite
the southern end of Madagascar) there are to be seen certain animals
that live on the land yet take pleasure also in the sea. Although they
are certainly not sea-horses, they have equine heads and manes.
This beast has a horn two palms in length, and the horn is movable
so that it can be turned to right or left and raised or lowered at will.
The animal fights fiercely with the elephant and its horn is considered good against poison.[15] A similar animal, called the campchurch, was reported eight years later by André Thevet. This
creature, he said, was to be found near the Strait of Malacca, large as
a stag and bearing on its brow a horn three feet and a half in length
and mobile like the crest of the Indian cock. The horn was efficacious
against poison. The campchurch had two web feet like those of a
duck which it used in swimming both in fresh and salt water, but
its forefeet were like those of the stag. (See the second figure in
Plate XIV.) It lived on fish.[16] This André Thevet, one must

remember, was a man "worthy of trust." He believed what was told him by a Turkish ambassador about the unicorns of Ethiopia and he thought also that the reindeer had only one horn. Caspar Bartholinus, who had seen reindeer, ridiculed this assertion, but John Johnston, who tried to please everyone in his *Historia Naturalis*, reconciled Bartholinus and Thevet by showing a picture of the reindeer with the two horns twisted together into one.

We have seen that Ambroise Paré disbelieved in the unicorn as firmly as his faith in the Bible would allow, but his fairness in controversy was such that he quoted against himself the testimony of an acquaintance of his, a physician named Louys Paradis, who said that he had actually seen the animal. This unicorn had been sent to Alexandria, where Paradis encountered it, as a gift to the Great Mogul from Prester John. It was about as large as a boar-hound, though not so slender in body, had a glossy coat like that of the beaver in colour, a slender neck, small ears, and one horn between the ears, very smooth, dark, and only one foot long. The head was short and thin, the muzzle round like a calf's, the eyes were very large and fierce in aspect, the legs lean, the hooves divided like a deer's. The animal was of one colour all over excepting one forefoot, which was yellow. It ate lentils and pease but lived chiefly on sugar-cane. Paradis was told by the men who brought it from Prester John that there were many others of the same kind in their country, but that they were so wild that they were hard to capture and that the people feared them more than any other beasts.[17] This account is more impressive in its minuteness and precision even than that of Vartoman, and one is surprised that Paré, who seems to have thought his informant trustworthy, could maintain his disbelief in the face of it.

In reading these accounts one cannot fail to be impressed by the number of unicorns coming from Prester John, who seems to have kept the neighbouring potentates regularly supplied with them. Vartoman's two unicorns came from the Court of Prester John, the numerous specimens seen by Edward Webbe were in a Park adjoining that monarch's palace, the unicorns reported by Leonard Rauchwolf as belonging to the Sophy came from there and so did the single animal seen at Alexandria by Louys Paradis. Let us turn directly to the source of supply and see what records can be found of unicorns in Ethiopia itself.

Most of these records were written by Portuguese and Spanish missionaries to Abyssinia, and they cover a period of about one hundred years. John Bermudez, who went on an embassy to Prester John in 1535, is the earliest member of the group. He says that in the province of Abyssinia, known in his time as Damute, there is found in the mountain districts a very fierce and wild unicorn shaped like a horse and as large as an ass.[18] Marmol Caravaial (often called Marmolius), who wrote forty years later, is much more specific: "Among the Mountains of the Moon in High Ethiopia", he says, "there is found a beast called the unicorn which is as large as a colt of two years and of the same general shape as one. Its colour is ashen and it has a mane and a large beard like that of a he-goat; on its brow it has a smooth white horn of the colour of ivory two cubits long and adorned with handsome grooves that run from base to point. This horn is used against poison, and people say that the other animals wait until this one comes and dips its horn in the water before they will drink. It is such a clever beast and so swift that there is no way of killing it, but it sheds its horns like the stag and the hunters find these in the wilderness." [19]

Fray Luis de Urreta, whose book on Ethiopia has already proved useful, also tells us that unicorns are found among the Mountains of the Moon. "The reason why so few men have ever seen them", he says, "is that these mountains are almost inaccessible. They are quite different from the pictures of them to be seen in Europe, for they are only slightly smaller than elephants and their feet are like those of the elephant. Their general characteristics remind one of swine, for they love to wallow in the mire. On the brow there is one horn, heavy and large but tapering to a point and black in hue. The animal's tongue is rough with spines that tear whatever it licks like a teasel—an excellent emblem of flatterers! . . . It is true that Saint Thomas and Saint Gregory and other holy men consider this unicorn identical with the Rhinoceros, but we must remember that they were chiefly concerned with moral matters and the welfare of the soul and that it was not their business to distinguish the species of animals." [20]

The most interesting of these travellers in Ethiopia was the Jesuit missionary Jeronimo Lobo (1593–1678). After sailing round the Cape in 1622 and spending some time in the Portuguese colonies of India he went to Abyssinia, the Negus Segued having recently been converted by the Jesuit Pedro Paez. There he spent several years in the district of Damute, where both he and John Bermudez place the unicorn, but in 1632 the Negus fell into heresy and banished all the Jesuit fathers. Lobo was captured by the Turks and sent to Goa to secure ransom money, after which he tried to get the Portuguese viceroy to declare war on Segued with the object of bringing him back to orthodoxy by force of arms. Failing at Goa, Lobo sailed for home, was wrecked and captured by pirates on the way, and laid the grievances of the Christian faith—mingled, perhaps, with others of a more private sort—before the Courts of Lisbon, Madrid, and Rome without avail. Disgusted by this irreligious pacifism, he returned to India and rose to high office in his Order. His last days were spent in Portugal.

Lobo left two accounts of Abyssinia, one of which was translated into French[21] from the unpublished manuscript and out of the French into English by Samuel Johnson in his Grub Street years. This familiar book contains the following passage: "In the Province of Agaus has been seen the Unicorn, that Beast so much talk'd of and so little known; the prodigious Swiftness with which this Creature runs from one Wood into another has given me no Opportunity of examining it particularly, yet I have had so near a sight of it as to be able to give some Description of it. The Shape is the same as that of a beautiful Horse, exact and nicely proportion'd, of a Bay Colour, with a black Tail, which in some Provinces is long, in others very short; some have long Manes hanging to the Ground. They are so Timerous that they never Feed but surrounded with other Beasts that defend them." [22]

It is pleasant to have this passage in Johnson's phraseology, and one would like to know what the man who kept an open mind about the Cock Lane Ghost thought concerning the unicorn. His *Dictionary*,

I think, forbids us to include him among the believers, but in his Preface to the Lobo translation he says that whatever the Jesuit relates, "whether true or not, is at least probable; and he who tells nothing exceeding the bounds of probability has a right to demand that they should believe him who cannot contradict him. He appears to have described things as he saw them, to have copied Nature from the Life, and to have consulted his Senses, not his Imagination."

One is glad to recall Johnson's measured assertion while considering Father Lobo's second passage on this topic, which appears in *A Short Relation of the River Nile*, edited, or perhaps one may say written, in 1669 by Sir Peter Wyche.[23] The contents of this book are: "A Short Relation of the River Nile; The True Cause of the River Nile Overflowing; Of the Famous Unicorn:—where He is Bred and how Shaped; The Reason why the Abyssine Emperor is Called Prester John of the Indies; A Short Tract of the Red Sea; A Discourse of Palm-Trees." All of this is obviously delectable matter, but the best chapter is that concerning "The *Unicorn*, the most celebrated among Beasts, as among Birds are the Phoenix, the Pelican, and the Bird of Paradise". This animal is "of the more credit because mentioned in holy Scriptures, compared to many things, even to God made man. None of the Authors who speak of the Unicorn discourse of his birth or Country, satisfied with the deserved eulogiums by which he is celebrated. That secret was reserved for those who travelled and surveyed many countries. . . . The country of the Unicorn (an African creature, only known there) is the Province of Agaos in the kingdom of Damotes; that it may wander into places more remote is not improbable. . . . A Father, my companion, who spent some time in this province, upon notice that this so famous animal was there, used all diligence to procure one. The natives brought him a very young colt, so tender as in a few days it died. A Portuguese Captain, a person of years and credit, told me that returning once from the army with twenty other Portuguese soldiers in company they one morning rested in a little valley encompassed with thick woods, designing to breakfast while their horses grazed on the good grass. Scarce were they sat down when from the thickest part of the wood lightly sprang a perfect horse of the same colour, hair, and shape before described. His career was so brisk and wanton that he took no notice of those new inmates till engaged among them; then, as frightened at what he had seen, suddenly started back again, yet left the spectators sufficient time to see and observe at their pleasure. The particular survey of these parts seized them with delight and admiration. One of his singularities was a beautiful strait horn on his forehead. He appeared to run about with his eyes full of fear. Our horses seemed to allow him for one of the same brood, curvetted and made towards him. The soldiers, observing him in less than musket shot, not able to shoot, their muskets being unfixt, endeavoured to encompass him, out of an assurance that that was the famous unicorn; but he prevented them, for, perceiving them, with the same violent career he recovered the wood, leaving the Portuguese satisfied in the truth of such an animal. My knowledge of this captain makes the truth with me undoubted. In another place of the same province (the most remote, craggy, and mountainous part, called Manina) the same beast hath been often seen grazing amongst others of different kinds. . . . To this place of banishment a tyrannical Emperor name Adamas Segued sent without any cause divers Portuguese, who from the top of these mountains saw the unicornes grazing in the plains below, the distance not greater than allowed them so distinct an observation as they knew him, like a beautiful Gennet, with a fair horn in his forehead."

More scholarly than any of these writings is the *New History of Ethiopia* by Job Ludolphus, which appeared in English in 1682. Here one finds a description of a beast "both Strong and Fierce, call'd *Arweharis* . . . which signifies one Horn. This beast resembles a goat, but very swift of foot. Whether it be the Monoceros of the Ancients I leave to the scrutinie of others. . . . However, the Portugals tell us that the report was not altogether vain, for one of them was seen by John Gabriel in the province of the Agawi in the kingdom of Damota. . . . The description of the Portugueses seems most agreeable to Truth." [24]

Robert Frampton, later Bishop of Gloucester, spent several years of his early life during the middle of the seventeenth century in the Orient, and while there he once met "a great officer of that country they call Ethiopia". This officer told him that "the most remarkable beast they had there was the Unicorn, which, though very wild and rarely taken, he had often seen, and described just as we paint him. And the man being utterly unacquainted with the European fancy made it, if not probable, at least possible that such a beast there might be, though in that little frequented country, not well known by us, it might escape the notice of those few that had been there." [25]

In October 1652 there arrived in Copenhagen an "African legate" by the name of Franciscus Marchio de Magellanes. He was much impressed by the alicorn in the royal museum, especially because it was so different from the horn of the unicorn that was familiar to him in his own land. This horn, he said, came from the Tirè Bina, a very fleet and wild beast about the size and shape of a small horse, which lived in the African desert. Shaggy about the head and legs and feet, the animal had a short mane and a tail like that of a horse, but not very full. Its hide, smooth and with very short hairs, was ashen in hue above, with a black line running along its back, and white from the lower jaw to the abdomen. There was a small bundle of hairs on the brow from the midst of which there sprang a single horn to which the hairs adhered. This horn, barely three spans in length, had not the spiral striae seen in European alicorns, but small protuberances running in a straight line from the base to the point. It was of a golden hue and hollow at the root. On the point of this horn there was another bundle of hairs, as large as a man's fist and reddish. The Africans made much of this horn, using it both internally and externally against poison. The legate told his friends in Copenhagen that the Tirè Bina always dipped the horn in the water before he drank of it, and that as soon as he did this the water was greatly agitated. The inhabitants were accustomed to dip the horn in their drinking-water in the belief that this made it more healthful. They also used the animal's flesh and the burned hairs of its tail as drugs.[26]

These reports of the Ethiopian and African unicorn, buried as most of them were in books that were seldom read, made little impression in northern Europe. In 1625 Purchas felt obliged to say: "As for the Unicorne, none hath beene seene these hundred yeares last past, by testimony of any probable Author (for Webb, which said he saw them in Prester John's Court, is a mere fabler.)" [27] James Primerose, thirteen years later, thought that although the animal was certainly not fictitious it must be excessively rare.[28] Aldrovandus said in 1639 that in spite of the fact that almost the whole surface of the globe had been explored hardly any man dared to affirm that he had seen the unicorn. John Ogilby, the bookseller-poet, by no means so ridiculous a person as Dryden and Pope managed to make him appear, shows in his *Africa* that his faith is slight.[29] After the middle of the seventeenth century, however, there was a decided tendency, somewhat difficult to explain, toward belief. This is clearly seen in Antony Deussing's monograph on the unicorn [30] and in all the other academic dissertations; but in these the "will to believe" is obviously actuated by fear of the effect that doubt of the unicorn would have upon faith in the Bible.

The eighteenth century, as I have said, was not a good time for unicorns. The general attitude of the period is well expressed in Benjamin Martin's once famous *Philosophical Grammar*: "The Scripture makes mention of the Dragon and the Unicorn, and most Naturalists have affirmed that there have been such creatures and have given Descriptions of them; but the Sight of these Creatures, or credible Relations of them having been so very rare, has occasioned many to believe there never were any such Animals in Nature; at least it has made the History of them very doubtful." [31]

John Bell of Antermony heard a "credible relation" in Tartary from a native hunter which is worth recording. This hunter said that "in the year 1713, being out a-hunting, he discovered the track of a stag, which he pursued. At overtaking the animal he was somewhat startled on observing it had only one horn, stuck in the middle of its forehead. Being near the village, he drove it home and showed it, to the great admiration of the spectators. He afterwards killed it and eat the flesh, and sold the horn to a comb-maker. I inquired carefully about the shape and size of this unicorn and was told it exactly resembled a stag. The horn was of a brownish colour, about one *archeen* or 28 inches long, and twisted from the root till within a finger's length of the top, where it was divided like a fork into two points very sharp." [32]

Faith in the unicorn was at a low ebb in Europe when Anders Sparrmann published in 1783 his account of travels in South Africa.[33] Without asserting that he had seen the animal, Sparrmann gave the impression that the unicorn was not uncommon near the Cape of Good Hope, basing his own belief upon the constant reports of natives and the observation of single horns that were shown to him. Half a dozen other travellers in South Africa during the next half-century reached the same conclusion. Thus Baron von Wurmb writes from the Cape in 1791 that he expects soon to see a unicorn, "which has just been discovered in the interior of Africa. A Boer saw a beast shaped like a horse and with one horn on its brow, ash-gray and with divided hoofs—his observation went no farther. A Hottentot has confirmed this report, and the people in these parts quite generally believe in the existence of the unicorn. . . . The future will decide. Various respectable natives have given their servants orders to bring in one of these beasts alive if possible, or else to shoot one, so that we shall soon see the question settled." [34] Cornelius de Jong, writing two years later from the same region, traces the quest for a South African unicorn to an elderly Dutchman of education and intelligence by the name of Cloete, who was offering three thousand florins to anyone who would bring him a live specimen. The offer was made hopefully, for Cloete and de Jong agreed that the evidence for the presence of the unicorn in the neighbourhood was convincing. Hottentots who could not possibly have heard the European legends about the animal described it exactly and even said that they had drawings of it in their caves and houses.[35]

One of these drawings was seen and copied, a few years later, by the English traveller, Sir John Barrow, who was completely converted by it to a belief in the unicorn.[36] His copy shows the head and neck of a creature with the general appearance of an antelope and with a single horn like that of the gemsbok rising, apparently, from the right side of the brow. This drawing was one of several thousands discovered by Sir John Barrow, all of them as realistic, he says, as the skill of the artists would permit. He makes it clear that in this instance there could be no possible confusion with the rhinoceros, which is also depicted in the South African caves, and he argues earnestly that the long tradition of the unicorn, taken together with what he has heard from the natives of Africa and with this drawing, should be sufficient to compel belief.

A man still better equipped than Barrow to judge this matter, Sir Francis Galton, was almost equally impressed by the evidence. "The Bushmen", says he, "without any leading question or previous talk upon the subject, mentioned the unicorn. I cross-questioned them thoroughly, but they persisted in describing a one-horned animal, something like a gemsbok in shape and size, whose one horn was in the middle of its forehead and pointed forwards. . . . It will be strange indeed if, after all, the creature has a real existence. There are recent travellers in the north of tropical Africa who have heard of it there, and believe in it, and there is surely plenty of room to find something new in the vast belt of *terra incognita* that lies in this continent." [37]

Among the rather numerous believers in an African unicorn the names of David Livingstone and Dr. Andrew Smith should not be forgotten. The *Athenæum* for December 22, 1860, reviewing *The Romance of Natural History*, by the father of Edmund Gosse, says that "the unicorn cannot be pronounced a fable, although our national representation of it may prove to be fanciful", expressing belief in a South African species "which appears to occupy an intermediate rank between the massive rhinoceros and the lighter form of the horse". Dr. William Balfour Baikie, the scientist and African traveller, writes in the same journal for August 16, 1862: "The constant belief of the natives of all the countries which I have hitherto visited have partly shaken my scepticism, and at present I simply hold that the non-existence of the unicorn is not proven. A skull of this animal is said to be preserved in the country of Bonú, through which I hope to pass in a few weeks, when I shall make every possible inquiry. Two among my informants have repeatedly declared that they have seen the bones of this animal, and each made a particular mention of the long, straight, or nearly straight, horn."

These persistent rumours of unicorns in South Africa seem to have revived the belief, which had died down since the seventeenth century, that the animal was to be found in the northern parts of the continent. Dr. Eduard Rüppell was told by the natives of Kordofan, without any question or suggestion from him, that there was in their country a beast about as large as a horse and of the same shape, with reddish smooth hide, divided hoofs, and one long slender straight horn on its brow.[38] Baron von Müller, travelling in the same district in 1848, was told by a native who had provided him with specimens of many other animals, about a beast called *a'nasa* which he described as resembling a donkey in shape and size but with a boar's tail and a single movable horn.[39] During his travels in Abyssinia A. von Katte heard repeatedly from soldiers drawn from all parts of the country "that the unicorn really exists in the wild valleys of the mountains. It is true that their reports are not entirely consistent, but neither are they contradictory. Those who assert that they have seen the animal give the same description of it that Pliny left us. They say, that is, that it has the hoofs of a horse and the same shape as a horse, that it is grey in colour and has a strong horn in the middle of its brow. Its size is that of a well-grown ass. They say also that it is very shy and therefore hard to approach. These people find great likeness between it and the unicorn shown on the English arms, but when I showed them a picture of the rhinoceros they said at once: 'That is not it; that is another animal.' . . . I am therefore strongly inclined to believe that the unicorn is really to be found in the high, inaccessible mountains of this country."[40]

The vast size and the mystery of the Dark Continent affected the imaginations of thoughtful and trained observers in the nineteenth century somewhat as America had affected the mind of Europe three hundred years before. "In a land like inner Africa", wrote Joseph Russegger, "in which Nature puts forth the strangest forms of life, we may expect that the larger and unknown quadrupeds which we have thought long since extinct will be discovered. Is it not possible that even the unicorn may be found there? Arabs, Nubians, and Negroes told me often and much about this animal, which resembled, according to their descriptions, either an antelope or a wild ass. Their reports were too contradictory and contained too much nonsense for me to reproduce them, but everywhere one hears

the refrain that the animal still exists. . . . To regard the unicorn
as wholly fabulous and a product of fancy is an absurd and arbitrary
position, and we do well to remember that if the elephant and
giraffe and camel should once die out they too, on account of their
strange forms, would be thought fabulous." [41]

The most interesting account of an African unicorn is that com-
municated to the *Journal Asiatique* by F. Fresnel in a letter written
in April 1843 and published in March of the following year.[42]
Fresnel was a consular agent of France at Djeddah, and his remarks
are based, not upon personal observation, but upon the testimony of
several Arabs in whose honesty and intelligence he firmly believed.
These men had often killed the animal in Dar-Bargou, north-west
of Darfour, a district still almost unknown and at the time when the
letter was written quite unexplored.

Fresnel's description is very minute. He says that the unicorn is
a pachyderm, but insists that it is not the rhinoceros. In appearance
somewhat like a wild bull, it has the legs and feet of an elephant,
a round and almost hairless body, a short tail, and a single horn one
cubit long and movable at the animal's will. This horn springs from
between the eyes and not from the end of the nose like that of the
rhinoceros. For two-thirds of its length it is of an ashen grey-colour,
like the rest of the animal, but the upper third is a vivid scarlet.
(One thinks of the splash of scarlet on the end of the horn described
by Ctesias, and of the words of Solinus, "*de splendore mirifico*.") When
the unicorn is not disturbed he swings this horn to right and left as
he walks, but he can fix it like a bayonet ready for action at a moment's
notice. Of vast strength and extremely fierce, he always charges at
the first sight of a man, and he charges with intent to kill. He is never
taken alive. Fresnel gives a minute account of the method of hunting
the beast which one can hardly read without recalling the lion-
capture story. One man on foot goes up to the unicorn's lair while
his fellows, on horseback and armed with lances, wait at a distance
near a tree. As soon as the animal sees the man he plunges toward
him, and the man turns and makes for the tree. The mounted hunters
lance the beast from behind while he is running, and while he turns
to face one after the other, until he drops from exhaustion.

Fresnel has perfect confidence in his sources of information. "There is nothing more animated and honest", says he, "than the descriptions given by a Bedouin, just as there is nothing more false and obviously absurd than those given by the inhabitants of eastern cities or by travellers who are only merchants." His informants had nothing to sell, they said nothing about the horn's medicinal value, they had hunted this beast and killed it, they knew the rhinoceros well and said that this unicorn was quite different. Fresnel was therefore thoroughly convinced that the *abou-karn* of eastern French Soudan was the same creature as the Hebrew *Re'em* and the monoceros of Ctesias and the unicorn of Pliny. One is reminded of Samuel Johnson's words with regard to Father Lobo: "He who tells nothing exceeding the bounds of probability has a right to demand that they should believe him who cannot contradict him."

In following the trail of the African unicorn I have neglected chronology and ignored important developments in other parts of the world. The nineteenth century studied the unicorn chiefly "in the field", yet there were a few scholars of the old school who still preferred the methods of the library. E. A. W. Zimmermann, after reviewing all the evidence available in 1780 to a patient German polymath, concluded that the unicorn legend must be founded upon zoological fact.[43] The French geographer Malte-Brun was deeply impressed by the rumours of unicorns emanating in his time from almost the whole continent of Africa, and he decided that although the existence of the animal had not been proved it was certainly not impossible. He said, furthermore—and I think he was the first to express this modern view—that whether unicorns were to be found in Nature or not, the legend concerning them was interesting and worthy of study for its own sake.[44] H. F. Link, a scholar of extraordinary caution and thoughtfulness, reached the conclusion, after many pages of argument, that the unicorn must be accepted as an actual though perhaps an extinct and certainly a very rare animal.[45]

Among these productions of the library one of the most interesting

is the *Notice en réfutation de la non-existence de la licorne*, by J. F. Laterrade, a professional scientist of literary talent.[46] This monograph is
well written and ingenious though not convincing. The author does
not assert that unicorns exist but contents himself with arguing that
they are not only possible but even probable. In the first place, he
says, the description of the animal is in no way fabulous and it
contains nothing contrary to Nature; secondly, many authors of
repute have written about it in full belief; thirdly, no proof has
been found that it does not exist. One does not feel that French
acumen is well represented in this argument, for each of Laterrade's
three points lies open to attack. Any comparative anatomist would
deny his first assertion, which no contemporary and countryman of
Cuvier should have allowed himself to make. The historian could
name a hundred exploded fallacies that have been supported by
authors of repute. As for the third point, absence of disproof is no
great assistance toward belief. One might write the word "witches"
in place of Laterrade's "unicorns" and get the same results.

In the year after that in which Laterrade's monograph appeared
Cuvier himself attempted to give the unicorn the *coup de grâce*.[47]
He was probably the first of all the writers on our topic who had
scientific knowledge adequate to the problems involved, and, in
addition, a clear mind of the highest order. Cuvier is strongly
inclined to think the unicorn a fairy tale, although he does not
positively affirm this. He believes that it was compounded out of
the oryx and the rhinoceros. Speaking as a scientist, he says that any
horn growing single would be perfectly symmetrical, and that no
such horn has ever been found. A cloven-hoofed ruminant with a
single horn, moreover, would be impossible, in his opinion, because
its frontal bone would be divided and no horn could grow above
the division.[48]

And yet the unicorn legend continued to show surprising vitality,
quite as many reports and rumours concerning the animal coming
from the Orient as from Africa. Captain Samuel Turner, writing in
the first year of the nineteenth century, records an interesting
conversation with the Rajah of Bootan. "He had a very curious
creature, he told me, then in his possession; a sort of horse, with

a horn growing from the middle of his forehead. He had once another of the same species, but it died. I could not discover from whence it came, or obtain any other explanation than *burra dure!* a great way off! I expressed a very earnest desire to see a creature so curious and uncommon, and told him that we had representations of an animal called an unicorn, to which his description answered; but it was generally considered as fabulous. He again assured me of the truth of what he told me, and promised I should see it. It was some distance from Tassisudon, and his people paid it religious respect; but I never had a sight of it." [49] This is an impressive story, but the force of it is somewhat weakened by the paragraph just preceding, in which the Rajah tells his English visitor about a race of men with short, straight tails, so inconvenient that they were obliged to dig small holes for them before they could sit down.

The *Quarterly Magazine* for December, 1820, quotes a letter from a Major Latter, stationed in the hill country east of Nepal, asserting that the unicorn had been discovered at last in Tibet. The Major writes: "In a Thibetan manuscript which I procured the other day from the hills, the unicorn is classed under the head of those animals whose hoofs are divided; it is called the one-horned *tso'po*. Upon inquiring what kind of animal it was, to our astonishment the person who brought me the manuscript described exactly the unicorn of the ancients, saying that it was a native of the interior of Thibet, fierce, and extremely wild, seldom ever caught alive, but frequently shot, and that the flesh was used for food. The person who gave me this account has repeatedly seen these animals and eaten flesh of them. They go together in herds, like our wild buffaloes, and are very frequently met with on the borders of the great desert about a month's journey from Lassa, in that part of the country inhabited by the wandering Tartars." The *Asiatic Journal*, after quoting this letter in December of the following year, remarks: "Our readers are aware that steps have been taken to obtain a complete specimen of the animal supposed to be the unicorn, which is said to exist in considerable numbers in Thibet." Seven years later the same periodical reported that Major Latter was still hunting for the unicorn but had nearly given up hope.

The most famous of earlier travellers in Tibet seems never to have had any doubts. "The unicorn", says Huc, "which has long been regarded as a fabulous creature, really exists in Thibet. You find it frequently represented in the sculptures and paintings of the Buddhist temples. Even in China you often see it in the landscapes that ornament the inns of the northern provinces. The inhabitants of Adtza spoke of it without attaching to it any greater importance than to the other species of antelopes which abound in their mountains. We have not been fortunate enough, however, to see the unicorn during our travels in Upper Asia." [50]

All this testimony regarding the unicorns of Tibet is illumined by a passage in Colonel Prejevalsky's *Mongolia*, which throws a beam of light, also, along the whole course of the unicorn legend as we have traced it from the *Indica* of Ctesias. This passage is concerned with a small, fleet, and very quarrelsome Tibetan antelope known to the Mongols as the *orongo* and to science as *Antholops Hodgsoni*. [51] It has slightly recurving black horns, twenty-three inches long, with rings—perhaps the ἑλιγμούς of Aelian—on the anterior surfaces. Prejevalsky says that "the orongo is held sacred by Mongols and Tangutans, and lamas will not touch the meat. The blood is said to possess medicinal virtues, and the horns are used in charlatanism: Mongols tell fortunes and predict future events by the rings on these, and they also serve to mark out the burial places, or more commonly the circles within which the bodies of deceased lamas are exposed: these horns are carried away in large numbers by pilgrims returning from Thibet and are sold at high prices. Mongols tell you that a whip-handle made from one will prevent a rider's steed from tiring. Another prevalent superstition is that the orongo has only one horn growing vertically from the centre of the head. In Kan-su and Koko-nor we were told that unicorns were rare, one or two in a thousand; but the Mongols in Tsaidam, who are perfectly well acquainted with the orongo, deny entirely the existence there of a one-horned antelope, though admitting that it might be found in South-western Thibet. Had we gone farther we should probably have heard that it was only to be found in India, and so on till we arrived at the one-horned rhinoceros." [52]

In the middle of the nineteenth century it was still possible for intelligent people to believe in the unicorn's existence; indeed, if the written records are a trustworthy indication, there seems to have been almost as much belief in the animal at that time as there had been two hundred years earlier, and decidedly more than in the eighteenth century. An amusing evidence of the public interest in the problem is found in a provincial English newspaper: "An Italian gentleman, named Barthema [Lewis Vartoman] said to be entitled to implicit credit, who has just returned from Africa, states that he saw two unicorns at Mecca which had been sent as a present from the King of Ethiopia to the Sultan." [53] This report was of course exactly true, and the only fault that could be found with it was that the news it contained was somewhat over three hundred years old. One of the foremost French archaeologists of the century went out of his way to declare his faith. "In spite of my unfitness to judge in such matters", wrote Charles Cahier, "and in spite of the formal denial by the learned Cuvier of all unicorns past or future, I admit that I do not despair of this animal which is so cried down at present after so many panegyrics. The horn may be movable or not, it may be persistent or caducous, for all this is not important; but I dare to hope that it will be single. The unicorn will have a place in our museums beside the ornithorhyncus, which was quite as improbable as the other before it was brought before us; or he may be placed near the pterodactyls, which would have seemed absurd until the moment when they were found." [54] A scholarly English writer of even more recent date conjectures that the unicorn may be "a hybrid produced occasionally and at more or less rare intervals, a cross between some equine and cervine species." Or the word "unicorn" may be "a generic name for several distinct species of (probably) now extinct animals—creatures which were the contemporaries of prehistoric man and which, before they finally expired, attracted the attention of his descendants, during early historic time, by the rare appearance of a few surviving individuals." [55]

CHAPTER VIII

CONJECTURES

HAVING considered some of the more important arguments and observations that have been advanced to prove the existence or non-existence of the unicorn, we may now assume the rôle of the sceptic who regards the whole legend as probably a product of the fancy, asking ourselves how the belief first arose. This question plunges us at once into the remote past; it forces us to think as much as possible in the way of men whose mental habit was very different from our own; it is a question, therefore, to which no conclusive answer, carrying final conviction to all, can be expected. I shall arrange my conjectures in the order of plausibility, passing from those one feels tempted to accept immediately to others that may seem at first highly dubious.

Several authoritative scholars have held that the unicorn legend derives entirely from Oriental beliefs about the rhinoceros. This was the opinion of Cuvier, for example, a man whose expert knowledge and good sense command respect, and it is an opinion in keeping with the tendency of our time to prefer the light of common day to "the light that never was". An impressive "case" can be made out for this view.

We have repeatedly seen the rhinoceros crossing the unicorn's path or plunging through the undergrowth in a direction remarkably parallel. Ctesias, Aelian, Pliny, and Isidore mingle large ingredients of rhinoceros with their unicorns. Learned Christian Fathers such as Tertullian, Jerome, Ambrose, and Gregory reject the unicorn entirely in favour of his *doppelgänger*, and later scholars had to exert constant effort to prevent the animal from slipping down—or back? —into the huge Indian hog. And this is not surprising when one considers that almost exactly the same beliefs were held in India about the one animal as those entertained in Europe about the other, and that from the beginning of the sixteenth century Portuguese commerce made possible a constant infiltration of Oriental super-stitions into the Western world. We cannot ignore the fact that Western interest in the alicorn increased at just the time when this infiltration began, and that rhinoceros horns were actually used in Europe, although to no great extent, precisely as alicorns were. A curious illustration of the uncertainty regarding the "true horn" is seen in the fact that the treasury of St. Mark's in Venice contains, beside the two famous alicorns brought from Constantinople and another one of later acquisition, the unmistakable horn of a rhinoceros, hanging with them. In this way the Cathedral assured itself against error, however the learned might eventually decide.

The parallelism between the two traditions may be shown in the words of a famous traveller of the sixteenth century. Linschoeten says of the rhinoceros that "some think it is the right Unicorne, because that as yet there hath no other bin found, but only by hearesay and by the pictures of them. The Portingalles and those of Bengala affirme that by the River Ganges in the Kingdome of Bengala are many of these Rhinoceros, which when they will drinke the other beasts stand and waite upon them till the Rhinoceros hath drinke, and thrust their horne into the water, for he cannot drinke but his horne must be under the water because it standeth so close unto his nose and muzzle: and then after him all the other beastes doe drinke. Their hornes in India are much esteemed and used against all venime, poyson, and many other diseases . . . which is very good and most true, as I myselfe by experience have found." [1]

After reading this passage one is disposed to agree with the assertion of de Laborde that the rhinoceros is the sole source of all the marvellous qualities attributed to the unicorn.[2] One is not surprised to find that Conrad Gesner used Dürer's famous drawing of the rhinoceros as the illustration accompanying his account of the monoceros, or that John of San Geminiano could say *"Christus assimilatur rhinocerote."* [3] Arabian writers constantly described the one animal under the name of the other,[4] and in Europe there seems never to have been a time when some one did not suspect that the two were identical.[5]

It is true that those who thought thus had always vigorous opponents. Andrea Bacci disposed of the notion to his own satisfaction by pointing out that the Romans knew the rhinoceros perfectly and yet believed in the unicorn as a totally different animal. He found the horns of the two animals in the treasury of Don Francesco and characterized that of the rhinoceros, a beast that he seems to have regarded with contempt, as black and thick and vulgar. Julius Caesar Scaliger fell foul of Cardan in this fashion: "By what evil fate does it happen that in spite of the frequent beatings you receive from the rods of grammarians you must now fall under the censure of naturalists? There is no help for you, Cardan, when you describe the monoceros under the heading of rhinoceros, for these two animals are entirely different." [6] This serious charge, like many another that Scaliger brought against his foe, was unjustified, for Cardan had said with all possible clearness that the two animals were quite distinct and that nothing but the vague similarity in their names had caused confusion.[7] But the most amusing of all those who strove to defend the unicorn from this contamination was Luis de Urreta. I have already quoted the passage in which he describes what he calls the unicorn in terms that apply exclusively to the rhinoceros and then refers with an indulgent smile to the belief of "certain holy men", who could not be expected to know better, that the two animals were really the same.

These passages show that the rhinoceros was as mysterious in Europe as the unicorn itself. Familiar to the Romans of the Empire, it was remembered in the Middle Ages chiefly because of a few references in Martial and other ancient writers. For a thousand years Europe forgot what the rhinoceros looks like. There is, to be sure, a curious little figure in the pavement of St. Mark's at Venice—near the Door of the Madonna—which seems, when one first comes upon it, to contradict this statement. This figure, the original of which seems to have been placed here in the thirteenth century, shows the unmistakable head of the rhinoceros with the horn properly placed, although the body is that of a bear, the feet are furnished with claws, and the ears are very large and shaped like those of a bat. The more learned *cicerones* of St. Mark's always refer to this pavement mosaic as the rhinoceros under the palm-tree, explaining that it symbolizes the wrath of God, but they do not tell us why the rhinoceros should stand so near the Madonna's door or how a mosaicist of the thirteenth century happened to know even thus much about the appearance of an Indian beast. Hazardous as it may seem, my conjecture is that the mosaicist did not intend to represent a rhinoceros at all but a unicorn. For an accurate description of the unicorn it is not unreasonable to suppose that he went to his contemporary and fellow-townsman, Ser Marco Polo, recently returned from India where he had seen the rhinoceros in the wild state and had come away with the belief that he had seen the unicorn—although he had to admit (Book III, Chapter 9) that it "is not in the least like that which our stories tell of as being caught in the lap of a virgin; in fact, 'tis altogether different from what we fancied".

The first rhinoceros seen in western Europe in modern times was brought round Cape Horn in 1498 and taken to Lisbon. The second, much better known and indeed a celebrated animal, arrived in the same city seventeen years later, where it became a great favourite at "the palace of the king" and on one occasion was pitted against an elephant, which it put to ignominious flight. A sketch of it sent to Albrecht Dürer was converted into the well-known engraving, delightfully inaccurate, which did duty for more than a hundred years in books of zoology. In 1517 this rhinoceros—whose name should have been Ulysses—set forth once more for Rome, intended as a gift to the Pope; but his ship was wrecked off Marseilles and in spite of his gallant effort to swim ashore only the dead body was recovered. The skin was stuffed and sent "to the palace of the King" of France.[8] It was a hundred and fifty years after this that England first acquired a live rhinoceros of her own.[9]

Some of the traits ascribed to the unicorn were almost certainly derived from facts observed by hunters of the rhinoceros. The hide of this beast is impervious to primitive weapons, so that the belief might well get abroad that it could be taken or killed only by stratagem. The people of India and China have long thought, indeed, that their beakers of rhinoceros horn were made of the horns of animals killed by elephants. Until the invention of the modern rifle the Indian rhinoceros had been killed or captured chiefly by great drives, such as that led by Tamerlane, in which many men and horses took part. Although not very swift of foot, the rhinoceros runs more rapidly than its bulk would lead one to expect, and it begins slowly, as early writers said of the unicorn, increasing its speed little by little. With reference to the Western belief that the virgin decoy attracts her victim by her odour it is worthy of remark that the eyesight of the rhinoceros is weak and his sense of smell very keen. The repeated statements that the unicorn belongs in some sense to the king reminds one that even in modern times Eastern potentates have been known to keep the rhinoceros in their parks and to take him with them on royal progresses as a symbol of power and sovereignty. Just as the unicorn came to represent chastity and solitude in Europe and became especially dear, therefore, to Christian monks, so the rhinoceros symbolized chastity and solitude in India and was regarded as a model of the ascetic life.[10] Alkazuwin says concerning the animal's solitude that when it has chosen a grazing ground it will not tolerate the presence of any other beast within one hundred parasangs on any side, and those who know the literature of solitude will understand how readily this trait would be accepted by the Forest Hermits as a mark of holiness and wisdom. Finally, there is to be considered the tradition of the unicorn's great strength which persisted even when the animal was likened by *Physiologus* to a kid. Does it not seem probable that there is some memory here of the elephant-fighter? Joshua Sylvester, after speaking in high commendation of the elephant, proceeds as follows:—

But his huge strength nor subtle witt can not
Defend him from the sly Rhinocerot,
Who never, with blinde furie led, doth venter
Upon his Foe, but, yer the Lists he enter,
Against a rock he whetteth round about
The dangerous Pike upon his armed snout;
Then buckling close, doth not at random hack
On the hard Cuirasse of his Enemies back
But under's bellie (cunning) findes a skinne
Whear (and but thear) his sharpened blade will in.[11]

Even more is claimed for the rhinoceros on the score of medicinal value than for the unicorn, for not his horn alone but his entire body is held to abound with magical virtues. These virtues, it would seem, were regarded as merely brought to a higher potency in the horn, according to a belief that his strength chiefly lay in the member with which he fought and defended himself. The hunting, transport, preparation, and sale of these horns has been one of the more romantic details of Oriental business activity for a very long time, comparable only, so far as the East is concerned, with the commerce in dragon's bones. There are even records showing that Occidental merchants shared in this business. Lying in the Strait of Malacca in 1592, James Lancaster sent commodities to the King of Junsaloam "to barter for Ambergriese and for the hornes of the Abath, whereof the king only hath the traffique in his hands. Now this Abath is a beast which hath one horn onely in her forehead, and is thought to be the female Unicorne, and is highly esteemed of all the Moores in these parts as a most soveraigne remedie against poyson." [12]

Caspar Bartholinus tells us that when he was in Italy about the year 1620 the rhinoceros horn was on sale in several of the larger cities and that it was recommended as a specific against poison and fevers, small-pox, epilepsy, vertigo, worms, impotence, and stomach-ache.[13] Forty years later Father Lobo could say that this horn, as compared with true alicorn, was "not so sovereign, though used against poison".[14] Pierre Pomet, writing in 1699, asserts that the rhinoceros horn is still used in the belief that it is as effective as alicorn.

This is what one would expect, but it is a little surprising to find precisely the same set of beliefs at the Cape of Good Hope in the eighteenth century, applied there to the white rhinoceros.[15] Whether to attribute this to a prehistoric transmission across the length of Africa or to the influence of the Dutch and Portuguese one is not quite sure. Charles Thunberg writes that in the region of the Cape the horns of the rhinoceros were kept "not only as rarities but also as useful in diseases and for the purpose of detecting poison. The fine shavings of the horns, taken internally, were supposed to cure convulsions and spasms in children, and it was firmly believed that goblets made of these horns in a turner's lathe would discover a poisonous draught by making the liquor ferment." [16]

With these facts and considerations in mind one is strongly inclined to agree with de Laborde that the rhinoceros is the sole source not only of the superstition regarding the alicorn but of the whole unicorn legend. Before committing oneself to the rhinoceros theory, however, there are a few questions that one would like to have answered. How did the unicorn acquire from this animal, so mild and phlegmatic when not molested, his reputation for extreme pugnacity? Does it seem likely that the rhinoceros suggested the unicorn's reputation for extreme fleetness? With the rhinoceros alone in mind, what sense can we make of Topsell's assertion, founded upon good ancient authority, that the unicorn "fighteth with the mouth and with the heels, with the mouth biting like a lion and with the heels kicking like a horse"? Again, what is the connection between the rhinoceros and the unicorn of *Physiologus*, of which we are told that it is like a kid? Finally, how is it possible to identify an animal of such delicacy and refinement as the unicorn's with the gross, grunting, slime-wallowing rhinoceros? One hesitates to think of him as related to that beast even in the way that the water-lily is related to the mud.

Looking for a way of escape from the almost inescapable evidence accumulated above, one recalls that the rhinoceros was not the only one-horned animal known to or imagined by the ancients. Both Pliny [17] and Aristotle [18] believed that the oryx was a unicorn.[19]

This animal, as we learn from Oppian's poem on the art of hunting,[20] was regarded in the ancient world as extremely formidable both to man and beast. Although it does not look much like a goat to the modern eye, the ancients, with their loose zoological terminology sometimes called it that, and certainly it is far more goat-like than the rhinoceros. The oryx, or rather a bronze figure of one, was probably the original of the drawing of a "monoceros" preserved in an early manuscript of Cosmas Indicopleustes. The nimble and delicate unicorns of mediaeval manuscripts are all of the same general kind—that is, they are all vaguely like antelopes. The painted figure of a unicorn found by Sir John Barrow in a South African cave was clearly that of some sort of antelope. The descriptions of unicorns left us by Vartoman, Thevet, Lobo, Francis Magellanes, Caravaial, Rüppell, and several others, suggest the oryx strongly, and in one of these descriptions—that of Magellanes—the same assertions are made regarding the medicinal value of the horn as those with which we are familiar. The horn of the rhinoceros was not the only one with which this superstition was connected, so that de Laborde may be wrong after all in asserting that it was the source of the whole belief concerning the alicorn. Aelian tells us that it was a custom of ancient hunters to reserve the oryxes they captured as presents for their kings.[21] It will be recalled that we have already been obliged to call in a large antelope of some sort to explain the unicorn of Ctesias. In short, almost if not quite as much may be said for the oryx as for the rhinoceros by one trying to find the source of the unicorn legend.

Almost as much has, in fact, been said. Samuel Bochart devoted twenty folio pages of amazing erudition [22] to an attempt to prove that both the Re'em and the unicorn derive from the oryx (Plate XV), basing his argument upon a firm belief—for which he had the authority of Aristotle and Pliny—that all oryxes are one-horned. (Such are the charming results of studying zoology in libraries.) Professor Martin Lichtenstein of Berlin, a far less learned man but better acquainted with antelopes, supported the oryx theory by citation of Egyptian monuments.[23] He reproduced a mural decoration found in the pyramid at Memphis showing five antelopes, one of them certainly intended as a unicorn, led by human figures, the whole scene representing a ritualistic offering. In another plate shown by Lichtenstein we see a god with a saw in one hand holding a one-horned antelope by the other, and the suggestion is that one of the horns has just been cut off. The antelope here shown is apparently the small and graceful dorcas, sacred to Isis, and it is significant, therefore, that in this second plate the god and the antelope stand before that goddess, enthroned. We may perhaps draw the inference that Isis preferred to have her antelopes appear before her with one horn.

Although Lichtenstein does not mention the fact, one cannot help remembering in this connection that the early Christians of Alexandria transferred to the Virgin Mary some of the attributes of Isis, the Egyptian Mother of God, and that even the conventional Christian paintings of Mother and Child are sometimes said to have had this pagan origin. A question grazes the mind whether we have found here the channel by which a heathen superstition was diverted to the uses of Christian symbolism. (This question arises with unusual emphasis when one stands before the beautiful painting of the Madonna and Child by Stefan Lochner in the Wallraf-Richartz Museum at Cologne. On the Madonna's bosom there is a large jewelled brooch which shows in the middle a seated maiden with a unicorn resting in her lap.) Here, at any rate, we have a unicorn vaguely *simile haedo* which belongs to the country of *Physiologus* and is in some way related to a goddess who, in spite of her own practice of incest, was regarded as a patroness of chastity. Bochart's argument would have been stronger if he had admitted a possibility that other antelopes beside the large and fierce oryx may have had some influence upon the unicorn legend. The dorcas is a smaller and more kid-like animal, altogether a more appropriate companion for virgins seated in the woods.

As we shall see, both Pallas and Cuvier admit that the oryx may now and then, as a *lusus naturae*, have only one horn, and far more frequent than such "sports" must be the animals that have had one horn broken off in conflict with their fellows. The most important consideration is, however, that when seen in profile the oryx really seems to have only one horn—a fact to which there is abundant testimony [24] and which anyone can test for himself by visiting a large menagerie.

The pertinence of this fact is made clear in a communication that appeared recently in a daily newspaper. Referring to the report that the present Duke of Gloucester had shot an oryx in Tanganyika Territory, the correspondent writes: "The African, even when he is a professional hunter, is not anything of a naturalist. One day a man passed me carrying in the manner of a sceptre or wand of office a long, straight horn. I asked my African companion about the horn and was assured that it was a very rare trophy indeed; it came off a great antelope that was only to be found, and then but rarely, in the desert country far to the North. When I asked whether the owner would not be better off with the two horns instead of with only half a pair, my companion said that the remarkable beast which provided the horn carried only one. . . . Some time later I moved to a part of the country where oryx were to be found. The animal is a very shy beast, not easy to approach. From a distance, and especially when broadside on, he certainly appears to have only one horn. Moreover, the first I saw head-on had, in fact, only one horn. But when I managed to drop that oryx and looked him over I found that, though the beast had only one horn, he had had two; there was a stump of the second, just where one would expect it. Male antelopes at times bicker with one another, and they do it with their horns; one can hear the rattle of them as their wearers battle together. In a bout of the sort the long slender horn is apt to snap off, and that, no doubt, was how the single-horned oryx came to be. Perhaps it was by some such means that the fabulous unicorn found its way into heraldry." [25]

Discoveries of this sort are made many times before they become common property. Sir William Cornwallis Harris made much the same remarks about the oryx seventy years ago, but with important variations. His passage, though wretchedly written and full of errors in statement of fact, deserves partial quotation. "Romance", says he, "aiding the skilful hand of nature with her richest embroidery, has succeeded in investing the group to which the Oryx belongs with a degree of interest that few other quadrupeds can

XXI. THE VIRGIN-CAPTURE

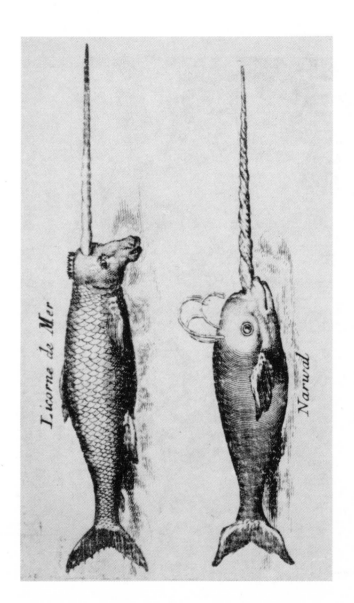

Licorne de Mer

Narwal

XXII. FACT AND FICTION

character alone, for these are obviously products of fancy, but his physical aspect—on the basis of a "horn" which never grew on his brow. A remarkable horn, or an object everywhere so-called, did certainly attract much attention in the Middle Ages, and there can be little doubt what sort of object this was. Representations of it in mediaeval manuscripts show that it had precisely those "anfractuous spires and cochleary turnings" which I see in the ivory stick on the desk before me and which are to be found in no other natural object. This ivory stick is perfectly straight, suggesting that it grew single and alone, as indeed it did. As I have already said, the Italian word *licorno*, "the horn", was almost certainly made at a time when the object was regarded as independent and no origin for it had been imagined. The rather awkward extension of this word to name the beast from whose brow the horn was supposed to spring suggests that the animal was deduced from the horn. If this could happen in Italy during the Middle Ages it may have happened elsewhere and much earlier. We do not know for how long such objects as my alicorn have been familiar in Mediterranean countries, but the commercial history of the race that chiefly purveyed them stretches back for a very long time. Furthermore, it is not necessary to this conjecture that the kind of horn before me and no other should have always served to suggest the unicorn; there are several horns, particularly those of certain antelopes, so straight and apparently independent as to suggest, when seen singly, that they grew alone. It is a matter not of conjecture but of fact that the single straight horns of antelopes have been used in Tibet during many centuries for magical and ritualistic purposes, and that these sacred horns have been dispersed by pilgrims over a wide territory, acquiring more and more, as they went farther from their source, the reputation of talismans and of being the horns of unicorns. Here we see a unicorn legend in the making.

The highly significant passage that I have quoted from Colonel Prejevalsky shows all the essential phases of the unicorn legend assembled in Tibet, and it shows also how they might be put together. We start, to be sure, with an actual animal, sacred and taboo. Its blood is thought to be medicinal; its long straight horn is used by priests in necromatic and religious rites; it has some sort of symbolism. In this same region there has been, since the time of Genghis Khan and probably for very much longer, a belief in one-horned antelopes. The priests who use the horns in divination may know that they grew in pairs, although they use them singly, but the pilgrims who buy these horns and carry them into the surrounding districts are probably not aware of this. At a distance from the distributing centre everyone is convinced that they are the horns of unicorns. The representations of salesmen praising their wares tend to increase belief in the magic powers of the horns, and this belief grows as it spreads West and East. Tibet lies between Persia, from which we get our first notices of the Western unicorn, and China, which has a highly developed unicorn legend not of native origin. Tibet was included in the "India" of Ctesias.—Why should we look farther for the sources of the unicorn?

There is a possibility, however, and one that must not be ignored, that unicorned animals actually exist in rare instances as *lusus naturae*. This possibility was urged by Peter Simon Pallas, one of the most competent zoologists of the eighteenth century, who believed that the legend of the unicorn sprang from chance encounters with such one-horned sports.[27] The theory is not unattractive, accounting as it does for the universal belief that the unicorn is exceedingly rare and also for the facts that it has been reported from many different parts of the world and has been described as resembling a wide variety of animals. A nineteenth century scholar points out that there are antelopes whose horns are joined for the first few inches from the base, and he asks what is to prevent nature from prolonging this juncture, now and then and as a freak, throughout the entire length.[28] These speculations are brought into the region of fact by an authentic record of a one-horned animal. In his *Natural History of Oxfordshire*[29] Robert Plot describes several sheep with six or eight horns kept in his time by Lord Norreys at Ridcot; "and there was one other sheep", says he, "that excelled them all in being a Unicorn, having a single horn growing in the middle of its forehead, twenty-one inches long, with annulary protuberances round it and a little twisted in the middle. There was, to be sure, another little horn growing on the same head, but so inconsiderable that it was hid under the wool."

This Oxfordshire unicorn seems to have been a freak, but others have been produced artificially by the deliberate man-handling of horns, of which there has been a good deal, early and late, in various parts of the world. "Among us", says a modern writer, "the horn does not seem capable of much modification, but a Kaffir can never be content to leave the horns as they are. He will cause one horn to project forward and the other backward.[30] Now and then an ox is seen in which a most singular effect has been produced. As the horns of the young ox sprout they are trained over the forehead until the points meet. They are then manipulated so as to make them coalesce, and so shoot upwards from the middle of the forehead, like the horn of the fabled unicorn." [31]

This passage is corroborated by another in a more recent book which seems to bring the unicorn almost to one's door: "Few domestic sheep are more remarkable, or have given rise to more controversy, than the Indian one-horned or unicorn-sheep, of which the first living specimens ever seen in this country formed part of a large collection of Nepalese animals presented to King George V when Prince of Wales, that were exhibited at the London Zoological Gardens in the year 1906. Although receiving the name of unicorn-sheep, these animals really possessed a pair of horns, for if we examine one of their skulls and remove the horn-sheath from its bony support it will be noticed that the latter is composed of two quite separate structures. . . . There appears to be a certain amount of mystery regarding the origin of these creatures, and some doubt as to whether their peculiar horn-formation is not the outcome of artificial manipulation." A letter from the British Resident at the Court of Nepal is then quoted in which these words occur: "There is no special breed of one-horned sheep in Nepal, nor are the specimens which have been brought here for sale natural freaks. By certain maltreatment ordinary two-horned sheep are converted into a one-horned variety. The process adopted is branding with a red-hot iron the male lambs when about two or three months old on their horns when they are beginning to sprout. The wounds are treated with a mixture of oil and soot and when they heal, instead of growing at their usual places and spreading, come out as one from the middle of the skull. . . . I am told that the object of producing these curiosities is to obtain fancy prices for them from the wealthy people in Nepal." The original writer then continues: "Notwithstanding the above explanation, the majority of naturalists are inclined to doubt whether a true understanding has even yet been arrived at concerning these sheep, for it has been pointed out that the mere fact of searing the budding horns would not result in those appendages sprouting out at the summit of the skull instead of towards the side, and moreover, if there is any secret attending their production it has been remarkably well kept from the ever-prying eyes of zoologists. It is true that the horns of a young animal might be induced to grow together by binding them up, but in that case we should expect the bony supports to be bent aside at their bases as a result of the unnatural strain put upon them, whereas on the contrary, those of the unicorn sheep arise in quite a straight manner from the skull." [32]

Whatever the process may be there is no doubt that the thing is done, and for the present purpose the motive is more important than the method. The British Resident at Nepal says that the artificial unicorns of that country are produced "to obtain fancy prices", but we should like to know why a sheep with one horn is thought to be worth more than a sheep with the normal equipment, and also why such a sheep was thought a suitable gift for the Prince of Wales. Some light is thrown upon this question by the fact that the tribe of Dinkas, who live just south of the White Nile, not only manipulate the horns of their cattle as the Kaffirs do but use this practice as a means of marking the leaders of their herds. [33] One can readily believe that the practice is one of great antiquity and that it was used as the Dinkas use it in many parts of the world during the pastoral ages. In the minds of primitive men living a pastoral life the leader of a flock or herd is a valuable possession and he is also a natural emblem of sovereignty and supreme power.[34] We have already seen that the unicorn has been used as such an emblem in lands far apart and during a great stretch of time, the remarkable vision in the Book of Daniel providing the most striking instance. It seems possible, therefore, that what I may call the unicorn idea, the notion that one-horned animals exist in Nature, arose from the custom of uniting the horns of various domestic animals by a process which is still in use but still mysterious to the civilized world. Here may be the explanation of the one-horned cows and bulls that Aelian says were to be found in Ethiopia and of the unicorned cattle reported by Pliny as living in the land of the Moors. The cows with single horns bending backward and a span long seen by Vartoman at Zeila in Ethiopia may have been of this sort. The one-horned ram's head sent to Pericles by his farm-hands may have been that of the leader of their flock, and so a perfect symbol of that leadership in Athens which, according to Plutarch's interpretation, they wished to prophesy for their master. Finally, the mysterious one-horned ox mentioned three times over in the *Talmud* as Adam's sacrifice to Jehovah may have been the most precious thing that Adam possessed, the leader of his herd of cattle.—Once more the question rises whether there is any need of seeking further.

One goes on seeking for the source or sources of the unicorn legend partly because other explanations of it, perhaps not so immediately plausible as those just considered but quite as able to stand scrutiny, continue to suggest themselves. Another reason for continuing the search is that none of the suggestions thus far made is completely convincing. They suggest no sufficient reason why the single horn—whether found alone or on the head of a beast, whether growing naturally or as the product of artifice—should have attracted so much attention and should have won such prestige as the horn of the unicorn has long had. Even if we accept one or all—for this too is possible—of the suggestions put forth above we feel that they are not primary or fundamental because they do not explain the strange fascination exercised by unicornity (if I may venture the neologism) upon the mind. They require explanation in their turn by something lying behind and towering above them all.

Among the ruins of the Palace of Forty Pillars at Persepolis, on the left-hand side of the western staircase constructed by Artaxerxes III, there is a bas-relief showing the figure of a lion with teeth and claws fastened upon a one-horned animal of uncertain species resembling at once a bull, a large antelope, and a goat. Three other treatments of the same subject are found in the corresponding positions, the figure of the unicorned animal varying slightly from one to another.[35] During the last century and a half these bas-reliefs have been studied minutely by many competent scholars and the suggestion has been made repeatedly that they may have some bearing upon the problem of the unicorn.[36]

No purpose would be served by a full survey of this extensive literature. I may say, however, that there has been much discussion concerning the species represented by the unicorn, some contending that it was intended for a goat, others that it is an antelope, and still others that it is certainly a wild ass. For my own part, dependent as I am upon the numerous photographs and drawings, I am chiefly impressed by the confidence in his own opinion displayed by each of the contenders, for it seems obvious to me that the animal was intended by the sculptor—who could be realistic enough when he chose, judging from his lion—to represent a composite beast in which ass and goat and antelope and bull were included. One of the most interesting of the conclusions upon which there is fairly general agreement is that Ctesias was influenced by these figures in writing his description of the unicorn. There seems to be no reason why we should not accept this opinion, provided that we see how little it signifies. Ctesias probably saw the bas-reliefs and others like them at Susa, and one cannot say that his one-horned onager is utterly unlike the rather nondescript animal of the Persepolis sculptures; but he certainly did not derive from these figures his precise ideas about the colours of the horn and of the astragalus, about the use of the horn by Indian princes, or about the unicorn's habitat and characteristics. From the bas-reliefs of Persepolis he

could have got little more than a belief that there existed somewhere
—and why not in "India", the home of wonders?—a beast vaguely
resembling the wild ass that he had seen in Persia but, unlike the
local variety, furnished with a single horn. For the appearance and
properties of this horn he would have had to inquire elsewhere.

Ctesias may well have accepted these figures as those of unicorns,
but did the sculptor intend that they should be so understood?
This is a question which one would suppose that any thoughtful
person sitting down before the present problem would try to answer
first of all, but on the contrary the question is not even stated or
grazed for over a hundred years by any of the writers engaged in
the main discussion. Niehbuhr, Rhode, Ker Porter, Heeren, Lassen,
and Robert Brown all tacitly assume that all representations of
animals in ancient sculpture that look like unicorns were intended
as such.[37] This strange ignorance or ignoring of an obvious art
convention vitiates some of their results and weakens confidence in
their powers of observation.[38]

The statement is often made that the artists of Egypt, the
Euphrates, and Persepolis knew nothing of perspective and that
they always showed two legs for four, one ear and one horn for
two, through sheer inability to represent the third dimension. This
statement is untrue. There was an artistic convention—which grew
up, probably, before the technic of representing perspective was
mastered—allowing the artist to show one horn or ear instead of
two when representing animals in profile, but this convention was
by no means universally followed, and the fact that ancient artists
were not consistent in observing it lends some excuse to the
enthusiasts named above who found unicorns everywhere in ancient
art, on coins and seals and gems as well as in sculptures, somewhat
as Sir Thomas Browne found quincunxes.[39]

The fact that the sculptors of the ancient world sometimes showed
two horns in representing animals in profile must not be taken as
proof that when they showed only one they had in mind an actual
unicorn. Far more important for our purpose than the sculptor's
intention, however, is the effect of his work upon the public mind,
the interpretation put upon it by ignorant laymen. We have just

seen that several acute modern scholars, most of them students of
ancient art, were convinced that the one-horned figures of Persepolis
were intended to represent unicorns. If this was true of them, what
are we to expect of ignorant men, for whom graphic and plastic art
is always a record of actuality? Millions of ignorant men saw the
unicorn bas-reliefs at Persepolis and Susa, and millions more saw
others almost exactly like them at Nineveh and Babylon, for these
figures, like almost everything else in Persian sculpture, were
derived from the remote Euphratean past. If these millions had not
believed in unicorns before they saw the figures, we may be quite
sure that they did believe after they had seen them. Whatever the
original artists meant to do, this is a part of what they accomplished:
either they corroborated an already existing belief in the unicorn or
else they gave the first hint leading to that belief.

Those who doubt whether this is possible will do well to read
Jean Wauquelin's *Merveilles d'Inde*, in which it is perfectly evident
that the six-handed men, the horned women, and the griffins with
lions' paws, all regarded by the fifteenth-century author as actual
creatures, derive ultimately from the symbolic monstrosities of
Indian religious art. It has even been suggested, quite credibly, that
the griffin itself was the imaginative creation of Indian tapestry
workers and that the Greeks, seeing these tapestries at the court of
Persia and elsewhere, thought the figures on them represented real
animals and described the animals in words as best they could.
The fact that esoteric symbols are constantly subject to exoteric
interpretation, that symbolic images are almost everywhere regarded
by most people as idols and these idols as physically present deities,
is familiar to every student of the history of religion, and purely
artistic representations of animals—if indeed there were any such
in the times of which we are speaking—were subject to similar
misinterpretation. We have seen that Arabian travellers, finding
certain figures carved on rhinoceros horn, thought that they grew
naturally in the horn, and that when Sir John Barrow, a highly
educated traveller of the nineteenth century, found in South Africa
a cave painting of an antelope showing only one horn he could only
infer that one-horned antelopes must exist in Nature. The numberless

millions of Persepolis and the Euphrates valley, who lived all their lives with powerful representations of one-horned animals constantly before them, may have been no more intelligent and cautious and critical.

Not only on the great public monuments were such apparently one-horned animals to be seen; figures of them were spread broadcast through the known world by the constant use of them on seal-cylinders in Persia, Assyria, Babylon, Chaldea, and Elam.[40] The spread of these cylinders was not confined even to the wide territory in which for many centuries they were in daily use, for the figures upon them, impressed on tablets of clay, were employed to identify and protect personal property, so that they must have had a dispersion similar to that of modern trade-marks. Almost indestructible by weather, seal-cylinders made over four thousand years ago lasted on into a time when the symbolism they at first conveyed was quite forgotten. Everywhere they went—and they went everywhere—they suggested the existence of one-horned animals, and they suggested also that these animals were in some way highly important. If there had been no belief in the unicorn before the use of these emblems on seal-cylinders or independent of it, they alone would have been sufficient to suggest and develop such a belief.

But the unicorn, like *das Ewig Weibliche*, lures us on and on. Although it seems likely that faith in the animal was corroborated by seal-cylinders and profile figures in bas-relief, I should be sorry to think that his first emergence wore such "hues of hap and hazard", that he was born of a mere blunder. If the facts point to that conclusion we must of course accept them, but I am not sure that they do. I venture to suggest that the ignorant millions of Persepolis and Nineveh and Babylon might have been justified and right in accepting these figures as representations of unicorns, and that the artists who made them intended that they should be so accepted.

I am well aware that this suggestion is counter to expert opinion. Early writers upon the one-horned figures at Persepolis and elsewhere assumed unanimously, as I have said, that they were always intended to represent unicorns, and later writers have assumed with the same unanimity that they never were. The second assumption seems to me hardly less hasty than the first. No one doubts that there was a widespread and long-enduring artistic convention by which one horn was commonly depicted to represent two, but this convention was often ignored, and furthermore its existence does not prove that none of the animals represented as unicorns were ever intended as such. Conclusive evidence of a pre-Ctesian belief in the unicorn would be given by a full-face figure dating from before the time of Ctesias and showing only one horn, but I am not aware that such a figure exists. We can do fairly well without it.

Strong probability that the unicorn legend is older than Ctesias and older than the Palace of Forty Pillars is indicated by many of the facts already discussed, but there is no need of resting the present argument upon anything in the slightest degree uncertain. It can be shown that animals clearly described as unicorns held a high position in the religion of Persia.

The basic idea of Zoroastrian religion is an intensely conceived dualism worked out in the moral sphere as a perpetual conflict between forces of good and of evil captained respectively by the primal gods Ormuzd and Ahriman. The forces comprise and the struggle involves not human beings alone but the whole animal creation, part of which is regarded as belonging to the god of virtue and light, part to his rival. All the creatures or "servants" of Ormuzd consider it their highest duty to cherish others of their own kind and to destroy the creatures of Ahriman. The division of the animal kingdom into pure and impure creatures is made, of course, according to the utility or hostility of different species to mankind. Thus the horse and the ass stand high among the servants of Ormuzd, but highest, king and progenitor of all, is the bull. The chief of the impure animals is either the martichore or the lion. In many primitive beliefs, probably in most, the snake is of good omen, primarily because a need is felt of placating it, but Zoroastrianism shows what seems to most modern minds the natural attitude in regarding it as evil, at war with all pure animals, who kill it when they can.[41]

In the sacred writings of Persia there are several references to an animal of Ormuzd's creation that is of utmost importance to the present problem. The context of one of these, a passage almost modern in feeling, brings together for adoration the beneficent forces and elements of nature, and then come the words: "We worship the Good Mind and the spirits of the Saints and that sacred beast the Unicorn which stands in Vouru-Kasha, and we sacrifice to that sea of Vouru-Kasha where he stands." [42] In another context, not unlike the sanitation chapters in Leviticus but on a much higher level, there is mention of water polluted by the creatures of Ahriman —that is to say, presumably, stagnant water, always mysteriously dangerous in a country such as Persia. But Ormuzd has provided against this danger, for "the three-legged ass sits amid the sea Varkash, and as to water of every kind that rains on dead matter . . . when it arrives at the three-legged ass he makes every kind clean and purified with watchfulness."[43] The most important text reads thus: "Regarding the three-legged ass they say that it stands amid the wide-formed ocean, and its feet are three, eyes six, mouths nine, ears two, and horn one. Body white, food spiritual, and it is righteous. . . . The horn is as it were of pure gold, and hollow. . . . With that horn it will vanquish and dissipate all the vile corruption due to the efforts of noxious creatures. When that ass shall hold its neck in the ocean its ears will terrify, and all the water of the wide-formed ocean will shake with agitation. . . . If, O three-legged ass! you were not created for the water, all the water in the sea would have perished from the contamination which the poison of the Evil Spirit brought into its water through the death of the creatures of Ahuramazd."[44]

These passages throw at least a glimmer of welcome light upon more than one aspect of the unicorn problem. Here we have an ass, although a supernatural and symbolic and celestial one, with a single horn, and that horn when dipped in water is thaumaturgic in its power against poison. Ctesias, physician to the Court of Persia, may have had something other than travellers' tales and bas-reliefs to work upon in his account of the one-horned ass, and in any case he was not the inventor of the unicorn. That animal has now definitely escaped from human records into timeless myth.

It will be recalled that after a laborious effort to explain the unicorn's water-conning trait in the terms of mediaeval theories of medicine I was obliged to abandon that problem—promising, however, to return to it later. The tentative explanation advanced at the end of the fifth chapter gave no clue, as I said, to the reason why the water is poisonous, and it did not include the other animals which, in nearly all versions of the story, wait beside the water for the unicorn's coming. The *Bundahis* suggests unmistakably that the water is poisonous because the impure creatures of Ahriman have in some way made it so, and it makes clear also that the animals waiting beside the water are the pure creatures of Ormuzd expecting the advent of their champion and preserver.

Lest there should linger any doubt that the three-legged ass of the *Bundahis* and the unicorn of Europe are of the same stock, let us place beside the third quotation just above, the account given by John of Hesse of the water-conning which he says he saw beside the bitter waters of Marah: "Even to-day the venomous animals poison the water after the going down of the sun, so that the good animals cannot drink of it; but in the morning after sunrise comes the unicorn, and he, dipping his horn in the stream, expels the poison so that during the daytime the other animals may drink." This is the unicorn of Europe in his most characteristic action, but this is precisely the action also of the three-legged ass. John of Hesse even speaks of *animalia bona* and *animalia venenosa* exactly as though he were a Zoroastrian worshipper of Ormuzd instead of a Christian priest, and it would be hard to find a stranger tangle of cultures and beliefs than his Christian use of an ancient Persian symbol to illustrate and enforce a Hebrew tale. How glibly we talk about "melting-pots" as though they had been invented in our own day!

With every wish to avoid the appearance of dogmatism, I cannot even pretend to doubt that the horned ass of the *Bundahis* and the unicorn of the West belong to the same tradition.[45] But here we seem to have come, at last, to something final. I cannot trace the three-legged ass—that is the unicorn, with a less euphonious name—to his origin, for he fades into the clouds of mythology and the distance blots him out. One may say that he bears some resemblance to the horned horse of Indra [46] and to the snake-killing horse of Pedu,[47] but these surrogates, if such they are, merely take him farther away. So little is known and heard of him in Persian literature that he is probably an importation from another culture, and it seems likely that his legend is older than the *Avesta*. James Darmesteter regards him as one of the many personifications of the storm-cloud,[48] and so considered by the people of a thirsty land a beneficent creature and a serpent-killer. Angelo de Gubernatis identifies him with the *gandharvâs* of Hindu myth who guard the sacred soma in the midst of the waters.[49] However this may be, the sea of Varkash in the midst of which he stands represents either the ocean as contrasted with the Persian Gulf, or else, more probably, the "waters of the firmament."[50] He is called three-legged for purely symbolical reasons, either because he is supposed to stand on air, earth, and sea, or because his reign is to endure for three Zoroastrian ages. As the guardian of the pure animals and chief antagonist of Ahriman he is usurping the position of the Primitive Bull which, according to the *Avesta*, is at the head of Ormuzd's creation. This usurpation carries one's thought back to the long controversy over the question whether the one-horned animal of the Persepolis bas-reliefs was intended to represent a bull, a goat, or an ass. Possibly the sculptor intended that it should represent all three of these and stand for the entire animal kingdom of Ormuzd. The pollution in the waters which the three-legged ass is said to destroy or disperse by dipping its horn need not be taken literally, for the myth is symbolic in every detail.[51] It may represent the darkness of night [52] dispersed by the first beams of dawn or by moonlight; it may stand for drought overcome by the golden horn of the lightning; ultimately, however, it is an emblem of evil overcome by good.

Like the unicorn of Europe, the three-legged ass is a symbol of purity and a champion of those oppressed by the devil. In him the Christian makers of *Physiologus* had ready to their hand a perfect emblem of a Saviour sent into the world for the healing of the nations, and the fact that they chose instead of this the trivial and inept tale of the virgin-capture merely shows again how puerile they were.—But perhaps they were not given the choice, for the Persian tale may have been one of the very few myths and legends that were never heard in Alexandria.

It is natural to suppose that the three-legged ass must have been a glorification of some actual animal, perhaps the onager of the Persian plains; and if that were so he would not stand at the end of our quest but would be merely another point of departure; his attributes, however magnified, would be those of some terrestrial creature which we should feel obliged to find. Fortunately for the present investigation, the mythopœic fancy did not work in this way. Difficult as the conception may be to us, the worshippers of the three-legged ass, instead of atributing to him the characteristics of actual asses, derived what they took to be those characteristics from what they knew of him, their divine prototype. The wild ass merely performs on earth the rôle created for him by the three-legged ass of Varkash, and if he kills serpents that is only because his celestial prototype destroys the poison that Ahriman has spread in the sea, annihilating evil-doers with his golden horn.[53] One might say, perhaps, that the three-legged ass is the Platonic idea to which all actual asses strive to conform. They are the shadow of which he is the substance. For this reason the myth of the three-legged ass may be regarded as one source of the unicorn legend.

But this is not the only unicorn referred to in the sacred literature of Persia. We are told that the race of goats is divided into five orders of which sheep-goats form the second, and that these are subdivided into five kinds, the second of which is the Koresck, which has "one great horn and dwells upon separate hills and takes its pleasure there." [54] We know also that the Koresck is of the fold of Ormuzd because it is said in the same passage that he educated one of the Zend kings. This helps to explain the fact that several of the one-horned animals represented at Persepolis have cloven hoofs and look far more like goats than like either the bull or the ass. From the time of Aristotle to that of the British College of Heralds scholars have been perplexed by the unicorn's combination of caprine with equine characteristics. The unicorn of Albrecht Dürer, for example, is a horse in most respects, but it has cloven hoofs and a goat's beard (see Plate XVII), and so has the unicorn of the British Royal

Arms.[55] This confusion, preserved by a surprising tenacity of tradition, may have been due originally to the effort of Zoroastrian artists to represent not any single species of animal but a combination of several species which they regarded as the leaders of the pure creation.

In thinking of the one-horned figures at Persepolis we are not to ignore the fact that they are grouped about the royal palace, just as were the four brazen unicorns seen by Cosmas Indicopleustes about the four-towered palace of the King of Ethiopia. The King of Persia was regarded as the general overseer of the realm of Ormuzd, and it was natural that his chief lieutenant, the king of pure beasts, should be associated with him. The relationship between unicorns and royalty is brought out again by the fact just mentioned that one of the Zend kings was reared by a Koresck. It may be implied by the symbolism of the Persepolis bas-reliefs, for we find that the same animal—closely resembling a lion but possibly intended to represent the martichore as well—which is seen springing upon the unicorn in some scenes is shown in others fighting with the King, who drives a sword through his body. Heeren and Porter would have us believe that this familiar group was originally intended merely to exhibit the King's prowess as a hunter;[56] to me it seems symbolic of the final victory of Ormuzd, just as the other scene represents, I think, his temporary defeat. The sculptors would scarcely have dared to show the King overcome even by the powers of darkness, and this may be the reason why they used his animal representative for the first scene; but it was natural that he should appear in person when victorious. In any case, the King here takes the place of his chief subaltern. Even at Persepolis kings and unicorns stand side by side, reminding one of the phrase recurring so frequently in the Bestiaries: "They lead him to the palace of the king."

The four brazen unicorns seen by Cosmas about the palace in Ethiopia may have been stationed there primarily as symbols of sovereignty, but it is probable that they had another more important function—that of guardians. For this belief I can advance no coherent evidence, yet I am more confident of it than of many assertions that I have "documented" heavily. I might show that the seal-cylinders on which apparently one-horned animals were so frequently represented were used not as trade-marks and substitutes for signatures only but as amulets, and I might speak of the human heads of stone equipped with formidable single horns that are set up at the corners of Chinese houses to keep away demons. In Italy to this day single horns set in heavy blocks of wood are placed against open doors, and I have seen in Italy three little bronze unicorns made and used for the same purpose. A dozen such parallels and examples would not amount to proof, but they may produce conviction. Recent excavations have shown that almost every private house in Nineveh and Babylon was protected against invasion from the unseen world not only by charms and ritual but by symbolic figures of various kinds buried in the floor or placed above the lintels. Now the king's house needed special attention because he bore the brunt of every attack from the forces of evil, and whatever harm came to him was a national calamity. Here I think we find a hint for the explanation of the colossal stone bulls that guarded the palaces of Assyria—bulls with human heads and faces of majestic power. The unicorn belongs with these. As the one-horned bull protects the herd of which he is the leader and as the three-legged one-horned ass protects the pure creation, so the unicorn protects the king and thereby the people. He is a devil-fighter.

Thus far we have paid no attention to the total scene, represented four times over in great prominence at Persepolis, in which a beast resembling a powerful lion attacks an apparently one-horned animal probably intended, as we have seen, to stand for the ass and goat and bull (Plate XVIII). Consciously begging several questions at once, I shall call these animals the lion and the unicorn. The delineation of their conflict was remarkably popular over a great extent of territory and of time. One sees it continually and with only slight variations on cylinder-seals of Babylon and Assyria, on coins of Mycene, and on *objets d'art* of uncertain origin that were spread through Europe and Asia during the Middle Ages by Scythian traders.[57] The inference is that it had more than a decorative value and was widely recognized as a symbol. But a symbol of what?

Here and there in the unicorn literature of Europe one finds references to a clever ruse employed by the lion in capturing unicorns. Little is made of this story because it has not the sanction either of *Physiologus* or of the Greek and Latin authorities, and as it has no Christian significance it seems to have been crowded out by the story of the virgin-capture, yet it may be much older than the Holy Hunt allegory and may have served for ages as a religious symbol in the East.

Several European writers assert that this story was first told in "a letter written in Hebrew by the King of Abyssinia to the Pope of Rome". This seems at first a rather obscure reference, and one has not much hope of discovering the letter referred to in the voluminous correspondence of the Holy See; but a little reflection breeds a little encouragement and one turns again to the celebrated "Letter of Prester John", which may be read, if not in Hebrew, in every important language of Europe.[58] Half-way through the French version [59] upon which I happen to pitch occur the words: *"Item sachez quen nostre terre sont les licornes qui ont sur le front une corne tout seulement; & en y a en touts maniers, cest assavoir de vers de noirs & aussi de blancs. Et occissent le lion aucune foys mais les lions les occisent moult subtilement, car quant la licorne est lasse elle se met du coste dung arbre & le lion va entour & la licorne le cuide frapp de sa corne, & elle frape larbre de si grant vertu quelle ne le peut oster; adonc le lion là tue."*

The Latin original of this passage seems to have been the source of all later European versions,[60] such as that of Edward Topsell, who says of the unicorn: "He is an enemy to Lions, wherefore as soon as ever a Lion seeth a Unicorn, he runneth to a tree for succour, that so when the Unicorn maketh force at him, he may not only avoid his horn but also destroy him; for the Unicorn in the swiftness of his course runneth against a tree, wherein his sharp horn sticketh fast. Then when the Lion seeth the Unicorn fastened by the horn, without all danger he falleth upon him and killeth him." [61]

Although this story never took deep root in Europe it had

sufficient vitality to spring up there, with variations, in the literature of the people, as we see in the following tale :—

" 'Before you win my daughter and the half of my kingdom,' said the King, 'you must accomplish yet another heroic deed. You must capture a unicorn that is at large in the wood and doing great harm there.'

"The tailor took a halter and an axe and started for the wood, telling the party that was with him to wait outside. The unicorn came in sight immediately, and made for the tailor as if to gore him without ceremony.

" 'Steady, steady,' cried the tailor. 'Not so quick !'

"He stood still and waited till the animal was quite close, and then sprang nimbly behind a tree. The unicorn made a frantic rush at the tree and gored it so firmly with his horn that he could not get it out again, and so was caught.

" 'Now I've got you, my fine bird,' said the tailor, coming from behind the tree. He put the halter round the beast's neck, cut its horn out of the tree, and when all this was done led the animal home to the king." [62]

If this has always been an idle and meaningless tale then it is a very strange one. It is so odd, so unlikely to occur to the free excursive fancy, that one suspects a symbolic significance. But what significance? Can this question be connected with that other, which we have left in suspense, concerning the symbolism of the lion and unicorn bas-reiefs at Persepolis and their innumerable congeners? They too present a version of the lion-capture story although they show, perhaps because of the limitations of plastic art, only the *dénouement*. We may be able to answer the two questions together more easily than we could either one of them separately.

As I have pointed out, the one-horned figures at Persepolis were imitations, both in subject and treatment, of others at Nineveh and Babylon. These in their turn were by no means original, for recent diggings at Ur of the Chaldees have shown that precisely the same conventional treatment of horned animals and the same interest in them that we have seen at Persepolis existed as far behind Persepolis

in time as it lies behind us. On the lid of a toilet-box found at Ur
there is worked in gold and lapis-lazuli exactly the same subject as
that presented in the gigantic bas-relief under the staircase at Persepolis—a lion gripping with teeth and claws the hind quarters of a
one-horned beast. A shell plaque of amazing delicacy in this collection [63] shows two one-horned goats standing back to back on either
side of a tree, and another shows a creature with the body of a goat
and the head of a man, in profile and one-horned, with a foreleg
thrown over the shoulder of a similar monster seen full-face and
with two horns.

Looking at these objects from the city of Abraham, one realizes
that, beautiful as they are, they were produced in a time long ante-
cedent to any nonsense about art for art's sake and were certainly
not intended as mere ornaments. Each of them had a meaning and
was a compact symbol or metaphor in a language now lost to us.
That meaning was evidently an important one, for the pattern or
theme of the lion and unicorn conflict can be shown to have endured
in art for at least twenty-five hundred years, and that of the two
unicorned goats on either side of the tree for somewhat longer.
Is it possible to make a plausible guess at the meaning these objects
had for their makers? The scholars who are best equipped to answer
this question are precisely those most reluctant to hazard even a
conjecture. Gazing at these ancient unicorns, however, one cannot
help recalling that they come from a region which we have always
considered, perhaps because of our ignorance, the very cradle of
astrology. Is it possible that the lion and the unicorn (I continue,
consciously, to beg the question), so strangely brought together in
that dim past, were solar and lunar emblems? Well aware as I am of
the bad reputation earned for all such theories by the wild excesses
of the "solar myth" euhemerizers of the nineteenth century, I am
willing to give this possibility its chance.

That there is some kind of connection between the moon and the
unicorn is not a theory but a fact (Plate XX). To be convinced of this
one need scarcely look farther than the miserere seat in the Parish
Church of Stratford-on-Avon which shows the figure of a unicorn
with a crescent moon over its head. On ancient cylinder-seals the

crescent moon frequently appears in conjunction with figures of animals which, whatever the original intention, are represented with single horns.[64] Selecting characteristics of the unicorn at random we see that the animal may be likened to the moon, as the astrologers see it, in several ways: The unicorn is commonly, though not always, thought of as white in body; it is an emblem of chastity; it is very swift; [65] according to the best authorities it cannot be taken alive.[66] The animal is most readily associated with the new or crescent moon, which might indeed seem to dwellers by the sea to be leading the stars down to the water and to dip its own horn therein before they descend. The crescent moon has been used for ages to represent both celestial motherhood and virginity, whether of Ishtar, Isis, Artemis, or the Madonna. In all his pictures of the Assumption at Madrid Murillo painted the crescent moon over Mary's head. Old alchemical charts commonly designate the figure of Luna by placing in her right hand a single horn. The ki-lin, or unicorn of China, is commonly represented in bronze, bearing a crescent moon among clouds on his back.

These matters may seem little to the purpose, and I mention them merely for their cumulative force; but when we turn to consider the unicorn's medicinal properties and to ask what parallel these may have in old beliefs about the moon we discover something more significant. According to astrological belief and also that of magic and early medicine, the moon's phases exercise controlling influence upon all "humours", including not only the waters of the earth but the juices of plants and the blood of animals and of man.[67] The close relationship between the moon and the tides, well known if not well understood from very ancient times, may have suggested this idea which later attained a surprising extension and complexity. Alkazuwin asserts that the vigour of all animals grows with the waxing moon, that the milk of kine and the horns of beasts and even the whites of eggs increase with it, that during the first half of every lunar month more snakes come from their holes than in the second half and that their venom is more deadly. He recounts also the belief, still current in rural England, that trees planted in the waning moon seldom come to any good.[68] Physicians of the Middle Ages foretold the results of illnesses and regulated their treatments with constant attention to the moon's phases.

But this mere swaying and increasing of tides and humours by the new moon, although it has intimate connections with medical theory, does not bring us closer to the unicorn's magic power of dispelling poison. For the parallel to that we must look to another astrological belief. It was thought by early astrologers, and therefore by most educated Europeans of four centuries ago, that the moon, either by virtue of its proximity to earth or by the swiftness of its course, purifies the air of the noxious vapours supposed to rise from the earth during the night. The belief in these poisonous fumes, which correspond to the venom of Ahriman in the *Bundahis* myth and to that left floating in water by serpents in the unicorn legend, is still strong enough to keep tightly closed at night the windows of three houses in every five throughout rural England, Europe, and America, but the faith in the moon's purifying power does not seem to have survived. That faith was destroyed, apparently, and the moon came to be regarded as positively unwholesome in her influence, by the same turn of thought that made many theorizers regard the unicorn's horn, once the very emblem of purity, as essentially poisonous. At first the moon's effect in dispersing noxious vapours was explained partly by the speed and proximity of her course which enabled her to f   the air and keep it in motion, and partly also by reference to her essential purity. "As Albumasar sayth, the mone clensyth the ayre, for by his contynuall mevynge he makyth the ayre clere & thynne. And soo yf mevynge of the spere of the mone were not the ayre sholde be corrupte wyth thyckenesse & enfeccion that sholde come of out-drawynge by nyghte of vapours & moystures, that grete corrupcion shold come thereof." [69] The more common and less learned view of the ancient world was, however, that the moon acted upon poisons by simple "antipathy", she herself remaining pure. By the time of Ptolemy the Geographer this opinion seems to have changed, in accordance with changes going on in medical theory, and the moon's effect upon noxious vapours was attributed to her "sympathy" with them; it was apparently ascribed to the high potency of poison in her own essence which enabled her to draw all lesser poisons into herself. Using the jargon of later times, her action was no longer explained by the principle of "allopathy", but was regarded as "homœopathic". For a long period, however, the two explanations overlapped and were used alternately as occasion served, just as they were in discussions of the alicorn's medicinal action and just as a modern physician may turn from one theory of medicine to the other with no feeling of inconsistency. We may surmise that the shift was not due so much to passage of time as to differences of latitude and climate, for the moon has always seemed beneficent and pure in the southern lands from which astrology came, but in northern countries it has usually been thought unwholesome, sinister, dangerous, while remaining unquestionably therapeutic.[70]

The pertinence of all this to the problem now in hand, whether the moon and the unicorn can be in any way identified with each other, is made clear by Ptolemy and two of his commentators. We are told in Ptolemy's *Tetrabiblon* that the chief influence of the moon is exercised upon "humours", and that it is able to wield this influence because it is nearer to the earth than other heavenly bodies and so can draw vapours from the earth into itself.[71] In another place the same author remarks that the moon is saturated with the exhalations of the earth.[72] The Arabian astrologer known to Europe as Albumasar doubted these assertions, holding that the earth's vapours cannot rise higher than sixteen stadia—less than two miles—and that the moon is considerably farther away than that.[73] Albumasar was triumphantly answered by Cardan, who says in his amplified translation of Ptolemy that we can actually see the moon drawing vapours and that she does this not by contact and immediate absorption, like a sponge, but by innate and essential power acting at a distance like the power of a magnet upon iron. In other words, her action is due to her *forma*, and is exactly analogous to that attributed by Andrea Bacci to the alicorn.

One comes upon these passages and fits them into their place with something like the thrill a mason may feel when he sees his key-stone slip smoothly down between the two halves of an arch on which he has been labouring with secret doubts of final success. (The petty triumphs of literary research are so minute and they are so commonly made in large libraries, where one is not allowed to shout "Eureka!" above a whisper, that this bit of confession may be pardoned.) For is not the belief in the moon's power to absorb poisons rising from earth during the darkness closely similar to the belief in the unicorn's water-conning? Does it not recall the vivid picture of the three-legged ass dipping his golden horn into the waters of the firmament and dispelling their corruption? One's fancy, warmed by exercise, rushes on into the Middle Ages and the Renaissance, almost ready to believe that in these ancient superstitions about the moon there may be found a source for the beliefs concerning the unicorn.

When fancy rushes forward at such speed, however, it is always well that some other faculty of the mind should hold back. Solar and lunar hypotheses, as we ought to know by this time, are dangerously seductive sirens, and many a tall ship has gone on the rocks just here, so that the voyager who will not stop his ears should lash himself to the mast. And yet I have agreed to give this hypothesis its chance. No harm can be done by a merely tentative and experimental assumption that the unicorn of the lion-capture story once stood for the moon. Let us make this assumption and see whither it will lead.

If the unicorn is to represent the moon, then the lion, a common solar emblem, should of course represent the sun, and we have only the tree left to be explained. Trees are involved in several problems concerning the unicorn. Many descriptions of the virgin-capture specify that the maiden must be seated either in a wood or under a tree, and nearly all the mediaeval illuminations place her there. (Plate XXI). Professor Otto Wiener has advanced an ingenious theory that in the original form of the story the animal was captured by the tree itself, and in the story now before us the tree does take the place of the virgin as the lion takes that of the huntsman and his dogs. Unicorned animals are often found on Assyrian cylinder-seals grouped with a single conventionalized tree in symbolical arrangement.[74] This tree of the cylinder-seals is usually called the Tree of

Fortune, but it seems to be ultimately indistinguishable from the Cosmogonic Tree, the Tree of the World, springing from the nether darkness and holding the earth and heavenly bodies in its branches, familiar in the myths of many peoples but best known to us by the Scandinavian name Yggdrasil.[75] If the lion and unicorn are to represent sun and moon they will need no less a tree than this as the scene of their encounter.

We are now prepared for a bald statement of the solar-lunar theory concerning the lion-capture, and I make it in the words of that theory's most enthusiastic exponent: "The Lion-sun flies from the rising Unicorn-moon and hides behind the Tree or Grove of the Underworld; the Moon pursues, and, sinking in her turn, is sun-slain." [76] In other words, just as the lion of our story slips behind the tree to avoid the unicorn's onrush, so the sun goes behind the Tree of the World, or perhaps into that western grove called the Garden of the Hesperides; and as the unicorn is caught by the horn so the moon is held fast during the interlunar period—at which time, as many myths assert, the sun eats it up.

To this audacious theory the cautious critic objects at once that the moon is two-horned and that a far more fitting emblem for her is the common one of the bull or cow; and yet the young crescent moon standing upright in the sky does suggest a single horn, and if we are to do justice to the lunar theory it is of the crescent moon that we must think, in spite of the awkward fact that only the old moon is slain by the sun. It is possible, furthermore, that the unicorn may symbolize a normally two-horned creature such as a bull or cow whose horns are being constantly brought together and twisted into one as the herdsmen of Africa still twist the horns of their herd-leaders. To a pastoral people it may have seemed that the moon was thus marked out as the leader of the herds of the sky that follow her down to the sea, but do not drink until she has dipped her horn.

Robert Brown, the chief contender for this lunar theory, makes much of the fact that the "unicorns" of Assyrian sculpture and gems and seals are for the most part "regardant"—that is, that they are shown with heads turned and looking backward. This is indeed a remarkable characteristic of these puzzling figures. Careful examination of hundreds of examples shown by Félix Lajard shows that almost but not quite all of the animals shown in profile and with two horns are looking forward, whereas almost all of those shown with only one horn are regardant. In explanation of this Brown says: "The unicorn-goat [that is, the moon] during the first half of its career bounds forward from the sun, at which and the earth it looks back, and hence it is regardant; during the second half of its career

it bounds back toward the sun, looking back to the point whence it has begun to return."

Brown also finds significance in the fact that many of these creatures are shown touching or nearly touching the symbolic tree with their horns, and that their heads are invariably turned toward this tree.[77] From this topic he turns, naturally, to the mysterious "Horn of Ulph", which is probably the most remarkable relic in unicorn lore.

This large drinking horn was given to the Church of Saint Peter, now York Minster, in the ninth century by a certain Prince of Deira named Ulph as a token of his donation to that church of all his lands; the See of York still holds by virtue of this horn several valuable estates called Terrae Ulphi.[78] The designs carved upon it, wherever and whenever they were made, are ancient and Euphratean in ultimate origin, highly symbolistic, apparently Byzantine in style. We may account for this fact, if we like, by recalling the influence of the Orient and the Near-East upon Scandinavian art which was made possible by the great overland routes, or we may explain it by reference to the activity of Scythian traders. At any rate, the designs include the favourite theme of the lion leaping upon a horned beast— in this case apparently a fawn. What is far more important, they include the symbolic Tree of the World and an unmistakable unicorn;[79] for there can scarcely be any doubt that the artist who carved this design was thinking of one horn and not of two. The end of this horn is embedded in, or at least is touching, the tree, so that the figure represents exactly the symbol of the setting moon already discussed. The body and legs and head are those of a cow or bull, but there are two additional details that prove beyond a doubt, in Brown's opinion, that the figure is a moon-emblem: the creature's tail is converted into a serpent by being equipped with a snake's head at the end, and beneath its belly there emerges from the earth the head of a dog.[80] Now it is a fact remarkable in this connection that the goddess Hecate Triformis appears in the *Argonautica* [81] in the three forms of horse, dog, and snake, which are usually interpreted as representing respectively the full, the waning, and the crescent moon.[82] If the unicorn of the Horn of Ulph—which Robert Brown manages to call a "horned horse"—does stand for the moon, its one horn must symbolize the two horns of the crescent coalesced.

This Horn of Ulph, one must admit, is an awkward obstacle for those who are determined not to believe anything that goes by the name of solar and lunar interpretation. And indeed such incredulity is often made to look like mere prejudice, for there are of course many myths based upon primitive attempts to explain the apparent motions of sun and moon. Robert Brown's effort to show that the unicorn legend is one of these is at least impressive in spite of its awkwardness and extravagance. If Brown had brought to bear such corroborative evidence as I have cited from Ptolemy and Cardan concerning early beliefs about the moon and if he had related his theory to the total sweep of the unicorn legend, I do not say that he would have established his thesis, but at any rate he would have left less room than he did for another book in English about the unicorn.

I find that I have suggested eight possible sources for the unicorn legend: the rhinoceros, the oryx, the separate horn, the freak of nature, horn-twisting, a misinterpreted art convention, the three-legged ass, and lunar myth. For each of these I have argued faithfully as though, for the time being, I believed in it alone. The fact is that I believe in them all, and I see no more necessity that the unicorn legend should have sprung from a single source than that the Nile should rise in a single spring or that an oak with fifty arms should have a single root. It is true that one stream out of all the many that are braided together at last in the Nile comes from farthest back in the mountains, so that all the others are reduced to the rank of affluents and tributaries, but men quarrelled and explored for ages before they could decide which stream that is. Similarly, there may have been a primitive unicorn, a unicorn almost divine, of which the rhinoceros and oryx were only the unworthy avatars, so nobly conceived that every object and creature that called it to mind— separate horns, single-horned sports, cattle with twisted horns, bas-reliefs that suggested one-horned animals—aroused a kind of awe, so holy that it gave rise to a Persian myth. The influence of these subsidiary sources may have been to revive the earlier belief when it was languishing and to provide fresh nuclei round which ideas that had at first no connection with them might cluster. The rhinoceros and the oryx, for example, may have been at first mere earthly representatives of the supreme unicorn, as the onager of Persia was a representative of the three-legged ass, acquiring later in popular belief some of the characteristics of their great progenitor, which was then forgotten. But through all these languishings and revivals the unicorn has maintained an amazing consistency.

From beginning to end of his long history he has been wild, fleet, chaste, solitary, and beneficent.

And now, having pursued the unicorn through the ages and seen him take refuge at last in the sky, we may end our search for the source of his legend. We end it not because we have plucked out the heart of his mystery but because there is no farther to go, seeing that we cannot enter the dark, brooding heart and mind of early man. The unicorn escapes us at last, as we should wish, for "he is not to be taken alive". Like every other thing or idea that we pursue to the limits of our powers and knowledge he goes forth into mystery.

CHAPTER IX

CERTAINTIES

THE zoologists of four hundred years ago believed that every terrestrial form of animal life had a marine counterpart. When men began to think, in the seventeenth century, that the land-surface of the globe had been fully explored and yet no unicorn was anywhere discovered, it was natural, therefore, that they should seek the animal beneath the ocean waves. They were justified by at least a partial success: the alicorn, whose origin had been concealed so long by the mists and dangers of the northern seas and by that old fear of the Atlantic sedulously propagated two thousand years before by Phoenician merchants, was traced at length to its source. The method of this discovery and the effects of it upon commerce and medicine and scholarship, the coincidence of it with the dawn of modernity, the light it threw backward over the way we have come— these things, which make up perhaps the most interesting department of unicorn lore, are what we have left to consider.

Near the end of an exceedingly dull history of Iceland [1] I find a vivid passage relating how Arnhald, the first Bishop of that country, was wrecked off the west coast of it in the year 1126, barely escaping with his life. There is a marsh on the mainland, the narrator tells us, near the spot where the shipwreck occurred, and this marsh was in his time still called the Pool of Corpses because of the many bodies of drowned sailors washed ashore there after the disaster. "And there also were found, afterward, the teeth of whales (*dentes*

balenarum,) very precious, which had gone down with the ship and
then had been thrown on shore by the motion of the waves. These
teeth had runic letters written on them in an indelible red gum [2]
so that each sailor might know his own at the end of the voyage,
for they had apparently been tossed into the hold helter-skelter as
though intended merely for ballast."

To one reader, at least, that passage is not merely vivid but
thrilling, for these "whales' teeth" were indeed very precious.
Shakespeare's Clarence saw no greater wealth in his gorgeous dream
of the under-sea than this that went down with the Bishop of
Iceland eight hundred years ago and was found again in the Pool of
Corpses. The fact that each man had his name written on the teeth
he owned shows that they were already valuable, but this was
in 1126; their market value was to increase for five centuries until
they were worth ten times their weight in gold. The "whales' teeth"
found in the Pool of Corpses were the "true unicorns' horns" of
kings' treasuries.

How many cargoes such as this were brought safely to port in
later years no one can say, for they belonged to a business in which
it did not pay to advertise. There were not enough of them, at any
rate, to glut the market, nor did they come in frequently enough to
attract the slightest attention in Europe. Four hundred and fifty
years after Arnhald's shipwreck there were scarcely more than twenty
famous alicorns in Europe, and although these were very famous
indeed no one had the faintest notion of their origin. If the situation
had been planned and prepared by a master of salesmanship it could
not have been arranged more admirably.

Four hundred and fifty years pass by, and in 1576 Sir Humphrey
Gilbert presents to Queen Elizabeth his famous argument to prove
that there must be a north-west passage to Cathay. He has to meet
the arguments in favour of a north-east passage made by Anthonie
Jenkinson, one of which is that a unicorn's horn has been picked
up on the coast of Tartary. Whence could it have come, Jenkinson
asks, unless from Cathay itself? Sir Humphrey replies: "First, it is
doubtful whether those barbarous Tartarians do know an Unicornes
horne, yea, or no: and if it were one, yet it is not credible that the

Sea could have driven it so farre, being of such nature that it will not swimme. . . . There is a beast called Asinus Indicus (whose horne most like it was) which hath but one horne like an Unicorne in his forehead, whereof there is great plent⁷ in all the north parts thereunto adjoyning, as in Lappia, Norvegia, Finmarke, etc. And as Albertus saieth, there is a fish which hath but one horne in his forehead like to an Unicorne, and therefore it seemeth very doubtful both from whence it came and whether it were Unicorne's horne, yea, or no."

In the following year Martin Frobisher set forth on his second voyage to discover a north-west passage, and during this voyage his men discovered, in the words of Master Dionise Settle: "A dead fish floating, which had in his nose a horn straight and torquet, of length two yards lacking two inches, being broken in the top, where we might perceive it hollow—into the which our sailors putting spiders, they presently died. I saw not the trial thereof, but it was reported to me of a truth, by the virtue whereof we supposed it to be the sea-unicorne." [3]

Eleven years later one of these "fish" was washed ashore on the coast of Norfolk so that England had only herself to blame if she continued to pay Danish fishermen the huge sums at which alicorns were then held. Englishmen did continue to pay such prices, however, and the credit for discovering, or at any rate for publishing, the true nature of the alicorn went to another nation.

The dead "fish" found by Frobisher's company belonged to the same species of whales from which the "teeth" collected by Bishop Arnhald's sailors had come, and that species was of course the narwhal—*monodon monoceros*. The adult males of these marine mammals, from ten to eighteen feet in length, have single teeth or tusks of pure ivory extending for half their length from the left side of the upper jaw, pointing forward and a little downward. [4] The fact that they are seldom seen south of Greenland explains the success of Scandinavian fishermen in keeping their lucrative secret for at least five centuries. Even after these animals had been closely examined and described by scholars of Copenhagen and Amsterdam curious misapprehensions concerning them held on well into the eighteenth century. In particular, it took over a hundred years to quell the belief that the narwhal's tusk was a "horn" and that it sprang from the middle of the forehead.

A well-written and sensible book published in 1665, for example, makes this assertion: "*Comme la Licorne de terre a une corne au front, cette Licorne de mer en avoit aussi une parfaitement belle au devant de la teste.*" [5] Thus far all is clear, but the reader is somewhat confused when he finds in the same chapter a good description of the actual narwhal. It happened that just when the author of this book, César de Rochefort, was writing the revision of his chapter on the *Licorne de Mer* for a second edition there arrived at Rotterdam a Flemish ship from Davis Strait which had on board many narwhals' tusks—"*une quantité bien considerable de ces dens ou cornes de ces Poissons qu'on appelle Licornes de Mer*". From these sailors he may have gained his correct notions of the narwhal, but he hands on to his readers without prejudice both the narwhal and the *Licorne de Mer*, giving pictures of both (Plate XXII). According to the economical customs of the times, these pictures did service in several other books, propagating error wherever they went. They were used by de la Martinière, for example, in his popular *Voyage des pays Septentrionaux*,[6] where confusion is worse confounded by the addition of a vigorous woodcut depicting the capture of a *Licorne de Mer* (Plate XXIII). The author informs us that he saw this capture—pretty certainly that of a cetacean because the harpoon was used—with his own eyes, and that he studied the head carefully, yet he allowed his engraver to place the "horn" in the middle of the brow. Furthermore, he says of the creature caught just after this one that it had no horn but that this was atoned for by the fact that its teeth were "*beaucoup plus grosses*". Now the fact is that the narwhal has only two teeth; in the young and in females both are rudimentary and in adult males one is enormously developed into the tusk. Unless de la Martinière's second *licorne* was a walrus I can make no sense of his passage, and even in that case it remains mysterious how an intelligent man can "study" the head of a narwhal and still believe that its "horn" springs from the brow.

XXIII. THE LICORNE DE MER

The unicorn was "an unconscionable time adying". No sooner was the narwhal discovered by Europeans—putting the legendary beast, as one might have thought, in deadly danger of being explained away—than they made a horn of its tooth and placed that horn where the horn of a unicorn ought to be. For was not the narwhal the *Licorne de Mer*, the unicorn of the sea? The rest followed, in spite of ocular evidence. A man who was by no means a fool could "study" the head of a narwhal, seeing clearly with his eyes if not with his mind that the creature's tusk issued from the upper jaw, and yet when he came to give directions to his engraver he was tricked by a mere word, the word "*Licorne*", into making that tusk a horn. There is no more vivid example of our inveterate tendency to see only what we expect to see, to think in terms of labels and phrases, to ignore the unfamiliar, to let the present be ruled by the past. One may judge what progress knowledge of the narwhal had made in England by the year 1721 from this definition: "*Unicorn Whale*— A fish eighteen feet long, having a head like a horse and scales as big as a crown piece, six large fins like the end of a galley oar, and a horn issuing out of the forehead nine feet long, so sharpe as to pierce the hardest bodies." [7]

About one hundred years later still "a sea-unicorn's horn, seven foot and a half long" was to be seen at a coffee-house in Chelsea. Thomas Roscoe was at this time working at his translation of Cellini's *Memoirs* in far-off Liverpool, and when he came across a note in which Cellini's Italian editor, Carpani, says that the unicorn is a wholly fabulous animal he wrote: "From all we hear of the fine specimen of a unicorn's head—an unique, we suppose, now in London—the Italian commentator will soon be obliged to change his tone." [8] These are the words, be it observed, of a highly educated Englishman of the nineteenth century.

Dutch and Danish scholars had told the world everything of importance about narwhal tusks and their relation to the traffic in alicorns two hundred years before the time of Roscoe. They had, to be sure, a definite advantage of position, for ships from the northern seas with narwhal tusks in their cargoes were frequently

calling at Copenhagen and Amsterdam, but their chief advantage
was that they read everything without believing all that they read,
that they were insatiably curious, and that they were rather more
disposed than any other body of scholars in Europe to try all things
and to hold fast only what seemed to be true.

Several early writers attribute to Pierre Belon, the sixteenth-
century traveller and zoologist, the first identification of the alicorn
with the narwhal's tusk.[9] Feeling that such a discovery would be an
important addition to the claims this bold and brilliant man already
has upon memory, I have searched his writing for confirmation, but
all that I find is his assertion that the alicorn is often merely the
"*dent de Rohart*".[10] This is not quite the same thing as the narwhal
discovery, for the *rohart* is the walrus or morse, concerning whose
tusks Hector Boëthius had made the same assertion some time before.
Olaus Magnus, Archbishop of Upsala, came closer to the truth in
saying that "the monoceros is a sea-monster that has in its brow
a very large horn wherewith it can pierce and wreck vessels and
destroy many men".[11] Perhaps we have here the literary origin of
the *Licorne de Mer* celebrated by de Rochefort and de la Martinière,
but Olaus Magnus is not entitled to the rank of discoverer for
Albertus Magnus was in advance of him by several centuries.
Closer to the fact than either of these remarks is the brief statement
of Amatus Lusitanus—who makes an excellent showing everywhere
by the unicorn test—that some fraudulent merchants "sell whale
bones in place of unicorns' horns".[12] Andrea Marini, writing in 1566,
suggests that the sea, "which often breeds animals very like those of
the land, and much more numerous", is the source of most of the
alicorns of Europe, and he suspects that all of those in England are
of marine origin because "there is not even a record of a one-horned
beast in that country". It seems probable to him that the sea has cast
up many objects with the shape and substance of horns, and he even
knows that there is "a sea-unicorn which has, as it were, a single
horn," though just what this horn is he cannot say. Three years
later the excellent Goropius of Antwerp goes a step beyond Marini.
After a close description of a great narwhal's tusk which was before
him as he wrote, one of three exposed for sale, he speculates about

its origin: "I sometimes suspect", says he with the caution of a scholar, "that this is the horn of some fish, because many remarkable horns are found among fishes and also because this horn at Antwerp was brought from Iceland. And yet it occurs to me, on the other hand, that this island is not far from the Pole, and that animals may be much more numerous there because of the absence of men, wherefore it is not absurd to suppose that the horn comes from a beast after all." [13]

The men thus far named had only glimmerings of the truth. We may learn from them by what slow processes the way is prepared for a slight advance in knowledge, how subject the knowledge once gained always is to relapses, and with what difficulty it was disentangled from old errors.

William Boffin, the English voyager, came a little closer in a letter written in 1615 concerning the north-west passage: "As for the Sea Unicorne", says he, "it being a great fish having a long horne or bone growing forth of his forehead or nostril (such as Sir Martin Frobisher in his second voyage found one) in divers places we saw of them, which if the horne be of any goode value, no doubt but many of them may be killed." [14] Not much credit is due to Boffin for these remarks, however, for he has not made up his mind whether the "horn" grows from the brow or the nostril and he does not know whether it is "of any goode value".

The earliest clear statement of all the essential facts that I have found is that of the great geographer Gerard Mercator. In one of his discussions of Iceland he says: "Among the fish is included the Narwhal. Anyone who eats its flesh dies immediately. It has a tooth in its head which projects to a length of seven cubits, and some sell this tooth as unicorn's horn. It is considered good against poison. The beast is forty ells in length." [15] Caspar Bartholinus, who wrote seven years later, in 1628, did not know so much as this, for he still calls the tusk a horn, [16] and if Mercator's statement had been somewhat ampler full credit for the discovery would be due to him. As it is, the man to whom that credit should be given acknowledges that Mercator had made a prior announcement of his own conclusions.

This man is Ole Wurm, Regius Professor of Denmark and a

zoologist and antiquarian of high attainment. Perhaps the most important event recorded in unicorn lore was his public delivery at Copenhagen in 1638 of his Latin dissertation on the narwhal's tusk.[17] The dissertation was called forth by a dispute among the merchants of Copenhagen about the true nature and origin of the substance they were selling as unicorn's horn—a quaint and antique situation indeed, when it is considered that the learned Professor was appealed to, so far as one can see, not for purposes of advertisement but actually to decide the question. If any of the alicorn merchants of the city expected Professor Wurm to put patriotism before truth and to "remember who paid his salary", they must have been grievously disappointed, for his remarks were decidedly "bad for business". He began with a careful description of the alicorns to be seen in his time all over Europe, everywhere regarded and highly treasured as horns of unicorns. So far are they from being such, he then says, that they are not horns at all. They have neither the substance, nor the shape of horns and they are not set in the animal's cranium as horns are. He asserts that they have all the characteristics of teeth and that teeth they must be called. In his third section Ole Wurm declares that the alicorns of Europe are the teeth of narwhals, citing as evidence the cranium of a narwhal, which he has recently examined. This cranium he describes, and also the tusk projecting from the left side of the upper jaw, with painstaking exactness. He concludes by saying that in the future those who do not care to deny the authority of witnesses and even of their own senses will be obliged to admit that the alicorn is really the tooth of the narwhal.

One might suppose that after such a public statement of the facts, iterated as it was by the author himself and by many others,[18] the vogue of the alicorn would have ceased and the whole unicorn legend would have begun to die away. On the contrary, the dissertation seems to have had little more effect at first than such productions usually have. Public faith in the unicorn was unshaken. The trust of physicians and princes in the alicorn remained. It is true that the price of narwhals' tusks fell off sharply at about this time, but that was chiefly due to a glutting of the market.[19] I have shown that the tusk was to be used in the royal household of France for one hundred and fifty years after Ole Wurm's dissertation was delivered and printed; it was to be kept on the official pharmacopœia of London for more than a century to come; good physicians continued for a long time to speak highly of its medicinal virtues. Ignorance and mental indolence, better known as conservatism, may have been chiefly responsible for this, but they were assisted by these two facts: the disclosure of the marine origin of most alicorns did not by any means disprove the existence of the terrestrial unicorn; on the contrary, if there was a unicorn of the sea it seemed to follow necessarily that there was one of the land as well. Further, the proof that the alicorns of Europe were whales' teeth did not cause people to abandon the belief in their medicinal virtues, for it seemed natural to suppose that the sea-unicorn would have all the properties attributed to his counterpart of the land.

We may infer that Ole Wurm's dissertation had little effect even in his own land from a remark made by de la Martinière about the disposition of the two "horns" taken by his company to which I have already referred: "One of the Principals of the Company was ordered by the rest in all their names to present to his Majesty [Frederic III of Denmark] the two sea-horses horns that we brought home with us, which his Majesty received as a most estimable present, supposing they had been Unicornes Horns, of the virtues of which so many authors had written. He ordered them presently to be laid up among the best of his rarities, promised the Company to do them what benefit he could, and presented the bearer with a Chain of Gold with his Picture hanging to it, and forgave him his Customes besides." [20] One can only surmise, reluctantly, that Frederic III did not read all the works of his Regius Professor.

The two "horns" presented on this occasion to the King of Denmark are heard of again in the *Travels* of Dr. Edward Browne, son of Sir Thomas. "Two such as these", he writes, "the one ten foot long, were presented not many years since to the King of Denmark, being taken near to Nova Zembla." But this Edward Browne is a scoffer, and his testimony is valuable chiefly as showing how plentiful alicorns became towards the end of the seventeenth century.

He asserts that he has "seen some full fifteen feet long, some wreathed very thicke, some not so much, and others plain: some largest and thickest at the end near the Head; others are largest at some distance from the Head; some very sharp at the end or point, and others blunt. My honoured Father Sir Thomas Browne had a very fair piece of one which was formerly among the Duke of Curland's rarities, but after that he was taken prisoner by Douglas it came into the hands of my Uncle Colonel Hatcher, of whom my Father had it. He also had a piece of this sort of Unicornes Horn burnt black, out of the Emperor of Russia's Repositorie. . . . I have seen a walking Staffe, a Sceptre, a Scabbard for a Sword, Boxes, and other Curiosities made out of this Horn, but was never so fortunate as from experience to confirm its medical Efficacy against Poisons, although I have known it given several times and in great quantity. Mr. Charleton hath a good Unicorn's Horn. Sir Joseph Williamson gave one of them to the Royal Society. The Duke of Florence hath a fair one. The Duke of Saxony a strange one, and besides many others I saw eight of them together upon one table in the Emperor's treasure, and I have one at present that for the neat wreathing and the elegant shape gives place to none. But of these Unicorns' Horns no man sure hath so great a Collection as the King of Denmark; and his Father had so many that he was able to spare a great number of them to build a magnificent Throne out of Unicorns' Horns." [21]

This alicorn throne of Denmark was in its time one of the chief wonders of Europe, and if Edward Browne mentioned it to show how cheap the material had become he did not choose a good example. It was begun by Frederic III and was long used as the Coronation Chair, the legs and arms and all the supporting pieces being made of alicorn. (If the construction of such thrones was at all common in the remoter past then it is clear why all captured unicorns were led at once "to the palace of the king".) Christian V was crowned in this chair in 1671 and the officiating bishop remarked: "History tells us of the great King Solomon that he built a throne of ivory and adorned it with pure gold, but your Majesty is seated on a throne which, though like King Solomon's in the splendour of its materials and shape is unparalleled in any kingdom." Whatever might be said of

the learned professions, Church and State had not abandoned
the unicorn.

The dissertation of Ole Wurm did not shake the faith of Europe,
as I have said, in any serious degree. Belief in the medicinal value
of narwhal tusk remained as strong as ever—and Ole Wurm, like
Caspar Bartholinus, seems to have shared this belief himself. And
after all this was a sensible attitude, for the substance remained the
same that it had always been, although a few persons now called it
by a new name and thought of it as coming from another part of the
world. César de Rochefort, in the passage in which he speaks of the
cargo of tusks just arrived at Amsterdam from the northern seas,
remarks that they are certain to bring a great price because all the
most celebrated physicians and apothecaries, having tested them in
various ways, assert *"qu'elles chassent le venin, et qu'elles ont toutes les
mêmes proprietez qu'on attribue communement à la Corne de la Licorne
de terre"*. And this in 1665 was still approximately true.

Eleven years after that date appeared the curious monograph by
Paul Ludwig Sachs, M.D.,[22] the main purposes of which are to
show that the unicorn really exists, that its true name is "narwhal",
and that the narwhal's "horn"—for Sachs rejects all theories about
"teeth"—has at least the alexipharmic if not the magic properties
formerly attributed to the alicorn. So much he has himself proved
by repeated scientific experiments, and he quotes in corroboration
of his belief a dozen of the most prominent physicians of the time
who used the "horn" in daily practice. Taking his point of view,
one smiles with sympathy at his pious outburst by way of peroration:
"Therefore we cannot sufficiently adore and wonder at the marvellous goodness of God, who has brought forth for us things useful
and beneficial to our health not only from the bowels of the earth
and from the mountain-tops but even from the abysses of the sea.
In the sea the unicorn is found. Those precious objects which have
long been kept like pearls in the treasuries of princes and which
our forefathers vainly sought among the wild forests and mountains
of Africa and America are now brought to us from the ocean waves.
This miraculous and never-enough-to-be-praised horn forces us to

cry out with the royal prophet: 'Praise the Lord from the deep, ye whales and all abysses; yea, all creatures, praise the Lord. Hallelujah!'"

The remarks of Pierre Pomet on this topic [23] are considerably more restrained. He has no more belief in the terrestrial unicorn than Paul Sachs had, and rather less confidence in the tusk, yet he hands on de Rochefort's *Licorne de Mer*, together with the inevitable picture, in addition to the narwhal, leaving the reader to suppose that there were two marine creatures with this medicinal horn. Nicolas Lemery, another French pharmacist of wide influence, says much the same things in 1733, although he tacitly ignores the *Licorne de Mer*.[24] He asserts that the narwhal tusk strengthens the heart, induces perspiration, cures epilepsy, and is *"propre pour resister au venin"*. These are exactly the same claims that had been made two hundred years before for the unicorn's horn, although nearly a century had passed since the appearance of Ole Wurm's dissertation. Lemery says that the reason for the alicorn's great rarity in former days was that the narwhal was then unknown, *"mais depuis qu'on a pêché beaucoup de ces poissons, cette corne n'est plus guéres rare; on en trouve chez plusieurs Marchands coupées par tronçons"*.

The remark of Lemery that by the year 1733 the alicorn was much more common than in former times leads one to ask what had been the narwhal tusk's commercial history. The materials for an answer to this interesting question are few, partly because that history belongs to a time when no trade records were kept and partly because those concerned had no desire that their transactions should be generally known. What little can be said on this topic, therefore, must be based primarily upon inferences.

One of the inferences to be drawn from the few facts at our disposal is as unquestionable as it is significant. I have already spoken more than once of the fact that in mediaeval pictures of the unicorn found in illuminated manuscripts that go back to the twelfth century, the animal's horn almost invariably shows the characteristic striae, the "anfractuous spires and cochleary turnings",[25] which are found on no object in nature except the narwhal's tusk. Now when we consider that the narwhal is almost never seen south of

Greenland,[26] that the seas in which it swims were utterly unknown to Europeans in the twelfth century—or, for that matter, in the fifteenth—and that its tusk will not float, we can reach only one conclusion: narwhal tusks have been articles of merchandise for at least eight hundred years. The same conclusion is indicated by the remarkable passage quoted above in which Arngrimr Jonsson records the loss, in 1126, of a cargo of tusks collected among the gulfs of Iceland. A study of the Mediterranean trade carried on during the Middle Ages in Scandinavian bottoms will show that there would be no difficulty, when once such tusks reached Norway or Denmark, for them to find their way into the treasure chests of Europe.

How much farther than that they went, and how much earlier than 1126 they set out on their travels, is harder to say. The overland routes by which the trade of Scandinavia was carried into Russia and southward toward the Black Sea must have absorbed many of them, and the tradition that the two alicorns of St. Mark's in Venice were taken at the division of spoils from Constantinople in 1204 is therefore, in itself, not incredible. In Arabia they had apparently ousted the rhinoceros horn as early as the fourteenth century, for Alkazuwin says that the unicorn has "one horn on his head, sharp at the point and thicker at the bottom, with raised striae outside and a hollow within". We may be fairly sure, however, that the tusks did not reach China in considerable numbers until the legend of the Ki-lin was complete, for there is no evidence of acquaintance with them in the descriptions and representations of that animal. Whether they gave rise to the Italian word *licorno* one cannot certainly say. One does not see how they could have had any dispersion whatever in Europe or Asia before the seas about Iceland became known at least to a few adventurers, and it is this fact, among others, that makes Aelian's word ἐλιγμούς so tempting to the historic imagination. If we translate that word cautiously and conservatively by "rings", as I have done, then it is fairly certain that Aelian had in mind the horn of an antelope; but if we translate it by "spirals"—a sense in which it was used by Aristotle, with reference to snail-shells, and also by Aelian himself

—then we must think of narwhal tusks as brought back from Ultimate Thule in the third century of the Christian era.

One thing is perfectly evident regarding this traffic: it never amounted to a regular trade. So much is made clear by the great prices commanded by the tusks in the sixteenth century, after they had been known for at least four hundred years. Even if we allow fifty per cent. for the goldsmith's work upon the Horn of Windsor or upon that for which Pope Julius III paid ninety thousand scudi, it is clear that the tusks had enormous rarity value. In the middle of the sixteenth century there were probably not more than fifty whole tusks in all of Europe and Great Britain, although the smaller pieces were more numerous, and these, seeing that they were precious and almost indestructible, represented certainly a large part of the total importation from the beginning. Taken together with the huge prices and the fact that the supply was almost unlimited,[27] this paucity is somewhat perplexing. We can scarcely believe that the middlemen who conducted the sales had the economic foresight and knowledge which would have made them refrain from glutting the market. Perhaps we need only remember that the voyage to Iceland and Greenland was a different thing in the centuries of which we are speaking from what it is now, that means of advertisement were almost entirely lacking,[28] and that the number of persons who would be practically interested, so to speak, in alicorns was always narrowly restricted. Furthermore, the maintenance of high prices for the tusks is partly explained by the fact that just when they began to be more plentiful in Europe a fresh impetus to the belief in their medicinal value was contributed by Portuguese travellers returning from India. The rhinoceros was introduced to Europe at about the same time, and it was felt that his horn would not meet the specifications because it was too short and not at all like the alicorns represented in pictures. Narwhal tusks on the other hand corresponded exactly, and for the best of reasons, with pictures of unicorns' horns that had behind them almost the authority of revelation.

We may be quite as certain of one other thing about this traffic: during the earlier centuries it did not involve conscious deceit on the part of anyone. The seamen of the North who collected the tusks may not even have known under what name and with what representations concerning their value they were finally sold.²⁹ Those who conducted the final sales may not have been aware, in the earlier centuries, of the tusks' origin.³⁰ Even if they had been aware of this, their notions of zoology and of *materia medica* were certainly no clearer than those of the scholars and physicians whose opinions we have examined, and they would have felt entirely justified in selling for ten times its weight in gold a substance for which such miraculous powers were everywhere asserted and accepted. There was a definite though restricted demand for alicorns, but there was no general agreement as to just what these were. Rhinoceros horns had a considerable following and walrus tusks, artificially straightened, had probably a greater; fossil bones and petrified wood and even stalactites were used in large quantities; after the end of the fourteenth century, however, the tooth of the narwhal defeated all competitors and was accepted by the experts as "true unicorn". A busy merchant could not trouble himself about such niceties. The public wanted unicorns' horns; his business was to give the public what it wanted and to get the best price he could.³¹

Before it established itself above all rivals the narwhal's tusk met with some opposition, as we have seen, from those who knew what the ancients had said about unicorn's horn. The chief objection was to its colour, for both Pliny and Aelian had said that the true horn was black. Boëthius de Boodt disposed of most of the horns to be seen in his time by saying that they were not of the right colour,³² and Amatus Lusitanus advised his readers to purchase the black variety—antelope or rhinoceros horn—when it could be had. Pietro della Valle, again, although much interested in the tusk shown him by Captain Woodstock, who had found it in Greenland in 1611, could not agree that it was the true horn, for this, if he remembered his Pliny correctly, had been described as black.³³ Another objection to the narwhal tusk was that it was not large enough, even at the base, to permit its being made into beakers such as those used by Indian potentates; but this difficulty was evaded by fitting together several laminæ sliced from the tusk and so constructing a tankard not unlike a German *stein*, or by inserting a single piece of the tusk in a cup made of other materials.

During the seventeenth century, however, those who had narwhal tusks for sale were confronted by more serious difficulties and objections. A probing, curious, sceptical spirit was spreading through northern Europe, inciting men to ask questions that had never been asked before and to deny beliefs that had been held for ages—beliefs that were still held, of course, by all but one or two in the million. Those who were infected by this new spirit laid a novel emphasis upon what they called "experience" and we call experiment, rating the evidence it provided almost as highly as that given by "authority" and by "reason". Not quite so logical as the Schoolmen, nor quite so erudite as their own immediate pre-decessors—although their book-learning was still enormous in comparison with that of those whom we call scientists to-day—they sought for evidence not so much in authority and tradition and the consent of the ages as in what they were more and more disposed to call "facts". Such a spirit was not good for the traffic in narwhal tusks. Very slowly but surely it diffused throughout Europe an intellectual climate in which the unicorn could not feel at home.

Like all transformations in the fundamental habits of our thought, this change was very gradual. Recent news from Tennessee and Oklahoma shows that it is far from complete to-day, and Europeans may reach the same conclusion upon evidence gathered nearer home. The mass of men, quite unaffected by Ole Wurm of whom they had never heard, went on buying powdered alicorn for more than a hundred years after his dissertation was delivered, went on drinking alicorn-water, went on believing what they were told as they always had done and as they always will do. Thomas Bartholinus certainly exaggerates the influence of the Danish discovery when he implies that it stopped the traffic in narwhal tusks. "Our merchants would have filled whole ships with this pretended horn", says he, "and would have sold it all through Europe as true alicorn, if the deceit had not been detected by experts." [34] Thus it is that scholarship constantly tends to over-estimate its own influence. The fact seems to be that if anything like whole cargoes of narwhal tusks had ever been brought to Europe they must have been brought at about the time when Bartholinus was writing, and in Danish ships. No; the scholars of Denmark may have done their best to kill the goose that laid their country's golden eggs, but the goose declined to die. All the little that may have been lost in British and European markets by Ole Wurm's unpatriotic disclosures was made up by new markets in Russia—or rather by old Russian markets first developed by the Scandinavian overland traders. When these were gone, there were still others, as we shall see, in lands much farther off where Latin dissertations were never read.

For all this, the difficulties encountered in selling the tusks at anything like the old prices did certainly increase as the seventeenth century wore on. Pietro della Valle gives us some significant information on this topic in his account of the efforts to dispose advantageously of the tusk found by Captain Woodstock. As he was bound to do by the terms of his agreement, the Captain turned this tusk over to his Company of Merchants, who sent it at once to Constantinople for sale. The best offer made for it there was only two thousand pounds.[35] Hoping to get more than this, the Company sent it to Russia, where about the same amount was offered, and in Turkey the bids were even lower. (The fact that no effort was made to sell the tusk in western Europe is significant.) At last it was cut into small pieces and disposed of bit by bit, realizing a total sum of only twelve hundred pounds.[36]

Even clearer evidence that the market was rapidly falling is found in de la Peyrère's *Relation de Groënland*, which first appeared in 1647. " 'Tis not long since", says this garrulous writer, "that the Company of New Greenland at Copenhagen sent one of their agents into Muscovy with several great pieces of these kind of horns, and amongst the rest one end of a considerable bigness, to sell it to the Great Duke of Muscovy. The Great Duke being greatly taken with the beauty thereof, he shewed it to his Physician, who, understanding the matter, told the great Duke 'twas nothing but the tooth of a fish, so that this agent returned to Copenhagen without selling his commodity. After his return, giving an account of the success of his journey, he exclaimed against the physician who had spoiled his market by disgracing his commodities. 'Thou art a half-headed fellow', replied one of the directors of the Company, as he told me since. 'Why didst thou not offer two or three hundred ducats to the physician to persuade him that they were the horns of unicorns?' " [37] If we have been right in saying that there was no conscious deceit in the earlier history of the traffic in tusks, that period is now definitely past.

There are several references to this Copenhagen Company of Greenland Merchants to be found in unicorn literature, although not so many as one could wish. It seems to have enjoyed something like a monopoly in the traffic for a time, and during a still longer period Denmark kept the business in her control. We read in *Purchas His Pilgrims*, for example, that in 1561 "a citizen of Hamburg begged the gift of a unicornes horne found in the ice of Iceland, and sold it after in Antwerp for some thousands of Florins. When this came to the King of Denmarkes eares he ruled that no Germaine should winter in Iceland in any cause." [38] Another record shows that "in the year 1606 a company of merchants in Copenhagen sent two ships into the straits under the patronage of the Chancellor Christian Fries, and they traded with the natives. . . . On this voyage the ship's company brought back the teeth or horns of the unicorn fish, which at that time were unknown, and were valued at twelve hundred pounds a piece in Copenhagen, and were sold in Russia for a great price as the horns of the land-unicorn." [39]

Although there was certainly a "period of depression", we are not to suppose that the unicorn, after his millenniums of glory, was snuffed out by a dissertation, or even that the traffic in his alleged horn was permanently disabled by the discovery that it was really the tooth of a small whale. Superstition is armed in triple bronze against all mere learning, and as for trade and commerce we should know that they will use science for their own ends precisely as far and as long as they find it lucrative. We reckon ill when we ignore the enterprise shown by modern business in finding and exploiting new markets. When it was found that western Europe would absorb no more alicorns at the old prices they were sent to Constantinople, Turkey, and Russia, and when even these markets began to fail others were discovered to take their places. One of the more amusing events in unicorn lore is the emergence of the alicorn, late in the eighteenth century, in the trade of the Far East.

The story is told by Charles Peter Thunberg, a traveller and botanist whose account of the medicinal use of rhinoceros horn in South Africa I have already quoted. He visited Nagasaki in 1775—at a time, that is, when the Dutch factory on the neighbouring island of Dezima still held a monopoly in the Japanese trade. This monopoly, which began in 1601, had formerly been of immense value, two voyages sufficing to make a Dutch captain wealthy for life; but it had recently fallen away for the sad reason that the Japanese had learned from their European visitors a few elementary tricks of trade. Among the articles imported by Japan in 1775 were camphor, tortoise-shells, spectacles, glass and mirrors, watches, chintz, and "unicorns' horns". The collocation is instructive.

"Unicorn's horn", writes Thunberg, "sold this year on Kambang very dear. It was often smuggled formerly, and sold at an enormous rate. The Japanese have an extravagant opinion of its medical virtues and powers to prolong life, fortify the animal spirits, assist the memory, and cure all complaints. This branch of commerce has not been known to the Dutch till of late, when it was discovered by an accident. One of the chiefs of the commerce here, on his return home, had sent out from Europe, amongst other rarities, to a friend of his who was an interpreter, a large, handsome, twisted Greenland unicorn's horn, by the sale of which this interpreter became extremely rich and a man of consequence. From that time the Dutch have written to Europe for as many as they could get, and made great profit on them in Japan. At first each catje [three-quarters of a pound] sold for one hundred kobangs or six hundred rixdollars, after which the price fell by degrees to seventy, fifty, and thirty kobangs. This year, as soon as the captain's wide coat had been laid aside and prohibited [to prevent smuggling] all the unicorn's horn was obliged to be sold on Kambang, the open market of Dezima, where each catje fetched one hundred and thirty-six rixdollars. . . . The thirty-seven catjes four thails which I had brought with me were therefore very well disposed of for five thousand and seventy one thails and one mas [the 'thail', in money, is about the equivalent of one rixdollar], which enabled me to pay the debts I had contracted and, at the same time, to expend one thousand two hundred rixdollars on my favourite study." [40]

Here we may close this inadequate outline of the narwhal tusk's commercial history, not because there is nothing left to say, but because we should find chiefly disillusionment in pursuing the research until we came to the hogsheads crammed with alicorns that may be seen stored to-day in the London docks. And here, too, we may as well end our sketch of the lore of the unicorn, although certainly not for lack of further materials. It is something to have shown how it happened that, perhaps on account of a curious set of beliefs about the moon worked out ages ago by Mesopotamian astrologers, a European scholar of the eighteenth century was able to equip himself for his botanical studies by selling bits of narwhal tusk at twelve rixdollars an ounce to credulous Orientals.

At any rate, I have accounted for the long, straight stick of ivory that lies before me on the table.

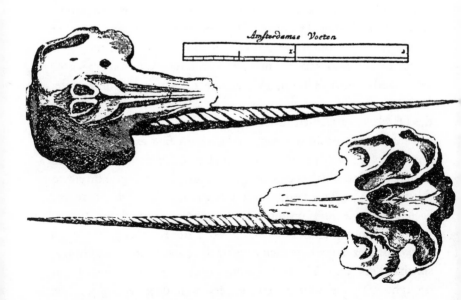

CHAPTER X

REFLECTIONS

I

RELIGIOUS history presents few stranger possibilities than this, that the beast sculptured on the staircases at Persepolis may have come at last, after as many changes as the Old Man of the Sea went through, to stand depicted in the windows of Christian cathedrals; that the three-legged ass may have been transformed eventually into a symbol of Christ; that a lunar myth of Mesopotamia may have produced after two thousand years an allegorical representation of the central Christian mystery. Whether these changes ever occurred or not, the unicorn has preserved through all his long history a character that would have made them possible.

For the most part we have made the beasts of fancy in our own image—far more cruel and bloodthirsty, that is to say, than the actual "lower animals". The dragons of the Western world do evil for evil's sake; the harpy is more terrible than the vulture, and the were-wolf is far more frightful than the wolf. Almost the only beast that kills for the pure joy of killing is Western civilized man, and he has attributed his own peculiar trait to the creatures of his imagination. There are a few exceptions, however, to this rule that our projection of ourselves is lower than the facts of Nature, and the unicorn—noble, chaste, fierce yet beneficent, altruistic though solitary, strangely beautiful—is the clearest exception of all. The unicorn was not conceived in fear. Our early sense of Nature's majesty and mystery is revealed in him. If he came from Ur of the

Chaldees, where the moon was a friend to man always contending against the demoniacal sun and the powers of darkness alike, his constant benevolence is more readily understood; but whatever may have been his first local habitation and whatever was his original name, this "airy nothing" was born and bred in the human mind. There are times when one takes hope and comfort in remembering the fact.

II

"Whoever has followed the development of a single department of knowledge", says Nietzsche, "finds in its history a clue to the understanding of the oldest and commonest processes of all intellectual life. There one finds the premature hypotheses, the idle fictions, the absence of distrust, the lack of patience, and the good stupid will to believe. Our senses learn late, and never fully learn, to be subtle, dependable, and cautious instruments of knowledge."

The legend of the unicorn is so old and it has been since its dim beginnings so close to human hearts and bosoms that it illustrates vividly Auguste Comte's three stages of intellectual "progress": the theological, the metaphysical, and the positivistic. Tracing it through the centuries, we have seen it remodelled again and again by the changing *Zeitgeist* or adjusting itself anew to the time-climates into which it has strayed. The historian of thought might find this legend, indeed, a serviceable thread upon which to arrange his generalizations, and it would save him from Comte's error, and ours, of supposing that the successive stages of human thought are stages of progress in the sense of amelioration. We do not think better about the unicorn than the men who made the myth of the three-legged ass; we think differently.

Although the conception of the unicorn does us credit, the total history of the animal's legend does not flatter our modern pride. In his beginnings, wherever and whatever they may have been, the unicorn was a symbol of beneficent power inhabiting the poetic imagination. The symbol expanded into myth and this myth was debased into fable. The unicorn next became an *exemplum* of moral virtues, then an actual animal, then a thaumaturge, then a medicine, then an article of merchandise, then an idle dream, and, last stage of all, an object of antiquarian research. Relics of the earlier stages are discoverable in the later, but what is most apparent is the steady intrusion of fact upon fancy and the invasion of what was once a sanctuary by the positivistic temper. We are accustomed to regard the growth of this temper as unqualified gain, and it has indeed brought us many advantages that no sensible man or woman would forgo, but it has not been good for unicorns or for the many holy and beautiful things that unicorns may be taken to represent. There are some quite sober moods in which one may sum up all the unquestionable advantages of modernity and calmly decide that he would "rather be a pagan suckled in a creed outworn".

Or, for that matter, a Christian of the ages when that name still connoted a rich and sufficient and poetic faith. It is true that the Middle Ages moralized the unicorn, thus contributing their share to his degradation, for Christianity inherited from the later Stoics a feeling that all nature is a vast copy-book of maxims designed for mankind's edification, a sort of subsidiary revelation of moral truths. Two thousand years have not quite rid us of that error: Wordsworth did not escape it, and even Emerson revealed his clerical upbringing by the naïve assertion that "Nature is ancillary to man". It was indeed a "pathetic" fallacy, but there are moods in which one would rather believe in even an emasculated and homiletic unicorn than in none at all.

It is not that the men of the Middle Ages who believed in the unicorn were less intelligent than we; their intelligence was trained in a different direction. A modern scientist might make the same havoc among the scientific beliefs of the Schoolmen that the Connecticut Yankee made in King Arthur's Court, but it would by no means follow that he had a better mind than that of Duns Scotus or Thomas Aquinas, any more than it follows that Mark Twain's low-bred Yankee is superior to the champions of chivalry. We care for facts, and are comparatively careless about ultimate meanings; the Middle Ages were regardful of meanings and careless about facts.

The Middle Ages saw the spiritual and physical worlds as two aspects of one thing—a view made easier by their revival of the Platonic doctrine of microcosm and macrocosm. We feel confident—although another century of scientific thought may convince us of error—that this view is hostile to the interests of science, but we should not be quite so sure that it is hostile to the interests of men and women. "By depriving objects of their share in the spiritual life of man," says Mr. Aldous Huxley, "by leaving to them only such characteristics as can be measured, physicists of the seventeenth and eighteenth centuries made possible the advance of modern science. A world regarded from the introvert's point of view, a subjectivized world, is unamenable to science. It may be picturesque and agreeable, but it is not a world for physicists and mathematicians."

Probably not, although this does not seem a serious objection to such a world, and one hopes that we have not yet fallen so low as to test the worth of this "world" and that by asking whether it has been made safe for mathematicians and physicists. Quite as reasonably one might demand assurance that a given world is safe for unicorns. But it is to Mr. Huxley's closing remark on this topic that I should like to call special attention: "The scientific theories of the Middle Ages were fruitless theories." Of course they were that in the sense that further scientific theories could seldom be deduced from them, yet there are other things to be asked about a theory than whether it is prolific of corollaries and consequences after its own image. We may ask, for example, how it is related to the total complex of human hopes and fears; and if, like the theories of the physicist and the mathematician, it has been carefully disassociated from these, then its fruit, however abundant, will be to us like Dead Sea apples and will furnish forth a Barmecide Feast. The scientific theories of the Middle Ages were not like this. They were framed, unconsciously, with human "values" always foremost in thought. When we have begun to correct our own extreme tendency in the opposite direction we can afford to be severe with them for this, but in the meantime we do well to remember that

> There are two laws discrete,
> Not reconciled,—

Law for man, and law for thing;
The last builds town and fleet,
But it runs wild,
And doth the man unking.

III

Is there no choice possible, then, except that between a docile and unquestioning acceptance of authority on the one hand and a world of physicists and mathematicians on the other? Because Ole Wurm has demonstrated that alicorns are really the teeth of whales, must we abandon the unicorn altogether? I do not see the necessity.

The higher and the enduring values of a belief—the faiths that we call religious provide the best examples—do not depend at all upon its congruity with actual fact, but upon its sway over the human heart and mind. They are grounded not upon fact, but upon what even we may perhaps still call "the truth". The question of historicity and actuality with regard to gods and unicorns is a relatively trifling matter which may be left to antiquarians and biologists, for both the god and the unicorn had a business to perform greater than any mere existence in the flesh could explain or provide a basis for. We wrong ourselves when we insist that if they cannot make good their flesh-and-blood actuality on our level we will have none of them.

The unicorn came to stand for Christ, and for that reason if for no other we can scarcely avoid passing in thought from the symbol to the symbolized. Here are two great and beautiful legends, to say no more than that, neither of which could have lived so long in the world if it had not contained a truth far higher than any historic or zoological fact could help us to understand. But legends and truths of this kind are in grave danger in a world increasingly adjusted to the requirements of physicists and mathematicians; there is question whether they can hold out against our tendency to accept no truths except those the senses seem to warrant—which is to say, no truths whatever, but only facts. The legend of the unicorn was assailed three centuries ago on the side of fact, and it gradually withered because there was no longer any sufficient capacity for a faith unsustained by the senses. That attack could never have been made if the unicorn had not first been dragged from the fastnesses of the imagination to take his chances in the mob of animals whose only claim upon our attention is that they happen to exist. Three centuries from now, if we continue to make the question of fact decisive where it should have least weight, the legend of Christ may be as outworn as that of the beast that was once His appropriate symbol. For the decline of the unicorn began with the affirmation that the animal must exist in nature, and just so, as Matthew Arnold saw with painful clearness, religion is declining because it has based its claim upon fact, or supposed fact, which is now crumbling. Our best hope seems to lie in the faith expressed by Arnold himself that in the years coming on poetry will be an ever surer and surer stay.

NOTES ON THE TEXT

CHAPTER I

1. *Anabasis*, i. 8, 26. Xenophon relates this on the authority of Ctesias himself, with obvious reference to his lost History of Persia.

2. *Ctesiae Cnidii Operum Reliquiae*, ed. Baehr, Frankfurt, 1824.

3. *Vide* Aristotle, *Hist. Anim.*, i. 8, 8.

4. *De Animalium Proprietatibus*, cap. 41 (or 40).

5. By adding the blue of the eyes, however, we get the four sacred colours of China, for the symbolic significances of which see Laurence Binyon's *The Flight of the Dragon*. Chinese writers and painters make much of the unicorn's (or Ki-lin's) colours, by which they suggest its power and nobility.

6. Arabian writers of the twelfth and thirteenth centuries tell us, for example, that when the unicorn's horn is cut longitudinally there are found within it the figures of men, trees, birds, and the like—an obvious mistaking of the products of Chinese carvers for the work of nature.

7. *Vide* Sir John Barrow's *Travels in South Africa*, London, 1808, vol. ii. p. 269.

8. *Anabasis*, i. 5, 2.

9. In a superb Assyrian frieze preserved in the British Museum the king Assur-ban-i-pal is shown hunting these animals, which are represented in bas-relief with astonishing vigour and fidelity.

10. The Zoroastrians probably did not eat or even hunt the wild ass, which was regarded as a beast of Ormuzd's creation, so that Ctesias may have had no opportunity to learn that its flesh, as a modern traveller says, is "one of the greatest delicacies of Persia". The Persian physicians of a much later date said that the flesh of the onager is sweet to the taste but bitter to digestion. The Laws of Manu (v. 11 and 18), on the other hand, after saying that it is unlawful to eat the flesh of animals with divided hoofs, mention the rhinoceros as one of the animals that may be eaten, and there is abundant proof in later literature that this animal was often eaten and was considered very wholesome.

11. This is the view taken by H. H. Wilson in his *Notes on the Indica of Ctesias*, Oxford, 1836, pp. 49–54.

12. The only careful description of this unfamiliar antelope that I have seen is in Sven Hedin's *Scientific Results of a Journey in Central Asia*, Stockholm, 1914, vol. vi. pp. 29 ff. In the photographs there given the unicorned appearance of this animal, when seen in profile, is most striking.

13. Confusion of the larger antelopes with asses is not so impossible as it may seem, for it is apparently just this confusion that Herodotus makes in his reference to the "horned asses"—probably oryxes—of "the eastern side of Libya where the wanderers live".—*History*, iv. 191.

14. *Hist. Anim.* ii. 2, 8 and vi. 36.

15. *Ibid.*

16. *Historia Animalium*, iii. 41.

17. *Ibid.*, iv. 52.

18. *Ibid.*, xvi. 20.

19. The temptation is strong to translate Aelian's ἑλιγμούς, not by "rings", but by the word "spirals", a sense which it will bear. Thomas Bartholinus, who was a good Grecian, took it in this sense. Aristotle—*Hist. Anim.* iv, 7, 11—uses it to name the markings on the snail-shell, and the basic word ἕλιξ signifies "spiral" in all its senses. The choice between the two translations has real importance in unicorn lore, as I shall show in later pages. Professor Gilbert Murray tells me that he thinks "rings" the more natural rendering, and I have decided to err, if err I must, on the side of caution.

20. This recalls the story, widely familiar even in the West because of its occurrence in the famous forgeries known as the Correspondence of Dandimus and Alexander, of the Brahmin hermits who lived apart from their wives during most of the year, but visited them once in every twelvemonth, remaining only until their wives had conceived. The parallel is interesting because the rhinoceros was sometimes held up as a model, or at least as a symbol, of the Indian sage's retirement and chastity. A vivid and beautiful example of this is seen in *Sutta-Nipâta* i. 3—*Sacred Books of the East*, vol. x. part 2, p. 6.

21. *Vide* Martial, *De Spectaculis*, 22.

22. *Hist. Nat.* viii. 33.

23. *Polyhistoria*, cap. 55.

24. *The excellent and pleasant worke of Julius Solinus Polyhistor* . . . translated by Arthur Golding, London, 1587, p. 198.

25. Philostratus, *Vita Apollonii Thyanei*, iii. 1.

26. *Cynegetica*, ii. 96.

27. *Est bos cervi figura, cuius a media fronte inter aures unum cornu existit, excelsius magisque directum his quae nobis nota sunt cornibus.—De Bello Gallico*, vi. 26.

CHAPTER II

1. I use the verse-numbering of the Oxford Edition, 1894.

2. In the Revised Version this word is consistently changed to "wild ox", glossed in the margin, not very helpfully, as "ox-antelope".

3. Gesenius, the Biblical scholar, asserted roundly that the *Re'em* of the Old Testament was identical with the unicorn described by Pliny.

4. The Seventy were led into manifest absurdity in their translation of Deuteronomy xxxiii. 17, where they write, following the original exactly, κέρατα μονοκέρωτος. The King James Version corrects this blunder as well as possible by making the name of the animal plural.

5. *De Bello Gallico*, vi. 26.

6. Sir A. H. Layard, *Nineveh and Its Remains*, London, 1849, vol. ii. p. 429. See also H. B. Tristram, *Natural History of the Bible*, London, 1867, p. 146, where the same identification is made, backed by more knowledge than Layard possessed.

7. *Yalkut Shim'oni*, ii. 97d.

8. *Zebahim*, 113b.

9. *Chulin* 60a; *Sabbat* 28b, and A; *Sara* 8a. For a full discussion of these dark matters see Dr. L. Lewysohn, *Die Zoologie des Talmuds*, Frankfurt, 1858. Rabbinical tradition says that Joshua coined money, B.C. 1440, bearing the head of a unicorn.

10. Charles Cahier does make this assumption, however, in his *Nouveaux Mélanges d'Archaeologie*, Paris, 1874, p. 106 ff., attributing some sort of editorship to Tatian. His view has not withstood criticism. The *Physiologus* has also been ascribed at various times to Saint Basil, Eustathius, Epiphanius, Chrysostom, and Isidore.

11. This *significatio* I have taken from the so-called *Physiologus* of Gottwieh, which is as simple and representative as any.

12. For a careful comparison of all existing versions see the still authoritative *Geschichte des Physiologus*, by Friedrich Lauchert, Strassburg, 1889.

13. Translated, into Latin, by J. P. N. Land in his *Anecdota Syriaca*, Lugd. Batav., 1870, vol. iv. p. 146

14. This is the view suggested, though not advocated, and rather in despair of finding any better solution than in the belief that it is correct, by Carl Cohn, *Zur Literarische Geschichte des Einhorns*, Berlin, 1883.

15. E.g., John of San Geminiano, *Summa de Exemplis*, ii. cap. 123, where it is said that she must be not only naked but bound to a tree.

16. In his *Quaestiones*, s.v. "unicornu" (Migne, *Patrol. Lat.*, vol. 210).

17. The passage was first printed by Leo Allatius in *S.P.N. Eustathii Archiepiscopi Antiocheni, et Martyris, In Hexahemeron Commentariis*, London, 1629, p. 40. It is also to be found in Migne, *Patrol. Graec.*, vol. 18, col. 744. As the Commentary is a patchwork of writings, many of which are of later date than 330, it cannot be the work of Eustathius. Dr. F. Zœpfl (*Der Kommentar des Pseudo-Eustathios zum Hexaëmeron*, Münster, 1927, p. 55) concludes that it was written between 375 and 500 at Antioch by an unknown person.

18. John of Trevisa's translation of Bartholomæus Anglicus, *De Proprietatibus Rerum*, Westminster (by Wynkyn de Worde), 1494, xviii. 90. The passage in Bartholomæus follows exactly Isidore's *Origines*, xii. 2.

19. *Rhinoceros a Graecis vocatus, Latine interpretatur in nare cornu. Idem et monoceros, id est unicornis, eo quod unum cornu in media fronte habeat pedum quatuor.*

20. By Peter Damian, Lib. ii. epistle 18; Rabanus Maurus, *Opus de Universo*, viii. 2; Bede, *Job*, cap. 39; Hugo de St. Victor, *De Bestiis et aliis Rebus*, ii. 6; Bartholomæus Anglicus, *De Proprietatibus Rerum*, xviii. 90; Albertus Magnus, *De Animalibus*, xxii. tract. ii. cap. 1; Johannes Tzetzes, *Chiliad* v. cap. 7; Gossouin, *L'Image du Monde* under rubric "*Des Bestes d'Ynde*"; Rudolf von Ems, *Weltchronik*, line 1767 ff. I mention here only the passages I have seen, but these are certainly only a small part of those that might easily be found.

21. *Speculum*, Lib. xix. cap. 114.

22. The text of the unicorn passage is given by Thomas Wright in *Popular Treatises on Science Written during the Middle Ages*, London, 1841, p. 81.

23. *Le Bestiaire Divin*, by Guillaume, Clerc de Normandie, Paris, 1852, p. 235 ff.

24. Richard de Fournival, *Le Bestiaire D'Amour*, Paris, 1860.

25. The unicorn legend was used in this way not infrequently in the erotic lyrics of the Renaissance. See e.g. *Poésies du roi de Navarre*, Paris, 1742, ii. 70, chanson 31. Johann von Antoniewicz—*Romanische Forschungen*, vol. v. p. 241 ff.—observes that the scene of the virgin-capture is frequently found on old treasure chests together with that of Tristan and Isolde in their forest bower. He says that he knows of no instance in which one of these scenes appears without the other, and he suggests that the juxta-position was meant to mark the contrast between the earthly and the heavenly love.

26. The confusion was assisted by the fact that several early and influential writers had believed the unicorn and the rhinoceros to be identical. Saint Jerome held this view. So did Tertullian (*contra Judaeos*, cap. 10), Gregorius (*Moralia*, iii. 13), and Bede (*Job*, 39).

27.
> Ist abir das sie ist ein wip
> und megde namin ir selbin giht,
> so lat er sie genesin niht
> und zeiget an ir grozin zorn:
> durch si so stichet er das horn
> und reichet an ir die volscheit
> die sie von ir selbir seit.
>
> *Weltchronik*, ll. 1792 ff.

28. Johannes Tzetzes, *Chiliad* V.

29. *Summa de Exemplis*, ii. cap. 123.

30.
> La met une pucele hors de sein sa mamele,
> E par odurement Monoceros la sent.

31. Hildegarde of Bingen, *Physica*, viii. 5.
32. But see Wolfram von Eschenbach's *Parzifal*, 613. 25:

> Das tier die meide solten klagn,
> Ez wirt durch reinheit erslagn.

33. An ivory carving in the South Kensington Museum shows the virgin crowning the huntsman with a chaplet in celebration of their mutual success. A window in the Cathedral of Lyons shows the virgin seated on the unicorn's back as a sign of her conquest. These and many similar representations show how inextricably the virgin-capture and the Holy Hunt themes—venery and Christian symbolism—were tangled together. One of the most striking examples of the virgin's duplicity that I have seen is that shown in Plate XXI, where she anoints the unicorn's head at the moment when the hunters are stealing upon him.

34. *Der beschlossen Gart des rosenkrantz Marie*, 1505, vi. folio ix. verso and ff.

35. *Sibylla Tryg-Andriana, Seu de Virginitate*, Frankfurt, 1629, cap 92. The whole book is based upon the mediaeval axiom: "*maior corona est virginum quam coniugatorum*". Kornemann is not responsible, however, for the mawkish prudery of his unicorn passage, for this follows closely Thomas Cantipré's *Miraculorum et exemplorum . . . libri duo*, caps 32 and 33.

36. The upright beam above the transverse bar in the Holy Cross was explicitly likened to the unicorn's horn by Tertullian, *Contra Judaeos*, cap. 11. This vivid metaphor, which may have been suggested by the text: "He hath raised up a mighty horn of salvation for us," became almost commonplace in the writings of the later Greek fathers.

37. An example of the use of it by the learned of western Europe is seen in a beautiful Chant Royal of the early sixteenth century, composed in honour of the Virgin by the Confrérie du Pays d'Amiens. Here occur the lines :—

> Dont de forest d'eternel prescavoir
> Clémence fit l'unicorne mouvoir
> Pour expurger l'intoxication
> De ce venin.

38. Natalis Comes (Noël Conti) *De Venatione*, Venice, 1551, iv. 1, 298 ff. The lines I have translated treat both the water-conning and the virgin-capture themes in an unusual way, as though with rationalizing intent. In the former it is not the beasts of Ahriman or the "serpents" that have poisoned the waters but *veneniferae gentes*. In the second there is no suggestion of religious allegory or of anything that would seem supernatural to the author. The virgin-capture is explained in terms of sexual attraction —an explanation studiously avoided by nearly all of the clerical writers for reasons that seemed to them binding. Natalis Comes ignores all monkish prudery and bluntly asserts: "*Virginis amplexum cupiit fera bellua*."

39. J. P. N. Land, *Anecdota Syriaca*, 1862–75, vol iv. p. 146.

40. In his ἰαμβικοι περι ζωων ἰδιοτητος, 41 (or 40). The hint is made only in the last two lines of the poem, and these may be an interpolation.

41. *Hierozoicon*, London, 1663, iii. cap. 26.

42. *Geschichte des Physiologus*, p. 24.

43. I should not wish to deny that he may have had some influence upon the minor details of the unicorn story.

44. *Contributions toward a History of Arabico-Gothic Culture*, New York, 1917. vol. iv. p. 71.

45. *Ibid.*, p. 252.

46. Taken in its entirety, Professor Wiener's argument is the reverse of simple—is indeed so complicated that after repeated re-readings I am not sure that I fully understand it. Like all this writer's work, it is characterized by great learning and amazing audacity of conjecture. In passages which I am reluctantly obliged to ignore in my text Wiener traces the unicorn through many languages and centuries, deriving him not only from the *antholops* but from the Arabian *yahmur*, from the *Urus* of Pseudo-Epiphanius, from the female kite who complained to Solomon that her mate would

not acknowledge his offspring, and from the narwhal that became the male progenitor of the Merovingian dynasty. He changes the kite into a stag without hesitation, and the stag, again, into a *bos cervi figura* with one horn. When he meets a contradiction of his theory in an old text he assumes an interpolation. The upshot of his whole argument is, however, what I have stated.

47. Old pictures of the unicorn sometimes, though very rarely, show a serrated edge on its horn. I have seen one such on a playing card of the fifteenth century and another in Johann von Cube's *Ortus Sanitatis*, 1491.

48. Al Damîrî, in *Hayât al-Hayawân* (Zoological Lexicon), 1371.

49. By Fray Luis de Urreta, Valencia, 1610, pp. 245 ff.

50. Copies of the engraving by Albrecht Dürer.

CHAPTER III

1. Besides the unicorn proper, to which he does full justice, Brunetto Latini describes also an *eglisserion*, a gigantic one-horned goat. (*Tresor*, s.v.) This seems to show that the distinction between the equine and caprine unicorns was kept alive until the middle of the thirteenth century. But Brunetto was an encyclopaedist and had need to be unusually precise and exhaustive. His eglisserion is heard of elsewhere but it had comparatively little vogue.

2. The statement is made in F. E. Hulme's *Symbolism in Christian Art*, London, 1891, p. 178, that "the unicorn is figured in the catacombs." This would be exceedingly interesting if it were true. I have searched Wilpert's exhaustive *Roma Sotteranea* and several other works on the catacombs without finding the slightest support for the assertion. In my own visits to the Roman catacombs and in conversation with men who have spent their lives among them I have convinced myself that the statement is unfounded.

3. Mrs. Jameson says in her *Sacred and Legendary Art*, London, 1848, near the beginning, that the unicorn is properly used in Christian art only as a symbol of the Virgin Mary and of Saint Justina of Antioch. Aside from the fact that the unicorn was never, properly speaking, the symbol of either of these persons, this statement ignores one of the supreme symbolisms of sacred art—that in which the unicorn stands for Christ.

4. *Legends of the Madonna*, London, 1852, p. 170.

5. *Vide* Charles Cahier, *Monographie de la Cathédrale de Bourges*, Paris, 1841, etc.

6. Several reproductions of these may be seen in the *Revue de l'Art Chrétienne*, vol. 38, January, 1888.

7. See the article *Die Jagd des Einhorns* in *Der Katholik* for 1880, describing two remarkably detailed frescoes found in a ruined castle in the Tyrol.

8. John Guillim, *A Display of Heraldry*, London, 1610, Section iii. cap 14.

9. T. D. Fosbroke, *Encyclopaedia of Antiquities*, London, 1840, vol. ii. p. 892.

10. This is seriously suggested by M. A. Lower in his *Curiosities of Heraldry*, London, 1845, p. 101. An interesting fact in favour of this view is that the tester spike was often twisted in exactly the fashion of the unicorn's horn. An example may be seen in the Armoury of the Tower of London.

11. *Observations on the Popular Antiquities of Great Britain*, London, 1870, vol. iii. chapter on "Popular Errors," article 23.

12. For accurate respresentations of the English unicorn as shown on the seals of James I, Charles I, and Charles II, see Sandford's *Kings of England*, plates 514, 515, and 517. The unicorns of James II and George I are depicted in Knight's *Old England*, ii. 192 and 256. Admirable examples of the Scottish unicorn are given on the title-page of the edition of Hector Boëthius published at Paris. Many characteristics of the English unicorn—the crown on the neck, for example, and the chain—are to be seen on the coins called "unicorns" struck for James III of Scotland about 1480, but there the

animal is "seiant." There is dispute regarding the origin of the Scottish unicorn, but apparently it came from the arms of the Dukes of Somerset and entered Scotland when Jane Beaufort of that house married James I, the poet-king. If this is true, the English unicorn originated in England. (Cf. Seton's *Law and Practice of Heraldry in Scotland*, Edinburgh, 1863, p. 274.) At the time of the union, 1603, a royal crown was added to the unicorn, but this was removed after the accession of the Hanoverians. The unicorn has always had the sinister position in England, but Scotland proudly kept it dexter until 1766 and for a long time refused to remove the crown. In 1853 Scotland petitioned for the retention of the crown. The petition failed.

13. The writer of this letter—which appears in *Notes and Queries*, Tenth Series, vol. 10, p. 208—wishes to know the origin of the nursery rhyme, but he gets no satisfactory answer in later numbers of the magazine. He does not deserve one.

14. L. Twining, in his *Symbols and Emblems of Early and Mediaeval Christian Art*, London, 1852, p. 172, says that the unicorn "was represented on the walls of Persepolis in battle with the lion, both with and without wings; it was also known to the Egyptians and is found amongst their hieroglyphics. With these nations it was the symbol of purity and strength." Every assertion in this passage is either doubtful or else false.

15. This detail is usually omitted by the mediaeval followers of *Physiologus* presumably because the illuminations almost always showed the hunter not capturing but killing the unicorn.

16. See, e.g., Marco Polo's *Travels*, ii. cap. 13.

17. *Life of Pericles*, vii.

18. In his gloss upon *Daniel* viii. 5, Pusey remarks: "The he-goat is represented according to the well-known symbol of Persepolis, with its one beautiful horn between its eyes." If this is true, then Daniel's vision is bitterly satirical, for he chooses for the overthrow of the Persian king the very animal by which that king's power was represented, suggesting strongly that the royal house of Persia was declining.

19. S. T. Coleridge, *Literary Remains*, i. 120.

20. *Iliad*, ii. 861.

21. *Odes*, iii. 21.

22. Revelation v. 6.

23. See Zornius, *Biblioth. Antiq.*, i. 121, for a list of authorities upon the horns of Moses. The literature is very extensive. Zornius concludes: "*Cornu enim potentiae symbolum fuisse norunt omnes.*"

24. If there is any reader of this book who can bear to hear more about horns, he will find "God's plenty" in *Horns of Honour*, by F. T. Ellworthy, London, 1900. But although this pleasant writer has ransacked the ages and spoiled the climes in quest of horns, although he has several illuminating and almost final things to say about the cornute processes of the cuckold, all his horns are double—a tautology hard to forgive.

25. Cf. note 3 on this chapter.

26. Leonardo's little Bestiary, which he wrote for some undiscoverable purpose, is in his *Frammenti Letterari e filosofici*, Florence, 1899.

27. In the *Physiologus* it is rather the wild ass that cannot endure the company of other beasts.

28. Tertullian, *Contra Judaeos*, x, and *Adversus Marcion*, iii. 18; Gregory Nazienzen, *Oratio*, xiii (sometimes numbered xxv), Theodoret, *In Numeros, Quaestio* 44; Clement of Alexandria, *Pedagogia*, i. 5; Hugo Rabensis, *De Universo*, viii. 1.

29. Irenaeus, ii. 42. Justinus, *Dialogus contra Tryphonem Judaeum*.

30. Commentary on Psalm xliii.

31. Commentary on Psalm xxviii. See also Gregory the Great, *Morales*, xxxii, cap. 15.

32. Pseudo Jerome, Commentary on Psalm xxi, 22. Cassiodorus somewhere expresses the same idea.

33. Not only the unicorn, but the elephant was sometimes used by very early writers as an emblem of Christ. This introduced a difficulty, for Pliny had made it clear that the two animals were enemies, and it may have been because of this incongruity that the elephant symbol had a comparatively short life.

34. The *Alexanderlied* of Pfaffen Lamprecht (twelfth century)—line 5427 ff. of the text published in 1850 by Heinrich Weismann.

35. *Parzifal*, 482, 24 ff.

36. *Alte hoch-und-niederdeutsche Volkslieder*, collected by Ludwig Uhland, 1844, No. 337.

37. *Poésies du roi de Navarre*, Tome ii, p. 70.

38. Works of Rabelais, translated by Urquhart and Motteux, London, 1846, v, cap. 30.

39. Composed during the first third of the fourteenth century. First edited and published at Dresden, 1908, by Friedrich Gennrich, for the *Gesellschaft für Romanische Literatur, Band* 18. The six tapestries now in the Musée de Cluny called *La Dame à la Licorne* were made in the fifteenth century to illustrate this romance. I am aware, however, that another explanation of them is often given in guide-books.

40. A romance of the fourteenth century first edited and published by Ferdinand Heuckenkamp, Halle, 1896.

41. Canto xiv, stanza 75.

42. Canto xviii, stanza 188.

43. *Driadeo*, Canto iv, stanza 56 ff.

44. *The Faerie Queene*, ii. 5, 10.

45. *Bussy D'Ambois*, Part I, ii. 1, 52 ff.

46. *Timon of Athens*, iv. 3, 339.

47. Among these, apparently, may be placed the name of Francis Bacon. See his *Historia Vitae et Mortis*, chapter on *Medicinae ad Longaevitatem*, 4, where the "*cornu monocerotis*" is referred to without any hint that the author questions the popular faith in its origin. The bezoar-stone is mentioned in the same context with approval.

48. *Julius Caesar*, ii. 1, 203–4.

49. *The Tempest*, iii. 3, 21–2.

50. *Under the Hill*, London, 1904.

CHAPTER IV

1. The probability is that the first reference to "India" was intended, as in Virgil, to indicate vaguely a far-distant land in which Ethiopia might well be included, and that the whole remarkable story of Prester John derives from some actual Christian king of Abyssinia. So long as Ethiopia was called India, however, one could cite excellent authority to show that it must contain unicorns.

2. *Op. cit.*, p. 247.

3. *Hayat al-haiwán*, Cairo, 1371. I depend upon the translation given by Samuel Bochart in his *Hierozoicon*.

4. *Breva relação da embaixada q̃ o Patriarcha dõ João Bermudez troxe do Emperador . . . Preste João*, Lisbon, 1565, cap. 51.

5. *Descripcion General de Affrica*, Granada, 1573, i, cap. 23, folio 30.

6. *Edward Webbe—His Travailes*, London, 1590.

7. *A Short Description of the River Nile . . . and Other Curiosities*, London, 1669 cap. 3—"Of the Famous Unicorn, Where He is Bred and Shaped."

8. *A New History of Ethiopia*, London, 1682, i. 10.

9. *Description du Tubet*, translated into Russian by Prince Hyacinthe Bitchourin and thence into French by M. Klaproth, Paris, 1831, p. 230.

10. Ssanang Ssetsen, *Geschichte der Ost-Mongolen und ihres Fürstenhauses*, St. Petersburg, 1829, p. 89. The same story is told in Chinese, but there the unicorn is coloured green and speaks four languages.

11. *An Account of an Embassy to the Court of the Teshoo Lama in Tibet*, London, 1800, p. 157.

12. Abbé Huc, *Travels in Tartary, Thibet, and China during the Years* 1844–5–6. Translated by W. C. Hazlitt, ii, p. 245.

13. *Quarterly Review*, December 1820, Also in *Asiatic Journal*, February 1821.

14. *Aromatum et Simplicium . . . apud Indos nascentium Historia*, Antwerp, 1567, i, cap. 14.

15. *A Voyage to Congo*, in Pinkerton's *Voyages*, vol. xvi, p. 211.

16. *Briefe des Herrn von Wurmb und des Herrn Baron von Wollzogen*, Gotha, 1794, pp. 412 ff.

17. *Travels into the Interior of South Africa*, London, 1808, vol. ii, p. 269.

18. *The Narrative of an Explorer in Tropical South Africa*, London, 1853, cap. 9.

19. *The Athenaeum*, August 16, 1862.

20. *Itinerarium Joannis de Hese presbyteri ad hierusalem*, first printed 1499.

21. *Evagatorium Terrae Sanctae*, ii, p. 441 in Hassler's edition. The same story is told by Bernhard von Breydenbach, who was of the party, in his *Sanctarum Peregrinationum, Libri Duo*, 1486.

22. *The Navigations and Voyages of Lewes Vertomannus*, translated out of Latine into Englyshe by Richard Eden, London, 1576, cap. 19.

23. *Les Voyages fameux de Vincent Le Blanc*, Paris, 1648.

24. John Bell of Antermony, *Travels from St. Petersburg in Russia to Various Parts of Asia in* 1716, etc., Part II, cap. 2.

25. *Mongolia*, English translation, 1876, ii. 207.

26. Leonhard Rauwolff, *Aigentliche beschreibung der Raiz*, etc., 1582, p. 231.

27. London, 1598, facing p. 10.

28. The name is strangely compounded, for the word *ki* (also transliterated as *khi* and *ch'i*) is the name of the male and *lin* that of the female. Similarly, the male phoenix is called the *fung* and the female the *hwang*, so that if one wishes to refer to the species in general he must say *fung-hwang*.

29. The *Spring and Autumn Annals*, commonly attributed to Confucius, end with a record of the animal's appearance.

30. Book vii, section 3, paragraph 10, in the French translation by J. M. Callery.

31. This is the assertion of Henri Doré in his *Recherches sur les Superstitions en Chine*, Chang-Hai, 1912, Part I, vol. ii, p. 446 ff. (This work is publication No. 34 in the *Variétés Sinologiques*.) A picture of the Ki-lin is given here in the natural colours.

32. See *A New General Collection of Voyages and Travels*, London, 1747, vol. iv, p. 315. The description of the Ki-lin there given is based upon Navarette.

33. For the symbolic significance attributed to colours in China, see Laurence Binyon, *The Flight of the Dragon*, London, 1911.

34. *Epitome of the Ancient History of Japan*, by N. McLeod, Nagasaki, 1875, p. 116. This highly "curious" book is so untrustworthy in general that one can have little confidence in the passage quoted. McLeod's quality is indicated by his declaration that the unicorn was "the ancient crest of the Kings of Israel, and is still retained by the Mikado." Upon this and a few other such discoveries he builds a conviction that the Japanese belong to the "Lost Ten Tribes".

35. These are all carefully distinguished and discussed, with ample citation of original authorities, by Charles Gould in his *Mythical Monsters*, London, 1886, pp. 348 ff. Gould's extraordinary book, containing great masses of undigested knowledge, is still the most important source of information about Oriental unicorns, chiefly because the author had assistance from Chinese scholars in preparing his chapter. Gould was an engineer and a surveyor of Tasmania. He had the easy credulity of men who attain erudition without being educated. Like his contemporary David Livingstone, he was a firm believer in the real existence of unicorns, and like Sir Charles Lyell and the father of Edmund Gosse he also believed in sea-serpents.

36. Although never confused with the rhinoceros, the Ki-lin did take on, about A.D. 1200, some of the characteristics of the giraffe. (See *Journal Asiatique*, IIᵉ Série, xii, p. 155, and *Journal of the Royal Asiatic Society* for 1925, pp. 247 ff.) This confusion was made possible by the grotesquely inaccurate descriptions of the latter animal. The giraffe was hardly better known in Europe than in China between the time of Lorenzo di Medici, who had one as a gift from the Soldan, and 1827, when two arrived from the Pasha of Egypt for the courts of England and France.

37. This one may say in spite of the probability that the "unicorn's horn" of Europe has been bought and sold in China for many centuries. It is certain that Dutch merchants carried on an active trade in this horn with Japan in the eighteenth century, and it seems likely that many horns reached China by overland routes. I have, in fact, seen one that was long used by a Chinese physician in his medical practice. The Japanese had taken over the legend of the Ki-lin long before this, but there is nothing to show that they identified the Western horn, for which they were glad to pay its weight in gold, with the horn of their own legendary animal. The Japanese Ki-lin seems to have had little place in popular belief, and it is important chiefly in painting. (See Basil Hall Chamberlain, *Things Japanese*, 1905, p. 444.) Two pictures of it are to be seen in the *Japanese Encyclopaedia*—French translation by L. Serurier, Leyden, 1875.

38. Amsterdam, 1673.

39. *Purchas His Pilgrimes*, Glasgow, 1906, vol. xviii, p. 62.

40. Hakluyt's *Voyages*, Extra Series, Glasgow, 1904, vol. x, p. 59.

41. *Ibid.*, vol. vii, p. 418.

CHAPTER V

1. Amatus Lusitanus, writing in 1554, advised his readers to purchase the black variety. (*In Dioscoridis Anazarbeide Medica Materia*, ii, *Enarratio* 52.) Boëthius de Boodt, a cautious and accurate man, rejected with contempt an alleged unicorn's horn shown him at Venice because it was not of the colour described by Aelian. (*Gemmarum et Lapidum Historia*, Leyden, 1609, ii. cap. 244.)

2. *Discorso . . . della Natura dell' Alicorno*, Florence, 1573.

3. *History of the Worthies of England*, chapter on London.

4. Wolfgang Frantze, *Historia Animalium Sacra*, Wittenberg, 1612, p. 131. This work was written chiefly for the use of the clergy in preparing sermons, and it contains many ingenious justifications of the ways of God toward man.

5. Thomas Bartholinus, as I have said, took the word to mean "spirals" in this instance. See note 19 on Chapter I.

6. Translated by M. J. de Goeje, *Mémoires d'histoire et de géographie orientales*, Leyden, 1862, p. 47. A similar assertion is made in *Relations des Voyages faits par les Arabs . . . dans l'Inde et à la Chine*, Paris, 1845, i. pp. 28 ff.

7. For this passage, as for most others from the Arabic, I depend upon the translation given by Samuel Bochart in his *Hierozoicon*, London, 1663, i. Lib. iii. cap. 16.

8. *Hist. Anim.*, iii. 9.

9. Pliny, *Nat. Hist.*, viii. 31, followed by Hugh de St. Victor (Migne, *Patrol. Lat.*, vol. 177, col. 86). See also Sir Arthur Shipley's delightful chapter on the Yale in *Cambridge Cameos*, London, 1924.

10. *Aromatum Historia*, i. cap. 14.

11. *La Cosmographie Universelle*, Paris, 1575, Tome V, Lib. ii, cap. 5.

12. Letter from F. Fresnel, *Journal Asiatique*, March 1844.

13. Pierre Belon, *Plurimarum Singularum et Memorabilium Rerum*, Antwerp, 1589, i. 1, cap. 19.

14. *Diary*, November 12, 1645.

15. *Loc. cit.*

16. According to Leon de Laborde, *Notice des Émaux*, Paris, 1852-3, vol ii. p. 361.

17. Joannes Jonstonus, *History of the Wonderful Things of Nature*, London, 1657, cap. 43.

18. *De Subtilitate*, x.

19. Franciscus Sansovinus, *Venetia Citta Nobilissima*, Venice, 1581, ii, folio 38 verso. This passage allows one to suppose that the horns were taken at Constantinople, although there is no such assertion. The local tradition in Venice, however, has always been, and is to-day, that Doge Enrico Dandolo brought these two horns with him as part of the spoil which he took with his own hands.

20. Recorded by Antonio Pasani in *Il Tesoro di San Marco*, Venice, 1886, p. 93.

21. Caspar Bartholinus, *De Unicornu ejusque Affinibus et Succedaneis*, Hafniae, 1628, cap. 3. Also Boëthius de Boodt, *loc. cit.*

22. The only evidence I have for this is the statement of Andrea Marini, *op. cit.*, p. 20, but he speaks as though he had seen them.

23. Frederick Chamier, *The Life of a Sailor*, London, 1832, p. 88.

24. *Discorso della Natura dell' Alicorno*, p. 51.

25. *De Monocerote seu Unicornu*, Wittenberg, 1660.

26. De Laborde, *Émaux*, ii. p. 362.

27. *Archaeologia*, vol. xxx. p. 334.

28. De Laborde, *loc. cit.*

29. *Archaeologia*, vol. xxvi. p. 277.

30. *Mémoires*, vii. 9.

31. *Histoire*, iii. 139.

32. *Memoirs of Benvenuto Cellini*, translated by Thomas Roscoe, London, 1822, vol. i. p. 213.

33. Hakluyt's *Principal Voyages*, Everyman's Library Edition, vol. ii. p. 272.

34. Immanuel Meteranus, *Historia Belgica Nostri*, 1599, Lib. xiii. p. 396.

35. *Archaeologia*, vol. xliv. p. 378.

36. *Itinerarium Germaniae, Galliae, Angliae, Italiae*, 1612. On p. 150: "*Monstrabatur hic inter cetera nobis monocerotis cornu, in longitudine* 8½ *spithamas excedens, valoris* 100,000 *librar. auri.*" In the quotation from Hentzner given in Dodsley's *Fugitive Pieces*, ii. p. 244, however, the value is said to be ten thousand pounds, still a satisfactorily large sum when multiplied by ten to get our present "buying power."

37. Hakluyt's account of Frobisher's second voyage for the discovery of a North-west Passage. The same statement is made in *Purchas His Pilgrimes*.

38. *History of the Worthies of England*, chapter on London, The Horn of Windsor was seen and admired in 1592 by Frederick, Duke of Wurtemberg, on his *Bathing Excursion . . to the Far-famed Kingdom of England*. The Prince of Anhalt, travelling in England four years later, said in his versified narrative that there were two horns at Windsor, one smooth and one wreathed :—

> Zwey lang' Einhörner seind daselbsten auch verwahrt,
> Das eine war gar glat, und eins gewundner art,
> Fast an vier ellen lang.

Henry Peacham, in the verses he wrote for *Coryat's Crudities* in 1611, speaks of the horn apparently with contempt :—

> Why doe the rude vulgar so hastily post in a madnesse
> To gaze at trifles and toyes not worth the viewing? . . .
> That horne of Windsor (of an Unicorne very likely . . .).

Foreign travellers, however, such as Justus Zinzerling and Peter Eisenberg, continued to speak of it with admiration.

39. W. B. Rye, *England as Seen by Foreigners in the Days of Elizabeth and James I*, London, 1865, p. 203.

40. Pegge's *Curalia*, iv. p. 122.

41. *Histoire Général des Drogues*, Paris, 1694, ii. cap. 2. This horn belonging to Charles I was the one chosen by Edward Topsell for his enthusiastic description : "I do also know that which the King of England possesseth to be wreathed in spires . . . and I never saw anything in any creature more worthy of praise than this horn. The substance is made by nature, not art, wherein all the markes are found which the true horn requireth. . . . It is of so great length that the tallest man can scarcely touch the top thereof, for it doth fully equal seven feet. It weigheth thirteen pounds. The figure doth plainly signifie a wax candle (being folded and wreathed within itself) being far more thicker from one part, and making itself by little and little less toward the point. . . . The splents of the spire are smooth and not deep, being for the most part like unto the

wreathing turnings of snails, or the revolutions or windings of wood-bine about any wood. But they proceed from the right hand toward the left, from the beginning of the horn even unto the very end. The colour is not altogether white, being a long time somewhat obscured. But by the weight it is an easy thing to conjecture that this beast which can bear so great a burden in his head, in the quantity of his body can be little less than a great ox."—*The History of Four-footed Beastes*, London, 1607.

The several horns in the Tower attracted almost as much attention as those mentioned above. In an account written in 1635 we read: "Not long after I went to the Tower of London, where I saw a Unicornes horne about 1½ yards in length and 2 or 2½ Inches diameter att the bigger end, goeinge Taperwise and wreathed, all somewhat smoothe (I thinck by often handlinge). It was white, resemblinge the substance of an Eliphants Tooth, estimated att 18 or 20,000 pounds sterlinge. This, as all the rest are, conceived to be rather the horne of some fish then of a beast, because such a beast now a dayes is not to bee found, although discoveries att present are in farre greater perfection than they were then."—Peter Mundy, *Travels*, publ. by the Hakluyt Society, 1907, etc., vol. iii. pp. 3–4.

This single horn was valued at eighteen thousand pounds or more in 1635. An inventory of the plate in the Lower Jewel House of the Tower taken in 1649 mentions "The unicornes hornes weighing 40 lb. 7 oz., valued at £600."—*Archaeologia*, vol. xv. p. 272. These horns probably included the one seen fourteen years before by Peter Mundy, and the four or five of them together were valued at only one-thirtieth of the sum that one had been thought to be worth.

42. Andrea Bacci, *op. cit.*, p. 72, says that in his time a pound of powdered alicorn was commonly sold in Florence for 1,536 crowns, the worth of a pound of gold at the same time being 148 crowns.

43. This assertion is made by the unknown antagonist of Ambroise Paré in the latter's *Discours . . . de la licorne*, Paris, 1582. Much curious information about the cost of alicorn is to be gleaned from the *Epistre* introducing this *Discours*, although Paré is not an original authority.

44. Jacobus Primerosius, *De vulgi erroribus in medicina*, Amsterdam, 1639, iv. p. 38.

45. *History of Four-footed Beastes*, chapter on the unicorn.

46. *Loc. cit.*

47. Andrea Bacci, *Discorso dell' Alicorno*, p. 72.

48. Zedler's *Grosses Universal Lexicon*, s.v. "*Einhorn*."

49. *In Dioscoridis de Materia Medica Libros quinque Enarrationes*, iv. cap. 71.

50. *History of Scotland*, Book I.

51. *La Cosmographie Universelle*, Paris, 1575, v. 5.

52. *De Unicornu et Lapide Bezaar*, 1659, p. 13.

53. *Op. cit.*

54. Caspar Bartholinus, *De Unicornu ejusque Affinibus*, 1628, cap. 7, and Jacobus Primerosius, *loc. cit.*

55. *Dittionario Novo Hebraico, Molto Copioso, Dechirato in Tre Lingue*, Venice, 1587.

56. Folio 182, counting from the right, column 1.

57. *Ein schöner newer . . . Discurs von der Natur, Tugenden, Eigenschafften, und Gebrauch dess Einhorns*, Frankfurt, 1625. I cite this translation because I have not seen the original *Histoire de la Lycorne*, which was published at Montpellier in 1624.

58. *Ca.* 1400. Modern edition, London, 1893, p. 59.

59. *Epistre* introducing his *Discours de la Mumie*, etc., Paris, 1582.

60. *The White Devil*, Act III.

61. *Op. cit.*

62. *De Rerum Varietate*, xvii. cap. 97.

63. *Discorso dell' Alicorno*.

64. John Swan, *Speculum Mundi*, Cambridge, 1635, p. 435.

65. Andrea Marini, *Discorso contra la falsa opinione dell' Alicorno*, Venice, 1566.

66. An interpolation by a later hand in the manuscript followed by Migne refers to he use of the hoof of the unicorn in just the way in which the horn was later employed.

67. *"aes."* Perhaps a scribe's error for *"os,"* a bone. It is obviously related to the "carbuncle" at the base of the horn mentioned by Pfaffen Lamprecht and others.

68. *Physica*, vii. cap. 5.

69. *De Animalibus Historia*, xx, Tract. 2, cap. 1. First printed at Rome, 1478. Modern edition by H. Stadler, Münster, 1920. A mark of Albertus's quality is seen in his contempt for the almost universal belief that the "barnacle goose" is produced by a tree. He had seen that goose lay eggs, and, what is even more remarkable, made the correct deduction.

70. Expressed in his *Tractatus de Venenis*, first printed 1473, the basis of most later writing on the topic.

71. *Boke of St. Albans*, xliii.

72. *Kingis Quaire*, clv.

73. Prescott, *Ferdinand and Isabella*, I, vii. p. 383.

74. Publications of the Hakluyt Society, 81, p. 259.

75. *Edward Webbe's Travels* (1590), Arber's edition, p. 35.

76. *Purchas His Pilgrimes*, London, 1625, p. 841.

77. This may be gathered, I think, from his words: *"Lapis Bezoar probatæ est virtutis; quod spiritus recreet et lenem sudorem provocet. Cornu autem Monocerotis de existimatione sua decidet; ita tamen ut gradum servet cum cornu cervi et ossi de corde cervi et ebore et similibus."*—*Historia Vitae et Mortis*, chapter on *Medicinae ad Longaevitatem*.

78. Several of these signs are preserved at the Wellcome Historical Medical Museum in London, probably the best place in the world in which to study the sort of beliefs with which we are here concerned.

79. *Op. cit.*

80. *Historia Animalium*, Lib. v, chapter *De Monocerote*.

81. Andrea Bacci, *op. cit.*

82. *De Vulgi Erroribus*, iv. cap. 38. Dr. Primerose of Hull took his medical degree at Montpellier, where he may have come under the influence of Laurens Catelan.

83. *Worthies of England*, chapter on London.

84. *History of Four-Footed Beastes*, *loc. cit.*

85. Such as Nicander of Colophon, who wrote, *ca.* 150 B.C., a highly rhetorical poem on Poisons and their Antidotes.

86. See, e.g., *Les Empoisonnements Criminels au XVIᵉ Siècle*, by Marc Robert, Paris, 1903.

87. For most of these details, which I have not attempted to verify, I depend upon Frantz Funck-Brentano's *Le Drame des Poisons*, Paris, 1900, and the book by Marc Robert cited just above. I have also used *Poison Romance and Poison Mysteries*, by C. J. S. Thompson, London, 1899.

88. Macaulay's *History of England*, edition of 1849, i. pp. 439 ff.

89. See his *Discours des Venins*, 1582, cap. 22.

90. A careful description is given in Linschoeten's *Voyages*, London, 1598, i. cap. 87.

91. George Jennison, *Noah's Cargo*, London, 1928, p. 156.

92. De Laborde—*Émaux*, ii. p. 354—cites descriptions of five of these, taken from royal and ducal inventories.

93. See de Laborde s.v. *"Salière."*

94. *Gemmarum et Lapidum Historia*, ii. cap. 168. The same topic is discussed in ii. cap. 279.

95. Those who think, with Mr. George Jennison, that the unicorn was originally a snake will find here the source of the virgin-capture story.

96. See *Notes and Queries*, Seventh Series, vol. 8, p. 63.

97. In *Purchas His Pilgrimes*, first edition, ii. p. 1169, there is a description of an Indian snake, clearly the cobra, "which they call of the Shadow, or Canopie, because it hath a skin on the head wherewith it covereth a very precious stone". Jordanus Catalanus, Bishop of Columban, reports in his *Mirabilia Descripta*, *ca.* 1450, that in the "Third India" there are many dragons with brilliant stones called carbuncles in their heads, besides a great quantity of serpents similarly adorned. Further information on

snake-stones is given by Cardinal Ponzetto in his *Libellus de Venenis*, Rome, 1521, Lib. ii. 1, 4, where we learn that the golden fibres in the stones were supposed to darken when poison was brought near.

98. Thomas Lupton, *A Thousand Notable Things*, London, 1595, vii. 18.

99. *Ibid.*, vii. 79.

100. *Heiligthumsbuchlein*, 1755.

101. The griffin's claw that once belonged to Corpus Christi College, Cambridge, is described by Tylor, *Early History of Mankind*, third edition, pp. 319-20. Three that were kept in the treasury at Bayeux and exhibited on the altar on feast days are mentioned by E. J. Millington, *Heraldry in History, Poetry and Romance*, p. 278.

102. See Albertus Magnus, *De Mineralibus*, ii. 2, and Boëthius de Boodt, *op. cit.*, ii. cap. 14. The "male" carbuncle was regarded as the king of stones. Whether used as an amulet or crushed in wine, it was held to withstand poison, preserve from plague, banish sadness and evil thoughts and terrifying dreams. A good one was supposed to shine by night and to be visible through clothing. It was occasionally made an emblem of Christ. In a few instances, all early, the carbuncle at the base of the unicorn's horn seems to have been regarded as the source of the horn's magic properties.

103. Boëthius de Boodt, *op. cit.*, ii. cap. 198.

104. Andrea Bacci, *De Venenis et Antidotis*, Rome, 1586, p. 52.

105. Hector Boëthius, *Scotorum Historiae Libri XVIII*, Paris, 1526. I paraphrase the passage from memory, having been unable to find it a second time. It should be in the first book. Those who believe, with Professor Wiener, that the *virgo* of *Physiologus* was originally a *virga* will see in this story a striking analogue of the capture of the unicorn by a tree.

106. Hakluyt's *Principal Navigations*, Everyman's Library Edition, ii. p. 284.

107. *La Cosmographie Universelle*, Paris, 1575, v. cap. 5.

108. Andrea Marini, *Discorso contra la falsa opinione dell' Alicorno*, Venice, 1566.

109. *Ibid.*, p. 8.

110. It was sometimes called a *tousche* (from *toucher*), and often simply *lincorne* or *licorne*, the word which names both animal and horn, as *alicorno* does in Italian.

111. *La Grande Encyclopédie*, art. *Licorne*.

112. *The Workes of Ambrose Parey*, translated by Th. Johnson, London, 1634, xxi. cap. 39.

113. Ambroise Paré, *Epistre* to his *Discours sur la Mumie*, etc., Paris, 1582.

114. A picture of such an alicorn tankard may be seen in *Poison Romance and Poison Mysteries*, by C. J. S. Thompson, London, 1899.

115. *Pell Records*.

116. De Laborde, *loc. cit.*

117. *Thyestes*, 453.

118. Palmarius Constantius, *De Peste*, 1610.

119. Ζωολογια, *or the History of Animals as they are Useful in Physick*, London, 1659, cap. 39.

120. *De Venenis et Antidotis*, Rome, 1586, p. 61.

121. *Pharmacopoeia Londiniensis*, published by the Royal Society of Physicians. Between 1651 and 1746 there were twelve or fifteen editions and reprints.

122. In his *Oecoïatrie*, Lyons, 1558. This is one of the strangest and one of the foulest books in the world, written by a remarkable man—a sort of minor Rabelais—of whom it is to be wished that we knew more.

123. *La première et seconde partie des Erreurs populaires touchant la medicine*, Rouen, 1601, i.

124. *Histoire Général des Drogues*, Paris, 1694, ii. 2.

125. An amusing illustration of this is seen in the *Declaration des Abuz et Tromperies que font les Apothicaires*, by Lisset Benancio, Lyons, 1557. This vigorous piece of vituperation was answered in kind by the opposing party.

126. See F. Gay, *Une lignée d'apothicaires*, Paris, 1896.

127. I guess that her views on the unicorn were derived from the Arabic through the

translations made by Gerard of Cremona, but I have been unable to confirm this conjecture.

128. One must not forget, however, that there had been Christian as well as Indian physicians in Bagdad almost from the first; neither should one ignore the probability that some notions of the Arabic unicorn were brought back by the Crusaders. The references to the horn's—or carbuncle's—therapeutic power in the Alexander cycle and in Wolfram von Eschenbach may well have had this origin.

129. *Op. cit.*, p. 5.

130. Such as those, for example, made by Andrea Bacci. I should say, however, that I have been unable to find any considerable statement of the horn superstition in the Arabic medical writings accessible to me in translation. Avicenna, *De Viribus Cordi*, often cited and quoted by Andrea Bacci, does not mention the alicorn at all in the versions I have seen, and it seems probable therefore that Bacci used a corrupt text. The great Canon of Medicine by Hali Abbās (Al Magusi), Venice, 1496, says nothing of the alicorn. These men, however, were greatly superior to the *setta de gli Arabi* held up to scorn by Marini. That sect need not have included any Arabs whatever, and probably it was chiefly composed of Italian quacks.

131. "*Pour le changement d'n en l*", says Littré, "*comparez orphelin*". I have compared *orphelin*, but with no enlightenment.

132. Marini—*op. cit.*, p. 8—obviously reverses the fact in saying that "*il volgo . . . danno al corno il nome dell' animale che l'ha*".

133. "It should be noted that *corno* in Italian argot means *phallus*, and hence it is the post powerful of prophylactics, especially *la corne torse*. We have remarked elsewhere [in *The Evil Eye*, p. 186] that in modern Italy all sorts and descriptions of charms are called *un corno*".—F. T. Ellworthy, *Horns of Honour*, London, 1900, p. 59. On this topic see Tuchmann in *Mélusine*, September 1896, p. 106.

134. Professor C. H. Grandgent of Harvard University writes in a private letter: "*Alicorno* looks to me like a cross between *unicornis* and *al-cornu*, the existence of which latter form I should like to verify." I have not been able to find *al-cornu*, but even if it does occur it does not affect my argument, for still we should have a hybrid word representing two stages of culture.

135. *In Dioscoridis Anazarbeide Medica Materia*, 1558, ii. 52.

136. See Xenophon, *Cyropaedia*, vii; Pliny, *Nat. Hist.*, xi. cap. 37; and Athenaeus, ii, where we are told of a banquet given by King Xanthus of Thrace at which every drinking vessel was of horn. Francis Alvarez reports that Prester John and all his great lords drink their wine from horn exclusively—*Purchas His Pilgrimes*, 1625, p. 1038.

137. By F. T. Ellworthy, *op. cit.* A compendium of what the ancient and mediaeval worlds observed, thought, and fancied about horns in general may be seen in Joannes Eusebius Nieremberg's *Historia Naturae*, Antwerp, 1635, vii. cap. 2.

138. *La Cosmographie Universelle*, Paris, 1575, v. 5.

139. Gordon Cumming, *Wanderings in China*, vol. i. p. 173.

140. Johannes Schenkius, in his *Observationum Medicalium Libri Duo*, 1565, lists eight different kinds of animals whose horns he considers alexipharmic. Seven of these are unicorns; the eighth is the stag.

141. Giovanni Battista della Porta, *Natural Magic*, English translation, London, 1658, i. cap. 7. The first edition of this very popular book was composed when the author was barely fifteen. Thirty-five years later he revised it slightly and published it at Lyons in 1651 as *Magiae Naturalis Libri Viginti*.

142. This assertion is made by Pliny, *Nat. Hist.*, viii. 23, and by many others.

143. Thomas Lupton, *A Thousand Notable Things*, London, 1595, xi. 14.

144. The "bone of the stag's heart" (*os cordis cervi*) enjoyed a high reputation extending into the eighteenth century, being prescribed exactly like alicorn for posion and plague. See P. A. Matthiolus, *Commentarii . . . de Medica Materia*, Venice, 1565, i. p. 357.

145. According to Mr. Harold Bayley—*New Light on the Renaissance*, p. 16—the figure of the stag was often used as an emblem of purity.

146. The belief that viper's flesh, or fat, is the sovereign cure for viper's bite is still

vigorously flourishing in Devonshire and Dorset. I have been told by more than one old man who has spent his life in the Rocky Mountains that the best remedy for rattle-snake bite is "rattle-snake oil".

147. *Hist. Animal.*, viii. 29.

148. *De Elia et Jejunio*, cap. 20. Hieronymus Mercurialis, *De Venenis et Morbis Venenosis*, Venice, 1601, gives the best doctrine of his times on the question "*Utrum Venenum à Venenis Extinguatur*".

149. *De Occultis Proprietatibus*, Lisbon, 1540, ii. cap. 19. Compare Bartholomaeus Maranta, *Libri duo de Theriaca et Mithridato*, 1576, i. cap. 3.

150. Pierre Pomet, *Histoire des Drogues*, Paris, 1694, article on the elk. Here is given a convincing picture of the animal preparing himself for flight.

151. *Op. cit.*, iv.

152. This trait is apparently transferred from that of the stag, yet Cardan says that the unicorn is found "*in Aethiopia inter solitudines, squalentemque terram, atque inter serpentes, mirumque modum venenis cornu eius adversari creditur*".—*De Subtilitate*, x. folio 326 of Basle edition.

153. London, 1598, i. cap. 47.

154. *Itinerarium Joannis de Hese presbyteri ad hierusalem*, first printed 1499. The several texts that I have seen vary in unimportant details. A good one is given by Friedrich Zarncke in his *Priester Johannis*, 1883, ii. pp. 162 ff.

155. Exodus xv. 23–25.

156. Frederick Walpole, *The Ansayrii and the Assassins*, London, 1851, vol. iii. p. 285.

157. *Nat. Hist.*, viii. cap. 33.

158. *De Occultis Proprietatibus*, iii. cap. 33.

CHAPTER VI

1. Sebastian Münster, *Cosmographiae Universalis Libri VI*, Basle, 1550, p. 1036.

2. *De Subtilitate Libri XXI*, Nuremberg, 1550, x.

3. Conrad Gesner, *Historia Animalium*, Frankfort, 1551.

4. Pierre Belon, *Observations de Plusiers Singularitez et Choses Memorables de Divers Pays Estranges*, Paris, 1553, i. 14.

5. *Discorso de Andrea Marini, Medico, Contra la Falsa Opinione dell' Alicorno*, printed by Aldus, Venice, 1566.

6. "*Andreas Marinus juratus cornutorum animantium hostis*", writes Thomas Bartholinus, *De Unicornu*, 1678, p. 151.

7. Ulysses Aldrovandus, in his *De Quadrupedibus Solidipedibus*, Bologna, 1639, p. 386, says that he made such a translation. I have not seen it. Possibly he refers to the extended outline in his own book.

8. Some of these are: *Pietre preziose che risplendevano nelle veste sacre del sommo sacerdote*, Rome, 1581; *Trattato delle gemme e pietre preziose*, 1603; *De venenis et antidotis Prolegomena*, 1586; *Della gran Bestia detta dagli antichi Alce e delle sue proprietà*, 1570.

9. *L'Alicorno, Discorso dell' Eccellente Medico et Filosofo M. Andrea Bacci, Nel Quale si Tratta della Natura dell' Alicorno & delle sue virtù Eccellentissime. Al Sereniss. Don Francesco Medici, Gran Principe di Toscana.* Florence, 1573. The first edition, in Latin, appeared in 1566. I give the title of the Italian edition because it is this that I have chiefly used.

10. Having failed to find this assertion in either of the two translations of Avicenna's treatise that I have seen, I suggest that Bacci used a corrupt version.

11. In Latin, Venice, 1566; in Italian, Florence, 1573, a quarto; in Italian, Florence, 1582, octavo; in Italian with other works of Bacci's, Rome, 1587; in Latin, Venice, 1586; in Latin, Stuttgart, 1598.

12. *Discours D'Ambroise Paré, Conseilleur et Premier Chirurgien du Roy, à Sçavoir: De la Mummie, De la Licorne, Des Venins, et de la Peste*, Paris, 1582.

13. Marini is mentioned, however, in Paré's *Replique* to his antagonist. Bacci, strange to say, is spoken of with praise.

14. Although I have not been able to find this reply, it must be extant, for Packard quotes from it in his *Life and Times of Ambroise Paré*, New York and London, 1922, p. 116.

15. *Replique D'Ambroise Paré . . . à la Response faicte contre son Discours de la Licorne* Paris, 1584.

16. It seems unnecessary to present Paré's other remarks on the unicorn, which add little to what he says in the *Discours*. The most important passage is to be found in *The Workes of the Famous Chirurgeon Ambrose Parey*, translated by Th. Johnson, London, 1634, xxi. cap. 39.

17. This chapter, the fifth of the fifth book, has the title : "*De l'isle de Cadamoth, avec un gentil traicté de la Licorne*".

18. Edward Topsell, *The History of Four-Footed Beastes*, London, 1607, s.v. "unicorn".

19. *Histoire de la Nature, Chasse, Vertus, Proprietez et Usage de la Lycorne, par Laurens Catelan, Apoticquaire de Monseigneur le Duc de Vendome. Et Maistre Apoticquaire de Montpellier*. 1624. The title of the German translation, 1625, is given in note 57 on Chapter V. This German translation has seven copper-plates, the original only one.

20. A study of Catelan's life and times is given in *Une lignée d'apothicaires*, by F. Gay, Paris, 1896.

21. *De Unicornu ejusque affinibus et succedaneis*, Copenhagen, 1628.

22. First edition, Patavii, 1645; second edition, augmented by Caspar the Younger, Amsterdam, 1678.

23. *Recueil Général des Questions traitées és Conférences du Bureau d'Adresse, sur toutes sortes de Matières. Par les plus beaux Esprits de ce Temps*. Six vols., Paris, 1633.

24. In his *De Quadrupedibus Solidipedibus*, Bologna, 1639.

25. *Pseudodoxia Epidemica: Or, Enquiries into Very Many received Tenents and commonly presumed Truths*, London, 1646, iii. cap. 23, *Of Unicornes Hornes*.

26. Boëthius de Boodt, *Gemmarum et Lapidum Historia*, 1647. The unicorn passage is ii. cap. 244—*De vero cornu menocerotis* (*sic*)*, et an id reperiatur*.

27. Joannes Jonstonus, *Historia Naturalis*, 1657.

28. J. F. Hubrigius, *De Monocerote seu Unicornu*, Wittenberg, 1660. Reprinted by G. C. Kirchmayer as his own in *Hexas Disputationum Zoologicum*, 1661. Attributed to Kirchmayer by Edmund Goldsmid in his translation, *Unnatural Natural History*, Edinburgh, 1886.

29. *De Monocerote*, Leipzig, 1667. *Praeses*, F. C. Berens.

30. *De Unicornu*, Wittenberg, 1679. *Praeses*, S. F. Frenzel.

31. *The Workes of Ambrose Parey*, London, 1634, xxi. cap. 39.

32. Frank Gibson, *Superstitions about Animals*, London, 1904, pp. 184-5.

33. See, however, Conrad Gesner's *De Figuris Lapidum*, 1551, p. 153, where the idea is clearly implied, and perhaps for the first time.

34. *Op. cit.*

35. *Exercitationes*, 1557, cap. 250.

36. Genesis vii. 14 and 16. This cogent citation was made by Hermann Suden in *Der Gelehrte Criticus*, Leipzig, 1704-6, *Frage* 78.

37. J. H. Homilius, *De Monocerote*, cap. 1.

38. *History of the World*, London, 1634, cap. vii, paragraph 9.

39. Aldrovandus, *loc. cit.*

40. *Truth of Revelation*, London, 1831, p. 132.

41. The very large alicorn that Albertus Magnus says he had in his hands may have been a stalactite, although he shows an acquaintance with such formations in his *De rebus metallicis* i. 2, 9.

42. This name seems to have originated with Conrad Gesner, who was followed by Boëthius de Boodt. Clusius calls it fossil ivory, and others *lithomarga*. Cæsalpinus (*De Metallis* ii. cap. 48) gives it the significant name *lapis Arabicus*.

43. *Gemmarum et Lapidum Historia* ii. caps. 241-43.

44. *Op. cit.*, cap. 10.

45. *Museum*, 1655, ii. 6.

46. *Scientia Naturalis* (In *Opera*, 1640) iv. 4.

47. See the latter's *De Peste*, Section 3.

48. *Schediasma Curiosum de Unicornu Fossili*, Jena, 1666.

49. *Monocerologia, seu de genuinis Unicornibus dissertatio*, 1676, p. 12.

50. For a detailed account of this medicine and of its use in China and Japan see H. N. Moseley, *Notes of a Naturalist on the 'Challenger'*, London, 1879, pp. 423–4.

51. *Natural History Magazine*, May–June 1924.

52. M. W. de Visser, *The Dragon in China and Japan*, London, 1913. See also Ernest Ingersoll, *Dragons and Dragon Lore*, New York, 1928, pp. 94–5.

53. Otto von Guericke, *Experimenta Nova . . . Magdeburgica*, Amsterdam, 1672, v. cap. 3.

54. *Protogaea*, 1749, section 35.

CHAPTER VII

1. *De Benedictionibus Patriarcharum* (Migne, *Patrol. Lat.*, vol. xiv), cap. 11.

2. κοσμα, Ἀιγυπτιου μοναχου, χριστιανικη τοπογραφια edited by J. W. McCrindle, for the Hakluyt Society, London, 1897, Book xi. The drawing of the unicorn is in the Appendix.

3. Vatican Gr. 699, an uncial manuscript of the eighth or ninth century. The drawings are generally accepted as close copies of those made by Cosmas himself. Thomas Bartholinus examined this manuscript when it was in the Medicean Library.

4. Ssanang Ssetsen, *Geschichte der Ost-Mongolen und ihres Furstenhauses*, St. Petersburg, 1829. The event is supposed to have occurred in 1206.

5. In a French manuscript of the Romance of Alexander preserved at Saint Germain des Prés there is a long appendix on the *Proprietez des Bestes* in which three kinds of unicorns are described: "*Aucunes ont corps de cheval et teste de cerf et queuhe de sanglier, et si ont cornes noires, plus brunes que les autres. Ceulx-ci ont la corne de deux couldees de long. Aucuns ne nomment pas ces licornes dont nous venons de parler licornes, mais monoceros ou monoceron. L'autre manière de licornes est appelée eglisseron, qui est à dire chievre cornue. Ceste-cy est grant et haulte comme ung grant cheval, et semblable a ung chevreul, et ha sa grant corne tres aguhe. L'aultre manière de licorne est semblable a un beuf et tachée de taches blanches. Ceste-cy a sa corne entre noire et brune comme la première. . . . Ceste-cy est furieuse comme ung thoreau quant elle veoit son ennemy.*"

6. *Evagatorium Terrae Sanctae* ii. p. 441 in Hassler's edition.

7. *Exercitatio* 205.—"*Sed Vartamano, viro optimo, qui sese duos vidisse scribit, habenda fides est.*"

8. *Itinerario* ii. cap. 15.

9. *Ibid.*, i. cap. 17.

10. *The Navigation and Voyages of Lewes Vartomannus, Translated out of Latine into Englyshe* by Richard Eden, London, 1576, cap. 19. Reprinted as Chapter 2 of Vartoman's Travels in *Purchas His Pilgrimes*, London, 1625, Part II, p. 1489. In the margin Purchas says: "The only report that I have found in any credible Author of Unicornes: neither in 120 yeares which have passed since have I found one Relation to second it."

11. *Edward Webbe, His Travailes*, London, 1590.

12. *Les Voyages fameux du Sieur Vincent le Blanc*, Paris, 1648, i. cap. 5.

13. *Ibid.*, cap. 33.

14. *Aigentliche beschreibung der Raiz*, etc., 1582, p. 231. Translated by John Ray and published in 1693 as *Travels into the Eastern Countries*. The unicorn passage is in ii. cap. 8.

15. *Aromatum et Simplicium . . . apud Indos nascentium historia*, Antwerp, 1567, i. cap. 14.

16. *Cosmographie Universelle* v. 2, 2.

17. Ambroise Paré, *Discours de la Mumie*, etc., cap. 4.

18. *Breva relaçao da embaixada*, etc., Lisbon, 1565, cap. 51.

19. *Descripcion General de Affrica*, Granada, 1573, i. cap. 23, folio 30, verso.

20. *Historia . . . de los . . . Reynos de la Etiopia*, Valencia, 1610, p. 247.

21. By Legrande, as *Voyage historique d'Abyssinie*, Paris and the Hague, 1728.

22. *A Voyage to Abyssinia, by Father Jerome Lobo, as translated by Sam'l Johnson*, London, 1735, ii. cap. 2.

23. *A Short Relation of the River Nile*, printed for the Royal Society, London, 1669. Sir Peter Wyche says in his Epistle Dedicatory that the papers he translates were procured "by the curious Sir Robert Southwell from an inquisitive and observing Jesuit at Lisbon who had lived many years in Æthiopia and the Indies". It is evident that he did not know this Jesuit's name. A German translation of Sir Peter's book— his work amounted almost to original authorship—appeared at Nuremburg in 1670 with the title *Neue Beschreibung und Bericht von der wahren Beschaffenheit des Mohrenlands*, etc., vaguely said to be the work of "*P. Hieronymi, eines Jesuiten in Portugal*". The fact that Father Lobo dictated the materials of the book was discovered by the French translator Thevenot, who used it in vol. iv of his *Relations de divers Voyages Curieux*, Paris, 1662. Thevenot learned this fact from correspondence with Lobo's friend, the Jesuit Baltasar Tellez.

These details are important for two reasons. Where the *Short Relation* speaks of a certain holy Father having seen unicorns, Lobo must have said to Sir Robert Southwell that he himself saw them. Further, James Bruce of Kinnaird, in his *Travels to Discover the Source of the Nile*, London, 1769–72, is obliged to deal with the first chapter of the *Short Relation*, in which Lobo lays modest claims to having seen the source of one of the main tributaries. Bruce, with his habitual amenity, meets this claim chiefly by calling Lobo "a lying Jesuit", a phrase which in England in 1769 amounted to conclusive argument. Since then Lobo's reputation has risen. See *Mémoire Justicatif en Réhabilitation des Pères Pierre Paez et Jerome Lobo*, by Charles T. Beke, Paris, 1848.

24. Job Ludolphus, *A New History of Ethiopia*, made English by J. P., Gent., London, 1682, i. cap. 10.

25. *Life of Robert Frampton, Bishop of Gloucester*, by T. Simpson Evans, London, 1876, p. 114.

26. This account, written out by Thomas Bartholinus at the command of his king, appears in his *Historia Anatomica*, Cent. II, *Hist.* 61, and also in his *De Unicornu*, cap. 24. It is given in almost the same words by Ole Wurm, *Museum* iii. cap. 13.

27. *Purchas His Pilgrimes*, 1625, v. cap. 11.

28. *De Vulgi Erroribus in Medicina*, 1638, iv. cap. 38.

29. John Ogilby, *Africa*, London, 1670, p. 21.

30. *De Unicornu et Lapide Bezaar*, 1659, p. 45.

31. *The Philosophical Grammar*, second edition, 1738, p. 359.

32. *Travels from St. Petersburg in Russia to Various Parts of Asia* in 1716, etc.—in Pinkerton's *Voyages*, vol. vii. p. 333.

33. *Resa till Goda Hopps-Udden*, 1783. Translated, London, 1785, as *A Voyage to the Cape of Good Hope*. James Bruce of Kinnaird remarks, *op. cit.*, v. p. 105, that Dr. Sparrman "has distinguished himself by his low illiberal abuse of learned foreigners", and then proceeds to show how learned foreigners should be treated by saying that Sparrman's publisher, "by way of apology, as I suppose, for his rusticity and ill-manners, says, that he was employed in labour to earn a sum sufficient upon which to travel. . . . I think his knowledge acquired seems to be pretty much in proportion to his funds".

34. *Briefe des Herrn von Wurmb und des Herrn Baron von Wollzogen*, Gotha, 1794, pp. 412–16.

35. *Reisen nach dem Vorgebirge der guten Hoffnung* (translated from the Dutch), Hamburg, 1803, i. p. 201.

36. *Travels in South Africa*, second edition, London, 1808, vol. i. p. 269.

37. *The Narrative of an Explorer in Tropical South Africa*, London, 1853, cap. 9.

38. *Reisen in Nubien, Kordofan*, etc., Frankfurt, 1829, p. 161.

39. See also the *South African Christian Recorder*, vol. i.

40. *Reisen in Abyssinien im Jahre* 1836, Stuttgart and Tübingen, 1838, p. 89.

41. *Reisen in Europa, Asien und Afrika*, Stuttgart, 1843, *Band* II, i. p. 474.
42. He wrote a second, briefer account of the *abou-karn* in *Comptes rendus de l'académie des sciences*, 1848, p. 281.
43. *Geographische Geschichte des Menschen und der vierfüssigen Thiere*, Leipzig, 1780, pp. 367 ff.
44. *Précis de la Géographie Universelle*, Paris, 1817, vol. v. p. 71.
45. *Die Urwelt und das Alterthum erläutert durch die Naturkunde*, Berlin, 1821, ii. pp. 171–81.
46. First published in *Bulletin d'Histoire naturelle*, and again in the author's *Œuvres Choisies*, 1862.
47. In *Excursus IV* of his edition of Pliny's *Natural History*, Paris, 1827.
48. This point had been made by several German scholars long before Cuvier's time.
49. *An Account of an Embassy to the Court of the Teshoo Lama in Tibet*, London, 1800, p. 157.
50. Abbé Huc, *Travels in Tartary, Thibet, and China during the Years* 1844-5-6. Translated by W. Hazlitt, vol. ii. p. 245.
51. See Sven Hedin's *Scientific Results of a Journey in Central Asia*, Stockholm, 1904, vol. vi. pp. 29 ff.
52. Lieutenant-Colonel N. Prejevalsky, *Mongolia*, English translation, ii. pp. 207 ff.
53. *Lincoln Herald*, July 1, 1831.
54. *Mélanges d'Archéologie*, Paris, 1847–9, vol. ii. p. 225.
55. Charles Gould, *Mythical Monsters*, London, 1886, p. 350.

CHAPTER VIII

1. Linschoeten's *Voyages*, London, 1598, i. cap. 47.
2. *Émaux*, ii. 366.
3. *Summa de Exemplis*, ii. cap. 123. The same symbolism is worked out, with characteristic fury of imagination, by Tertullian, in *Adversus Judaeos*, x.
4. E.g., *Account of the Travels of Two Mohammedans through India and China in the Ninth Century*, Pinkerton's *Voyages*, iii. 189. See also the second voyage of Sinbad the Sailor in the *Arabian Nights*.
5. The evidence for this is too dispersed to be given in full. In No. 97 of the *Carmina Burana* various birds and beasts are named in Latin with glosses in High German; the gloss for Rhinoceros is *Ainhurn*. Marco Polo may have assisted somewhat, for he reports of the "unicorn" he saw in eastern India: "'Tis a passing ugly beast, and not at all like that which our story-tellers say is caught in the lap of a virgin. In fact it is entirely different from what we had supposed". Further details prove that what he saw was the rhinoceros. (Book iii. cap. 9) The strangest mingling of the two animals is that in the Travels of Vincent le Blanc.
6. *Exercitationes*, 205, sect. 1.
7. *De Subtilitate* x.
8. Amatus Lusitanus, *In Dioscoridis . . . Materia Medica* ii. 52.
9. "I went to see the Rhinoceros or Unicorn, being the first that I suppose was ever brought to England." Evelyn's *Diary*, October 22, 1684.
10. Cf. the third chapter of the *Uragavagga*, Sacred Books of the East, vol. x, part 2.
11. Joshua Sylvester's *Du Bartas His Divine Weekes*, the sixth day.
12. Hakluyt's *Principal Navigations*, Glasgow, 1904, vol. vi. p. 399.
13. *De Unicornu ejusque Affinibus*, folio 17.
14. *Short Relation of the River Nile*, cap. 7.
15. A species distinct from those of India, having two horns and differing in size and general appearance. The white rhinoceros, r ow greatly reduced in numbers and territory, had once a great spread. Its remains have been found in the London clay.

16. Charles Peter Thunberg, M.D., *Travels in Europe, Africa, and Asia between the Years 1770 and 1779.* London, 1795, vol. i. pp. 246 ff.

17. *Nat. Hist.* ii. 37 and 46, and xi. 106.

18. *Hist. Anim.* ii. 8 and 3.

19. The species known to the ancients was the *oryx beisa*, a large antelope of east and north-east Africa with almost straight horns three feet long. It is replaced in South Africa by the *oryx gazella*, or gemsbok.

20. *Cynegetica* ii, lines 445 ff.

21. *Hist. Animal.* xiii. 25 and xv. 14.

22. *Hierozoicon* i. lib. 3, cap. 16.

23. Lichtenstein's theory was first put forward in *Verhandlungen der Königliche Akademie der Wissenschaften*, 1824, pp. 207 ff. It was amplified in his book *Über die Antelopen des Nördlichen Afrika*, Berlin, 1826, and in *Darstellung neuer oder wenig bekannter Säugethiere*, Berlin, 1829-34. The plates referred to are Nos. I and V in the third of these publications.

24. "Anyone who has seen a wild sable antelope galloping cannot fail to be struck by its resemblance to the unicorn."—J. G. Millais, *Breath from the Veldt*, 1845, p. 133.

"There is in the Museum at Bristol a stuffed antelope from Caffraria. . . . It is of the shape and size of a horse, with two straight horns, so nearly united that in profile it shows only a single horn."—A. Brunet, *Regal Armourie of Great Britain*, 1839, p. 218.

25. *The Daily Telegraph*, London, December 12, 1928.

26. Sir William Cornwallis Harris, *Portraits of the Game and Wild Animals of Southern Africa*, London, 1840, cap. 9.

27. Peter Simon Pallas, *Spicilegia Zoologica*, Berlin, 1774, Fasc. xii. p. 35 ff. Cuvier accepted Pallas's conjecture.

28. Malte-Brun, *Précis de la Géographie Universelle*, Paris, 1817, *livre* 92. The passage is directed against Cuvier's contention that the single horn is anatomically impossible.

29. Second edition, Oxford, 1705, cap. 7, paragraph 40.

30. Sir Arthur Shipley—*Cambridge Cameos*, 1924, cap. 4—finds in this practice the origin of the belief in the "yale", an imaginary animal with horns pointing fore and aft, reported by Pliny, and not infrequently met with in mediaeval illustrations and carvings.

31. John G. Wood, *Natural History of Man*, London, 1868, i. cap. 8. The passage in Wood is based upon one in Le Vaillant's *Travels in Africa* (English translation, 1796), where the process of cutting and twisting is described. Wood gives a picture of several Kaffir cows with horns twisted into fantastic shapes, and one is a unicorn.

32. W. S. Berridge, *Marvels of the Animal World*, London, 1921, pp. 47 ff.

33. I owe this detail to a private letter quoted by Sir Arthur Shipley, *loc. cit.*, from Dr. C. G. Seligman.

34. This recalls a curious passage in Albertus Magnus, *De Animalium* xii. 244. Here he writes: *Aliquando sunt duo cornua in capite animalis, et aliquando unum solum, sicut . . . animal quod quidam antiquorum archos quasi principem vocaverunt.*" The probability is that the oryx is here referred to and that the name has been changed to suit a fanciful etymology; but it is possible that Albertus had seen a reference to a herd-leader distinguished by a single horn, for such a leader would naturally be called ἄρχων or *princeps*.

35. See photographs in Stolze and Andreas, *Denkmäler und Inschriften von Persepolis*, Band I, Plate 42 and Band II, Plate 76.

36. Perhaps the first traveller to make this suggestion was Carsten Niebuhr, *Reisebeschreibung*, 1778, *Band* II, pp. 126 ff. He was followed by J. G. Rhode, who developed the theory ingeniously and at length in his *Uber Alter und Werth einiger Morgenländischen Urkunden*, 1817, pp. 86 ff., making, however, a less impressive case than he might have done if better informed about the unicorn legend of Europe. Sir Robert Ker Porter (*Travels in Georgia, Persia*, etc., 1821, pp. 585-600) attempts an adverse criticism of Rhode's theories, I think unsuccessfully. A. H. L. Heeren (*Historical Researches into the Politics, Intercourse, and Trade . . . of Antiquity*, Oxford, 1833, i. 150 ff.) disagrees with Rhode in details, but accepts his main conclusions. Christian Lassen (*Indische Alterthumskunde*, Bonn, 1849, *Band* ii. pp. 646 ff) disagrees only in minor respects. Robert Brown (*The Unicorn*, London, 1881) accepts the main theses of Rhode and his successors

as proved. E. Schröder (*Sitzungsberichte der Königlich Preuss. Akad. der Wissenschaften zu Berlin*, xxxi, 1892, pp. 573–81) accepts and slightly extends the earlier conclusions without giving due credit to his sources. I am indebted to all of these writers, and particularly to Rhode, for much of the matter in the present section, although advantages of date and a wider knowledge of unicorn literature enable me to go somewhat beyond them.

37. The earliest clear statement I have found of the fact, now generally understood, that the sculpture of Persepolis and the Euphrates Valley commonly showed only one of the two horns and ears of an animal seen in profile when two were intended is in Sir A. H. Layard's *Nineveh and Its Remains*, 1849, ii. p. 430.

38. Robert Brown, for example, treats as a unicorn every animal he finds presented in profile with one horn on ancient bas-reliefs, seal-cylinders, gems, or coins. He cannot understand why others do not do the same, and he says with special reference to C. W. King's *Antique Gems and Rings*: "It is singular how rarely those who reproduce these representations have noticed their unicornic character."

39. Considering that this has an important bearing upon my topic, I have examined several thousands of plates showing horned animals as depicted in ancient art. (Perhaps the best single work for such investigation is the volume of *Planches* accompanying Félix Lajard's *Introduction à L'Étude du Culte . . . de Mythra*, Paris, 1847.) I have found no example of a unicorned animal shown in "full-face".

40. See *The Seal Cylinders of Western Asia*, by W. H. Ward, Carnegie Institute of Washington, Publication 100, 1910, where hundreds of representations of such animals are shown.

41. *Bundahis* iii. 15; *Vendidad* xiv. 5. Compare *Herodotus* i. 140. Among the several animals created by Ormuzd for killing serpents are the boar and the stag—*Bundahis* ii. 47.

42. *Yasna* xlii. 4 (*Sacred Books of the East*, vol. xxxi. p. 291).

43. *Dînâ-î Maînôg-î Khirad*, cap. 62, 26. (S. B. o. t. E., vol. xxiv.)

44. *Bundahis* xix. 1–12. (S. B. o. t. E., vol. v.)

45. All the commentators upon the three-legged-ass that I have seen—Rhode, Frederick Creuzer (*Religions de l'Antiquité*), Darmesteter, and De Gubernatis—are content to assert its identity with the unicorned figures of Persepolis and, in the case of Creuzer, with the unicorn of Ctesias. Not one of them mentions the striking fact that its characteristic action is also that of the Western unicorn.

46. *Rig Veda* i. 163, 9.

47. *Hymns of the Atharva Veda* vii. x. 4.

48. *Ormuzd et Ahriman*, Paris, 1877, pp. 148 ff.

49. *Zoological Mythology*, London, 1872, i. p. 53.

50. "The fyrste Heven is watry other crystalline. And is made by the myght of god waters which ben sette above in the fyrmament".—Bartholomaeus Anglicus, John of Trevisa's translation. Compare Genesis i. 7.

51. One may recall, however, that the characteristic of the serpent, according to *Physiologus*, is that it lays aside its poison before drinking. Thus the Chinese dragon leaves its spittle—an important article of commerce—floating on the sea. Ahriman is represented in Zoroastrian myth by serpents and dragons.

52. De Gubernatis says—*op. cit.*, ii. 391—that it is customary in German and Slavonic countries to bless the water so as to charm away the monsters or serpents, originally spirits of darkness. These monsters are thought to swallow all bright and beautiful things—or, as dragons, to hide them. They hide or swallow the sun. The three-legged ass may be regarded as the power that brings back the lights and colours of day by frightening the evil powers that have hidden or eaten them.

53. Darmesteter, *op. cit.*, p. 280.

54. *Bundahis* xiv. 3.

55. The hoofs of the unicorn have given much trouble. Aristotle, Pliny, Solinus, and Aelian all say that they are solid. Strabo, Albertus Magnus, Vartoman, Cardan, and many others say that they are divided. In some pictures the fore-feet are solid and the

hind feet cloven, so as to "split the difference". Thomas Bartholinus (*De Unicornu*, p. 241) thinks that both kinds may occur according to differences of climate without indicating any distinction of species.

56. This view is vigorously opposed by J. G. Rhode, *Die Heilige Sage ... des Zendvolks*, Frankfurt, 1820, pp. 214 ff.

57. See M. M. Rostovtzeff, *Iranians and Greeks in South Russia*, Oxford, 1922, Plate VII.

58. The date of this forgery is indicated by the fact that it was first addressed to Emmanuel of Constantinople, who reigned 1143–1180.

59. Printed at Paris in black letter ca. 1490.

60. The Waldensian *Physiologus*, to be sure, says that the unicorn *"ha un corn al front cun loquel el romp li arbre"*, but it proceeds no farther.

61. *History of Four-Footed Beastes*, London, 1607, s.v. *"unicorn"*.

62. Grimm's Fairy Tales—"The Brave Little Tailor".

63. Made by the Joint Expedition of the British Museum and the University of Philadelphia and exhibited at the British Museum in 1928–29.

64. See Félix Lajard, *Introduction à L'Étude du Culte de Mythra, Planche* xvi. 7b and liv. B 3.

65. Astrologers have always made much of the great speed, compared with the apparent speed of the other heavenly bodies, with which the moon runs her course.

66. Just as the moon cannot be "taken alive" by the sun but, according to primitive belief, is eaten by him at the end of its last phase.

67. The most familiar expression of this belief is in Pliny, *Nat. Hist.* ii. 220 ff.

68. *Kosmographia*, translated by Herman Ethé, Leipzig, 1868, pp. 40 ff.

69. *Batman uppon Bartholme*, London, 1582, viii. cap. 17. In making this delightful book Batman added a great deal to Bartholomaeus Anglicus, but usually from recognized authorities. Here, however, he has carelessly misread Albumasar, who really opposed the view attributed to him.

70. "In Oldenburg a peasant related how he rid himself of a bony excrescence by stroking it thrice crosswise in the name of the Trinity, and then making a gesture as if he were seizing the deformity and hurling it toward the moon. In the same part of Germany a cure for warts is to stand in the light of the waxing moon ... then hold the disfigured hand toward the moon. . . . Some say that in doing this you should pronounce these words: 'Moon, free me from these vermin'."—J. G. Frazer, *The Golden Bough*, Part VI, p. 54.

71. *Tetrabiblon*, commonly known as the *Quadrupartite* i. 4.

72. Ptolemy, *De Judiciis*.

73. *Introductorium in Astronomiam*, Auguste Vendelicorum, 1498, iv. cap. 1.

74. See Félix Lajard, *op. cit., Planches, passim*.

75. See Alexander Porteous, *Forest Folklore, Mythology, and Romance*, London, 1928, pp. 191–202.

76. Robert Brown, *The Unicorn, A Mythological Investigation*, London, 1881, p. 86. This book is badly written and arranged; the author shows little knowledge of the European legend of the unicorn and he says nothing about the astrologico-magical ideas of the moon which are most germane to his thesis; he is inaccurate, incautious, disposed to generalize upon insufficient data, and not above wrenching disputed or disputable points to his purpose. It is, in short, a wild book, but, like all its author's productions, a brilliant one, full of recondite learning and startling surmises.

77. His knowledge of these figures was based largely upon C. W. King's *Antique Gems and Rings*. If he had seen the far more inclusive and more accurate studies of the same objects that have appeared since 1881 he might have been less positive in his assertions; yet, on the whole, his statement holds true.

78. Winkle, *Cathedral Churches of England* i. 62. In Dugdale's *Monasticon* we read: "About this time (1006) Ulphe, the son of Thorald, who ruled west of Deira, by reason of the difference which was like to arise between his sons about the sharing of his lands and landships after his death, resolved to make them all alike; therefore, coming to York with that horn wherewith he used to drink, filled it with wine, and before the

altar of God and Saint Peter . . . drank the wine, and by that ceremony enfeoffed this church with all his lands and revenues."

79. Ludicrously conventionalized as this tree is, one can still see that it was intended to represent the date-palm, which was also used on the cylinder-seals of Assyria to represent the "Tree of Life" or the "Tree of Fortune". One could not ask for a better proof that the whole design is Euphratean in ultimate source.

80. For Brown's discussion see *op. cit.*, pp. 44 ff.

81. Lines 925 ff.

82. Sir G. W. Cox, *Mythology of the Aryan Nations*, ii. 142.

CHAPTER IX

1. *Specimen Islandiae Historicum*, by Arngrimr Jonsson (or Jonas), Amsterdam, 1643, p. 155.

2. Thomas Bartholinus says that he read on the unicorn's horn kept in the Cathedral of Utrecht the name of the Norse King Sverri, written in runic letters.— *De Unicornu*, p. 257.

3. Hakluyt's account of Frobisher's second voyage. Also given in *The History of East India*, Pinkerton's *Voyages*, vol. 12.

4. The earliest accurate description of the narwhal and its tusk that I have seen is that in William Scoresby's admirable *Account of the Arctic Regions*, Edinburgh, 1820, i. pp. 486 ff. Long before this, however—not to mention the seventeenth-century descriptions in Latin—a careful account had appeared in Nicolaus Witsen's *Noord en Oost Tartarye*, 1705, ii. p. 903. This, like the discussion by Thomas Bartholinus of sixty years earlier, was illustrated by excellent plates showing the narwhal's skull and tusks.

5. César de Rochefort, *Histoire naturelle et morale des Isles Antilles*, second edition, Rotterdam, 1665, i. cap. 15. The passage is based upon an account by one du Montel of a "Licorne de Mer" that was taken at San Domingo in 1644. The head of this creature, apparently a swordfish, was shipped to Europe in 1646 but was lost on the way. Du Montel did not assert that he had seen this marine *licorne*. He said that it wore a crown on its head, that it had large scales, that its flesh was delicious. The horn, which he described as rising from the brow, was exactly that of the narwhal. The belief in a *licorne de mer*, which lasted for many decades after the narwhal was well known, was due, apparently, to this account which du Montel made up from hearsay of the San Domingo swordfish.

6. Third edition, 1682. The voyage was taken in 1653.

7. Nathan Bailey's *Universal Etymological English Dictionary*, London, 1721.

8. *Memoirs of Benvenuto Cellini*, London, 1822, i. p. 213. I have no certain evidence that Roscoe's "unicorn's head" was the same as the "horn" displayed at Chelsea.

9. E.g., Samuel Bochart, *Hierozoicon*, 1663, col. 955.

10. In his *Observations des plusieurs singularitez*, Paris, 1553, i. cap. 14. In this same chapter Belon describes the narwhal's tusk belonging to the King of France without the slightest notion of its origin and true nature.

11. *Historiae Septentrionalium Gentium*, Rome, 1555, xxi. cap. 10.

12. *In Discoridis Anazarbeide Medica Materia*, 1558, ii, *Enarratio* 52.

13. Joannes Goropius Becanus, *Origines Antwerpiae*, Antwerp, 1569, p. 1039. It is this account of the unicorn that Sir Thomas Browne chiefly follows in the *Vulgar Errors*.

14. *Purchas His Pilgrimes*, Glasgow, 1906, vol. xiv. p. 399.

15. Gerard Mercator, *Atlas Minor*, 1621, p. 28: "*Inter quae Piscis Nahual. Hujus carnem si quis comedat, statim moritur. Habetque dentem in interiori capitis parte prominentem ad septem cubitos. Hunc quidam pro Monocerotis cornu vendiderunt. Creditur venenis adversari. Quadraginta ulnarum longitudinem habet bellua.*"

16. *De Unicornu ejusque affinibus*, cap. 1: "*Marina Borealia, quorum cornua iam potissimum apud magnates reperiuntur et pro veris venditantur.*

17. *An os illud quod vulgo pro cornu Monocerotis venditatur, verum sit Unicornu.* Most of the text is given by Thomas Bartholinus in his *De Unicornu.* The dissertation was called forth by a dispute among the merchants of Copenhagen about the nature of the substance they were selling as unicorn's horn.

18. A restatement of Wurm's discovery, longer than the dissertation itself, appears in I. de La Peyrère's *Relation de Groenland*, 1647, reprinted in English in the second volume of *A Collection of Voyages and Travels*, London, 1704. Here the whole history of the discovery is related in a letter from Ole Wurm.

19. See Thomas Bartholinus, *op. cit.*, p. 264.

20. Pierre Martin de la Martinière, *A New Voyage into the Northern Countries*, London 1674, at end of cap. 44.

21. *A Brief Account of Travels in Divers Parts of Europe*, London, 1685, pp. 102 ff.

22. *Monocerologia, seu de Genuinis Unicornibus*, 1676.

23. *Histoire Générale des Drogues*, Paris, 1694, s.v. *Licorne*, and cap. 33, *de Narwal.*

24. *Dictionnaire Universelle des Drogues Simples*, Paris, 1773, s.v. *Narwal.*

25. Harley 4751.

26. Several dead narwhals were washed ashore on the coast of England during the period when their horns were of great value—one in 1588 and another in 1644—but I have seen no record of their being found farther south.

27. An American ship exploring the coasts of Greenland in 1923 picked up scores of tusks. Hundreds of them are to be seen at present in the London docks.

28. Catelan's book was pretty certainly written to advertise the author's alicorn. The long digression in De Rochefort's book on the Antilles seems to have had a similar purpose.

29. It may be worth pointing out, however, that the northern fishermen were probably not ignorant of the unicorn. An Icelandic Bestiary, preserved in a Copenhagen manuscript of the thirteenth century, is to be seen in the *Analecta Norroena* edited by Mobius, 1877.

30. The dispute among the merchants of Copenhagen from which Ole Wurm's dissertation arose indicates that even in the city where we might expect to find the fullest knowledge of the alicorn's origin there was at least uncertainty.

31. Laborde implies not only that there was a rather extensive trade in narwhal tusks, but that, after the beginning, it was carried on with deliberate deceit. Both implications, I think, are due to the common error of over-estimating the age of modern business methods and conditions.

32. *Historia Gemmarum* ii. cap. 244. Pierre Belon was one of the first to point out the discrepancy—in his *Plusieurs Singularitez*, 1553.

33. *De' Viaggi, Lettera de' 22 di Marzo*, 1623.

34. *De Unicornu*, second edition, p. 110.

35. Pietro writes "*due mila Lire delle loro*", but it is evident from his definition that he means by the English "*Lira*" (*Libra*) the pound sterling.

36. Pietro della Valle, *loc cit.*

37. I quote, as before, from the English translation, given in vol. ii of *A Collection of Voyages and Travels*, London, 1704, p. 460.

38. Edinburgh, 1904, xiii. p. 510.

39. David Crantz, *The History of Greenland*, London, 1767, p. 278.

40. C. P. Thunberg, *Travels in Europe, Africa, and Asia Between the Years* 1770 *and* 1779. Second edition, London, 1795, vol. iv. p. 49.

NOTES ON THE ILLUSTRATIONS

Frontispiece.—*Millefleur* tapestry—see below, plates V–VI.

Chapter-heads.—The tracings of old watermarks used at the chapter-heads are all taken from *Les Filigranes, Dictionnaire Historique des Marques du Papier*, by C. M. Briquet, Paris, 1907, vol. iii, where some 540 figures of unicorns are given. They range in date from the end of the fourteenth to the end of the sixteenth century and are found in paper manufactured in many different places. Mr. Harold Bayley (*Lost Language of Symbolism*, ii. 98–99, and *New Light on the Renaissance*, 14–15) thinks that watermarks were used as secret symbols by the Albigensian paper-makers and that the unicorn was their emblem of purity. If so, it was widely imitated, for it was by far the most popular animal of those represented in watermarks. In a single copy of the *Fayt of Arms* printed by Caxton in 1489 there are twenty-one unicorns. The 540 figures in Briquet show many different ideas of the unicorn's appearance. The equine form predominates in the later examples, but usually with divided hoofs and often with the goat's beard. The caprine form is early and Italian. German paper-makers sometimes had in mind the chamois of the Alps, and there are several forms resembling the rhinoceros. There was no steady effort, however, to be realistic, and many of the marks are primarily decorative.

Plate I.—A beaker of rhinoceros horn. British Museum.

Plate II.—Royal MS. 973. 12, folio xiii, British Museum. An Italian manuscript of the fourteenth century.

Plate III.—Woodcut representing the Holy Hunt from *Der beschlossen gart des rosenkrantz Marie*, 1505, on folio x of *Das sechst buch*. The design belongs to a type frequently used in stained-glass and wood-carving as well as in books. Mary sits in a *hortus inclusus* (*Song of Solomon*, iv. 12), and behind her is one of her chief insignia, the Fleece of Gideon (*Judges* vi. 40). The sealed fountain (*Song of Solomon* iv. 12) and the Altar of Aaron are also symbolic.

Plate IV.—Flemish tapestry of the sixteenth century, based upon an Italian cartoon, now in the Accademia di Belle Arti, Florence.

Plates V–VI.—*Millefleur* tapestries woven about 1480, probably in Touraine, for François de la Rochefoucauld. Two pieces in the set of six are of later date. The combination, in the whole amazingly sumptuous series, of Christian symbolism and the cult of the Virgin with the pride of life and the "lust of the eye" is most striking. The recurring monogram, "A.M.", reminds one that the Ave Maria had been sanctified by Papal Bull only five years before these tapestries were begun.

Plate VII.—This scene appears in the strange, beautiful, and, as Dibdin called it, "enchanting" book, *Poliphili Hypnerotomachia* (The Combat of Love in a Dream), published by Aldus in 1499. Curious and recondite as the text is—written in a compound of Italian and Greek and Latin—the fame of this book is chiefly due to its physical beauty, and especially to the 172 woodcuts. These have never been certainly assigned to any artist, and conjecture has ranged from Raphael and Carpaccio to Mantegna and the Bellinis. Some believe that they were done by the "Master of the Dolphins", who made the familiar Aldine trade-mark. The triumphal car drawn by six unicorns illustrates the Third Triumph in honour of Jupiter, and it celebrates Jupiter's love for Danaë. The author—Fra Francesco Colonna, 1433–1527—says of it: *"Questo pomposamente trahevano sei atrocissimi monoceri, cum la cornigera fronte cervina, alla gelida Diana riverenti.* The six unicorns do not look *"atrocissimi"* and one fears that they are forgetting the gelid Diana a little in lending themselves to a celebration of the loves of Jupiter and Danaë. Their hoofs are cloven and they are slightly bearded. The design is obviously related to the illustrations of Petrarch's *Trionfi*.

Plate VIII.—This famous painting, known as the Santa Giustina of the Belvidere, now in Vienna, is the work of Alessandro Buonvicino, called Moretto, a member of the Venetian school. Moretto was at first a follower of Titian and then of Raphael, but before his death, *ca.* 1560, he struck out a style of his own of great nobility. There are two important saints, both virgin martyrs, named Justina. The unicorn was first used as the emblem of Justina of Antioch and was later transferred to Justina of Padua. The former has the more interesting legend. A youth of her city, having fallen in love with her but being unable to break her vow of chastity, sought assistance from a magician named Cyprian. The wizard himself lost his heart to her and plied her with sensual temptations with the devil's aid. When the devil finally gave up, Cyprian burnt his books and turned Christian. He and Justina were later thrown together into boiling pitch, but escaped miraculously. They were beheaded at the same time during the Diocletian persecutions. In all Justina's pictures the unicorn lies at her feet. The male figure in Moretto's painting is that of Alphonso I, Duke of Ferrara, and the model for the female figure was Laura Eustochio, a peasant woman, mistress to this Duke and later his wife, after the death of Lucrezia Borgia. Often painted in the nude by Titian —once in the Louvre picture called "Titian's Mistress"—she was a woman greatly beloved by the people of Ferrara and one quite worthy, in their opinion, to be represented as a Saint.

Plate IX.—This spirited engraving by Albrecht Dürer, dated 1516, is called by Bartsch "The Abduction of a Young Woman". Others have christened it "Pluto Stealing Proserpine" and "Dejaneira Carried off by the Centaur Nessus"; but the rider is distinct from the steed, so that the "centaur" title does not apply. The unicorn has cloven hoofs and a beard. Its short horn curves downward, is serrated on the lower edge, and vaguely suggests the walrus tusk. Otherwise the animal is a shaggy horse. Dürer's well-known rhinoceros engraving was executed in the previous year.

Plate X.—A Chinese carving, in ivory, of the Ki-lin. The original, in the British Museum, is less than three inches tall.

Plate XI.—From *Die Unbekante Welt*, by Dr. Olfert Dapper, Amsterdam, 1673.

Plate XII.—From a collection of tracts and broadsides in the Bodleian Library made by Anthony à Wood and bound in with several other papers emanating from quack doctors of the seventeenth century. This broadside was intended to be pasted in prominent places about London. The rude picture of the alicorn shows the common way of preparing "unicorn water".

Plate XIII.—This frontispiece of Thomas Bartholinus's *De Unicornu*, second edition, is the work of Romeyn de Hooge (*ca.* 1650–1720), a Dutch engraver of note. Among many other works of similar extent, he illustrated the *Decameron*, the *Heptameron*, the *Cent Nouvelles Nouvelles*, and La Fontaine's *Contes*. He was much censured in his own time for following too freely "*la fougue de son génie*". In the present engraving he has entered admirably into the spirit of his author's profuse, erudite, and not wholly serious work. At least seventeen different varieties of unicorns are represented.

Plate XIV.—A woodcut at the end of Bernhard von Breydenbach's *Perigrinationes ad Terram Sanctam*, Mainz, 1486. This is the earliest illustrated book of travel. The drawings for the woodcuts, which are numerous and excellent, were made from nature by Erhard Reuwich of Utrecht, who was one of the 150 members of the pilgrimage. This artist must have been one of the company who saw the unicorn described by Felix Fabri in the book he wrote about the same expedition, and it was probably on the strength of that observation that he included the unicorn among the beasts "truthfully depicted as we saw them in the Holy Land".

Plate XV.—From the *Historia Naturalis* of Joannes Jonstonus, 1657, vol. i. It is remarkable that the horns show no striae.

Plate XVI.—One of the two illustrations—the other being a rude engraving of narwhal tusks—in Samuel Bochart's *Hierozoicon*, London, 1663, columns 955–6. The engraving represents Bochart's notion, worked out entirely in the library, of the appearance of the Biblical *Re'em*, which he confidently identifies with the oryx.

Plate XVII.—From a painting, by Sir William Cornwallis Harris, of the *Oryx Capensis* or Gemsbok, reproduced in his *Portraits of the Game and Wild Animals of Southern Africa*, London, 1840.

Plate XVIII.—From *Travels in Georgia, Persia*, etc., by Sir Robert Ker Porter, London, 1821, facing page 598.

Plate XIX.—From a sheet of the so-called "Satirical Papyrus", in the British Museum. This papyrus is composed of parodies upon scenes in the "Book of the Dead" and is of

Græco-Roman date. The scene here represented parodies one in which the soul of the deceased is shown playing draughts. Sir Flinders Petrie tells me that in his opinion the animal to the left was intended to represent an antelope, but Sir Wallis Budge speaks of the two animals as "lion and unicorn".

Plate XX.—Reverse of a medal by Pisanello, now in the British Museum, struck in 1447 in honour of Cecilia Gonzaga, whose portrait is given on the obverse. One should observe not only the symbolic crescent moon, but the fact that the unicorn is entirely goatlike.

Plate XXI.—From Fabro's translation of Catelan's *Histoire de la Licorne*. In some early pictures the virgin holds a vessel containing the blood of the animal, whose head is still in her lap, but in others, such as the one here shown, she anoints him from a flask. This probably arose from a misunderstanding of the earlier symbol.

Plate XXII.—From Pierre Pomet's *Histoire Général des Drogues*, Paris, 1694, ii. p. 78. The picture is of earlier date than this, however, as shown in the text.

Plate XXIII.—From Pierre Martin de la Martinière's *Voyage des pays Septentrionaux*, third edition, 1682, page 261.

Figure 1, *page* 89.—From Montfaucon's *L'Antiquité Expliquée*, 1724, *Supplement, tome III, Planche* XI. Montfaucon regarded this plaque as ancient, and Charles Cahier was inclined to agree with him. Certainly it is either ancient or of the Renaissance, and if it belongs to the latter period one does not see why the horn should show no striae. The unicorn shows none of the influence of *Physiologus*. Montfaucon, who knew and cared nothing about unicorns, used the plaque merely to illustrate feminine costume of the ancient world.

Figure 2, *page* 249.—Detail from the "Horn of Ulph" as given in Robert Brown's *The Unicorn.*

Figure 3, *page* 272.—Drawings of the narwhal's cranium and tusk, from *Noord en Oost Tartarye*, by Nicolaus Witsen, 1705, vol. ii, p. 903. A curious error in these drawings is that the striae are made to run clockwise, as they never do in nature.

Figure 4, *page* 278.—This design, which is found in several variant forms—the one here shown is that reproduced by Fabro in his translation of Laurens Catelan—has been the occasion of much learned controversy. Andrea Bacci believed that the medal was struck for Alexander the Great to celebrate his conquest of the region about Mount Nysa, the twin-peaked mountain on which Bacchus was born. There is uncertainty about the inscription, some holding that Sigma should stand in the place of the Kappa and that the Epsilon should be Alpha Epsilon. The vessel from which the unicorn drinks is of the sort associated with Bacchic worship. It is true that Alexander discovered Nysa and the town of the Nysaeans in the north-west of India, but it is also true that he founded the city of Nicaea in Bithynia. The first suggestion that the medal may have been Alexander's seems to have been made by Pirro Ligorio in his *Libro Miracoloso*. Bartholinus accepted the view, as did most other writers who mentioned it during the seventeenth century. It seems to me obviously a production of the sixteenth century, and probably Italian.

L

INDEX

A CATALOG OF SELECTED
DOVER BOOKS
IN ALL FIELDS OF INTEREST

DRAWINGS OF REMBRANDT, edited by Seymour Slive. Updated Lippmann, Hofstede de Groot edition, with definitive scholarly apparatus. All portraits, biblical sketches, landscapes, nudes. Oriental figures, classical studies, together with selection of work by followers. 550 illustrations. Total of 630pp. 9⅛ × 12¼.
21485-0, 21486-9 Pa., Two-vol. set $29.90

GHOST AND HORROR STORIES OF AMBROSE BIERCE, Ambrose Bierce. 24 tales vividly imagined, strangely prophetic, and decades ahead of their time in technical skill: "The Damned Thing," "An Inhabitant of Carcosa," "The Eyes of the Panther," "Moxon's Master," and 20 more. 199pp. 5⅜ × 8½. 20767-6 Pa. $4.95

ETHICAL WRITINGS OF MAIMONIDES, Maimonides. Most significant ethical works of great medieval sage, newly translated for utmost precision, readability. Laws Concerning Character Traits, Eight Chapters, more. 192pp. 5⅜ × 8½.
24522-5 Pa. $4.50

THE EXPLORATION OF THE COLORADO RIVER AND ITS CANYONS, J. W. Powell. Full text of Powell's 1,000-mile expedition down the fabled Colorado in 1869. Superb account of terrain, geology, vegetation, Indians, famine, mutiny, treacherous rapids, mighty canyons, during exploration of last unknown part of continental U.S. 400pp. 5⅜ × 8½. 20094-9 Pa. $7.95

HISTORY OF PHILOSOPHY, Julián Marías. Clearest one-volume history on the market. Every major philosopher and dozens of others, to Existentialism and later. 505pp. 5⅜ × 8½. 21739-6 Pa. $9.95

ALL ABOUT LIGHTNING, Martin A. Uman. Highly readable nontechnical survey of nature and causes of lightning, thunderstorms, ball lightning, St. Elmo's Fire, much more. Illustrated. 192pp. 5⅜ × 8½. 25237-X Pa. $5.95

SAILING ALONE AROUND THE WORLD, Captain Joshua Slocum. First man to sail around the world, alone, in small boat. One of great feats of seamanship told in delightful manner. 67 illustrations. 294pp. 5⅜ × 8½. 20326-3 Pa. $4.95

LETTERS AND NOTES ON THE MANNERS, CUSTOMS AND CONDITIONS OF THE NORTH AMERICAN INDIANS, George Catlin. Classic account of life among Plains Indians: ceremonies, hunt, warfare, etc. 312 plates. 572pp. of text. 6⅛ × 9¼. 22118-0, 22119-9, Pa., Two-vol. set $17.90

ALASKA: The Harriman Expedition, 1899, John Burroughs, John Muir, et al. Informative, engrossing accounts of two-month, 9,000-mile expedition. Native peoples, wildlife, forests, geography, salmon industry, glaciers, more. Profusely illustrated. 240 black-and-white line drawings. 124 black-and-white photographs. 3 maps. Index. 576pp. 5⅜ × 8½. 25109-8 Pa. $11.95

THE BOOK OF BEASTS: Being a Translation from a Latin Bestiary of the Twelfth Century, T. H. White. Wonderful catalog of real and fanciful beasts: manticore, griffin, phoenix, amphivius, jaculus, many more. White's witty erudite commentary on scientific, historical aspects enhances fascinating glimpse of medieval mind. Illustrated. 296pp. 5⅜ × 8¼. (Available in U.S. only) 24609-4 Pa. $6.95

FRANK LLOYD WRIGHT: Architecture and Nature with 160 Illustrations, Donald Hoffmann. Profusely illustrated study of influence of nature—especially prairie—on Wright's designs for Fallingwater, Robie House, Guggenheim Museum, other masterpieces. 96pp. 9¼ × 10¾. 25098-9 Pa. $8.95

FRANK LLOYD WRIGHT'S FALLINGWATER, Donald Hoffmann. Wright's famous waterfall house: planning and construction of organic idea. History of site, owners, Wright's personal involvement. Photographs of various stages of building. Preface by Edgar Kaufmann, Jr. 100 illustrations. 112pp. 9¼ × 10. 23671-4 Pa. $8.95

YEARS WITH FRANK LLOYD WRIGHT: Apprentice to Genius, Edgar Tafel. Insightful memoir by a former apprentice presents a revealing portrait of Wright the man, the inspired teacher, the greatest American architect. 372 black-and-white illustrations. Preface. Index. vi + 228pp. 8¼ × 11. 24801-1 Pa. $10.95

THE STORY OF KING ARTHUR AND HIS KNIGHTS, Howard Pyle. Enchanting version of King Arthur fable has delighted generations with imaginative narratives of exciting adventures and unforgettable illustrations by the author. 41 illustrations. xviii + 313pp. 6⅛ × 9¼. 21445-1 Pa. $6.95

THE GODS OF THE EGYPTIANS, E. A. Wallis Budge. Thorough coverage of numerous gods of ancient Egypt by foremost Egyptologist. Information on evolution of cults, rites and gods; the cult of Osiris; the Book of the Dead and its rites; the sacred animals and birds; Heaven and Hell; and more. 956pp. 6⅛ × 9¼. 22055-9, 22056-7 Pa., Two-vol. set $21.90

A THEOLOGICO-POLITICAL TREATISE, Benedict Spinoza. Also contains unfinished *Political Treatise*. Great classic on religious liberty, theory of government on common consent. R. Elwes translation. Total of 421pp. 5⅜ × 8½. 20249-6 Pa. $7.95

INCIDENTS OF TRAVEL IN CENTRAL AMERICA, CHIAPAS, AND YUCATAN, John L. Stephens. Almost single-handed discovery of Maya culture; exploration of ruined cities, monuments, temples; customs of Indians. 115 drawings. 892pp. 5⅜ × 8½. 22404-X, 22405-8 Pa., Two-vol. set $17.90

LOS CAPRICHOS, Francisco Goya. 80 plates of wild, grotesque monsters and caricatures. Prado manuscript included. 183pp. 6⅝ × 9⅝. 22384-1 Pa. $5.95

AUTOBIOGRAPHY: The Story of My Experiments with Truth, Mohandas K. Gandhi. Not hagiography, but Gandhi in his own words. Boyhood, legal studies, purification, the growth of the Satyagraha (nonviolent protest) movement. Critical, inspiring work of the man who freed India. 480pp. 5⅜ × 8½. (Available in U.S. only) 24593-4 Pa. $6.95

CATALOG OF DOVER BOOKS

ILLUSTRATED DICTIONARY OF HISTORIC ARCHITECTURE, edited by Cyril M. Harris. Extraordinary compendium of clear, concise definitions for over 5,000 important architectural terms complemented by over 2,000 line drawings. Covers full spectrum of architecture from ancient ruins to 20th-century Modernism. Preface. 592pp. 7½ × 9⅜. 24444-X Pa. $15.95

THE NIGHT BEFORE CHRISTMAS, Clement C. Moore. Full text, and woodcuts from original 1848 book. Also critical, historical material. 19 illustrations. 40pp. 4⅝ × 6. 22797-9 Pa. $2.50

THE LESSON OF JAPANESE ARCHITECTURE: 165 Photographs, Jiro Harada. Memorable gallery of 165 photographs taken in the 1930s of exquisite Japanese homes of the well-to-do and historic buildings. 13 line diagrams. 192pp. 8⅜ × 11¼. 24778-3 Pa. $10.95

THE AUTOBIOGRAPHY OF CHARLES DARWIN AND SELECTED LET-TERS, edited by Francis Darwin. The fascinating life of eccentric genius composed of an intimate memoir by Darwin (intended for his children); commentary by his son, Francis; hundreds of fragments from notebooks, journals, papers; and letters to and from Lyell, Hooker, Huxley, Wallace and Henslow. xi + 365pp. 5⅜ × 8. 20479-0 Pa. $6.95

WONDERS OF THE SKY: Observing Rainbows, Comets, Eclipses, the Stars and Other Phenomena, Fred Schaaf. Charming, easy-to-read poetic guide to all manner of celestial events visible to the naked eye. Mock suns, glories, Belt of Venus, more. Illustrated. 299pp. 5¼ × 8¼. 24402-4 Pa. $8.95

BURNHAM'S CELESTIAL HANDBOOK, Robert Burnham, Jr. Thorough guide to the stars beyond our solar system. Exhaustive treatment. Alphabetical by constellation: Andromeda to Cetus in Vol. 1; Chamaeleon to Orion in Vol. 2; and Pavo to Vulpecula in Vol. 3. Hundreds of illustrations. Index in Vol. 3. 2,000pp. 6⅛ × 9¼. 23567-X, 23568-8, 23673-0 Pa., Three-vol. set $41.85

STAR NAMES: Their Lore and Meaning, Richard Hinckley Allen. Fascinating history of names various cultures have given to constellations and literary and folkloristic uses that have been made of stars. Indexes to subjects. Arabic and Greek names. Biblical references. Bibliography. 563pp. 5⅜ × 8½. 21079-0 Pa. $8.95

THIRTY YEARS THAT SHOOK PHYSICS: The Story of Quantum Theory, George Gamow. Lucid, accessible introduction to influential theory of energy and matter. Careful explanations of Dirac's anti-particles, Bohr's model of the atom, much more. 12 plates. Numerous drawings. 240pp. 5⅜ × 8½. 24895-X Pa. $6.95

CHINESE DOMESTIC FURNITURE IN PHOTOGRAPHS AND MEASURED DRAWINGS, Gustav Ecke. A rare volume, now affordably priced for antique collectors, furniture buffs and art historians. Detailed review of styles ranging from early Shang to late Ming. Unabridged republication. 161 black-and-white drawings, photos. Total of 224pp. 8⅜ × 11¼. (Available in U.S. only) 25171-3 Pa. $14.95

VINCENT VAN GOGH: A Biography, Julius Meier-Graefe. Dynamic, penetrating study of artist's life, relationship with brother, Theo, painting techniques, travels, more. Readable, engrossing. 160pp. 5⅜ × 8½. (Available in U.S. only) 25253-1 Pa. $4.95

CATALOG OF DOVER BOOKS

HOW TO WRITE, Gertrude Stein. Gertrude Stein claimed anyone could understand her unconventional writing—here are clues to help. Fascinating improvisations, language experiments, explanations illuminate Stein's craft and the art of writing. Total of 414pp. 4⅝ × 6⅜.   23144-5 Pa. $6.95

ADVENTURES AT SEA IN THE GREAT AGE OF SAIL: Five Firsthand Narratives, edited by Elliot Snow. Rare true accounts of exploration, whaling, shipwreck, fierce natives, trade, shipboard life, more. 33 illustrations. Introduction. 353pp. 5⅜ × 8½.   25177-2 Pa. $9.95

THE HERBAL OR GENERAL HISTORY OF PLANTS, John Gerard. Classic descriptions of about 2,850 plants—with over 2,700 illustrations—includes Latin and English names, physical descriptions, varieties, time and place of growth, more. 2,706 illustrations. xlv + 1,678pp. 8½ × 12¼.   23147-X Cloth. $75.00

DOROTHY AND THE WIZARD IN OZ, L. Frank Baum. Dorothy and the Wizard visit the center of the Earth, where people are vegetables, glass houses grow and Oz characters reappear. Classic sequel to *Wizard of Oz*. 256pp. 5⅜ × 8.
24714-7 Pa. $5.95

SONGS OF EXPERIENCE: Facsimile Reproduction with 26 Plates in Full Color, William Blake. This facsimile of Blake's original "Illuminated Book" reproduces 26 full-color plates from a rare 1826 edition. Includes "The Tyger," "London," "Holy Thursday," and other immortal poems. 26 color plates. Printed text of poems. 48pp. 5¼ × 7.   24636-1 Pa. $3.95

SONGS OF INNOCENCE, William Blake. The first and most popular of Blake's famous "Illuminated Books," in a facsimile edition reproducing all 31 brightly colored plates. Additional printed text of each poem. 64pp. 5¼ × 7.
22764-2 Pa. $3.95

PRECIOUS STONES, Max Bauer. Classic, thorough study of diamonds, rubies, emeralds, garnets, etc.: physical character, occurrence, properties, use, similar topics. 20 plates, 8 in color. 94 figures. 659pp. 6⅛ × 9¼.
21910-0, 21911-9 Pa., Two-vol. set $15.90

ENCYCLOPEDIA OF VICTORIAN NEEDLEWORK, S. F. A. Caulfeild and Blanche Saward. Full, precise descriptions of stitches, techniques for dozens of needlecrafts—most exhaustive reference of its kind. Over 800 figures. Total of 679pp. 8⅛ × 11.   22800-2, 22801-0 Pa., Two-vol. set $23.90

THE MARVELOUS LAND OF OZ, L. Frank Baum. Second Oz book, the Scarecrow and Tin Woodman are back with hero named Tip, Oz magic. 136 illustrations. 287pp. 5⅜ × 8½.   20692-0 Pa. $5.95

WILD FOWL DECOYS, Joel Barber. Basic book on the subject, by foremost authority and collector. Reveals history of decoy making and rigging, place in American culture, different kinds of decoys, how to make them, and how to use them. 140 plates. 156pp. 7⅞ × 10¾.   20011-6 Pa. $8.95

HISTORY OF LACE, Mrs. Bury Palliser. Definitive, profusely illustrated chronicle of lace from earliest times to late 19th century. Laces of Italy, Greece, England, France, Belgium, etc. Landmark of needlework scholarship. 266 illustrations. 672pp. 6⅛ × 9¼.   24742-2 Pa. $16.95

ILLUSTRATED GUIDE TO SHAKER FURNITURE, Robert Meader. All furniture and appurtenances, with much on unknown local styles. 235 photos. 146pp. 9 × 12.   22819-3 Pa. $8.95

WHALE SHIPS AND WHALING: A Pictorial Survey, George Francis Dow. Over 200 vintage engravings, drawings, photographs of barks, brigs, cutters, other vessels. Also harpoons, lances, whaling guns, many other artifacts. Comprehensive text by foremost authority. 207 black-and-white illustrations. 288pp. 6 × 9.
24808-9 Pa. $9.95

THE BERTRAMS, Anthony Trollope. Powerful portrayal of blind self-will and thwarted ambition includes one of Trollope's most heartrending love stories. 497pp. 5⅜ × 8½.   25119-5 Pa. $9.95

ADVENTURES WITH A HAND LENS, Richard Headstrom. Clearly written guide to observing and studying flowers and grasses, fish scales, moth and insect wings, egg cases, buds, feathers, seeds, leaf scars, moss, molds, ferns, common crystals, etc.—all with an ordinary, inexpensive magnifying glass. 209 exact line drawings aid in your discoveries. 220pp. 5⅜ × 8½.   23330-8 Pa. $5.95

RODIN ON ART AND ARTISTS, Auguste Rodin. Great sculptor's candid, wide-ranging comments on meaning of art; great artists; relation of sculpture to poetry, painting, music; philosophy of life, more. 76 superb black-and-white illustrations of Rodin's sculpture, drawings and prints. 119pp. 8⅜ × 11¼.   24487-3 Pa. $7.95

FIFTY CLASSIC FRENCH FILMS, 1912–1982: A Pictorial Record, Anthony Slide. Memorable stills from Grand Illusion, Beauty and the Beast, Hiroshima, Mon Amour, many more. Credits, plot synopses, reviews, etc. 160pp. 8¼ × 11.
25256-6 Pa. $11.95

THE PRINCIPLES OF PSYCHOLOGY, William James. Famous long course complete, unabridged. Stream of thought, time perception, memory, experimental methods; great work decades ahead of its time. 94 figures. 1,391pp. 5⅜ × 8½.
20381-6, 20382-4 Pa., Two-vol. set $25.90

BODIES IN A BOOKSHOP, R. T. Campbell. Challenging mystery of blackmail and murder with ingenious plot and superbly drawn characters. In the best tradition of British suspense fiction. 192pp. 5⅜ × 8½.   24720-1 Pa. $4.95

CALLAS: Portrait of a Prima Donna, George Jellinek. Renowned commentator on the musical scene chronicles incredible career and life of the most controversial, fascinating, influential operatic personality of our time. 64 black-and-white photographs. 416pp. 5⅜ × 8¼.   25047-4 Pa. $8.95

GEOMETRY, RELATIVITY AND THE FOURTH DIMENSION, Rudolph Rucker. Exposition of fourth dimension, concepts of relativity as Flatland characters continue adventures. Popular, easily followed yet accurate, profound. 141 illustrations. 133pp. 5⅜ × 8½.   23400-2 Pa. $4.95

HOUSEHOLD STORIES BY THE BROTHERS GRIMM, with pictures by Walter Crane. 53 classic stories—Rumpelstiltskin, Rapunzel, Hansel and Gretel, the Fisherman and his Wife, Snow White, Tom Thumb, Sleeping Beauty, Cinderella, and so much more—lavishly illustrated with original 19th-century drawings. 114 illustrations. x + 269pp. 5⅜ × 8½.   21080-4 Pa. $4.95

SUNDIALS, Albert Waugh. Far and away the best, most thorough coverage of ideas, mathematics concerned, types, construction, adjusting anywhere. Over 100 illustrations. 230pp. 5⅜ × 8½. 22947-5 Pa. $5.95

PICTURE HISTORY OF THE NORMANDIE: With 190 Illustrations, Frank O. Braynard. Full story of legendary French ocean liner: Art Deco interiors, design innovations, furnishings, celebrities, maiden voyage, tragic fire, much more. Extensive text. 144pp. 8⅜ × 11¾. 25257-4 Pa. $10.95

THE FIRST AMERICAN COOKBOOK: A Facsimile of "American Cookery," 1796, Amelia Simmons. Facsimile of the first American-written cookbook published in the United States contains authentic recipes for colonial favorites—pumpkin pudding, winter squash pudding, spruce beer, Indian slapjacks, and more. Introductory Essay and Glossary of colonial cooking terms. 80pp. 5⅜ × 8½. 24710-4 Pa. $3.50

101 PUZZLES IN THOUGHT AND LOGIC, C. R. Wylie, Jr. Solve murders and robberies, find out which fishermen are liars, how a blind man could possibly identify a color—purely by your own reasoning! 107pp. 5⅜ × 8½. 20367-0 Pa. $2.95

ANCIENT EGYPTIAN MYTHS AND LEGENDS, Lewis Spence. Examines animism, totemism, fetishism, creation myths, deities, alchemy, art and magic, other topics. Over 50 illustrations. 432pp. 5⅜ × 8½. 26525-0 Pa. $8.95

ANTHROPOLOGY AND MODERN LIFE, Franz Boas. Great anthropologist's classic treatise on race and culture. Introduction by Ruth Bunzel. Only inexpensive paperback edition. 255pp. 5⅜ × 8½. 25245-0 Pa. $6.95

THE TALE OF PETER RABBIT, Beatrix Potter. The inimitable Peter's terrifying adventure in Mr. McGregor's garden, with all 27 wonderful, full-color Potter illustrations. 55pp. 4¼ × 5½. (Available in U.S. only) 22827-4 Pa. $1.75

THREE PROPHETIC SCIENCE FICTION NOVELS, H. G. Wells. *When the Sleeper Wakes, A Story of the Days to Come* and *The Time Machine* (full version). 335pp. 5⅜ × 8½. (Available in U.S. only) 20605-X Pa. $8.95

APICIUS COOKERY AND DINING IN IMPERIAL ROME, edited and translated by Joseph Dommers Vehling. Oldest known cookbook in existence offers readers a clear picture of what foods Romans ate, how they prepared them, etc. 49 illustrations. 301pp. 6⅛ × 9¼. 23563-7 Pa. $7.95

SHAKESPEARE LEXICON AND QUOTATION DICTIONARY, Alexander Schmidt. Full definitions, locations, shades of meaning of every word in plays and poems. More than 50,000 exact quotations. 1,485pp. 6½ × 9¼. 22726-X, 22727-8 Pa., Two-vol. set $31.90

THE WORLD'S GREAT SPEECHES, edited by Lewis Copeland and Lawrence W. Lamm. Vast collection of 278 speeches from Greeks to 1970. Powerful and effective models; unique look at history. 842pp. 5⅜ × 8½. 20468-5 Pa. $12.95

THE BLUE FAIRY BOOK, Andrew Lang. The first, most famous collection, with many familiar tales: Little Red Riding Hood, Aladdin and the Wonderful Lamp, Puss in Boots, Sleeping Beauty, Hansel and Gretel, Rumpelstiltskin; 37 in all. 138 illustrations. 390pp. 5⅜ × 8½. 21437-0 Pa. $6.95

THE STORY OF THE CHAMPIONS OF THE ROUND TABLE, Howard Pyle. Sir Launcelot, Sir Tristram and Sir Percival in spirited adventures of love and triumph retold in Pyle's inimitable style. 50 drawings, 31 full-page. xviii + 329pp. 6½ × 9¼. 21883-X Pa. $7.95

THE MYTHS OF THE NORTH AMERICAN INDIANS, Lewis Spence. Myths and legends of the Algonquins, Iroquois, Pawnees and Sioux with comprehensive historical and ethnological commentary. 36 illustrations. 5⅜ × 8½.
25967-6 Pa. $8.95

GREAT DINOSAUR HUNTERS AND THEIR DISCOVERIES, Edwin H. Colbert. Fascinating, lavishly illustrated chronicle of dinosaur research, 1820s to 1960. Achievements of Cope, Marsh, Brown, Buckland, Mantell, Huxley, many others. 384pp. 5¼ × 8¼. 24701-5 Pa. $7.95

THE TASTEMAKERS, Russell Lynes. Informal, illustrated social history of American taste 1850s–1950s. First popularized categories Highbrow, Lowbrow, Middlebrow. 129 illustrations. New (1979) afterword. 384pp. 6 × 9.
23993-4 Pa. $8.95

DOUBLE CROSS PURPOSES, Ronald A. Knox. A treasure hunt in the Scottish Highlands, an old map, unidentified corpse, surprise discoveries keep reader guessing in this cleverly intricate tale of financial skullduggery. 2 black-and-white maps. 320pp. 5⅜ × 8½. (Available in U.S. only) 25032-6 Pa. $6.95

AUTHENTIC VICTORIAN DECORATION AND ORNAMENTATION IN FULL COLOR: 46 Plates from "Studies in Design," Christopher Dresser. Superb full-color lithographs reproduced from rare original portfolio of a major Victorian designer. 48pp. 9¼ × 12¼. 25083-0 Pa. $7.95

PRIMITIVE ART, Franz Boas. Remains the best text ever prepared on subject, thoroughly discussing Indian, African, Asian, Australian, and, especially, Northern American primitive art. Over 950 illustrations show ceramics, masks, totem poles, weapons, textiles, paintings, much more. 376pp. 5⅜ × 8. 20025-6 Pa. $7.95

SIDELIGHTS ON RELATIVITY, Albert Einstein. Unabridged republication of two lectures delivered by the great physicist in 1920–21. *Ether and Relativity* and *Geometry and Experience*. Elegant ideas in nonmathematical form, accessible to intelligent layman. vi + 56pp. 5⅜ × 8½. 24511-X Pa. $3.95

THE WIT AND HUMOR OF OSCAR WILDE, edited by Alvin Redman. More than 1,000 ripostes, paradoxes, wisecracks: Work is the curse of the drinking classes, I can resist everything except temptation, etc. 258pp. 5⅜ × 8½. 20602-5 Pa. $4.95

ADVENTURES WITH A MICROSCOPE, Richard Headstrom. 59 adventures with clothing fibers, protozoa, ferns and lichens, roots and leaves, much more. 142 illustrations. 232pp. 5⅜ × 8½. 23471-1 Pa. $3.95

PLANTS OF THE BIBLE, Harold N. Moldenke and Alma L. Moldenke. Standard reference to all 230 plants mentioned in Scriptures. Latin name, biblical reference, uses, modern identity, much more. Unsurpassed encyclopedic resource for scholars, botanists, nature lovers, students of Bible. Bibliography. Indexes. 123 black-and-white illustrations. 384pp. 6 × 9. 25069-5 Pa. $8.95

FAMOUS AMERICAN WOMEN: A Biographical Dictionary from Colonial Times to the Present, Robert McHenry, ed. From Pocahontas to Rosa Parks, 1,035 distinguished American women documented in separate biographical entries. Accurate, up-to-date data, numerous categories, spans 400 years. Indices. 493pp. 6½ × 9¼. 24523-3 Pa. $10.95

THE FABULOUS INTERIORS OF THE GREAT OCEAN LINERS IN HISTORIC PHOTOGRAPHS, William H. Miller, Jr. Some 200 superb photographs capture exquisite interiors of world's great "floating palaces"—1890s to 1980s: *Titanic, Ile de France, Queen Elizabeth, United States, Europa,* more. Approx. 200 black-and-white photographs. Captions. Text. Introduction. 160pp. 8⅞ × 11¾. 24756-2 Pa. $9.95

THE GREAT LUXURY LINERS, 1927–1954: A Photographic Record, William H. Miller, Jr. Nostalgic tribute to heyday of ocean liners. 186 photos of *Ile de France, Normandie, Leviathan, Queen Elizabeth, United States,* many others. Interior and exterior views. Introduction. Captions. 160pp. 9 × 12. 24056-8 Pa. $10.95

A NATURAL HISTORY OF THE DUCKS, John Charles Phillips. Great landmark of ornithology offers complete detailed coverage of nearly 200 species and subspecies of ducks: gadwall, sheldrake, merganser, pintail, many more. 74 full-color plates, 102 black-and-white. Bibliography. Total of 1,920pp. 8⅝ × 11¼. 25141-1, 25142-X Cloth., Two-vol. set $100.00

THE SEAWEED HANDBOOK: An Illustrated Guide to Seaweeds from North Carolina to Canada, Thomas F. Lee. Concise reference covers 78 species. Scientific and common names, habitat, distribution, more. Finding keys for easy identification. 224pp. 5⅜ × 8½. 25215-9 Pa. $6.95

THE TEN BOOKS OF ARCHITECTURE: The 1755 Leoni Edition, Leon Battista Alberti. Rare classic helped introduce the glories of ancient architecture to the Renaissance. 68 black-and-white plates. 336pp. 8⅜ × 11¼. 25239-6 Pa. $14.95

MISS MACKENZIE, Anthony Trollope. Minor masterpieces by Victorian master unmasks many truths about life in 19th-century England. First inexpensive edition in years. 392pp. 5⅜ × 8½. 25201-9 Pa. $8.95

THE RIME OF THE ANCIENT MARINER, Gustave Doré, Samuel Taylor Coleridge. Dramatic engravings considered by many to be his greatest work. The terrifying space of the open sea, the storms and whirlpools of an unknown ocean, the ice of Antarctica, more—all rendered in a powerful, chilling manner. Full text. 38 plates. 77pp. 9¼ × 12. 22305-1 Pa. $4.95

THE EXPEDITIONS OF ZEBULON MONTGOMERY PIKE, Zebulon Montgomery Pike. Fascinating firsthand accounts (1805–6) of exploration of Mississippi River, Indian wars, capture by Spanish dragoons, much more. 1,088pp. 5⅜ × 8½. 25254-X, 25255-8 Pa., Two-vol. set $25.90

A CONCISE HISTORY OF PHOTOGRAPHY: Third Revised Edition, Helmut Gernsheim. Best one-volume history—camera obscura, photochemistry, daguerreotypes, evolution of cameras, film, more. Also artistic aspects—landscape, portraits, fine art, etc. 281 black-and-white photographs. 26 in color. 176pp. 8⅜ × 11¼.
25128-4 Pa. $14.95

THE DORÉ BIBLE ILLUSTRATIONS, Gustave Doré. 241 detailed plates from the Bible: the Creation scenes, Adam and Eve, Flood, Babylon, battle sequences, life of Jesus, etc. Each plate is accompanied by the verses from the King James version of the Bible. 241pp. 9 × 12.
23004-X Pa. $9.95

WANDERINGS IN WEST AFRICA, Richard F. Burton. Great Victorian scholar/adventurer's invaluable descriptions of African tribal rituals, fetishism, culture, art, much more. Fascinating 19th-century account. 624pp. 5⅜ × 8½. 26890-X Pa. $12.95

FLATLAND, E. A. Abbott. Intriguing and enormously popular science-fiction classic explores the complexities of trying to survive as a two-dimensional being in a three-dimensional world. Amusingly illustrated by the author. 16 illustrations. 103pp. 5⅜ × 8½.
20001-9 Pa. $2.50

THE HISTORY OF THE LEWIS AND CLARK EXPEDITION, Meriwether Lewis and William Clark, edited by Elliott Coues. Classic edition of Lewis and Clark's day-by-day journals that later became the basis for U.S. claims to Oregon and the West. Accurate and invaluable geographical, botanical, biological, meteorological and anthropological material. Total of 1,508pp. 5⅜ × 8½.
21268-8, 21269-6, 21270-X Pa., Three-vol. set $29.85

LANGUAGE, TRUTH AND LOGIC, Alfred J. Ayer. Famous, clear introduction to Vienna, Cambridge schools of Logical Positivism. Role of philosophy, elimination of metaphysics, nature of analysis, etc. 160pp. 5⅜ × 8½. (Available in U.S. and Canada only)
20010-8 Pa. $3.95

MATHEMATICS FOR THE NONMATHEMATICIAN, Morris Kline. Detailed, college-level treatment of mathematics in cultural and historical context, with numerous exercises. For liberal arts students. Preface. Recommended Reading Lists. Tables. Index. Numerous black-and-white figures. xvi + 641pp. 5⅜ × 8½.
24823-2 Pa. $11.95

HANDBOOK OF PICTORIAL SYMBOLS, Rudolph Modley. 3,250 signs and symbols, many systems in full; official or heavy commercial use. Arranged by subject. Most in Pictorial Archive series. 143pp. 8⅜ × 11. 23357-X Pa. $7.95

INCIDENTS OF TRAVEL IN YUCATAN, John L. Stephens. Classic (1843) exploration of jungles of Yucatan, looking for evidences of Maya civilization. Travel adventures, Mexican and Indian culture, etc. Total of 669pp. 5⅜ × 8½.
20926-1, 20927-X Pa., Two-vol. set $11.90

DEGAS: An Intimate Portrait, Ambroise Vollard. Charming, anecdotal memoir by famous art dealer of one of the greatest 19th-century French painters. 14 black-and-white illustrations. Introduction by Harold L. Van Doren. 96pp. 5⅜ × 8½.
25131-4 Pa. $4.95

PERSONAL NARRATIVE OF A PILGRIMAGE TO AL-MADINAH AND MECCAH, Richard F. Burton. Great travel classic by remarkably colorful personality. Burton, disguised as a Moroccan, visited sacred shrines of Islam, narrowly escaping death. 47 illustrations. 959pp. 5⅜ × 8½.
21217-3, 21218-1 Pa., Two-vol. set $19.90

PHRASE AND WORD ORIGINS, A. H. Holt. Entertaining, reliable, modern study of more than 1,200 colorful words, phrases, origins and histories. Much unexpected information. 254pp. 5⅜ × 8½.
20758-7 Pa. $5.95

THE RED THUMB MARK, R. Austin Freeman. In this first Dr. Thorndyke case, the great scientific detective draws fascinating conclusions from the nature of a single fingerprint. Exciting story, authentic science. 320pp. 5⅜ × 8½. (Available in U.S. only)
25210-8 Pa. $6.95

AN EGYPTIAN HIEROGLYPHIC DICTIONARY, E. A. Wallis Budge. Monumental work containing about 25,000 words or terms that occur in texts ranging from 3000 B.C. to 600 A.D. Each entry consists of a transliteration of the word, the word in hieroglyphs, and the meaning in English. 1,314pp. 6⅝ × 10.
23615-3, 23616-1 Pa., Two-vol. set $35.90

THE COMPLEAT STRATEGYST: Being a Primer on the Theory of Games of Strategy, J. D. Williams. Highly entertaining classic describes, with many illustrated examples, how to select best strategies in conflict situations. Prefaces. Appendices. xvi + 268pp. 5⅜ × 8½.
25101-2 Pa. $6.95

THE ROAD TO OZ, L. Frank Baum. Dorothy meets the Shaggy Man, little Button-Bright and the Rainbow's beautiful daughter in this delightful trip to the magical Land of Oz. 272pp. 5⅜ × 8.
25208-6 Pa. $5.95

POINT AND LINE TO PLANE, Wassily Kandinsky. Seminal exposition of role of point, line, other elements in nonobjective painting. Essential to understanding 20th-century art. 127 illustrations. 192pp. 6½ × 9¼.
23808-3 Pa. $5.95

LADY ANNA, Anthony Trollope. Moving chronicle of Countess Lovel's bitter struggle to win for herself and daughter Anna their rightful rank and fortune—perhaps at cost of sanity itself. 384pp. 5⅜ × 8½.
24669-8 Pa. $8.95

EGYPTIAN MAGIC, E. A. Wallis Budge. Sums up all that is known about magic in Ancient Egypt: the role of magic in controlling the gods, powerful amulets that warded off evil spirits, scarabs of immortality, use of wax images, formulas and spells, the secret name, much more. 253pp. 5⅜ × 8½.
22681-6 Pa. $4.50

THE DANCE OF SIVA, Ananda Coomaraswamy. Preeminent authority unfolds the vast metaphysic of India: the revelation of her art, conception of the universe, social organization, etc. 27 reproductions of art masterpieces. 192pp. 5⅜ × 8½.
24817-8 Pa. $6.95

CHRISTMAS CUSTOMS AND TRADITIONS, Clement A. Miles. Origin, evolution, significance of religious, secular practices. Caroling, gifts, yule logs, much more. Full, scholarly yet fascinating; non-sectarian. 400pp. 5⅜ × 8½.

23354-5 Pa. $6.95

THE HUMAN FIGURE IN MOTION, Eadweard Muybridge. More than 4,500 stopped-action photos, in action series, showing undraped men, women, children jumping, lying down, throwing, sitting, wrestling, carrying, etc. 390pp. 7⅞ × 10⅝.

20204-6 Cloth. $24.95

THE MAN WHO WAS THURSDAY, Gilbert Keith Chesterton. Witty, fast-paced novel about a club of anarchists in turn-of-the-century London. Brilliant social, religious, philosophical speculations. 128pp. 5⅜ × 8½.   25121-7 Pa. $3.95

A CÉZANNE SKETCHBOOK: Figures, Portraits, Landscapes and Still Lifes, Paul Cézanne. Great artist experiments with tonal effects, light, mass, other qualities in over 100 drawings. A revealing view of developing master painter, precursor of Cubism. 102 black-and-white illustrations. 144pp. 8¾ × 6⅝.   24790-2 Pa. $6.95

AN ENCYCLOPEDIA OF BATTLES: Accounts of Over 1,560 Battles from 1479 B.C. to the Present, David Eggenberger. Presents essential details of every major battle in recorded history, from the first battle of Megiddo in 1479 B.C. to Grenada in 1984. List of Battle Maps. New Appendix covering the years 1967–1984. Index. 99 illustrations. 544pp. 6½ × 9¼.   24913-1 Pa. $14.95

AN ETYMOLOGICAL DICTIONARY OF MODERN ENGLISH, Ernest Weekley. Richest, fullest work, by foremost British lexicographer. Detailed word histories. Inexhaustible. Total of 856pp. 6½ × 9¼.

21873-2, 21874-0 Pa., Two-vol. set $19.90

WEBSTER'S AMERICAN MILITARY BIOGRAPHIES, edited by Robert McHenry. Over 1,000 figures who shaped 3 centuries of American military history. Detailed biographies of Nathan Hale, Douglas MacArthur, Mary Hallaren, others. Chronologies of engagements, more. Introduction. Addenda. 1,033 entries in alphabetical order. xi + 548pp. 6½ × 9¼. (Available in U.S. only)

24758-9 Pa. $13.95

LIFE IN ANCIENT EGYPT, Adolf Erman. Detailed older account, with much not in more recent books: domestic life, religion, magic, medicine, commerce, and whatever else needed for complete picture. Many illustrations. 597pp. 5⅜ × 8½.

22632-8 Pa. $8.95

HISTORIC COSTUME IN PICTURES, Braun & Schneider. Over 1,450 costumed figures shown, covering a wide variety of peoples: kings, emperors, nobles, priests, servants, soldiers, scholars, townsfolk, peasants, merchants, courtiers, cavaliers, and more. 256pp. 8⅜ × 11¼.   23150-X Pa. $9.95

THE NOTEBOOKS OF LEONARDO DA VINCI, edited by J. P. Richter. Extracts from manuscripts reveal great genius; on painting, sculpture, anatomy, sciences, geography, etc. Both Italian and English. 186 ms. pages reproduced, plus 500 additional drawings, including studies for *Last Supper, Sforza* monument, etc. 860pp. 7⅞ × 10¾. (Available in U.S. only) 22572-0, 22573-9 Pa., Two-vol. set $31.90

THE ART NOUVEAU STYLE BOOK OF ALPHONSE MUCHA: All 72 Plates from "Documents Decoratifs" in Original Color, Alphonse Mucha. Rare copyright-free design portfolio by high priest of Art Nouveau. Jewelry, wallpaper, stained glass, furniture, figure studies, plant and animal motifs, etc. Only complete one-volume edition. 80pp. 9⅜ × 12¼. 24044-4 Pa. $10.95

ANIMALS: 1,419 Copyright-Free Illustrations of Mammals, Birds, Fish, Insects, Etc., edited by Jim Harter. Clear wood engravings present, in extremely lifelike poses, over 1,000 species of animals. One of the most extensive pictorial sourcebooks of its kind. Captions. Index. 284pp. 9 × 12. 23766-4 Pa. $10.95

OBELISTS FLY HIGH, C. Daly King. Masterpiece of American detective fiction, long out of print, involves murder on a 1935 transcontinental flight—"a very thrilling story"—*NY Times*. Unabridged and unaltered republication of the edition published by William Collins Sons & Co. Ltd., London, 1935. 288pp. 5⅜ × 8½. (Available in U.S. only) 25036-9 Pa. $5.95

VICTORIAN AND EDWARDIAN FASHION: A Photographic Survey, Alison Gernsheim. First fashion history completely illustrated by contemporary photographs. Full text plus 235 photos, 1840–1914, in which many celebrities appear. 240pp. 6½ × 9¼. 24205-6 Pa. $8.95

THE ART OF THE FRENCH ILLUSTRATED BOOK, 1700–1914, Gordon N. Ray. Over 630 superb book illustrations by Fragonard, Delacroix, Daumier, Doré, Grandville, Manet, Mucha, Steinlen, Toulouse-Lautrec and many others. Preface. Introduction. 633 halftones. Indices of artists, authors & titles, binders and provenances. Appendices. Bibliography. 608pp. 8⅜ × 11¼. 25086-5 Pa. $24.95

THE WONDERFUL WIZARD OF OZ, L. Frank Baum. Facsimile in full color of America's finest children's classic. 143 illustrations by W. W. Denslow. 267pp. 5⅜ × 8½. 20691-2 Pa. $7.95

FOLLOWING THE EQUATOR: A Journey Around the World, Mark Twain. Great writer's 1897 account of circumnavigating the globe by steamship. Ironic humor, keen observations, vivid and fascinating descriptions of exotic places. 197 illustrations. 720pp. 5⅜ × 8½. 26113-1 Pa. $15.95

THE FRIENDLY STARS, Martha Evans Martin & Donald Howard Menzel. Classic text marshalls the stars together in an engaging, nontechnical survey, presenting them as sources of beauty in night sky. 23 illustrations. Foreword. 2 star charts. Index. 147pp. 5⅜ × 8½. 21099-5 Pa. $3.95

FADS AND FALLACIES IN THE NAME OF SCIENCE, Martin Gardner. Fair, witty appraisal of cranks, quacks, and quackeries of science and pseudoscience: hollow earth, Velikovsky, orgone energy, Dianetics, flying saucers, Bridey Murphy, food and medical fads, etc. Revised, expanded In the Name of Science. "A very able and even-tempered presentation."—*The New Yorker*. 363pp. 5⅜ × 8. 20394-8 Pa. $6.95

ANCIENT EGYPT: Its Culture and History, J. E. Manchip White. From predynastics through Ptolemies: society, history, political structure, religion, daily life, literature, cultural heritage. 48 plates. 217pp. 5⅜ × 8½. 22548-8 Pa. $5.95

SIR HARRY HOTSPUR OF HUMBLETHWAITE, Anthony Trollope. Incisive, unconventional psychological study of a conflict between a wealthy baronet, his idealistic daughter, and their scapegrace cousin. The 1870 novel in its first inexpensive edition in years. 250pp. 5⅜ × 8½. 24953-0 Pa. $6.95

LASERS AND HOLOGRAPHY, Winston E. Kock. Sound introduction to burgeoning field, expanded (1981) for second edition. Wave patterns, coherence, lasers, diffraction, zone plates, properties of holograms, recent advances. 84 illustrations. 160pp. 5⅜ × 8¼. (Except in United Kingdom) 24041-X Pa. $3.95

INTRODUCTION TO ARTIFICIAL INTELLIGENCE: Second, Enlarged Edition, Philip C. Jackson, Jr. Comprehensive survey of artificial intelligence—the study of how machines (computers) can be made to act intelligently. Includes introductory and advanced material. Extensive notes updating the main text. 132 black-and-white illustrations. 512pp. 5⅜ × 8½. 24864-X Pa. $10.95

HISTORY OF INDIAN AND INDONESIAN ART, Ananda K. Coomaraswamy. Over 400 illustrations illuminate classic study of Indian art from earliest Harappa finds to early 20th century. Provides philosophical, religious and social insights. 304pp. 6⅜ × 9⅜. 25005-9 Pa. $11.95

THE GOLEM, Gustav Meyrink. Most famous supernatural novel in modern European literature, set in Ghetto of Old Prague around 1890. Compelling story of mystical experiences, strange transformations, profound terror. 13 black-and-white illustrations. 224pp. 5⅜ × 8½. (Available in U.S. only) 25025-3 Pa. $6.95

PICTORIAL ENCYCLOPEDIA OF HISTORIC ARCHITECTURAL PLANS, DETAILS AND ELEMENTS: With 1,880 Line Drawings of Arches, Domes, Doorways, Facades, Gables, Windows, etc., John Theodore Haneman. Sourcebook of inspiration for architects, designers, others. Bibliography. Captions. 141pp. 9 × 12. 24605-1 Pa. $7.95

BENCHLEY LOST AND FOUND, Robert Benchley. Finest humor from early 30s, about pet peeves, child psychologists, post office and others. Mostly unavailable elsewhere. 73 illustrations by Peter Arno and others. 183pp. 5⅜ × 8½. 22410-4 Pa. $4.95

ERTÉ GRAPHICS, Erté. Collection of striking color graphics: *Seasons, Alphabet, Numerals, Aces* and *Precious Stones*. 50 plates, including 4 on covers. 48pp. 9⅜ × 12¼. 23580-7 Pa. $7.95

THE JOURNAL OF HENRY D. THOREAU, edited by Bradford Torrey, F. H. Allen. Complete reprinting of 14 volumes, 1837–61, over two million words; the sourcebooks for *Walden*, etc. Definitive. All original sketches, plus 75 photographs. 1,804pp. 8½ × 12¼. 20312-3, 20313-1 Cloth., Two-vol. set $130.00

CASTLES: Their Construction and History, Sidney Toy. Traces castle development from ancient roots. Nearly 200 photographs and drawings illustrate moats, keeps, baileys, many other features. Caernarvon, Dover Castles, Hadrian's Wall, Tower of London, dozens more. 256pp. 5⅜ × 8¼. 24898-4 Pa. $6.95

AMERICAN CLIPPER SHIPS: 1833–1858, Octavius T. Howe & Frederick C. Matthews. Fully-illustrated, encyclopedic review of 352 clipper ships from the period of America's greatest maritime supremacy. Introduction. 109 halftones. 5 black-and-white line illustrations. Index. Total of 928pp. 5⅜ × 8½.
25115-2, 25116-0 Pa., Two-vol. set $17.90

TOWARDS A NEW ARCHITECTURE, Le Corbusier. Pioneering manifesto by great architect, near legendary founder of "International School." Technical and aesthetic theories, views on industry, economics, relation of form to function, "mass-production spirit," much more. Profusely illustrated. Unabridged translation of 13th French edition. Introduction by Frederick Etchells. 320pp. 6⅛ × 9¼. (Available in U.S. only)
25023-7 Pa. $8.95

THE BOOK OF KELLS, edited by Blanche Cirker. Inexpensive collection of 32 full-color, full-page plates from the greatest illuminated manuscript of the Middle Ages, painstakingly reproduced from rare facsimile edition. Publisher's Note. Captions. 32pp. 9⅜ × 12¼.
24345-1 Pa. $5.95

BEST SCIENCE FICTION STORIES OF H. G. WELLS, H. G. Wells. Full novel *The Invisible Man*, plus 17 short stories: "The Crystal Egg," "Aepyornis Island," "The Strange Orchid," etc. 303pp. 5⅜ × 8½. (Available in U.S. only)
21531-8 Pa. $6.95

AMERICAN SAILING SHIPS: Their Plans and History, Charles G. Davis. Photos, construction details of schooners, frigates, clippers, other sailcraft of 18th to early 20th centuries—plus entertaining discourse on design, rigging, nautical lore, much more. 137 black-and-white illustrations. 240pp. 6⅛ × 9¼.
24658-2 Pa. $6.95

ENTERTAINING MATHEMATICAL PUZZLES, Martin Gardner. Selection of author's favorite conundrums involving arithmetic, money, speed, etc., with lively commentary. Complete solutions. 112pp. 5⅜ × 8½.
25211-6 Pa. $3.50

THE WILL TO BELIEVE, HUMAN IMMORTALITY, William James. Two books bound together. Effect of irrational on logical, and arguments for human immortality. 402pp. 5⅜ × 8½.
20291-7 Pa. $8.95

THE HAUNTED MONASTERY and THE CHINESE MAZE MURDERS, Robert Van Gulik. 2 full novels by Van Gulik continue adventures of Judge Dee and his companions. An evil Taoist monastery, seemingly supernatural events; overgrown topiary maze that hides strange crimes. Set in 7th-century China. 27 illustrations. 328pp. 5⅜ × 8½.
23502-5 Pa. $6.95

CELEBRATED CASES OF JUDGE DEE (DEE GOONG AN), translated by Robert Van Gulik. Authentic 18th-century Chinese detective novel; Dee and associates solve three interlocked cases. Led to Van Gulik's own stories with same characters. Extensive introduction. 9 illustrations. 237pp. 5⅜ × 8½.
23337-5 Pa. $5.95

Prices subject to change without notice.

Available at your book dealer or write for free catalog to Dept. GI, Dover Publications, Inc., 31 East 2nd St., Mineola, N.Y. 11501. Dover publishes more than 175 books each year on science, elementary and advanced mathematics, biology, music, art, literary history, social sciences and other areas.